HIBERNIA.
Dives Lactis ac Mellis Insula
Cervorum venatu insignis.

EDITED BY BRIAN DE BREFFNY

340 illustrations, 62 in color

278 photographs, drawings and a map

The Irish World

THE ART AND CULTURE OF THE IRISH PEOPLE

TEXTS BY E. Estyn Evans
Kathleen Hughes
Roger Stalley
Brian de Breffny
Rosemary ffolliott
Anne Crookshank
Gearóid Ó Tuathaigh
Phillip L. Marcus
Jeanne Sheehy
William V. Shannon
Kevin B. Nowlan

HARRISON HOUSE/HARRY N. ABRAMS, INC.
NEW YORK

Endpapers: Detail of a page from the *Book of Durrow*
Half-title page: Hibernia; engraving by W. Hollar from *De Hibernia et Antiquitatibus eius*
by Sir James Ware, 1658

[handwritten call number: Oversize DA 925 .I75 1986]

Copyright © Thames and Hudson Ltd., London
This 1986 edition is published by Harrison House/Harry N. Abrams, Inc.,
distributed by Crown Publishers, Inc.,
225 Park Avenue South, New York, New York 10003

All rights reserved.

Printed and bound in Yugoslavia

ISBN 0-517-62499-0

h g f e d c b a

CONTENTS

FOREWORD

BRIAN de BREFFNY

Some psychologists now believe that the traditional images of the hard-working German, the hot-blooded Italian, the brooding Slav or the phlegmatic Englishman may not be as silly as we thought. Professor Lynn of the New University of Ulster suggests that racial, cultural and climatic factors may account for the existence of national stereotypes. Certainly to attempt to understand 'Irishness' one must know something of Ireland's geography and also trace a long series of causes and effects, examining the artistic as well as the political legacy which each generation bequeathed to its successors.

Irishmen have always been acutely, some would say morbidly, aware of their past. Today the country still carries the burdens of history, epitomized by the seemingly insoluble problem of Ulster which Professor O'Driscoll of Toronto University sees as 'inevitable . . . the final working out of the Irish system of the ideas of the Celtic Literary Revival'. The psychic bond which made the people into a spiritual and physical unit was forged, in his opinion, not by the nationalist politicians but by the writers and artists who transformed a distant, even fictional, national past into a living presence in the Irish mind.

Centuries of introspection, introversion and brooding preceded the Celtic Revival. Their roots can be traced beyond the indignities of the years of economic, social, cultural and political oppression lived in the shadow of an attractive and boisterous ascendancy, beyond the birth of Ireland's passionate attachment to the Holy See and the blood-curdling power struggle of the 16th and 17th centuries and beyond the Middle Ages, to that aristocratic pastoral civilization which escaped the influence of the Roman Empire – just as Ireland was later to escape the secularization of the Renaissance, thus preserving unique elements of an ancient heroic culture.

The inheritance of the Druids is not entirely spent in Ireland nor has the melancholy gaiety of the wake completely vanished. Its ambiguity, like the streak of violence which flashes like quicksilver across the placid island, is only one of the many dualities which haunt the Irish scene. Ireland emerges in a recent international survey as the least neurotic country in the world yet with the world's highest rate of chronic psychosis.

In his *Autumn Journal* the poet Louis MacNeice asked 'Why do we like being Irish?' and answered:

> 'Partly because
> It gives us a hold on the sentimental English
> As members of a world that never was,
>   Baptized with fairy water;
> And partly because Ireland is small enough
>   To be still thought of with a family feeling,
> And because the waves are rough
>   That split her from a more commercial culture;
> And because one feels that here one can
>   Do local work which is not at the world's mercy
> And that on this tiny stage with luck a man
>   Might see the end of one particular action.
> It is self deception of course;
>   There is no immunity in this island either;
> A cart that is drawn by somebody else's horse
>   And carrying goods to somebody else's market.
> The bombs in the turnip sack, the sniper from the roof
>   Griffith, Connolly, Collins, where have they brought us?
> Ourselves alone! Let the round tower stand aloof
>   In a world of bursting mortar!
> Let the school-children fumble their sums
>   In a half-dead language;
> Let the censor be busy on the books; pull down the Georgian slums;
>   Let the games be played in Gaelic
> Let them grow beet-sugar; let them build
>   A factory in every hamlet;
> Let them pigeon-hole the souls of the killed
>   Into sheep and goats, patriots and traitors.

I hope that in this book some clues will be found to explain his equivocal reply and the ambiguity of the images of Ireland which crowd into my mind – the 'Englishtown' and the 'Irishtown' of the straggling townships of Ulster; Tuam Cathedral on a Sunday morning with six indomitable Protestants singing 'Change and decay in all around I see'; Mass in western Mayo with the women inside the church and the men lingering outside the doors; the bowler-hatted marcher in an Orange parade who thought 'King Willy' was mentioned in the Bible; echoes of a ballad 'It's to hell with the future and live in the past, May the Lord in His mercy be kind to Belfast'; Catholic priests and nuns in the Quaker Meeting House in Dublin giving utterance to ecstatic praise of God in ecumenical unison with Presbyterians, Pentecostals and Evangelical firebrands; four high-ranking government officials fighting-drunk at a polite party in what was once the Pale; garish grottoes with simpering Madonnas; the smell – at once familiar and exotic – of burning turf and baking soda-bread in a one-room thatched cabin, in a ducal castle, in a rot-ridden Munster mansion furnished with the frayed remains of a chaste and genteel past. And the fragmented remembrances of the enchantment of the spoken word in Ireland – a stout Cork taxi-driver who described himself as 'obese'; the Tipperary shopwoman who cautioned me on a fine July day, 'The heat is destructive, the hospitals are totally replenished, the people are succumbing in the streets'; the South Dublin matron admiring her neighbour's new hat: 'It is both elegant and bizarre without being chronic or massive.'

Ireland still stands today on the edge of Europe and on the edge of the modern world, beckoning and hospitable, but jealous of her individuality, eager but uncertain in her anticipation of the future, yet strangely immersed in her ubiquitous past. A few miles from the traffic jams of Dublin or Belfast and the fragile pretensions of a self-conscious permissive society is the peaceful mystery of the mountains and lakes, townlands where the old values are cloistered and the other world never seems distant.

6

INTRODUCTION

The Irish – Fact and Fiction

E. ESTYN EVANS

IT IS DIFFICULT and perhaps impossible to be neutral in writing about Ireland and Irish affairs. The Irish themselves hold many divergent views, while the English are understandably bewildered and on the whole tolerant, forgetful of their long involvement and bitter experience in 'the other island'. The Irish do not so readily forget the past and have found consolation for their long subjection in an exaggerated version of former glories, of an island united, peaceful and thronged with heroes, of a past that never was. It was an image that inspired the Easter Rising of 1916 and still moves minority groups to periodic violence. For them the past is ineradicable. Lying as it were in the lap of the larger island, Ireland's contacts with the outside world, whether social, cultural, economic or political, became largely concentrated in one direction, and an obsession with – or reaction against – links with Britain was correspondingly sharpened. But whatever view may be taken, there can be no dispute as to the island's charm, its powers of seduction, or the outstanding contributions the Irish world has made through the centuries to the larger world outside.

The purpose of this Introduction is not to attempt a summary of the specialist chapters which follow but first to give some idea of the geological structure and environment of the island, and then to isolate the essential qualities of Irish culture – to try to account for the Irishness of the Irish. There are some who would invoke the racial inheritance of the Irish people, the so-called 'racial mind', but I suspect that they really mean culture, not race; and culture has more to do with place than with race. As is shown in Chapter 8, the characteristics of Irish-Americans are on the whole very different from those of the Irish at home. What do we know about the racial composition of the Irish people? It is a subject that requires what might be called an antagonizing reappraisal. Popular writers contrast the 'Celtic race' with the 'English race', but historical records lead us to suspect what studies of blood groups in Ireland confirm, that about a quarter of the genes in the people of the Republic are derived from Anglo-Norman and English settlers, and this is almost certainly a higher percentage than any derived from the 'Celtic race'.

Some anthropologists have claimed that at least half the genetic ancestry of the composite modern Irishman derives from the native Irish stock, the pre-Celtic inhabitants who, through millennia, had become partly adapted to the peculiarities of the Irish environment. The adjustment may have included a lessening of eye pigmentation under cloudy skies; at any rate one of the commonest Irish traits is the combination of dark hair and light eyes. The facial features caricatured in the stereotyped stage Irishman probably derive from an ancient stock. The most distinguishing genetic feature of the Irish people, especially in the western parts, is the high frequency of Blood Group O, which is probably the highest in Europe. High frequencies of O are common in the people of many other peripheral parts of the Old World, and in Europe are found among the Basques and in Scotland and Iceland. We cannot properly speak of a 'Celtic race': the Irish people are of mixed ancestry and, while a heritage of ancient genes may have contributed to their vitality, such qualities as may reside in physical inheritance are more likely to be derived from hybridization than from any supposedly pure race.

Irish history has been written mainly in terms of politics and personalities – and they have their place in the chapters that follow – but while we cannot doubt that men's deeds and words have had a powerful influence on the course of Irish history, its general pattern must be seen in the light of the Irish environment and the enduring heritage of its people, of what I have called the personality of Ireland. Patriotic writers have seen their homeland as a tragic mother-figure bearing poetic names which became, in English, Dark Rosaleen and Kathleen ni Houlihan. Attitudes to the land and to the landscape have been emotional and even sentimental, based on literary and traditional associations rather than observation and experience. The mountains most Irishmen know best are spiritual heights such as Croagh Patrick. For many, the other world – the world of legend – has seemed more real than the living world around them. The first chapter in Edna O'Brien's *Mother Ireland* has the promising but misleading title, 'The Land Itself': but it is in fact full of fictitious Firbolgs and mythical Milesians. I would see 'the land itself' as a part of Irish history, and the spirit of place as a key to the understanding of the Irishness of the Irish.

Who were these mysterious peoples, the Firbolg, the Tuatha dé Danann, the Milesians and the rest? These were the names, apparently derived from pagan deities, given in the Irish world annals to successive prehistoric invaders of Ireland as enshrined in oral tradition. Perhaps because this pseudo-history carried the authority of the Christian scribes who recorded it, the Firbolg and the Milesians have been held in a reverence that was never given to later invaders; the invasions, although clearly mythological, came to be accepted almost as gospel truth, all the more readily, perhaps, because they were sufficiently remote to seem heroic, whereas the historic invasions which followed had brought the remembered humiliation of conquest or at least half-conquest. Based as they were on oral traditions, however much they were doctored to fit in with Biblical records and to provide an impeccable ancestry for the claimants to the High Kingship, the world annals, like the Homeric

7

epics, probably contain a substratum of truth, if only it could be disentangled. Many attempts have been made to equate the invasions of the annals with the findings of archaeologists, linguists, ethnologists, anthropologists and historians, but there is little agreement on possible correlations, and the feuds among Irish scholars in this field are about as bitter as those among politicians. Whereas the English saw nothing but barbarism and obscurity in Ireland before the coming of the Anglo-Normans, the Irish cherished their ancient literature, and the pseudo-history of the annals was uncritically espoused by romantic nationalists such as the New Irelanders; and, astonishingly, it long remained the standard textbook version of early Irish history and has kept alive dangerous passions of pride and hatred.

It is hard for an Englishman to comprehend the Irishman's view of the past, for all time appears to be foreshortened into the living present. 'We Irish,' wrote Dr Lloyd Praeger, 'can never let the past bury its dead. Finn McCoul and Brian Boru are still with us . . . the Battle of the Boyne was fought last Thursday week, and Cromwell trampled and slaughtered in Ireland towards the latter end of the preceding month.'

I have suggested that 'the land itself' has had much to do with Irish history and character. We should look, first of all, at Ireland's position on the far Atlantic edge of the Old World. Early wanderers who reached the island found that they could go no farther. Successive immigrants into this cul-de-sac have tended to cling to the customs and traditions of their homelands, and perhaps the outstanding characteristic of Irish culture has been its conservatism, its retention of old-fashioned ways of life. From this comes its capacity to hand back to the outside world cultural loans which have been enriched by the Irish experience. For the price of survival was coming to terms with the Irish environment and way of life. The Gaelicization of the Anglo-Normans in Ireland is proverbial, and so it was with many earlier intrusive peoples and cultures. As many of us know, the same forces affect individuals. It was Edmund Spenser who wrote, in the 16th century, 'Lord, how quickly doth that country alter one's nature!' However long they resist and however loud their protests, sooner or later newcomers are absorbed. I would maintain that in some ways the Protestants of Ulster are more Irish than the Irish, always mindful of the past and celebrating it with slogans and annual parades. Over and over again, cultures have taken on an Irish shape as they were poured into the Irish mould.

The land of Ireland

Despite its small size and elegant compactness of shape, the island is characterized by great geological diversity and topographical variety. What distinguishes it from the sister isle of Great Britain is the broken nature of the upland areas, thanks mainly to the intense erosion associated with an oceanic climate. Thus we cannot simplify Irish geography and history by distinguishing, as we can in Britain, highland and lowland zones. Instead, there is a broken ring of uplands, many of them ending in spectacular sea-cliffs, and a lowland heart; but the hills are rarely out of sight and they crop up in unexpected places. The Wicklow Mountains, the largest

mass of mountain granite in the British Isles, directly overlook the capital city. And Belfast, not to be outdone, nestles in its narrow valley under the largest expanse of basaltic lavas in these islands – the Antrim plateau. This juxtaposition of upland and lowland areas, with their contrasted modes of life, has allowed different groups of people and different cultures to co-exist in a tiny island, has encouraged administrative and political fragmentation, and has long delayed the attainment of political unity. If, as pious politicians have proclaimed, Ireland is a 'god-given island', I suggest that the edict 'divide and rule' has its source in higher authority than the English Crown. A mosaic of varied local environments and inter-tribal feuds were realities which English political manipulation could exploit but could hardly create.

While one might suppose that the predominance of lowland would have facilitated communication and integration – for all the uplands put together would not cover more than one-eighth of the island – the largest (central) lowland is in no sense a meeting-place: it is imperfectly drained by the mighty Shannon and strewn with a profusion of lakes and bogs that have impeded movement. The Central Lowland thus never became a seat of political power, and the centrally placed Athlone became a major communication centre only when it was given the freedom of the air through Radio Eireann.

A brief geological excursion will help us to understand both the structural build of the island and its physical resources. Most of the uplands are the denuded remnants of two major phases of mountain-building. In the north, and extending far down the east and west coasts, are the remains of the immensely ancient Caledonian fold-mountains – a continuation of the Scottish uplands – oriented north-east/south-west and consisting of shales, schists, quartzites and granites. In the south, mainly in Waterford, Cork and Kerry, are the post-Carboniferous east-west Armorican folds, consisting of ribs of Old Red Sandstone flanked by Carboniferous Limestone. In these fold systems, mineralization brought concentrations of copper ore (in the Armorican folds) and of gold (deposited in the streams of the Wicklow and other Caledonian mountains) which contributed greatly to Ireland's first (prehistoric) Golden Age.

Between these converging mountain girders, as though caught in mighty pincers, lie the unfolded limestones of the Central Lowland, covering almost half the island and constituting the largest continuous stretch of Carboniferous Limestones in the whole of Europe. The most conspicuous exceptions to the levelled limestones occur where cappings of impervious rocks have preserved high plateaux such as the Burren of Clare or such dramatic landmarks as the great escarpment of Benbulbin in Sligo. For good or ill, however, the usually overlying coal measures have, thanks to excessive erosion, almost entirely disappeared. Thus, Ireland was destined to remain essentially rural and to be spared the devastation brought about in Britain by palaeotechnic

A ring of uplands encircles a great part of Ireland, often ending in spectacular sea-cliffs. Horn Head, Co. Donegal (opposite) rises more than 600 feet from the water. It includes one of the country's natural curiosities – MacSweeney's Gun, a huge blow-hole which produces a deafening report in stormy weather. (1)

The central lowlands might have been a means of contact between the inhabitants of early Ireland. Instead they were a means of division, being broken up by spurs

of mountain and large areas of impassable bog. Except in a few favoured areas, agriculture has counted for less than stock-raising. Shown on these pages are Bantry Bay, Co. Cork (above left), a bog near Salley Gap, Co. Wicklow (left), and Luggala, Co. Wicklow, a valley nestling in its hills. (2–4)

Benbulbin, Co. Sligo, is among the most dramatic of Ireland's mountains, and holds a special place in legend and history. Here, legend says, Diarmuid was slain by the soldiers of Finn MacCoul, and here, in the green valley at its foot, is the grave of Ireland's greatest poet, W. B. Yeats. (5)

The lakes could also be barriers to communication, but were sometimes living sites and highways. Below: the Upper Lake, Killarney, Co. Kerry. Killarney's rich scenery and gentle climate have made it a key region in Ireland's expanding tourist industry. (6)

industry and carboniferous capitalism. But there were compensations. The Central Lowland has been directly linked with Ireland's reputation, going back to early Celtic times at least, for quality livestock. The sweet, bone-building pastures of the limestone soils have had much to do with it. In another climate they would be producing wheat or wine, but, under the prevailing oceanic climate, which brings rain throughout the year, grass is the most profitable crop. Irish folk-tales, no less than the epics of her heroic age, are full of the lowing of kine, the bellowing (and the stealing) of bulls, the magic speed of horses and the terror of mythical beasts.

The pastoral heritage has not favoured the growth of towns or even of the agricultural villages that have long characterized the English lowlands and much of the European mainland. Most Irish towns are post-medieval in date and long remained very small. The strength of Irish culture has not manifested itself in great works of architecture or other massive cultural achievements demanding concentrations of wealth, but in personal craftsmanship and the creative arts. Family and kin have mattered more than community, and the ties of blood have often proved stronger than the claims of more abstract loyalties.

The limestone provided durable construction stone whether for megaliths, field walls, farmsteads or churches. Like the tough grey granite which is its closest rival as a native building stone, the hard Carboniferous Limestone does not lend itself to deep carving or delicate tracery, but rather to austerely simple architectural forms. It is only in the north-east that younger sedimentary rocks occur, but they do not include, to Ireland's great loss, that most valuable of freestones, the Jurassic Oolite.

We shall have to refer in Chapter 1 to the north-east because of the outstanding role it played in the earliest phases of Irish prehistory. Apart from the easy contacts facilitated by its close proximity to Britain, it had a near monopoly of the sort of hard cutting-stones required by man in the pre-metal age. It owed this advantage to its involvement in the igneous activity of the Scoto-Icelandic region – the columnar phenomena of Staffa, for example, being repeated in the Giant's Causeway in Co. Antrim. Successive sheets of basaltic lava poured out in geologically recent (Tertiary) times over the last remaining fragment of chalk in Ireland, including flints, and thus preserved it from further denudation. The white cliffs of the Antrim coast, with their abundance of exposed flints, are a great rarity in Atlantic Europe, and since they are easily visible across the narrow North Channel they may well have attracted questing fisherfolk to the island to become the first Irishmen. Even more valuable for the manufacture of cutting axes were certain rare sources of fine-grained sedimentary rocks that had been hardened by igneous contact and could be shaped by flaking and polishing; chief among them the 'bluestone' of Tievebulliagh, a conspicuous peak near Cushendall, whence stone axes were exported to many parts of the British Isles in neolithic times, from 3500 to 2000 BC. Tievebulliagh axes were evidently highly prized, and they were sometimes made for ritual purposes: witness the hoard of nineteen outsize axes found in 1872 in Malone, a southern suburb of Belfast.

We must now set the Irish stage, so far as it may be reconstructed, at the time when men first made their homes here some eight or nine thousand years ago. The finishing strokes in the shaping of the natural landscape were the work of ice in the Pleistocene period. Thanks to the excessive precipitation, which now fell as snow, no part of the island escaped the invasion of ice-sheets, and these have left their characteristic imprint on upland and lowland alike. Two depositional land-forms are so characteristic of the island that their anglicized names, 'esker' and 'drumlin', are perhaps the only Gaelic words to be adopted internationally in scientific nomenclature. Eskers are steep, narrow, winding ridges of sand and gravel, some fifty feet high and sometimes many miles long, that litter the Central Lowland and stand out as 'green hills' when they run through areas of bog or of naked limestone pavement. Because they provided dry footing for travellers, they have served as natural lines of communication in difficult country.

The drumlins provide a very different kind of environment. They are little rounded hills of boulder clay, up to half a mile long and a hundred feet high, running in the direction of the ice-flow and sometimes packed so closely together – a dozen or more to the square mile – that they block the natural drainage and make movement of any kind difficult. A great swarm of drumlins – one of the largest in the world – traverses Ireland in a broad loop from south Co. Donegal to Co. Down, representing the dumping of glacial clay and boulders as the ice-sheets tumbled from the Ulster uplands towards the Central Lowland. Archaeologically, this difficult border country was late to be opened up to settlement, and it had much to do with the historical isolation of the province of Ulster from the rest of the island.

Finally, in post-glacial times, there were further additions to the natural environment in the form of forests and bogs, and they have been closely involved in the human story. How, it may be asked, did plants and animals get into the island? Before the final ice-melt had raised the world sea-level to approximately its present position by about 6000 BC, Ireland was for some millennia joined to Britain by morainic land-bridges, and these allowed plants and animals to colonize what had been, after the retreat of the ice, tundra landscapes. In general, then, the native flora and fauna are those of north-western Europe, but there is less variety. The chief trees, in order of arrival, were willow, birch, hazel, pine, alder, oak, elm and ash. Some latecomers and slow-movers failed to make the crossing: among trees the beech, lime and hornbeam, and among animals the toad, the mole, the vole, the weasel, all species of snakes – and man himself, for we have as yet no evidence that he had reached Ireland much before 7000 BC. By that time the forest had spread wherever it could get a foothold, avoiding only swamps and the most exposed mountain tops. Nothing is now left of the primeval forest except for the fossil trunks of oak and pine in the bogs: already in neolithic times, extensive clearings were made for arable and pastoral husbandry, and forest destruction by man and grazing animals went on through the centuries until Ireland became the least wooded country in Europe.

But the Irish climate was also partly responsible. No less than one-sixth of the island is or has been covered with turf (peat). The bogs are of two kinds – lowland or 'raised' bogs and upland or 'blanket' bogs – and they appear to have grown most vigorously during what is called the 'sub-Atlantic' climatic phase, from about 600 BC onwards, when the climate is thought to have been even wetter than it is today. Under 'Atlantic' climates, when the surface soil for any reason becomes water-logged, organic matter decomposes very slowly and accumulates as peat, reaching an average depth, in the lowland bogs of central Ireland, of some eighteen feet. Important both scenically and economically, the bog-lands are also of great scientific interest, and not least to archaeologists. Thanks to their preservative powers, they contain a record of vegetational history and not infrequently of human history as well. Like the folk memory, they hold the golden past in their depth, preserving intact the once-golden pollen grains of identifiable trees and plants as well as the ever-golden ornaments and artefacts made by Bronze Age craftsmen. Some of these bog-finds have been interpreted as ritual offerings, but they are so numerous that if, anthro-pologically, man is defined as a tool-user, I suggest that the Irishman might be termed a tool-loser. By correlating pollen studies and carbon-dating with the horizons marked by archaeological finds, it has been possible to build up a chronology of prehistory and a picture of the succession of plants and types of land-use throughout the life of the bogs. The upland blanket-bogs are thinner and cannot always be explained either by the natural in-filling of lakes or by climatic change; they seem to be best developed in areas where man had been actively engaged in forest-clearing and farming during the neolithic and Bronze ages, from about 3500 to 600 BC, when the climate is thought to have been drier and warmer than it is today.

Myth-making

We have looked briefly at Ireland's positional geography and at its physical attributes, but another geographical factor must be taken into account. If the Irish world transcends space, it is partly because the Irish homeland is a small world, a tiny island no larger than thousands of other little islands scattered through the oceans, and its population of 4.5 millions is much less than that of many of the world's multi-million cities. Small islands if long occupied tend to become over-populated and to export people. Movements from Ireland into Britain are attested from the early centuries AD, and while in the succeeding centuries Irish influences were carried into Europe mainly by missionaries, adventurers and political refugees, it was emigration to Britain, beginning as a seasonal exodus of harvesting labourers and, after the great famine, mass emigration to North America (which had been preceded by a substantial and significant 18th-century outflow of protesting Presbyterians from Ulster), that carried Irishmen and Irish influences overseas on an unprecedented scale and at times sapped the vitality of the island. Not least among Ireland's paradoxes is its demographic history. Whereas the population of most countries has multiplied in the last century or so, that of Ireland, after trebling in less than a

century to reach a maximum of some 8.5 million in 1845, is now almost halved, and is no greater than it was at the end of the 18th century. Population has continued to fall until quite recently. In the 1950s the Republic was losing fifty thousand people every year, mostly to Britain, and won for itself, at a time when Northern Ireland (and the Irish immigrants in Britain) were enjoying the relative prosperity of the Welfare State, the unflattering nick-name of 'the Farewell State'. The tide of emigration has now slackened, however, and the population of the Republic is once more increasing, while that of troubled Northern Ireland is declining.

The 'soft' evergreen climate – and the soft accents and a leisurely pace of life – have earned the western isle yet another label, 'Europe's decompression chamber'. But Atlantic depressions appear also to bring psychological depression, which is given as the main cause of an excessive consumption of alcohol, estimated to account for 10 per cent of all personal spending in the Republic. I suspect that alcohol has long been one of the ingredi-ents in Irish wit and Irish bellicosity. I do not cite it as evidence, but there is a story of a well-known scholar who, well soaked after a day in the country investigating Gaelic names, came to the conclusion that the name of the mythological hero who appears in the literature as Con of the Hundred Battles might just as well have been Con of the Hundred Bottles!

From early times types of settlement and societal patterns in Ireland were those proper to herdsmen rather than arable farmers. Thus the historic village-system of England and much of Western Europe, with its hallowed institutions, its peaceful village green and its sense of community, was unknown in Gaelic Ireland, where society, while no less hierarchical, was based on family and clan. Blood ties were strong and patronymics almost universal, and the isolated farmstead and, in former times, the untidy clustered cabins of peasant kinsmen, were the normal types of settlement. (It was these clusters or 'towns', that gave the Irish 'townland', a minute territorial subdivision averaging about half a square mile in area, its English name.) Family ties, though weakened, remain surprisingly strong, even in urban areas, and they were an important element in the social, economic and political life of the Irish in America. In many parts of the Irish countryside, the extended family retains much of its traditional strength, and even 'far out' blood relations are referred to as 'friends'. Things of the spirit – things which have little to do with access to capital or technology – remain powerful integrating forces, as is shown by the great gatherings at country funerals.

If the Irish at home lacked the experience of traditional village life and loyalty to a mixed community, equally they had little opportunity of urban living. Native monastic towns were hardly worthy of the name, and towns established by the Anglo-Normans or the English were long regarded as foreign institutions. It has been said that the Irish have excelled not in building towns but rather in turning towns built by others into slums: it would be fairer to say that they have put their own stamp on the towns and cities they have adopted.

The strength of the blood tie has been evident at all levels of society and the principle of hereditary succession was adopted by the early Church (though it was quite alien to Christian teaching) as well as by the Anglo-Normans. In the election of the secular leaders who were local kings, struggles between rival contestants were the more bitter because they were between kinsmen. A caste-like system obtained in many sections of society. The Brehons, for example, were hereditary lawyers as well as judges, interpreters of an archaic body of laws which were regarded as immutable. It would seem that the prestige of the Brehons, who had inherited something of the mystery of the pagan Druidic guardians of the law, was in turn passed on to later generations. At any rate the Irish seem to have an aptitude for legal affairs, for arguing about (and evading) the law, and a fondness for litigation which have long brought profitable business to Dublin, and small towns throughout the country.

The gift of words, of imaginative and persuasive oratory and colourful language, is of course not the monopoly of lawyers and politicians. I recall the reply of a Mayoman to an English visitor who, hopefully taking out his watch, wanted to know at what time a certain local incident had occurred: 'It was in the heel of the evening,' was the leisurely response, 'about the time when the dew was *thinking* of falling.' Many Irish countrymen have remarkable powers of memory which testify to the strength of oral tradition in a world lacking material goods but cherishing things of the spirit. From early times transmission by word of mouth of a vast body of lore had been facilitated by the use of alliteration and rhythm. It was because, under the influence of the monastic schools, much of this material was committed to writing from the 6th century onwards, that early Irish literature is 'the earliest voice from the dawn of West European civilization'. Much of it is in verse form, which came to include rhyme as well as rhythm. The Irish clerics thus ensured the survival in written form of a wealth of traditional lore that perished elsewhere in Western Europe, for the urban culture of the Roman Empire which dominated most of the old Celtic lands had no place for pagan bards, seers and jurists.

We have already touched on the oral content of the Irish world annals, but these were only part of a vast assemblage of mythological lore, of fairytales and stories which find parallels, and possibly origins, not only in the old Celtic world but also in lands as distant as Eastern Europe, India and North Africa. They were part of the repertoire of the Gaelic story-teller until yesterday, and to them were added countless tales, ballads, legends and heroic sagas which grew out of the Irish experience or were borrowed from the literature of medieval Europe, which in turn was enriched by contributions from the Gaelic world. Ireland is thus a fascinating treasure-house of oral traditions, of highly imaginative tales concerning heroes, fairies, giants, demons, witches, hags, spirits and of course leprechauns, those impish manikins who, despite their popularity among devoted Irish-Americans, appear to be peripheral to the main body of native lore and may owe something to Scandinavian influences. In this world of magic, birds and animals, trees and flowers, the wind and the rain, were endowed with miraculous powers of speech and were treated with due respect. Legends grew around every element in the environment, whether natural or man-made, and as might be expected there is a wealth of lore associated with the milk cow. The blossoming fairy whitethorn and the golden flowers of May, with their symbolic promise of a full flow of milk and butter, were regarded with reverence as bringers of good luck. Flowering plants – whitethorn, blackthorn and furze – were significantly the companions of the earliest neolithic farmers, spreading as clearances were made in the closed forest that was once almost universal. Although fairytales and superstitious beliefs and customs lost much of their appeal after the tragedy of the famine and 'the devotional revolution' which followed, they are not entirely gone. Not long ago a friend collecting folklore in the Ulster hills was given this advice: 'Leave old thorns and priests alone: pay them their dues and leave them alone.'

Story-telling no doubt provided an escape from a hard life and material poverty into an unseen world of the imagination, but it was more than this. It was part of a heritage that stressed the spiritual aspects of life and emphasized personal accomplishments in an environment where a scattered population and limited resources made joint enterprise difficult and massive investment in urban forms of cultural expression impossible. Irish folk tunes are considered to be among the finest in the world. Singing or playing them on the fiddle is an individual accomplishment, without chorus or orchestra. But despite this wealth in non-material matters, there was, at the folk level, little in the way of visual art.

Traditional craft products tend to be severely functional and to derive their quality from fitness for purpose rather than artistic finish: textiles are plain; and there is no wood-carving and very little in the way of ceramics or metal-work. In general early Irish art is abstract and non-representational, and characterized by a superstitious *horror vacui*; but the intricate skills shown in the metalwork no less than in the illuminated manuscripts of early historic and early medieval Ireland left no mark in folk tradition. The splendid high crosses are interlaced with pagan and Christian motifs – an illustration of the way Christianity adapted itself to the pagan Celtic world. It seems that the main periods of artistic achievement have been the result of intrusive influences affecting élites. It is doubtful if the poverty of folk art as compared with that of most other parts of Europe can be attributed to the evil effects of conquest and the social submergence of the native people. Rather, the genius of the Irish has been expressed in spiritual forms, above all in poetry and the cultivation of conversation and story-telling as a fine art.

The New Society and 'hidden Ireland'
Very different were the cultural values of the New Society which was finally firmly established in 18th-century Ireland after the victories of William III. Its greatest triumph was Georgian Dublin, but it also left a lasting mark on the landscapes and townscapes of much of the country. It was almost entirely an imported culture and it turned its back on the Irish heritage, the pre-Reformation medieval and prehistoric heritage of myth and poetry which was preserved in the impoverished 'hidden Ireland' of the Gael. In domestic architecture its gracious Palladian and Georgian imprint is dominant

because earlier centuries had bequeathed comparatively little in the way of urban architecture and almost no grand houses in the countryside. Down to the end of the 17th century the country gentry clung to their fortified tower houses to give them the security which the state could not provide: there are no less than four hundred examples surviving in one county alone, Co. Limerick. The development of domestic architecture as illustrated in much of Europe and in England and Wales, where the age of fortification virtually ended with the great medieval stone castles, was in Ireland arrested for some three centuries by the prevailing conditions of anarchy. For much the same reasons there is little good-quality oak furniture or fine craftsmanship in other materials surviving from earlier times. Moreover there is little in the way of vernacular building older than the 18th century. The humble single-storey thatched dwellings were generally built of wattles, sods or clay and lacked the tradition of good carpentry which in England and Wales is often displayed in the furniture as well as the structure of farmhouse and cottage.

The Neo-Classical phase left a lasting mark on the cultural landscape. In domestic architecture the fashion of symmetry about a central doorway spread to the small farmhouse, particularly in those areas where English influences had long been dominant. Where the traditional thatched house survives – there are many parts of the country where it has almost disappeared in the last quarter-century – it will be noticed that the type with hipped roof and central chimney is virtually confined to the south-eastern half of the country. Only in the north and west, where English influence was weaker, did the traditional long-house derived from a combined living-room and byre, with its native end-chimney asymmetry, live on. And some of these houses still retain the oven-less open hearth around which the old stories are told.

Most of the cultural components of the Georgian era in Ireland were imported – as were many of the artists and silversmiths, architects and stuccadores. Although some of its products had an Irish flavour, for example the distinctive mahogany 'hunting table', it would be misleading to see the great popularity of architectural 'follies' as a special Irish trait; but it is characteristic that the fashion persisted far into the 19th century, just as urban terrace-houses retained the Georgian style into Victorian times. From about 1780 onwards the Georgian box-house, with its graceful fanlight door, its walled 'demesne' and its elegant glass and silverware and mahogany furniture, became the genteel standard throughout the country for all who could afford it, including the clergy of the Established Church. This gentility, like the splendour of Dublin, although it rested on and depended on a foundation of grinding poverty, had a strong appeal to the Irish merchants as they began to prosper and to the rising professional classes, who had lived a generation or two earlier in conditions of squalor. If the New Society left a lasting mark on Irish life and landscape, the gentry stock came in time to be profoundly affected by the older Irish heritage and to provide leaders for the nationalist cause; and in the end, in the last hundred years, some of its members were to prove their Irishness by making brilliant contributions to creative writing.

The wooded demesnes of the gentry have in many instances been taken over by the state to become the nuclei of much-needed forestry plantations; but it was not only the demesnes, the landscaped gardens and elegant gentry houses that left an enduring imprint on the countryside. The rectangular hedged fields gave the 'champion' country that had been dear to the Anglo-Normans a new pattern of domesticated order, while even in the Gaelic-speaking hill country landlords (and later the state) began to discipline the untidy 'through-other' system of scattered rundale plots by an overlay of 'straight marches'. But still, in almost all the Irish hills, one may see enduring traces of the old system of irregular patches of arable land so scarred with abandoned spade-dug ridges that the face of old Mother Ireland might be said to be wrinkled with their marks.

In parts of the country where grazing animals had ranged freely and left the landscape almost naked the new concern for wooded estates brought welcome relief. Many of the trees, shrubs and garden flowers imported from England or farther afield – among them the beech, the lime and exotic conifers – provided an appropriate setting for the Neo-Classical culture. Among the fashionable vegetables brought from southern Europe were globe artichokes (a favourite delicacy of the ancient Greeks and Romans) described by an Irish countryman as 'playthings for the gentry', a phrase that might be applied to many of the frills of 18th-century Anglo–Irish society.

Famine and 'the devotional revolution'

If few of the gentry's playthings were adopted by the Irish – I have heard carrots, for instance, described in Co. Cavan as only fit for horses – there was one exotic root crop, the Latin-American potato, which fitted so well into the Irish environment, climatically and socially, that it was fated to send back millions of Irishmen to America in return. Possibly introduced by Raleigh to his Munster estates towards the end of the 16th century, the potato was adopted by the peasants of that region as a supplementary crop; but it became the staple diet of the country as a whole only in the last quarter of the 18th century, when it was a major contributor to population growth. A gastronomic Gresham's Law was at work, for the prolific potato, which had only to be boiled to be eaten, became almost the only food of masses of the population, and the skills and lore associated with some traditional sources of food were almost forgotten. The potato was supplemented where possible, however, by milk and buttermilk, and today, despite the low per capita income of the Irish people, their consumption of milk and milk products – other than cheese – is one of the highest in the world. It was of course the disastrous failure of the potato crop after 1845 that led to the mass emigration of Irishmen, and it was their familiarity with spade and shovel that brought them ready employment as navvies.

The great famine was a major turning-point in Irish demographic, social and political history. It left much of the landscape ruined and deserted. The process of recovery and modernization which followed went on alongside mass emigration. Many old crafts, customs and magic practices decayed, together with a wealth of lore and legend that bound the peasant to his townland and homeland and to the numerous festivals held at the turning-points of the year, such as midsummer and the beginning of the pagan Celtic half-years in May and November. Some of these, however, and notably the mountain-top and lake-island gatherings at Croagh Patrick and Lough Derg, had been sufficiently Christianized as pilgrimages to survive and even grow in strength as acts of penance. Faction fighting lost its popularity and its meaning, and violence was channelled in other directions. At the same time under the influence of French Jansenism, of Victorian evangelism, and especially the reforming zeal of Paul Cullen, who became Archbishop of Armagh in 1849, there were dramatic changes in the devotional practices of the Catholic population, particularly in the remaining Gaelic-speaking areas. It has recently been suggested that one of the factors favouring what has been called 'the devotional revolution' was the manifest failure of 'the elder faiths' to avert the great famine: traditional piety, it is argued, thereafter flowed in more orthodox spiritual channels. Regular church attendance, which had been as low as 30 per cent on average in the Gaelic-speaking west when statistics were collected in 1834 – and there is no reason to dismiss them as 'Irish statistics' – rose to a very high figure and has remained uniquely high throughout the country. The figure given today for the Catholic population as a whole is well over 90 per cent. After Daniel O'Connell's campaign for 'a Catholic parliament for a Catholic people' the Catholic faith, growing in strength, increasingly became the main mark of patriotic identification. Unfortunately this not only weakened the bond of the total Irish heritage but, with the involvement of many priests in political agitation, alienated the Protestants of Ulster, who in earlier periods had mixed freely, and not infrequently intermarried with Catholics. Ironically, though this is now often forgotten, it was among the Presbyterian burghers of Belfast, in close touch with republican movements in Philadelphia and Paris, that the idea of an Irish nation uniting all creeds, classes and traditions originated towards the end of the 18th century.

By the middle of the 19th century Romantic writers were projecting contemporary concepts of nationhood into Gaelic Ireland of the High Kings; and at the same time, with the devotional revolution, early Christian Ireland, the land of saints and scholars, came to be revered as a model of orthodox piety, as devoutly observant as the Ireland of Victorian times. The monastic ideal was seen as a continuing guiding force in Irish life, a manifestation of 'the Celtic spirit'. But although there were ascetics among the monks, many were married and the rules of marriage and divorce were quite alien to Christian teaching. There was more scholarship than sanctity, although many men of humble birth 'walked the world' and achieved fame as missionaries. From the beginning, it seems, most of the converts came from families possessing hereditary power, and the clerics tended to be a social élite. The more Irish Christianity in Ireland became, the more closely did piety become linked with status, prestige and the control of supernatural power. It seems unlikely that the mass of the population was deeply affected by the new faith.

A well-known student of early Ireland used to say, in private, that if you knew the number of Irish saints you would know approximately the number of believing Christians! He would add that anyhow most of the '10,000 Irish saints' were very dubious figures, quite unknown to history, many of them mythological ancestral tribal heroes.

But if modern Irish piety cannot be linked with that of the early Christian period, there can be no denying the underlying continuities in folk ways and in devotion to the spiritual world. One of the most remarkable features of the devotional revolution was its puritanical attitude towards sex and its insistence on sexual purity and orthodoxy. The relationship between spirituality and sexuality has been explored by some Irish poets, and it might be suggested that the devotional revolution was in part a readjustment of these forces. So long as the elder faiths kept their appeal the promotion of fertility was a major concern, and the Church, however unwillingly, had come to terms with it. It was exhibited, for example, at the 'patterns' held at holy wells, and particularly at wakes for the dead. The pagan wake, with its megalithic memories, is now almost dead, but it has been said that the cult of death is still a strong force in Irish life. Before the upheavals of the mid-19th century, sexual activity, it seems, supported by many magical practices, was regarded not only as a means of procuring an annual birth but also as a sympathetic procedure for promoting a like fertility in crops and livestock.

Sexual repression has been seen by some critics as partly responsible for such varied traits as the prevalence of alcoholism, the fondness for intrigue and mischief-making, the sadism evidenced in the harsh treatment of animals and the appalling acts of violence committed in the name of political ideologies; but it must be said that these characteristics were all commented on long before the devotional revolution.

The new emphasis of sexual morality coincided with demographic and economic changes brought about by the famine, and must be related to them as well as to the influence of religious puritanism and the weakening of immemorial magic. It had been the practice in the countryside, especially during the period dominated by a potato economy, for young people to marry 'whenever they took a notion' and to be given a portion of the parental holding by subdivision. After the famine, to avoid the disaster of further impoverishment by land fragmentation, the pattern of family behaviour changed dramatically, conforming to the custom among land-owners of arranged marriages, and the change was accelerated as land legislation brought 'peasant proprietorship' in place of insecure tenancies. For many countrymen the practice of long and often life-long celibacy began in the period after the famine. Even so recently as 1945 one in four Irish farmers was still a bachelor at the age of seventy! Many young people of both sexes found relief in emigration, while others have dedicated their virginity to the Virgin Mother.

Great prestige attaches to families who have a son or daughter in the service of the Catholic Church, and if they sometimes fall by the wayside the explanation offered may well be, 'T'was his (or her) mother had the vocation!' 'Do ye call that hillside barren?' said a

Corkman to a visitor who had commented on the barren poverty of a mountainy landscape dotted with small farms: 'Let me tell ye that five priests and seven nuns came out of it!'

The strength of Irish Catholicism is perhaps best exemplified in the extent of its diffusion overseas, where it has been carried by missionaries and emigrants into every continent, most recently and most powerfully into North America. At home the faith was strengthened by Protestant, and particularly Nonconformist, opposition, and here religious zeal has manifested itself in schismatic movements; and they too have spread outside Ireland. It was from Co. Armagh, where the Orange Order originated in 1795, only a few miles from the primatial city, that Thomas Campbell, a Presbyterian minister, emigrated in 1807 to Pennsylvania in the wake of a massive exodus of Ulster Scots (from whose stock came a surprising number of American Presidents), and established a schismatic group, the Campbellites, out of which grew that distinctively American evangelical movement, the Christian Church (Disciples of Christ). It was in Dublin that the Plymouth Brethren had their origins in the early 19th century, before transferring to Devon; and it was in Dublin that the Exclusive Brethren broke away from them.

In the last twenty years, with government guidance, Ireland has been transformed from an agricultural to a primarily industrial country, and although nearly half its population is still classed as rural-dwelling, the number of industrial workers is now double the number engaged in agriculture. Since 1960 the rate of economic growth has been unmatched in Europe, but despite this the Republic is regarded as the weakest member of the European Economic Community, with heavy rates of inflation and unemployment. The process of modernization has made little impression on traditional Irish piety, and conservative attitudes are evident in the generally low status and rewards accorded to women, in restrictions on family planning and divorce. Membership of the EEC, while it has brought rewards, has also brought a challenge to the Gaelic west, for this Atlantic fringe of Europe is envisaged as a playground for tourists from the congested heart of the Continent, and one to ask how this can be reconciled with the preservation, still less the restoration, of the Gaelic language.

It could be argued that by adopting the concept and the apparatus of the European nation-state, and joining the EEC, Ireland has committed itself to becoming part of the Western European world, a role for which neither habitat nor heritage has fully equipped it. Yet, whatever changes may occur – and cultural change is inevitable – its own culture-pattern is so deeply bedded that many of its values and qualities are likely to persist in an environment of strong emotional appeal where traces and memories of the past are ever present, and where the other world seems but a step away. The characteristics of Irishness, it seems to me, are a respect for the past, an indifference to present time, a sense of the unseen world, intellectual curiosity, the gift of poetic imagination, a cynical sense of humour, a brooding melancholy, a subtle conception of what constitutes truth, an ingenious casuistry and a deviousness which are perhaps related to historical experience, and above all, an inexhaustible interest in words, in people and in spiritual matters: 'The English worship the law,' said Charles Stewart Parnell, 'but I am glad that Ireland has a religion.'

I

PREHISTORIC IRELAND

From the earliest migrations
to about AD 500

E. ESTYN EVANS

I speak for Erin,

Sailed and fertile sea.

Fertile fruitful mountains,

Fruitful moist woods,

Moist overflowing lochs,

Flowing hillside springs, . . .

From the incantations of the bard Amergin in
the *Leabhar Gabhála*, The Book of Invasions. tr. John Montague

The haunting relics of Ireland's prehistoric past have become almost symbols of another world. The old sites were held in veneration by the Celtic-speaking people who came to Ireland probably in the last centuries of the 1st millennium BC, and many of the myths that gathered around them survived into Christian times, often becoming associated with the saints. Even today a sense of the supernatural may be hard to overcome in their presence, and archaeological investigation fails to disperse the mists of legend. Some of that power no doubt resides in the mystery that still surrounds them. Date and purpose are often equally speculative. The so-called portal-dolmens, for instance, were no doubt basically single-chambered graves covered with a mound of earth and stones. But do they come at the beginning of neolithic man's occupation of Ireland, as their primitive

shape seems to imply, or relatively near the end, as the latest research is beginning to suggest? The one shown here is at Proleek, Co. Louth. Deprived of its encasing mound it stands stark and dramatic, the massive capstone, estimated to weigh forty tons, perched on three pointed megaliths.

Other types of prehistoric burial chamber can more confidently be fitted into chronological sequence. Court-graves and passage-graves date generally from the 3rd millennium BC. Wedge-graves do not appear until the beginning of the 2nd, and were probably introduced from France. Most stone circles and standing stones seem to date from the Bronze Age, but the tradition of erecting large stones was maintained in Celtic times and survived to emerge in the Christian era in the high crosses that are among the glories of the early Church. (1)

Court-graves are elaborate structures consisting of unroofed 'courts' from which segmented gallery graves open, set in a long cairn. At Malinmore, Co. Donegal (left), we are looking towards the court from one of its galleries— formerly roofed but now exposed to the sky. (2)

Passage-graves are large circular mounds containing a burial chamber reached by a passage. At New Grange, Co. Meath, the entrance (far right) is marked by a large stone covered with incised spirals. The chamber to which this passage leads is roofed by a sophisticated corbel vault (right) nearly 20 feet high. The large photograph (below) shows the interior of the main chamber looking back down the passage to the entrance. (5–7)

A stone saddle-quern found at New Grange was probably used for grinding wheat and barley. Oats were introduced much later, in the early Iron Age. It is from such domestic articles left in graves—they include arrow-heads, polished stone axes and simple pottery—that our knowledge of these early farmers is drawn. (3)

Inside the mound of Fourknocks, Co. Meath, lies a large chamber (below) roughly circular and about 20 feet in diameter. Originally it probably had a wooden roof resting on a post in the middle. As at New Grange there are three tomb chambers opening off it, two of them with carved lintels. In them and in the passage leading to the central chamber, excavations revealed over sixty burials. (4)

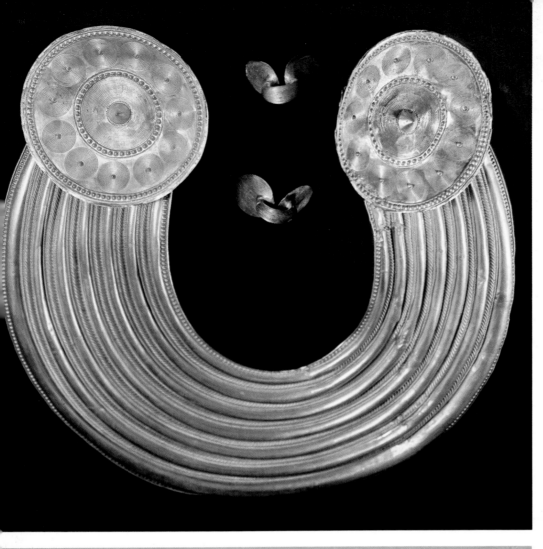

Alluvial gold was recovered from the rivers of the Wicklow mountains and elsewhere, and from 1800 BC onwards we find gold ornaments of astonishing splendour and artistic skill.

Gorgets, dating from the late Bronze Age, were worn below the chin, with the discs on the shoulders. This example (left), from Gleninsheen, Co. Clare, is over 30 centimetres wide. The ornament was shaped in repoussé and then finished with knife or chisel. (8)

'Lunula'—crescent moon—is the name given to another typical Irish gold ornament (lower left), characteristic of the early Bronze Age. The sheet was hammered flat, and a series of simple geometrical patterns traced on its surface. (9)

The golden boat found at Broighter, Co. Londonderry, is unique, with its mast, oars and seats for the rowers. A real boat, or means of journeying to the other world? Its date may be around the 1st century AD. (10)

Torques or collars belong mainly to the Bronze Age but some date from the early Iron Age. They may have had a special social or religious significance among the Celts, and images of gods are sometimes shown wearing them (the Roman sculpture known as the Dying Gaul has one). The most usual type was made by twisting a thin gold bar, as in that from Inishowen, Co. Donegal (below). The one shown bottom right is also part of the Broighter hoard. The ornamental motifs are traditionally Celtic. (11, 12)

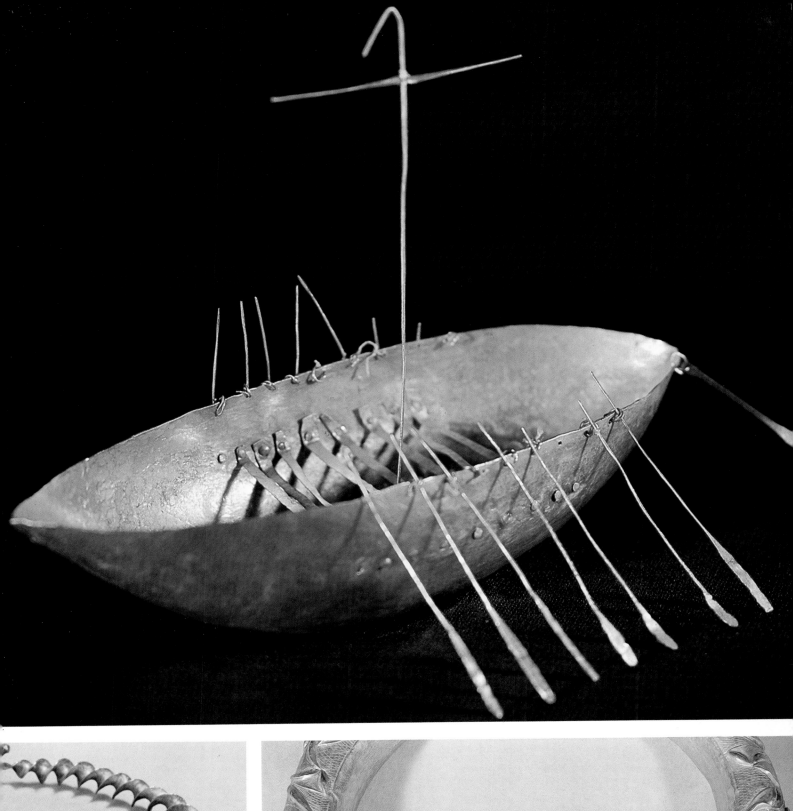

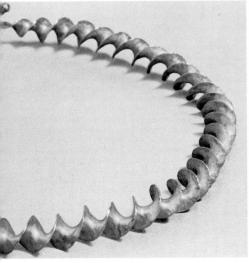

Circles, spirals and waves are among the favourite ornamental motifs of primitive peoples everywhere. The Irish passage-graves particularly abound in them, as we have seen at New Grange, but if they had any further meaning for their builders that meaning is now lost. Those on this page all come from Knowth, Co. Meath, with the exception of the example upper right. This is a much-magnified detail from a gold dress-fastener found near Clones, Co. Monaghan. The large stone (above) combines the spiral and two circles in a way that suggests a human form. One of the most interesting objects at Knowth is the stone basin (bottom right), found in a recess of one of the two main chambers; the ornament here sets a circular motif in the middle of horizontal grooves running round the basin. (13–18)

26

Loughcrew, Co. Meath. The Loughcrew Hills, and ridge more than 2 miles long, are crowned by over thirty cairns covering passage-graves—a vast prehistoric cemetery. This air photograph shows about a dozen of the most prominent. One near the centre has been excavated, revealing the familiar cross-shaped passage-grave inside. (19)

The hill of Tara, Co. Meath, perhaps the most famous of ancient Irish sites, goes back at least to the early 2nd millennium BC; the Mound of the Hostages (the small mound to the right) was discovered to be a passage-grave of that date. The larger circles are ring forts (raths) and all are enclosed within a hill fort ('the royal enclosure') dating from the early Iron Age (compare pl. 30). The left-hand circle is traditionally the coronation place of the pre-Christian Irish Kings. (20)

The farmers of the Bronze Age have left ridge and furrow patterns strikingly like those of the Middle Ages, but narrower and probably spade-made. The ridges are about $4\frac{1}{2}$ feet wide. The examples shown here were exposed by turf-cutting in Carrownaglogh, Co. Mayo. (21)

27

The 'forts'—as they are popularly called—which are such a feature of the Irish countryside were in fact for the most part not defensive works but farmsteads or enclosures for animals. They usually take the form of circular rings of grass-grown earth (raths) or dry-stone walls (cashels). Staigue Fort, Co. Kerry (left), however, was clearly built for defence; the wall stands up to 18 feet high and 13 feet thick. (22)

On an island cemetery, Boa Island in Lough Erne, Co. Fermanagh, stands a mysterious double figure of which one side is illustrated (right). It is probably a Celtic cult idol, since similar two-faced heads are common on the continent of Europe, but who do they represent—gods, heroes, ancestors? The riddle will probably never be solved. (23)

A royal site: the stone fort known as the Grianan of Ailech, Co. Donegal, which stands inside an old hill-fort, is documented as the capital of the kings of Western Ulster. It went on being used until at least the 12th century, and was drastically restored in the 19th. The ramparts contain galleries and have three internal terraces connected by steps. (24)

Standing stones are as mysterious as the stone circles. The alignment on the left is near Waterville, Co. Kerry, the single stone on the right at Punchestown, Co. Kildare. The latter is of granite and 20 feet high; there was a Bronze Age burial cist beside it. Some single stones certainly marked the sites of graves. (25,26)

Cairns, piles of stones on the summits of hills, are among the most prominent features of the Irish landscape. Most of them cover prehistoric burials. That of Ballymacgib-bon (below) possibly contains a passage-grave. (27)

Ogham stones belong to a twilight world between prehistory and Christianity. The 'Ogham' script is explained on p. 39. The cemetery at Kilcoolaght contains six of them, one of which is shown below. (28)

Stone circles go back to the Bronze Age and possibly earlier. They are usually unconnected with either burial or habitation and this makes dating exceptionally difficult. At Drombeg, Co. Cork, there are seventeen stones, one of them 'recumbent'. The date suggested is around the last century BC or the first AD. (29)

The circular enclosure known as Navan Fort (Emhain Macha), Co. Armagh, figures prominently in one of the old heroic narratives. It is a circular hill-fort, the fortress-palace of the Gaelic Kings of Ulster. Recent excavation of the tree-ringed mound inside the enclosure has shown that it was an ancient ritual structure 'spoiled' before our era. The smaller circle to the left is a rath of the Early Christian period. (30)

On a cliff edge on Inishmore, in the Aran Islands, 280 feet above the sea, stands Dun Aengus (left)—a strongly defended fort. There are three rings of stone walls (originally four), and beyond the third is an abattis—thousands of upright stone pillars placed to make access difficult for the attacker. (31)

Mysterious carved stones from the last centuries of paganism give tantalizing glimpses into the world of Celtic religion, but their meaning is lost. Above: a three-faced head from Corleck, Co. Cavan. (32)

The elegant spirals on this massive granite standing stone, at Turoe, Co. Galway, show that it belongs to Celtic Europe and to the style known as La Tène. It is about three feet high. (33)

Chapter 1

From the earliest migrations to about AD 500

E. ESTYN EVANS

Part of the spiral pattern carved on the large stone at the entrance to New Grange (see p. 51, pl. 6), Co. Meath. (1)

THE REPUBLIC OF IRELAND, as the only independent European nation having a strong Celtic heritage, is proud of this inheritance, and generations of Irish folk have been taught to think of Ireland as essentially a Celtic land. In this chapter, however, we shall be concerned mainly with the land, the people and the cultures of pre-Celtic Ireland, for chronologically the Celtic component begins to make itself felt only in the last centuries BC, about midway in the development of Irish culture from its neolithic beginnings. Thus the fabric of Irish life, fashioned in response to distinctive environmental forces, was of millennial antiquity when it had to face the challenge of Continental invaders speaking a strange language, experienced in the arts of war and possessing highly developed styles of art and exotic forms of religious observance. The Celtic impact, like the later Anglo-Norman intrusion, was essentially military and aristocratic in character, and it is reasonable to suppose that the ground-pattern of native culture lived on and in time reasserted itself. The newcomers, like later conquerors, were destined to become more Irish than the Irish. Their language, for instance, suffered a sea-change here along the Atlantic edge of Europe: it was so deeply affected by grammatical and phonological adjustments to native linguistic habits that Gaelic became 'one of the most bizarre branches of the Indo-European family'. In much the same way, as we shall see, the megalithic sites of an older Ireland came to be held in great veneration in Celtic tradition. Ancient beliefs connected with water, stones and trees seem to have been strengthened, as was the belief in magic and the supernatural. Celtic faith in an after-life, already attested in ancient Gaul, was surely quickened in Ireland in the presence of majestic megalithic tombs. The cult of death is to this day a strong motive force in Irish life, and the supernatural is never far away. One has to spend but a short time in the far west of Ireland to experience a sense of the invisible world and to realize that the end of the real world is in truth very near. The legendary voyages of St Brendan remind us that men had long been tempted to explore the unseen world beyond the western horizon, but effectively, until the Elizabethan age of maritime expansion, the finger-tips of western Ireland, reaching out into the unknown, were the very ends of the European world. Here were the last refuges of old-fashioned modes of life and here today is the last fragmented home of the Gaelic tongue.

Men and megaliths

Critics of the Irish climate have asked how early man could conceivably have been tempted to settle in the island! In the beginning, because of its remoteness, the island was not peopled throughout the lengthy palaeolithic period. It was left to roving fisherfolk and fowlers from Scotland, and possibly farther afield, to discover the untapped resources of its woods and waters. They may well have been attracted by the beckoning white cliffs of Antrim; but inland, in Lough Neagh and the River Bann, they found eels, salmon and waterfowl in enormous quantities and exploited them from waterside camps, where the remains of their wattled huts have been dated to the period 7000–4000 BC. During the following two millennia, these mesolithic food-gatherers, following coastal routes and inland waterways, penetrated westwards into Fermanagh, thence down the Shannon and into Co. Limerick and also down the east coast to Dublin and Wexford; but much of the south, on present evidence, was unoccupied. Although these first Irishmen left behind no visible habitation sites or burial monuments for archaeologists to excavate, it seems likely that some of the most enduring features of Irish life will be found to stem from the native substratum. If left to themselves, they might have stagnated in the isolation of a European Tierra del Fuego; but the opening up of the seaways in the 4th millennium BC brought multiple contacts which diversified their economy and allowed them to multiply.

Genetically, these first Irishmen, together with the pioneer farmers who followed them, have left a deeper mark on the general population of the country than any of the later arrivals, whether Celtic, Viking or English. The relatively high proportion of Irishmen, particularly in the north and west, having Blood Group O, points to a strong native (pre-Celtic) physical inheritance. We can only guess at the skills, aptitudes and beliefs which these roving pioneers may have contributed to Ireland's cultural pool – in the imaginative story-telling of fisherfolk, in folk-song, in a sense of kinship with nature, in beliefs about the unseen world. They made extensive use of wattles, fibres and small timber, of nets and baskets and vessels of wood and leather. When they acquired the art of making pottery, they decorated their round-bottomed vessels with impressions of materials at hand (string, cord and bone-ends) and archaeologists have named this class of pottery 'Sandhills' ware, from one of the characteristic coastal habitats of these fisherfolk. Sandhills ware was to become widespread by the late neolithic period (c. 2500–1800 BC), and its distribution affords evidence of the expansion of an acculturated population of mesolithic stock. They seem to have been the first to exploit the salmon of the Boyne, and it is a singular fact that the fisherfolk of the lower Boyne valley retained a mesolithic artefact – the skin-covered curragh – into modern times. The fisherfolk soon acquired the skill of shaping stones by grinding to make serviceable clubs and tools for splitting wood.

From about the middle of the 4th millennium, we begin to find archaeological and palaeo-botanical evidence of a new economy and of neolithic settlements in forest clearings in many parts of the Ulster uplands. If this was, as many prehistorians think, a period of relatively warm, dry 'continental' climate, we can more easily understand the great outburst of activity and the extensive forest-clearing that followed. Farmers and stockmen were evidently tapping the accumulated fertility of untouched forest soils. At Ballynagilly in Co. Tyrone the remains included the foundations of a rectangular timber house dated to 3280 BC. These farmers and stock-raisers used large quantities of plain round-bottomed pottery and flint artefacts, such as leaf-shaped arrowheads; and their characteristic tool was that of the pioneer farmer everywhere, the woodman's axe – the neolithic axe of polished stone.

Pottery of the neolithic period has been found in great quantities on scores of sites. Its makers must be regarded as newcomers, for they avoided the occupied river valleys. Many details of their material culture can be compared with those of the 'western neolithic' colonists who spread northwards from Europe through the chalk downs of England and who are well represented in the Yorkshire Wolds. They brought their domesticated animals with them – cattle, pigs, sheep and goats. Their domesticated seed-crops (wheat and barley) could not have been found wild in Ireland but were native to the eastern Mediterranean, and moreover the Irish settlers seem to have been physically mainly of Mediterranean (Iberian) stock.

Well before the end of the 4th millennium, these vigorous colonizers were constructing megalithic monuments of a distinctive type – the court-graves of Ulster and north Connacht – of which well over three hundred examples have been identified and some thirty excavated in recent decades. Nearly all occur north of a line from Clew Bay to Dundalk Bay. They date, on present evidence, from the last quarter of the 4th millennium and the first half of the 3rd. The graves display considerable variety in plan and architectural elaboration, but essentially they consist of segmented gallery-graves built of great stone slabs, set in long cairns, and conspicuously provided with unroofed megalithic courts or fore-courts, oval or semicircular in plan, which had ritual functions. The deposits placed in the gallery-chambers consist largely of domestic debris, discarded artefacts such as arrowheads and broken carinated pots typical of the pioneering settlers, and their purpose would seem to have been to serve not simply as burial-places but as shrines to ensure the continuity of farming life and the maintenance of fertility. Lingering folk customs and beliefs make it clear that the megaliths were associated with human fertility as well as with the well-being of crops and herds.

While some features of the court-grave seem to derive from the Irish experience (the rapid loss of soil fertility under the climatic conditions of the Ulster uplands may well have exercised the minds of settlers from warmer climates), the associated long cairn seems to embody ancestral memories of the English long barrow; and the skills required in clearing fields of glacial boulders may well explain the substitution of stone uprights for timber – which in the long barrows was used for building façades as well as mortuary houses – and of stone cairns for earthen barrows. An excavated monument at Bally-macaldrack in Co. Antrim (Doey's cairn) is just such a transitional monument as one would expect to find in east Ulster. Here, a megalithic chamber with forecourt leads into a cremation trench or mortuary house whose abundant charcoal has given a date of *c*. 3000 BC.

In discussing the megalithic idea we must also think of maritime connections with western Europe, particularly with Brittany, where some megaliths date from before 4000 BC. Receptive mesolithic folk who had acquired peasant skills but who still roved the seas may well have had contact with European megalith-builders in Brittany or beyond. This seems to be the likeliest explanation, as we shall see, for the origin of passage-graves such as New Grange, and such contacts could have affected the north of Ireland even earlier.

We should look a little closer at the problem of the megaliths. The great stone monuments and hill-top cairns are the most enduring and spectacular contributions of prehistoric man to the Irish scene. Most of the megaliths have a distinctive stamp by which they can be labelled Irish, and, although not numerous by the standards of Brittany or Denmark, some of the chambered graves, especially the majestic tombs in the Boyne valley and the great court-graves such as Creevykeel in Sligo, are of outstanding quality. They have long attracted attention and have been explained in a dozen romantic or fantastic ways, as the names commonly given to them, such as Druids' Altars and Giants' Graves, imply. But despite several decades of intensive scientific research and excavation, their origins are obscure and they keep something of their mystery still.

The distribution of the great stone monuments is closely bound up with the use of the western seaways, with coastwise trade and with the spread of the arts of husbandry. In Ireland, then, we see them not as relics of a forgotten people or an exotic cult but as part of the cultural apparatus of ordinary farming folk in the early days of their adjustment to the environment, and as an essential part of the Irish heritage. Most archaeologists have explained them either as the work of colonists from Brittany or Iberia or as the hallmark of missionaries, traders or 'prospectors' from some far-off, unspecified Mediterranean shore. Yet no one appears to have asked why, if the colonists or traders came from the south, it was not in the nearer and more inviting parts of the country that the building of megaliths began. It is in the less accessible and climatically less attractive northern half of Ireland, north of the River Boyne, that most of the 1,250 or so surviving megalithic tombs – and nearly all the earliest examples and types – occur. Only in the latest phase of megalithic culture, when the Metal Age was in sight, can we think of direct colonization – by builders of wedge-graves – and identify its probable source in France. In my view both types of early megalithic tombs – court-graves and passage-graves – were the work of established native farmers, for their material culture

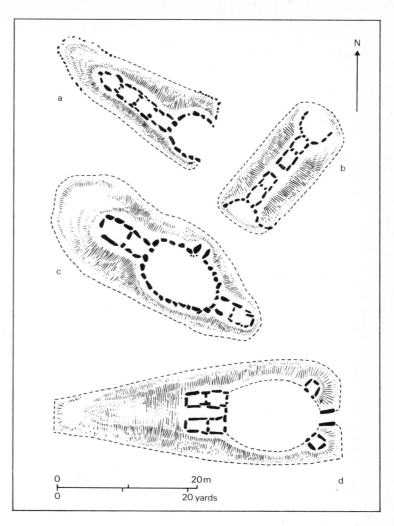

Plans of four types of court-grave: (a) Single court-grave at Browndod, Co. Antrim. (b) Dual court at Ballywholan, Co. Tyrone. (c) Full central court at Ballyglass, Co. Mayo. (d) Full end court at Malinmore, Co. Donegal. All the gallery chambers would have been covered with roofing stones, omitted here for the sake of clarity. Over 300 of these court-graves (so-called from the oval or semi-oval courts from which the galleries open) have been discovered in the northern half of Ireland, dating from the end of the 4th and the first half of the 3rd millennia. (2)

remained essentially Irish when they learnt the megalithic habit. The passage-grave cult differed in many ways from that of the court-graves. The tomb itself, carefully protected from damp and roofed in the classic examples on the Boyne with a high corbelled vault, was cruciform in plan and was entered by a long orthostatic passage, the whole being protected by a massive round cairn. The tombs are usually sited on elevated ground and often on hill-tops. They tend to be grouped in cemeteries, and the settlements of their builders are thought to have been nucleated rather than isolated. Burial rites also differed. Here are no tomb deposits of ancestral settlement-debris, but multiple cremations accompanied by abundant personal ornaments (bone pins and beads and miniature axe-pendants of bone or stone) and sometimes placed in large stone basins in the tomb chambers.

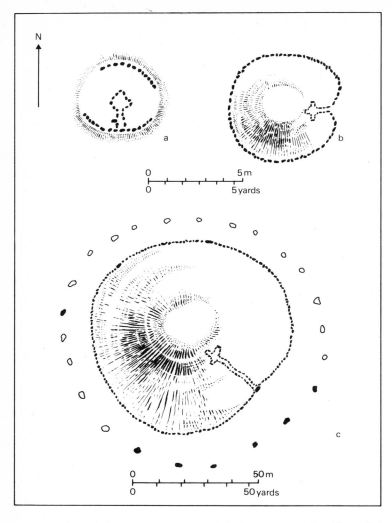

Plans of three passage-graves: (a) Carrowmore, Co. Sligo. (b) Loughcrew, Co. Meath. (c) New Grange, Co. Meath. Passage-graves consist of large circular cairns with a passage leading from the exterior to the tomb chamber. They are the grandest of prehistoric monuments in Ireland. The New Grange cairn has a diameter of over 85 yards, and is 45 feet high. (3)

About twenty such basins are known and they have no close parallels overseas. The Boyne culture is altogether more flamboyant and sophisticated than the earthy and puritanic peasant culture of the court-grave builders, which had little use for jewellery or art. The most astonishing feature of the finest passage-graves is the display of megalithic art: essentially abstract though suggestively anthropomorphic, it consists of engraved (pecked) spirals, concentric circles, rayed circles, lozenges, triangles, chevrons and serpentiform lines, usually covering the exposed surface of the stones in a way that foreshadows the overall decoration of Irish Bronze Age pottery or the intricate inspired doodling of Celtic Christian scribes, characterized by a *horror vacui*. Architecturally these corbel-roofed chambers have close parallels in Brittany and Iberia. While Iberian inspiration has also been claimed for Irish passage-grave art, the designs are not found there on tombstones and many of the most convincing parallels come from the Breton megaliths which are

also sited on elevations. But the spiral, all-important in the Boyne tombs, is rare in Brittany, and much of the Irish repertoire is native and cannot be matched overseas: nor can the use of profuse decoration on the kerbstones, notably at Knowth.

Moreover, the material culture of the passage-grave builders was essentially native and derived from the north of the country, as is shown by their 'Sandhills' pottery, the 'hollow scrapers' of flint and the leaf-shaped arrowheads. The colossal cairns covering the three most famous Irish passage-graves (New Grange, Knowth and Dowth) are without parallel in Brittany, and the patient excavations conducted at the two former sites by Professor O'Kelly and Dr Eogan have shown them to be unusual in several ways. The New Grange mound, for example, has a diameter of over eighty yards, covers an acre of ground and contains many thousands of tons of pebbles carried from the Boyne river terraces below. The layers of stones are interleaved with and stabilized by layers of sods, and old forest clearings covering many acres would have been required to provide sufficient sods. The hand-cutting and turning of sods to make cultivation ridges is to this day a traditional Irish method of preparing agricultural ground, and the ability to cut sods is of prehistoric antiquity, ecologically adapted, like the 'mounding' of tropical cultivators, to areas of heavy rainfall. The construction of New Grange, calculated by Dr Herity as requiring nearly a million man-days, presupposes a large established population, and one thinks of simple farmers and salmon-fishers, overawed by the promise of megalithic magic, being involved in the task. At the same time I have wondered whether the conspicuous display illustrated in the Boyne tombs could be related to the extravagant demonstrations of wealth characteristic of the Coast Indians of British Columbia, which were based on vast seasonal surpluses of salmon.

I would not think, then, of direct colonization from Brittany as the source of the Boyne culture. I prefer the explanation put forward by Humphrey Case – of multiple contacts made by adventurous fishermen who may have long been in contact with Breton fishermen in the Morbihan ('the little sea') and who could have invited missionary priests and skilled Breton craftsmen to assist them in their fashionable megalithic enterprise.

The Irish passage-graves, which flourished in the period 2500–2000 BC, number about three hundred, or much the same count as the court-graves. From the Boyne valley, which must be regarded as their Irish home, they spread in various directions, southward through Meath to the storied hill of Tara (in the very heart of what was to become Ireland's metropolitan region) and thence to the northern foothills of the Wicklow Mountains, northward into the Ulster hills, and westward by way of the cemetery of over thirty cairns on the summits of the Lough Crew Hills to the great cemeteries of Co. Sligo. The most celebrated of these is Carrowmore, near Sligo town, where about sixty round cairns can still be seen scattered over a wide gravel plain. The most conspicuous feature of the cairns is the kerb of ice-carried gneissic boulders from the Ox Mountains. While some cruciform chambers and the grave-goods recovered from them link Carrowmore with the Boyne valley, the small slab-roofed 'dolmenic' chambers and some other features suggest possible contacts with Scandinavia via the western ocean. Overlooking Carrowmore is the impressive landmark of Maeve's cairn, an enormous pile of stones crowning the hill of Knocknarea, which has a number of satellite cairns around it. And still in Co. Sligo, on the Bricklieve Mountains some fifteen miles to the south, is Carrowkeel, from which the typical highly decorated passage-grave pottery takes its name. Here some fifteen chambered cairns are dramatically perched on high parallel limestone ridges overlooking Lough Arrow.

Finally, how did the passage-grave cult fare in the heart of the Ulster court-grave territory? The tomb which crowns Slieve Gullion in Co. Armagh has a missionary orthodoxy to the extent of being cruciform in plan and having no fewer than three stone basins. Good examples of passage-grave art are to be seen at Knockmany and Sess Kilgreen in Co. Tyrone, and the chambered hill-top cairns even reached the north coast. The new idea in megalithic practice seems to have gained ground at the expense of the court-grave, but we have as yet few firm dates to guide us. Or the two religions, as today, may have existed side by side in Ulster through the late neolithic period, reflecting, then as now, cultural links on the one hand with the south and on the other with Britain. It may be significant that the passage-grave movement hardly touched Donegal in the far north-west or north Connacht, where the court-graves are most numerous and are thought by some Irish scholars to have been introduced by colonists from the European mainland. My own view is that this was the end of the line for a movement of megalith builders from the east, and that the concentration of sites in this area shows not that this was the first home but rather that it was the last refuge of the court-grave. Mayo would then have been what it became again in the 19th century AD – a congested district, at the world's end, preserving its old faith and keeping out the new-fangled passage-graves.

Portal-dolmens and wedge-graves

The word 'dolmen' ('stone table') was borrowed from Brittany by romantic antiquarians, and although the implication that the megaliths were Celtic in origin and that they once dripped with the blood of druidic sacrifices is nonsense, the word has the advantage of being unambiguous when applied, as it generally is, to single-chambered graves composed of three or more uprights roofed by a large capstone. Because of their simplicity and architectural naivety, dolmens have long been regarded as the prototypes from which the more elaborate chambered tombs evolved. More recently the view has been taken that the simple dolmen comes near the end of an evolutionary series, from a time when the art of roofing by corbels had been lost. From recent excavations it seems that the best-known variety of dolmen in Ireland does indeed come late in the megalithic age. This is the type to which, many years ago, I gave the name portal-dolmen (or portal-grave). In this type the capstone is massive (it may weigh up to one hundred tons) and is raised high at one end on two matched stone pillars to give a dramatic architectural form to monuments which are among the best-known relics of Irish prehistory. About 150 examples survive, in various stages of destruction, though their skeletons have a built-in stability and have generally withstood the ravages of time. Spectacular examples are to be seen at Legananny in Co. Down, Brennanstown in Co. Dublin, Proleek in Co. Louth, Drumanone in Co. Roscommon and Knockeen in Co. Waterford. Many of them were originally bedded in a stone cairn of which portions may remain, and this was in most cases a long cairn. For this reason and from their distribution (mainly in the north though extending thence down the west and east coasts respectively to Galway and Waterford) – and also from the miniature façade or court that sometimes survives at the entrance – I have suggested that they had their origin in the court-grave culture, and represent a late stage in its development, making their appearance at the beginning of the late neolithic. The portal-dolmens may perhaps be seen as the triumphant mark of a resurgent mesolithic (or 'secondary neolithic') culture which had been won over to husbandry, for the burials they contain were accompanied by native tool-kits and 'Sandhills' pottery. Whereas the court-graves are usually sited fairly high on the hillsides, the dolmens are generally at low elevations and are often sited near water.

To complete a summary of the varieties of burial monuments that can be given a neolithic date, we must also refer to a less spectacular and rarer form of burial, this time by inhumation, in a sub-megalithic cist under a round barrow, which, while its origins are obscure, seems also, from the associated tools and highly decorated heavy-rimmed pottery, and from a preference for lowland sites, to belong to a

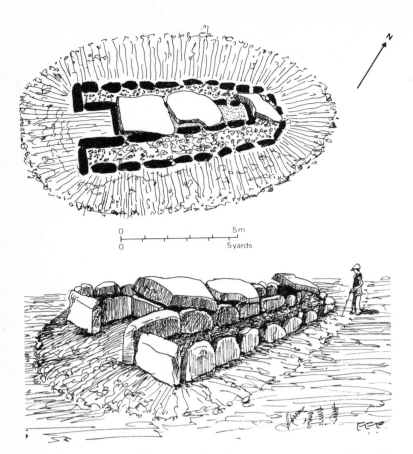

Plan and sketch of a typical wedge-grave as it survives today, with remains of the cairn. Graves of this type were probably introduced from France about 2000 BC, and soon became widespread all over Ireland. (4)

secondary neolithic culture. Portal-dolmens persisted to the end of the neolithic and became widely diffused, but they never reached the south-west, where by this time the fourth and last type of Irish tomb – according to our classification, the wedge-grave – was probably already established.

The far south-west (Cork and Kerry) hardly comes into the prehistoric picture until the very end of the neolithic and the dawn of the Metal Age, for although we date the Bronze Age from about 1800 BC a knowledge of copper may have reached Ireland by 2000 BC. The wedge-graves appear to be related to tombs in north-west France (compare the *allées couvertes* of Brittany) and to have been introduced into Ireland, for they have no native antecedents, and the presence of copper ores in the south-west may offer sufficient explanation for the settlement of a colony of gallery-grave builders from Brittany. The shallow pits and stone tools of prehistoric miners may still be found on Mount Gabriel in the Skull Peninsula in Co. Cork, near Killarney in Co. Kerry and at Bunmahon in Co. Waterford.

Wedge-graves are readily recognized, being long stone galleries divided into main chamber and antechamber, roofed with slabs and set in low cairns often reflecting the shape of the gallery, which tends to be wedge-shaped both in plan and side-elevation, the wider end usually facing west. About four hundred examples are known, and they are not only the commonest but the most widely distributed of all Irish megalithic tombs. The interests of their builders were trade – in copper and flint – as well as farming and stock-rearing, and they seem to have spread fairly rapidly, especially in areas of good grazing such as the Burren of Clare, where about a hundred of their tombs survive. But they quickly went native, borrowing the rite of cremation and many items of material culture from earlier settlers. Such tombs persist well into the Bronze Age, and they may contain the tell-tale 'Beaker' pottery and Beaker-type flint artefacts, and even an occasional metal object. The most imposing of the wedge-graves is Labbacallee ('The Hag's Bed') in Co. Cork, where the proportions of the gallery and the size of the roof slabs recall some of the monster galleries of France.

Stone circles

Stone circles have a strange fascination which is partly explained, in these days of precise dating and explanation in prehistory, by the difficulty of obtaining datable material or other information from sites which normally contain neither habitation debris nor burials. A single standing stone or *gallán* is often associated with them as pointer or outlier, but more often the single stone is a solitary monument, and being without associations its purpose is even more obscure. Both traditions are rooted in megalithic practice, and the great circle of (originally) thirty-four large uprights surrounding New Grange is an early example of well-spaced monoliths making a circle. Standing stones are often regarded as anthropomorphic, and there are suggestions that their sex is symbolized by their shape. They were apparently erected throughout the Bronze Age – one of the most impressive, the twenty-three-foot Longstone in Co. Kildare, marks the site of an early Bronze Age cist burial – and through the early Iron Age to give way to the Ogham-inscribed commemorative pillar stones of late pagan and early Christian times, to cross-inscribed stones, and ultimately to the full flowering of cross-carving and the transfiguration of the standing stone into the high cross.

The high crosses are unmistakably Christian but the Ogham stones, belonging to the twilight world of the 4th to the 6th centuries, are without history. The Ogham script, based on the Latin alphabet and invented in Ireland, was the island's first experiment in literacy. The inscriptions are in an archaic form of Irish, and they commemorate the dead, typically incorporating the word MAC (son). Most of the three hundred or so Ogham stones known in Ireland come from the south, from the area, between Waterford and Kerry, where pre-Patrician Christianity was established. The inscriptions are cut in parallel grooves and notches on the vertical edge of a standing stone. Outside Ireland, Ogham inscriptions occur in the Isle of Man, Scotland, Cornwall and Devon, and in particular South Wales, and this distribution is a fair reflection of the migrations of the Irish which took place in early Christian times, when the Romans were leaving Britain.

Associated with stone circles in various ways, as at Avebury in Wiltshire and at Lough Gur in Limerick, are earthen ring-banks with an internal fosse, and to these monuments the name 'henge' has been given. They were places of ceremony rather than burial, though the two purposes often go together. The massive earthen Giant's Ring near Belfast has a dolmen near the centre of the ring. The largest of the Lough Gur circles consists of an earthen bank nine yards wide, lined on the outside with tall contiguous uprights making a stone ring fifty yards across. Another variant occurs at Ballynoe in Co. Down, where fifty large uprights form a ring thirty-six yards across, enclosing a smaller circle superimposed on a long cairn covering cists which contained cremations and a sherd of passage-grave pottery. Truly a hybrid monument! When we come to look at the 'fortress-palaces', which were the royal seats and assembly places of early Celtic times, we shall see from examples which have been investigated that they were not so much hill-forts as henge-like ceremonial centres and that much use was made of timber circles which may prove to be related to the stone circles of the native Bronze Age.

The greatest concentration of stone circles in the country occurs in the uplands of mid-Ulster, where dozens of circle complexes have been uncovered in the process of peat-cutting. The most elaborate is at Beaghmore near Cookstown, where several circles are associated with cairns and alignments which date from the second half of the Bronze Age, and which are thought to have had a calendrical purpose. Certainly the 'recumbent-stone circles', of which about seventy are known in Co. Cork and which resemble in some ways the recumbent circles of Aberdeenshire, had to do with observations of the winter solstice. A preoccupation with the measurement of the passing year hints, perhaps, at declining fertility and restricted supplies of food.

Copper, bronze and gold

The cultural momentum of nearly two millennia of neolithic settlement and trade was maintained into, and quickened by, the Early Metal Age, beginning not long after 2000 BC. Through much of the Bronze Age the seaways were open, not only in the Irish Sea but along the Atlantic coasts to Scandinavia on the one hand and deep into the Mediter-

Ogham is not a language but an alphabet; the language is Old Irish. The system uses the corner of the stone as a dividing line, with straight or oblique strokes carved on either side. The letters HDTCQ *also stand for the numbers 1–5. In memorial stones the inscriptions run from bottom to top, continuing if necessary down the other side. The majority of Ogham stones come from Ireland, but about forty have been found in Wales, ten on the Isle of Man and a few in England. A well-preserved example from the cemetery at Kilcoolaght, Co. Kerry, is shown on p. 30. (5)*

ranean world on the other. After an experimental copper-using phase, mainly represented by plain flat axes in the ore country of Co. Cork, it is the north-east that comes into prominence in the Early Bronze Age, a reminder that its established trade connections in the Irish Sea and beyond facilitated the necessary import of tin (for the production of bronze requires the addition of 10 per cent of tin to copper), while a long tradition of craftsmanship in stone was applied to the making of moulds for casting. It is here in the north-east that intrusive elements are most apparent in the archaeological record and that fusion with native elements produced distinctive insular cultures. There was much prospecting for metals, and among newcomers were the eager Beaker-folk. The characteristic decorated drinking vessels that give them their name, which are best known in Britain for their inclusion with inhumations in single graves, appear with cremation burials in late megalithic tombs such as the wedge-graves. Throughout the Irish Bronze Age, burial by cremation in short cists, often under a hill-top cairn, demonstrates the fusion of old and new. Hill-tops had been the favourite sites for passage-graves, but the single graves marked a break with the passage-grave tradition of multiple burials. The accompanying 'food vessels' show in their function, and to some extent in the style of the impressed decoration which is now applied to native bowls, the impact of the prestigious beaker on the traditions of the late neolithic. It is surmised that the metal-workers who produced bronze implements and gold ornaments were itinerants, like the Irish tinkers of recent times, and indeed it is thought that society as a whole became more mobile thanks to a predilection for herding. Abandoned clearings in the woodlands and rough pastures among the hills and bogs would have provided extensive grazing grounds, and it is argued that the hill-top cairns would have served as landmarks and as permanent points of reference in a shifting world. They were the outstanding contribution of the Bronze Age to the landscape, and they have been conspicuous through all the ages since, some of them, with their bleached boulders of granite or quartzite, shining like beacons. There are few Irish hill-tops that do not have, if not a high-piled cairn, at least traces of one.

On the other hand Bronze Age habitation sites are hard to find except where continuity of settlement from neolithic times can be shown, as at Lough Gur in Co. Limerick. Many cist graves, however, and indeed many unprotected urn burials such as are found in lowland gravel banks, were presumably adjacent to fairly permanent habitations. Elsewhere some Bronze Age cultivated fields are now buried in blanket-bog, which would seem to raise the question of climatic change. Metal objects are very rarely found either on settlement sites or (unlike the expendable pots of clay) as grave-goods, and except when found at datable levels in the turf-bogs their age must be determined by their stylistic features or their position in a typological series. The Irish bronze-smiths were highly proficient at casting edge-tools and weapons – axes, spearheads, halberds, daggers, rapiers – and quite early in the Bronze Age decorated flat axes became a speciality of north-east Ireland. They were exported to Britain and several parts of the Continent. To the same period belong some of the finest ornaments of hammered gold, decorated 'sun discs', and collars known from their crescent-moon shape as *lunulae* which found their way to Scotland and Denmark and, in another direction, to Cornwall and France as well. They include also dainty basket-shaped earrings which even reached the eastern Mediterranean.

The skills of Irish craftsmen in gold in the 18th century BC or again in the last centuries BC and the 8th century AD, can perhaps be compared with those of Irish craftsmen in silver in the 18th century AD! Throughout the Bronze Age Britain continued to be the market for much of the work exported by Irish goldsmiths. One of their specialities was the torque, made from a bar of gold twisted and secured by elaborate fastenings, serving as a neck ornament, armlet or girdle. Two very large examples were found near and are named after Tara, but they were not directly associated with, and should be older than, the Celtic monuments on the hill. Typically Irish also are several types of smaller personal ornaments: bracelets, cupped rings and dress-fasteners. The latter, which were also made of bronze, resemble large single-piece cuff-links, and they seem to have taken the place of buttons or pins as fashionable dress-fastenings.

The coming of the Celts

The Late Bronze Age, from about 900 BC onwards, is marked by the appearance of many new and more efficient types of tools and weapons, and of novel techniques of metal-working such as hollow-casting by the *cire-perdue* method, and the hammering and riveting of sheet bronze to make large cauldrons. These handsome vessels stand in succession to the round-bottomed pottery vessels that had characterized the neolithic: they were made for suspension over an open fire, as if intended for outsize Irish stews, and they foreshadow the traditional round-bottomed iron cooking pot. The cauldron in folklore came to be endowed with many magic properties. Such weapons as socketed spearheads and long leaf-shaped slashing swords, presumably used from horseback, point to new methods of armed combat, and many decorative trappings for horses and warriors, in bronze and gold, provide archaeological evidence for the glorification of war. At the same time novel forms of burial, in urnfields, point to social groupings larger than the family; but characteristically, by the end of the period, it was defensive earthworks rather than burial monuments that were to leave their mark on the landscape. Another innovation was the use of water – of which there was never a shortage – to provide defence for settlements on artificial islands to which the name 'crannog' is given. For the first time, it seems, we begin to hear the clash of arms and the din of battle above the pastoral sounds of lowing kine, the music of the shepherd's pipe and the chanting of mourners among the cairns.

Another sign of unsettled times, from which the archaeologist has profited, was the custom of hiding great hoards of prized metal objects in the hope of recovering them. One such hoard, known as the Great Clare Find, was discovered near Newmarket in 1854 during the construction of the celebrated West Clare Railway. Consisting mainly of personal ornaments, most of which were sold as bullion, it was described as 'the largest assemblage of gold objects yet found in Northern Europe'. On the other hand some of the gold objects found in the bogs, such as those recovered from what came to be called the Golden Bog of Cullen on the borders of Limerick and Tipperary, may have been ritual or votive deposits, suggesting comparison with the early Celtic custom, well attested in Gaul, of making offerings to springs or lakes.

We are here on the edge of the ancient Celtic world, and must consider the difficult question of how and when Ireland acquired not only a Celtic language but new systems of religious belief, art, laws and social organization. It was a slow process and involved all kinds of compromises, but it is generally agreed – though it is frankly impossible to correlate linguistic changes in prehistory with changes in material culture – that Celtic influences began to reach Ireland in the Late Bronze Age, say after 600 BC, and they became unmistakable when iron-working was introduced, probably not far from 200 BC. When this happened, bronze was not abandoned, for it long continued to be used for ornaments and refined castings, and became, like gold, the mark of privilege; but iron was cheaper and more abundant than bronze – for iron-ore is common in nature, occurring even in the bogs – and iron was better suited to the making of edge-tools.

We know from classical writers as well as from other kinds of evidence that, beginning to expand from about 700 BC, the Celtic languages spread over much of western Europe in the second half of the last millennium BC from their cradle north of the Alps. The Celtic diffusion, which some writers have called an explosion, was in many ways a folk-movement, led by aristocratic warriors; but when we come as far afield as Ireland, which of course could only be reached by water, we must think rather of small conquering bands who succeeded because of their superior arms, their powers of organization and probably their superior language. But it was a somewhat archaic and conservative form of Celtic culture that reached Ireland.

The 19th-century belief that Ireland was over-run by 'a vast pastoral race' has done untold harm in distorting Irish history and encouraging the myth that the Irish people are a distinct and in some strange way pure Celtic race. The immensely rich and ancient Irish heritage came to be identified with a language which was painfully acquired by the natives and which became transformed in the process. The Celtic invaders brought a great cultural enrichment, material as well as spiritual, but Celtic culture in Ireland came to have a strong Irish flavour. One of their gifts, for example, was a new cereal, oats, a crop that was to become the grain of Ireland as of Scotland. Oats began their wild career as weeds in fields of wheat and barley and gradually established themselves as a crop better adapted ecologically to the damp climates of Atlantic Europe than the older cereals. Being sown in spring, oats could benefit from one of the few blessings of an Atlantic climate, the relatively dry spring. Providing food for beast as well as man and requiring less care in cultivation than wheat or barley, they fitted well into the flexible and mainly pastoral pattern of rural life in Ireland, and remained until quite recently, in many parts of the country, an essential ingredient of the rather rough, untidy (if egalitarian) system of rundale husbandry and seasonal nomadism (transhumance) and part of a domestic way of life that revolved around the ovenless open hearth – a symbol of griddle-baking as well as of hospitality – and a diet of oatcakes, milk, butter, porridge and stews. All this contrasts with the open wheatfields of the manorial English village system with its oven bread and (to the Irishman) its solid industry and servile conformity. These are themes that run right through the largely unwritten rural history of the two countries.

There is some evidence to suggest that the crisis through which Ireland and much of Europe north of the Alps was passing in the period of change during the second half of the last millennium BC was accompanied and aggravated by climatic deterioration and the growth of blanket-bogs in what is termed the sub-Atlantic period. Nature, however, may not be entirely to blame for the Irish blanket-bogs. Man himself, by prolonged attacks on the forest cover, and by overgrazing and over-intensive cultivation of long-settled patches of land, may have been partly responsible for his deteriorating environment. In several parts of western Ireland extensive walled enclosures, some with unmistakable traces of ridge-cultivation, have been discovered buried under vast stretches of blanket-bog which may well hide other remains, and it is argued that the leaching of the exposed over-cultivated soil could by itself have resulted in the formation of iron-pan with subsequent water-logging and the initiation of the bog-forming process. The normal climate of western Ireland, in this view, is so near the point of being too wet for profitable arable husbandry that the upsetting of the ecological balance may be as easily explained by human carelessness or excess as by climatic change. Later on it was no doubt partly because the alien potato ripened underground, was adapted to poor acid soils, and did not depend on good harvest weather, that it was eagerly adopted as a staple food-crop in this and other damp, infertile parts of Europe.

The earliest examples of both hill-forts and crannogs date from the Late Bronze Age; but it was probably the coming of iron, and of the warrior-chiefs to whom the name Celtic can properly be given, that speeded up the construction of defensive earthworks and lake-dwellings in the last two or three centuries BC. The élitist tradition of living in a defended habitation, whether protected by a *vallum* or by lake waters, persisted far into the Christian era. Iron digging implements and heavy iron axes – though, unlike older tools of lasting bronze, they have not survived – would have greatly facilitated construction work. The very word 'crannog' comes from the Irish *crann*, a tree, for the making of these artificial lake-dwellings consumed large quantities of timber.

Conspicuous among the defensive works of the early Celtic period, though they have not been precisely dated, are several stretches of linear or 'travelling' earthworks, built on the grand scale and sometimes apparently reinforced by clusters of ring-works (raths) and in one instance supplemented by a very large enclosure – the Dorsey in south Armagh. Consisting for the most part of an earthen bank (dyke) with a fosse on one side or on both sides, some portions have three parallel banks, standing up to six yards high and covering a width of a hundred yards. The most celebrated of these earthworks, known variously in folklore and legend as the Worm Ditch, the Black Pig's Dyke or the Great Wall of Ulster, supposedly runs in a continuous line from Co. Sligo to Co. Armagh, but in reality consists of a series of separate lines, up to six miles long, closing gaps between lakes or defending other weak points on routeways between north and south through the border belt of lakes and drumlins in south Ulster. The work was evidently intended not as a continuous military or political frontier but as a means of checking the movement of invaders, and especially cattle-raiders, from the south.

These linear defences apart, the earthworks of the early Celtic period were nearly always circular. And through a period of a thousand years that followed, when Gaelic culture was at its strongest, the preferred shape of enclosures, large or small, was circular or nearly so. That this tradition is Irish rather than Celtic is suggested by the henge-like arrangement of bank and fosse – the fosse being inside the bank – at two of the most famous Celtic 'hill-forts', Tara and Emain Macha, which seem to have had mainly ceremonial functions. Abundant evidence of Late Bronze Age activity was found under the great mound at Navan, while at Tara the Royal Enclosure surrounds, among other things, the so-called Mound of the Hostages which in fact covers a late megalith of passage-grave type ($c.$ 2000 BC). The continued sanctity of the site through the Bronze Age is shown by a succession of later burials in the mound.

The hill-fort at Downpatrick, probably from its location one of the first to be built, is more orthodox, consisting of a fosse which was strengthened by an internal timber-laced bank. In its simple form it may be as early as the 3rd or even the 6th century BC. Here, too, there had been previous occupation of the undefended hill-top, and in close proximity was found a hoard of sixteen Late Bronze Age gold bracelets. The cathedral church of Down, dedicated to St Patrick, stands inside the enclosure on the site of what was by tradition one of the Saint's first foundations. Another famous site of the Early Iron Age, again in the north-east, was the now completely destroyed crannog of Lisnacrogher in Co. Antrim, from which came three bronze sword-scabbards superbly decorated in the style of the abstract, curvilinear art called after La Tène in Switzerland. Among the finest bronzes of the early Celtic period are horse-bits, harness decorations and various ornaments of uncertain purpose which display novel skills not only in false-relief casting but also in more sophisticated ways of producing such effects, and in the use of red enamel. And here we must mention another first-period work of Celtic craftsmanship with elegant La Tène designs – the

splendid gold collar from Broighter, Co. Londonderry. It was found early this century with two torques and other gold objects, including a model boat complete with mast and oars, and, stranger still, two plaited wire chains of the style known as Trichinopoly work and similar to examples found in Egypt in the 1st century BC. The hoard, now in the National Museum, Dublin, was the subject of a famous lawsuit to determine ownership. It was declared to be treasure trove and therefore Crown property, but King Edward VII personally ordered its return to Ireland, and it was placed in the custody of the Royal Irish Academy.

Seat of the Celtic kings
Several sites of the early Christian period besides Downpatrick – one may cite Clogher in the north and Cashel in the south – were closely associated with hill-forts or royal seats. The primatial cathedral of St Patrick, Armagh, on its hill-top is itself inside a small circular hill-fort or large rath, but the storied pagan capital of Ulster, Emain Macha, which bears the name of the Celtic goddess – Macha – is some two miles to the west. Navan Fort, to give it its usual name, is a great circular bank of earth with a deep internal fosse enclosing an area of eighteen acres on a drumlin-top. Set eccentrically within the enclosure is a large mound sixty yards across and six yards high, reputed to be the burial mound of Queen Macha. It has been completely and most carefully excavated in recent years by Mr Dudley Waterman with results that are as remarkable as they are unexpected.

According to the Irish annals and hero-tales, in which Emain Macha figures prominently, the royal site was founded in the 3rd century BC and abandoned following its destruction by the men of Connacht in AD 332. There is no reason to accept this seemingly precise date and indeed some modern historians would place this event more than a century later. The great mound, however, if we can trust the dates supplied by its burnt timbers, was abandoned as early as the 2nd century BC and, what is more surprising, the first stages in the use of the site date from the 7th century BC. It thus looks as if Celtic beginnings go back chronologically to the full Bronze Age, and that deep native roots nourished the Celtic culture of Ireland from the start. Indeed this hill-top yielded the tell-tale flint tools and sherds of round-bottomed neolithic pottery, and the soil under the great mound bore the marks of Bronze Age ploughing. In the 7th century a shallow circular trench thirty-five yards in diameter was dug and a ring of large timber uprights erected just inside it. Inside this were several smaller rings of posts, some ten yards in diameter, which had been rebuilt repeatedly over a period of two or three centuries.

These structures do not seem to have been roofed or to have had a domestic purpose, but a scatter of Late Bronze Age potsherds was recovered. A find of unusual interest from this horizon was the skull of a Barbary ape, though its identification awaits confirmation. Remembering the great fairs that, we are told, were held at Emain Macha in the days of its glory, we may imagine a 'travelling man' bringing his pet here to amuse the crowds, never to return to its sunny home in North Africa.

Finally, about 200 BC, a much larger timber structure was erected on the site. Around a tall central post, four rings of heavy upright posts were sunk in deep holes, and outside was a fifth ring having a diameter of forty yards consisting of very massive posts joined together with horizontal planks. All the timber was oak, and in trying to interpret this strange site one naturally thinks of artificial druidical groves. Yet in the background is the sacred henge and the circle of stones. The end of the site was stranger still. About 150 BC the whole structure was burnt and buried under a great cairn of limestone boulders forty-five yards across, capped by a thick pile of sods rising to an estimated original height of nine yards.

Dun Ailinne, another legendary royal site at Knockaulin in Co. Kildare, is an even larger hillfort, and it too has its fosse inside the bank. Here again excavations have yielded evidence of some neolithic occupation and have also uncovered a mound under which were the remains of palisaded enclosures of the Early Iron Age, succeeded by a massive timber circle which in time was buried in a mound – in this case quite low.

The later Bronze Age: raths and cashels
There is little doubt that throughout the early period of Celtic or proto-Celtic intrusion the main point of entry was the north-east, as it had been from the beginning; but there were also movements into Leinster, and for a time during the Late Bronze Age the Shannon estuary came into prominence, probably as a back door or tradesman's entrance during those disturbed times. Among Late Bronze Age artefacts common in the Shannon basin are certain types of bronze sword, some of which seem to have been bog-offerings. This entry remained important during the Early Iron Age and evidently, to judge from the fame of the lower Shannon in the early monastic period, far into the Christian era. One of the novelties of the Late Bronze Age was the bronze horn, no doubt a forerunner of the war trumpet, and many examples come from the lower Shannon region, its only rival being the north-east. It was on the strength of these instruments that a learned German archaeologist concluded that 'the ancient Irish excelled in wind music'.

It is in the region west of the lower Shannon, too, that the finest and best-known decorated granite cult-stones are located, at Turoe near Loughrea and Castlestrange near Roscommon. They belong to the Early Iron Age and resemble in some ways the early Celtic *stelae* of Brittany, which are also made of granite and which are frequently associated with burials. These Irish examples are not known to have been linked with burials but both have been removed from their original sites. The Turoe stone, a massive pillar one-and-a-quarter yards high, has a domed top covered with abstract ornament in La Tène style and may date from the 1st century BC. This most impressive monument is proudly phallic in appearance.

Also from the Shannon basin, particularly from the upper region and the adjoining lake country of Roscommon, Cavan and Fermanagh, come several one- or two-headed or two-faced wooden or stone carvings of early Celtic style, though it is typical of our ignorance and of the manifest continuities between the pagan and the Christian worlds that some of them have been considered to be Romanesque. Co. Armagh also has many examples. The best-known three-faced head comes from Corleck, Co. Cavan, the legendary 'land of idols', but the most massive and the most mysterious is that on Boa Island in Lough Erne, Co. Fermanagh. Like the cult of the severed head, the Janus head is well attested in early Celtic times on the Continent. In this north-western part of Ireland many pagan elements lasted into the Christian period and today it has many survivals, for instance in folk medicine. As an example of ancient practices which persisted in this region we may cite the sweating cure. Many examples of corbelled sweathouses which have every appearance of antiquity but which were used into the last century can be seen here.

Another region which is known to have been an entry in early Celtic times was the east coast of Leinster between Dundalk and Dublin, the region known to history as Meath or the Middle Kingdom. Here Tara was well placed to aspire to become the first national capital. The Laginians who, according to the legendary histories, invaded Leinster and gave it its name, also conquered Connacht, but it was the area first settled, the favoured triangle of lowland between Dundalk and Dublin, that was destined to become the melting-pot out of which flowed a new alloy – the mould into which Celtic culture was poured to become Irish. The Celtic newcomers, it seems, were fascinated by the megalithic marvels of the Boyne, much as modern visitors from the German lands feel the magic of the west of Ireland. 'Brugh na Boinne', the lower valley of the Boyne, was regarded as the sacred burial-place of early Celtic kings, the great tombs as fairy mounds

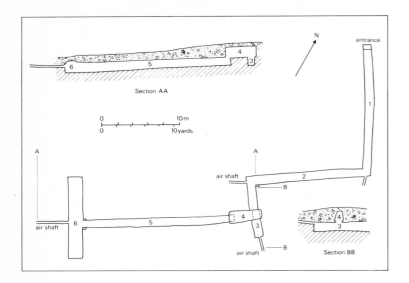

Key: Passage—1, 2, 3, 4, 5. Chamber—6
Plan and section of a souterrain at Donaghmore, Co. Louth. The purpose of these structures is still something of a mystery. They were probably primarily food-stores (prehistoric 'deep freezes') but could also be used as refuges in times of danger. (6)

and entrances to the other world. Whether deliberately or not, the newcomers profited by taking over the prestige attached to megalithic sites here and at Tara, and the vitality of old faiths was renewed under new masters. This metropolitan triangle was to be the base not only of Tara of the kings, but of some of the richest Christian sites (Kells, Monasterboice, Mellifont) and, from Viking beginnings, the city of Dublin.

The face of Ireland is spotted with ring-works of earth or dry stone enclosing the remains of dwellings dating from late prehistoric and early historic times. Estimated to number between 30,000 and 40,000, they can best be observed from the air. Their great profusion is partly explained by the fact that this type of habitation is representative of a way of life, established in early Celtic times, that persisted with little change, in the north and west at any rate, down to the end of the Middle Ages and even into the early 17th century. To judge from those that have been excavated, the majority of these structures belong to the early centuries of Christianity, when there seems to have been a population explosion. But there is another factor accounting for their great numbers, and that is the survival rate. They are most abundant in areas of good pasture, and both the historical and archaeological evidence suggests that they were the hallmark of a pastoral society with a mixed economy in which cattle-herding predominated.

Although in some areas later arable farming has resulted in the 'ploughing out' of such earthworks, in general, because of the grazing tradition and the superstitious beliefs that go with it (for example, it is thought to be very unlucky to destroy a 'fairy fort')

great numbers survive, and they are often marked by a ring of thorn bushes which are also superstitiously preserved. The popular name given to the rings (forts or forths) is misleading, for the great bulk of them were peaceful farmsteads, and the defences, usually a fosse with a single bank inside, were designed more as protection against wolves and other cattle thieves than against armed raiders. The Gaelic names for them, which are often incorporated in place-names, are anglicized as 'rath', 'liss' and 'dun', and the word 'rath' has generally been adopted by archaeologists. The diameter of these earthen-rings or raths may be anything from twenty to seventy yards and the larger examples may have two or three rings, depending perhaps on the social grade of the occupant. The general conclusion of archaeologists, which is supported by references in the annals, is that the raths were the homes of substantial farmers or ranchers, while larger examples, if appropriately sited, are almost indistinguishable from the small hill-forts which were royal sites. The mass of the people, commoners or churls, were outside the law and have left no trace in history or archaeology.

In stony ground, especially in the hills, the rings take the form of dry-stone walls, and the structure is then known as a 'cashel' or 'caher'. These too were sometimes royal sites, for example the hill-top cashel near Londonderry (but in Donegal) known as the Grianan of Ailech. This is mentioned in the annals as late as 1100, and reminds us that such royal sites (this cashel lies inside an older three-ringed hill-fort) were sometimes rebuilt long after the coming of Christianity. The Grianan, indeed, was largely rebuilt by an enthusiastic restorer a century ago, though wisely he was careful to distinguish his work from the original. A feature of these sophisticated cashels, best seen at Staigue Fort in Kerry, is the arrangement of stone stairways leading to wall-walks, and the cells and galleries inside the wall. With its strongly battered walls, Staigue Fort has the appearance of a huge, squat, truncated broch; but in the absence of modern excavation we cannot say to what period of prehistory or early history it and similar structures belong. Nowhere are the stone forts better displayed than on the Aran Islands, where the finest of them, Dun Aengus, better described as a promontory fort, is defended on one side by a two-hundred-and-eighty-foot cliff rising vertically from the Atlantic and facing the fierce south-westerly seas. Dun Aengus is the most splendidly sited of some two hundred promontory forts in Ireland, most of them on the coast but some of them on inland headlands, and it seems that, unlike the ordinary ring-works, their purpose was defensive. A striking feature at Dun Aengus which confirms this view is its protective girdle of pillar stones set firmly in the joints of the bare limestone plateau to act as deterrents. These stone *chevaux de frise*, named after the Frisian device of anti-cavalry spikes, are found at two or three other Irish stone forts and seem to be derived from prehistoric Spain, though it is doubtful if the Irish examples are as old.

Tradition says that the Aran forts were erected by refugees from the Boyne valley. Certainly they were strong refuges, but their builders and their date remain a mystery. The smaller raths and cashels usually contain the remains of a single dwelling house, typically round in plan or rectangular with rounded corners. In the rath it was built of light timbers and sods or clay and roofed with thatch: in the cashels it was often a corbelled stone beehive structure or *clochan*. Both raths and cashels are frequently equipped with one or more underground chambers and connecting passages usually lined with large stones, roofed with slabs and known to archaeologists as souterrains. Often these structures occur in the open countryside, where there is now no trace of rath or cashel, but in some such cases excavation has shown that a flimsy, undefended homestead originally stood nearby. In a few areas which were evidently densely settled in the early Christian centuries, they are so common that farmers lost livestock when their roofs collapsed and they were reluctant to use their horses to plough new ground. The Six Mile Water valley in Co. Antrim is one such locality and another is near Dundalk in north Louth, where the most elaborate souterrain known to me is to be seen at Donaghmore. It is over eighty yards long and is provided with three ventilation shafts, with a device to trap the unwanted visitor and also with a secret chamber built at a lower level.

Such sophisticated underground structures seem to be most common near the coast and to have been designed as places of refuge, presumably against the Norsemen, but this explanation will not serve for the thousands of souterrains ranging over many centuries, which are found in every county and which must have had a more domestic purpose. While this common variety could have served in emergency as a convenient hiding place from unwelcome visitors, the original and primary purpose was probably to preserve food and to store it for the lean winter months. Milk products in particular – for 'whitemeats' were universally consumed down to the coming of the potato – could have been kept cool and safe from theft whether by animals or humans.

Souterrains are so widely found that they must have been regarded as a cultural necessity by the more prosperous farmers, the equivalent, perhaps, of a 'deep freeze' in our own time. They are also among the pagan accessories adopted by the early Church, for they are found on a number of early church sites. Some examples, indeed, came to have religious significance and to have been regarded as entrances to the underworld, where supernatural manifestations occurred, as at St Patrick's Purgatory on an island in Lough Derg, Co. Donegal.

Art, religion and institutions

In Ireland the period from about 200 BC to AD 400, which we call Early or Pagan Celtic, is frankly prehistoric, though in much of Europe it would be illuminated by historical records. Thus, while classical writers tell us a good deal about the Continental Celts and druidism, we know almost nothing historically about the Celts in Ireland. The popular image of the druids as venerable robed and bearded figures of wisdom, hung with golden ornaments and parading with sprigs of mistletoe in a circle of stones, is largely the invention of the Romantic period. The accounts we have of Irish druidism date from medieval times and are deeply coloured by ecclesiastical prejudice, although they are based on far older oral traditions. Yet the very fact that the churchmen persisted in the oral transmission of the laws of poetry, genealogy and mythology is itself due to the perpetuation of the druidic method. To facilitate memorizing, the material was put into verse, making use of rhythm and alliteration, and the bardic tradition, which thus goes back to preliterate times, was to survive in Gaelic Ireland not only in the Celtic Church but in places into the 17th century. The Christian priests also took over the supernatural function of the druids.

Druidism, like so much else that is called Celtic, seems to have absorbed native traditions in Ireland, some possibly of mesolithic origins. In relation to the European Celtic world, anyhow, the Irish experience was late and marginal. It is an error to suppose, though by backward projection this is the popular view, that Ireland had some kind of monopoly of Celtic culture in prehistoric times. In early Celtic art, for example, while the Irish material clearly belongs to the family of art known as La Tène, it is comparatively rare, late and distinctly insular and idiosyncratic. And it was tenaciously conservative, handing on long-fossilized stylistic elements, for example, for the Christian scribes to play with. It has been pointed out that Gaelic society here in the far west retained many features which could be paralleled in another peripheral part of the Indo-European world – India. For example, the custom of 'fasting unto death' as a means of redress is not quite defunct either in Ireland or in India. More particularly, the druids, who were charged with the task of transmitting judicial as well as sacred learning, had their counterpart in the highest caste of Hinduism, the Brahmins. Some learned classes in ancient Ireland, such as the poets and satirists, long retained their functions as 'reformed druids', but the druidic rites of divination and astrological computation were apparently abandoned. The other high caste, the equivalent of the Hindu Kshatriya, was composed of land-holding warrior kings who had various grades of nobility and freemen beneath them. The kings, of whom there were about 150 when we get our first knowledge of them, were closely identified with a particular *tuath* or tribe, a word which came to be applied to the tiny kingdoms which passed into history more or less directly as the Norman baronies. The king was the embodiment of his people, was held to be descended from an ancestral deity and derived his sovereignty from inauguration rites performed at the royal places of assembly. In these rites, fertility was emphasized and the well-being of king and *tuath* was magically linked. These rites survived in attenuated form down to the destruction of the Gaelic order. Succession to the kingship was open to anyone within the four-generations group, the normal property-owning kinship unit, and the succession was therefore almost always disputed. 'The course of dynastic history', wrote Professor Hayes-McCoy, 'reeks with bloodshed, disorder and internecine war.'

Much that was frankly pagan passed into Celtic Christendom and was given a Christian façade, so that it is often difficult to disentangle the two inheritances. The lives of the 'ten thousand Irish saints' are related in such extravagant terms – mythology and magic being strangely mingled with piety – that one has the feeling that anything was acceptable if it could pass as history. Most of the saints in fact seem to be pagan gods, local deities or tribal ancestors in disguise. The need to establish a respectable ancestry for kings, and especially for the High Kings as they emerged, was a source of much learned but imaginative nonsense. On the other hand there is often a hard core of truth in some of the orally transmitted lore. The setting of the oldest hero-tales of the Ulster cycle is clearly the Ulster border and the state of endemic warfare that existed between 'the men of Ulster' and 'the men of Ireland'. In this warfare the inter-tribal cattle-raid was a prominent element, a proof of manhood and of the personal courage that was so highly prized in Celtic tradition, as well as a source of booty. As we shall see in the next chapter, so well did the Church adjust itself to native ways that the monastic houses were much given to raiding one another, and it is claimed that at least half the burnings and pillages of churches during the Norse period and indeed back to the 7th century were the work of the Irish themselves. And the abbots would unashamedly claim their tithe of the spoils of royal cattle-raids.

In the epics emphasis is placed on single combat, and it was the two-horse, two-wheeled chariot that carried the hero into battle. Handsome decorated horse-bits, often found in pairs, are about the only archaeological evidence for this. Even so, in the archaeological record, as in the historical, it is only the upper classes of society that are represented. The aristocratic dress, as described in the tales, consisted of a short tunic over which was a long woollen mantle fastened with a brooch at the neck. The descriptions of the rath-dwellings, however, are so poetic and highly coloured that they do not square with the wretched living conditions revealed by excavations. Such evidence as there is for diet, for cooking and eating customs, and for dress accords well with what we know from other sources about the cultural environment of late prehistoric Ireland. We note, for example, the popularity of meat in the diet, especially pork and beef, and the prestige attaching to the possession of a great cauldron from which portions of meat were obtained by 'dipping', apparently in prescribed order. The most popular ball-game was clearly related to hurling or shinty.

A characteristic feature of pagan Celtic society was the itinerant habit of the learned and of the craft castes; and the wandering scholar as well as a number of travelling men, such as the tinkers, have no doubt come out of this tradition. 'Dealing-men' and those who engaged in competitive sport and entertainment were also mobile and they did their business at the various royal places of assembly. Since these activities, like warfare, were essentially inter-tribal it was common for the assembly places to be located towards the borders of the little kingdoms, and it has been suggested that this may be one reason for the attraction of the early Church to such border areas.

The culture of the Early Iron Age, for all its martial splendour and its high achievements in art and oral literature, was essentially barbaric and lacked political, administrative and judicial institutions. It was, in the words of Professor Binchy, 'tribal, rural, hierarchical and familial', and the nearest approach to urban forms were the 'temporary towns' or great fairs held at the royal seats. It remained faithful to rath and *tuath* and hostile to urban life far into the Middle Ages. Its virtues as well as its failings sprang from its 'tribal' pattern: while despising urban life it accorded high status to priests and poets, to men of learning and skilled craftsmen. Inspired by the new ideas and the Graeco-Roman heritage brought by Christianity, this insular Celtic-Irish culture blossomed again in the Celtic Church. And thanks to an inherited tradition of learned itinerancy now extended overseas, it was to have a profound influence in many parts of Europe.

2

THE EARLY IRISH CHURCH

From the coming of Christianity to the end of the Viking Era

KATHLEEN HUGHES

On some island I long to be,
A rocky promontory, looking on
The coiling surface of the sea

To see the waves, crest on crest
of the great shining ocean, composing
a hymn to the creator, without rest.

Colmcille, 6th century, (?) tr. John Montague

Prestige, power and wealth had been attained by the Church in late 7th century Ireland, after two centuries of struggling evangelization. Irish monks were active in Scotland, Northumbria, the English Midlands and East Anglia, and also in Europe, and in the 8th century Ireland, Scotland and Northumbria still shared a common cultural heritage.

Among the most impressive relics of that great age today are a small number of very richly illuminated manuscripts, of which the *Book of Kells* (opposite) is one of the most splendid. It was produced in the 8th or early 9th century, it is difficult to say where, though it was almost certainly at Kells by 1007. It consists (or consisted: some pages have been lost or destroyed) of the Latin text of the four gospels together with summaries, commentaries and tables of parallel passages. It is illustrated with pages of geometric decoration, full-page portraits and symbols of the evangelists, illuminated capitals and numbers of small animals and human figures. *The Arrest of Christ* is one of the three pictures which actually illustrate the gospel story. Two insignificant soldiers seize the much larger Christ, whose attitude already prefigures the Crucifixion. The whole group is set within an arch covered with interlace and geometric patterns. The text at the top reads: 'Et ymno dicto exierunt in montem Oliveti' (And after reciting a hymn they went out into the Mount of Olives). (1)

48

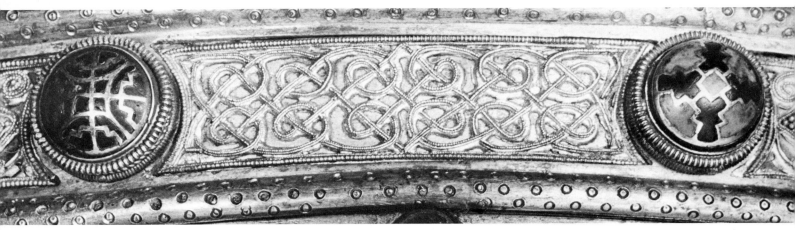

The repertoire of ornament which characterizes the art of the early Irish Church reflects both the pre-Christian Celtic tradition and foreign influences. The ornament of the *Cathach* (top left), from the early 7th century, ante-dates Northumbrian contacts, and comparable motifs appear on a slightly earlier ring-brooch (top right). Northumbrian influence appears in the studs of millefiore glass on the rim of the Ardagh Chalice (above), one of the most beautiful objects of insular art; the use of these glass studs, gold-wire interlace and punched-out dots entailed a variety of techniques. Lower left: the Athlone plaque, probably a book cover, adapts early designs to depict the crucifixion. Bottom right: the Moylough belt-shrine, made to hold a relic. (2–6)

The spirals of La Tène art are given a practical purpose in this bronze strainer of the 7th or 8th century, from Moylarg Crannóg, Co. Antrim. It has an iron handle, but exactly how it was used remains obscure; probably it served in the preparation of food. (7)

The high crosses of Ireland form an exceptionally fine group of monuments. Usually between twelve and seventeen feet high, they were erected in the precincts of monasteries and are often the only part to survive. The arms of the north cross at Ahenny (right) are enclosed in a ring and the cross is topped by a conical cap-stone. Shaft and cross are carved with interlace and running spirals reminiscent of metalwork and are surrounded by a moulding like rope; the round bosses may derive from metal studs or rivets. The relief at the bottom, showing a man standing under a palm tree and facing a group of animals, is still a mystery. (8)

A great flowering of manuscript illumination took place between the 7th and 9th centuries in Ireland. Influences from England and Europe seem to have converged to create a style that was as fertile in imagination as it was assured in technique. Left: a page from the *Book of Durrow* which is among the most traditionally Celtic. It is one of the earliest of the great insular manuscripts, written in the mid 7th century. Above left: St John, from the *MacDurnan Gospels*, probably late 9th century. Above right: David and Goliath, from the *Southampton Psalter*, 10th century. David holds a crook; Goliath, upside down on the ground, still puts his hand to his face to protect himself from the stone. (9–11)

The Tara Brooch is one of the great masterpieces of insular art. The front of the brooch has sunken panels which contain filigree designs on a gold-foil base. Circular and rectangular studs of amber and domed hemispheres of glass are set in silver-gilt depressions. The back is also ornamented. Outstanding virtuosity of technique and versatility of design are enclosed in this circle, $3\frac{1}{4}$ ins in diameter. (12)

The monasteries, though rich and powerful, were not remarkable architecturally. Early churches were usually of wood, and stone-building seems to have grown in the Viking Age. The small oratory of Gallarus, Co. Kerry (top left) is corbelled, made of stones without mortar, as were some monastic cells in stony areas. (13)

Contemporary dress and hair styles are reflected on a book shrine (*Breac Maodhóg*). Some of these figures carry books or crosses, and seem to be clerics. They probably demonstrate the secularization of many monastic communities by the 11th and 12th centuries. At the bottom of the page is an air view of the monastic site of Kiltiernan, Co. Galway. The outer enclosing wall, inner divisions, and remains of buildings can be seen, with the graveyard. Today only the ruined church is standing. (14–16)

Abbot Muiredach of Monasterboice, Co. Louth, was among the leaders of the Irish church in the 10th century. He died in 922. The sculptured cross which bears his name (right) makes an interesting contrast to the earlier Ahenny cross illustrated on p. 51. Where that had been covered in abstract patterns, this has figure reliefs. The central area represents the crucifixion; at the top there may possibly be depicted Moses between Aaron and Hur; and on the shaft, in descending order, Christ giving the keys to St Peter and the Law to St Paul, doubting Thomas, and (certainly) the arrest of Christ. On the other side are Old Testament scenes including (above) Adam and Eve and the murder of Abel. (17–18)

A mingling of cultures is evident in the works of the 11th and 12th centuries, after the Vikings had become firmly established in Ireland. The crozier of the abbots of Clonmacnoise (below), with its animal head, has suggestions of the Scandinavian Urnes style, derived from Norwegian prototypes. (19)

In the rugged west of Ireland a few relics of the Church's heroic age can still be found. Temple Benen, Inishmore, on the Aran Islands (left) is a single chamber of massive stone with originally a steeply pitched roof. Even more evocative is Skellig Michael, a lonely island off the coast of Kerry (below). Settled early by ascetic monks, it remained inhabited until the 12th century. The remains of six beehive houses, a small church and an oratory survive. (20, 21)

Chapter 2

From the coming of Christianity to the end of the Viking Era

KATHLEEN HUGHES

A gravestone from Clonmacnoise, Co. Offaly. Beneath the cross, which uses the typical interlace patterns, are the words (partly abbreviated) OR AIT DO D AINÉIL, 'A Prayer for Daniel'. (1)

IRELAND received her first bishop in 431. He was Palladius, sent by Pope Celestine I to the Irish 'believing in Christ'; probably that same Palladius who three years before, when he was a deacon, had (according to the chronicler Prosper) encouraged the Pope to send Germanus and Lupus, bishops of Auxerre and Troyes, to extirpate heresy in Britain. The Pope was following conventional practice in sending a bishop to an already established group of Christians. We cannot be certain where in Ireland they were located, but it seems very likely that it was somewhere in the south, for Cashel seems to have had a Christian kingship at an early date when other kings in Ireland were following pagan initiation rituals. Christianity may have entered by aristocratic contacts with the Continent or with Britain, or perhaps by the coming and going of traders.

The first stages of the Church

There can be no doubt that Palladius came in 431, but we know very little about his career in Ireland. One of the most puzzling problems is his relationship with Patrick, for tradition says that Patrick arrived in 432. This date comes from the annals, but the chronology of the 5th-century annals is very doubtful, as one can see by looking at the dates given to various generations of the family of Niall of the Nine Hostages. Annals began to be drawn up in the 7th century, or possibly in the 6th, and they were later extended backwards, using any oral and written sources available. Genealogy and tradition provided a fairly consistent and probably fairly reliable record as far back as about 500, but before then chronology is necessarily extremely vague.

If the date of the beginning of Patrick's mission is dubious, so is that of its end. The annals differ by more than thirty years – from 457 to 492 – over the date of his death. A mission of sixty years seems most unlikely. One hypothesis, more plausible than most, is that his arrival took place a considerable time after Palladius, but that the Armagh chroniclers, anxious to exalt his reputation, placed it earlier. Indeed, some of the legends concerning Palladius seem to have been transferred to Patrick. In Muirchú's *Life*, for instance, Patrick is supposed to have stayed for some time at Auxerre, which seems implausible in view of his defective Latin: whereas Palladius may on good grounds be associated with Auxerre. As far as we can picture him at all, Palladius would seem to be the conventionally educated Gallo-Roman bishop.

But who was Patrick? He came from a Christian family living on or near the west coast of Britain. At the age of sixteen he was carried off as a slave to Ireland, where he remained for six years. Then he escaped and eventually returned home. He describes graphically how in a vision he received a call to Ireland, and subsequently set off there as a missionary.

However obscure are his life and career, his writings are unique in the vivid impression they give of a personality. He knew, none better, his inadequacies, his lack of learning and education, his youth in exile and slavery, his unworthiness, his sin; but he was absolutely certain that it was God who had called him, given him to the Irish to serve them 'for the duration of my life'. 'I was like a stone lying in deep mire,' he says, 'and He that is mighty came and in His mercy lifted me up. ... Who was it that roused up me, fool that I am, from the midst of those who in the eyes of men are wise? ... *He* inspired me.' And it is because of this summons that he preaches, that regardless of danger he must make known the gift of God, which is the bequest he leaves to the thousands whom he has baptized. The tone of the *Confession*, in spite of its obvious defects, is one of complete certainty.

It seems very likely that Patrick's sphere of activity was mainly the northern half of Ireland. In the 7th century he was claimed by Armagh which, established within three miles of the ancient Ulster capital of Emain Macha, must have been an early foundation. The place-names which include the word *domnach* (deriving from the Latin *dominicus*) form a very early stratum, and are heavily concentrated in the north and in Brega, the kingdom on the central-eastern seaboard; their distribution suggests that they are to be associated with the church of Armagh, which was certainly claiming control over them in the 7th century. The area in which Patrick worked was pagan, and the episcopacy of Palladius and the mission of Patrick can best be explained by assuming that one was resident in the south, where a Christian community was already established, the other moving around the north, which was still pagan.

Patrick did not act like the conventional bishop. He was not ministering to Christians but converting the heathen; he mentions no seat but was merely 'resident in Ireland'; travelling on a mission of conversion, he was accompanied by a band of young princes and made gifts to the powerful. Some churchmen at least, presumably in Britain, rejected him. It is clear from his own writings that his education had been sparse, that he knew one book only, the Bible, and that once away from its familiar phrases he often expressed himself obscurely.

The confusion of the records is not surprising when one considers the political situation. In the 4th century, Ulster had been a large and powerful province, stretching as far south as the Boyne. When Armagh was founded it was probably still within the borders of Ulster. But by the early 7th century Ulster had shrunk to a much smaller area in the north-east corner of Ireland. The Uí Néill had established themselves in the central north, and under the new regime Armagh found itself in the kingdom of the Airgialla, vassal kingdom of an Uí Néill overlord. It must have been a period of political disturbance, which is reflected in the stories of Patrick's burial. The *Book of the Angel* claims Patrick's body for Armagh, but the continuation of Muirchú's *Life* says that he was buried in Downpatrick (in the later kingdom of Ulster) and that there was war between the Uí Néill and the Ulstermen over possession of the body. It was not until the 7th century that Armagh succeeded in establishing itself, claiming primacy in Ireland and presenting Patrick as the apostle to the Irish.

The 7th-century legend portrays Patrick as the successful missionary, converting all the Irish,

worsting the druids of the Uí Néill overlord, forcing the king to submission and triumphantly securing the acceptance of the faith. This is still the picture drawn in many modern books, but 6th-century Church legislation shows that it is false. The canons known as the First Synod of St Patrick (which probably belong to the 6th century) show a quite well-established Christian community with seven orders of clerics and various sees, each under its own bishop. But the Christians were still only a minority within a pagan society. The Church was not as yet integrated with the legal institutions of that society or protected by it; its members were forbidden to call each other before the secular courts and were to hold themselves separate from the world; they might not accept alms from pagans.

There is other evidence which suggests that the triumph of Christianity was a long-drawn-out process, lasting well over a century. The early kings of Tara were inaugurated by a pagan rite known as the *feis Temro*, 'feast of Tara'. *Feis* is the verbal noun of the Old Irish *fo-aid*, 'sleeps with', signifying that at this ceremony the king was united with his land in a ritual marriage. The last time it is mentioned in the annals is at the inauguration of Diarmait mac Cerbaill in 558 or 560, by which time the record is fairly reliable. Diarmait lived two generations after Patrick, and was the grandson of a brother of Lóegaire, the king whom the Patrician legend makes submit to Patrick. In the annals both Lóegaire and his successor, Ailill Molt, are inaugurated with a *feis Temro*. Little confidence can be attached to the dates of these 5th-century ceremonies, but the information is so contrary to Patrician propaganda as later accepted that it seems likely to be genuine. It bears out the clear evidence of the ecclesiastical legislation that Irish society remained predominantly pagan until the mid-6th century.

The rise of the monasteries
It was probably the advance of monasticism about the middle of the 6th century which completed the process of conversion. The Church founded by Palladius and Patrick had been organized under bishops in territorial dioceses, like the Church elsewhere. Although monasticism was known and practised, and a few people followed an ascetic life in their own homes or in small groups, it is clear from the language of the *Confession* and from the earliest Church legislation that it did not yet dominate the organization of the Church. By the middle of the 6th century, however, it was a growing force, and it surged forward especially after the devastating plague which hit Ireland in 548. The great monastic founders (two of whom, Finnian of Clonard and Ciarán of Clonmacnoise, died in the plague) were revered as saints, and families bequeathed property

for the foundation of new houses. Primarily intended as they were to serve an ascetic ideal, they also, probably from the beginning, supported married laymen who farmed the land. Thus the monastery was an estate with a religious purpose, a self-supporting farm, a kind of village.

Nearly all the monastic founders belonged to the aristocratic class of society, and it is clear from the 7th-century legislation that they and their successors were familiar with the secular law. The early 6th-century episcopal Church had tried to encourage a Christian society separate from the world. In the 7th century one group of churchmen continued a conservative policy, emphasizing the authority of the bishops, trying to follow the practices of the Continental Church; but another party was attempting to integrate the Church with the secular law and with native customs of status, evidence and surety. The Roman party succeeded in bringing the Irish Church into line with Continental practice on the date of Easter (a very heated issue in the 7th century); but in matters relating to ecclesiastical organization the Irish party prevailed and the Church adapted itself to native legal practices. By the time the 7th-century canons were drawn up, the clergy were no longer ordinary private citizens but were accorded a high honour price (which provided the basis for assessing the compensation to be paid if they were killed or injured) and monasteries were protected by laws of sanctuary. They were in fact fulfilling some of the same social functions as a secular lord and rights of inheritance within them can sometimes be discerned.

Such changes in the Church's position may have come about partly because of the spiritual and social prestige enjoyed by the monastic founders. Even in the present day there is good evidence for thinking that some individuals have gifts of healing which are not rationally explicable; early medieval accounts of miracles of healing, even when due allowance has been made for exaggeration, borrowing and literary convention, seem to preserve a core of truth. It was a period when people were on the look-out for miracles. Druids had had supernatural powers of prophecy and second sight, so it is not surprising that when between 688 and 704 Adomnan, abbot of Iona, wrote his *Life of Columba* he devoted his first book to the saint's prophetic revelations, the second to his miracles and the third to his visions.

At the same time, saints' Lives nearly all stress the noble ancestry of their heroes, and it is clear that Columba, in a hierarchical society, was the equal of the kings and overlords to whom he was related. At Iona, all of the first twelve abbots except two belonged to the same family. This is not surprising. In early Ireland a man's kin was the passport which demonstrated his status, secured him protection and

justice, and gave him his sense of identity. Thus a monastery which had had so distinguished a founding abbot might well look to his kindred for his successors.

The Irish monastic system was unlike that which prevailed elsewhere in Western Europe. The Benedictine Rule, which was to be accepted in all countries under Roman jurisdiction, was based on a strict and uniform organization and a meticulous daily schedule of work and prayer. Irish monasticism, on the other hand, never adopted a standard formula, and the monastic rules were as much spiritual exhortation as practical legislation. Many of the monasteries were supported by *manaig* (a word translated as *monachi*, 'monks'), married laymen who lived on the monastic estate with their wives and children, farming the land. The number of ascetics in a monastery varied from time to time. In the 8th century some houses were composed entirely of ascetics; others were governed by ordained abbots and had a strong ascetic tradition; yet others had lay abbots but supported separate groups of ascetics.

In the 5th- and early 6th-century Church the episcopal divisions, or sees, seem to have coincided with the areas of the petty kingdoms. Monastic territories were more fragmented: a monastery would be founded on family land, but might then acquire subsidiary houses, separated from it by some distance, but forming part of that monastery's *paruchia* and owing allegiance to the abbot or *comarba*, the founder's 'heir'. The *paruchia* of Iona, for instance, included houses in both Scotland and Ireland, and the abbots are recorded as visiting them. During the 6th and 7th centuries there was evidently some ambiguity about the relative authority of abbots and bishops. One party, the *Romani*, looked to the bishops as its leaders; the other, the *Hibernenses*, to the abbots. Ultimately it was monastic *paruchiae* which prevailed while the old episcopal sees disappeared. A big monastery kept its own bishop, but his functions were sacramental; the abbot, who was often a priest, was in charge of administration.

The 7th century saw a great surge of activity in the Irish Church. The monasteries provided motives and opportunities for writing and recording which seem to have been wanting earlier. Churches needed Gospel books and service-books; masters needed grammar books to teach Latin, the language of the monastic schools. There were synods of clerics which passed canons, some of which have come down to us, and churchmen drew up disciplinary manuals, the penitentials. The major controversy in the 7th-century Church concerning the date of Easter has been mentioned. It gave rise to writings. People became aware that their monasteries had histories, and began to write the Lives of their saints. And, most important of all for the historian, continuous year-by-year annals now began to be kept, certainly at Iona, very probably at Bangor, possibly elsewhere. All this means that the 7th-century Irish Church is surprisingly well documented.

It was during this period, in 634, that Aidan, invited by King Oswald of Northumbria, went with a party of monks from Iona and took up residence on Lindisfarne, near the royal fortress of Bamburgh. Bede describes how the monks travelled from place to place converting the Angles. Perhaps British Christianity had not entirely died out in the north, but even so it was the Irish missionary movement which gave it new impetus and the Irish monks were firmly established as leaders of the Northumbrian Church for a generation. In 664 came the Council of Whitby at which the Roman system of calculating Easter prevailed. Many Irish monks returned, first to Iona and subsequently to Ireland, though some stayed on at Lindisfarne, and there were certainly Irish scholars in Northumbria in the 8th century, playing a leading part in some of the monastic schools.

The arts of an expanding Church
Contact with Northumbria had a major effect on the cultural development of Ireland, for it meant that Irish and English styles in art became interchangeable, and that Ireland, Scotland and northern England formed a single culture-area.

Before the Irish went to England in 634 their scribes had developed an elegant, clear and vigorous hand. This they taught to the English, and it is often impossible to tell now whether manuscripts are Irish or Anglo-Saxon, so the word used for them today is simply 'Insular': The *Cathach* or 'Battler' of Columba, a psalter written in the early part of the 7th century before the mission to Northumbria, shows us a manuscript unaffected by English art. The fine

hand is already developed, the initials are incorporated into the text as they are in later books and are decorated, but the repertoire of decorative motifs is taken from La Tène art; trumpet patterns, peltas and spirals. Perhaps a generation or so later the *Book of Durrow* was written, and it is immediately noticeable how all is changed. This book still has the old Celtic designs, but it also has pages of animal interlace derived from Anglo-Saxon art, and Gospel symbols which show the influence of Anglo-Saxon millefiori jewellery and also of Pictish sculpture. Whereas the *Cathach* is an Irish book, the *Book of Durrow* belongs to the Anglo-Celtic world of the north.

There has been great controversy about where the *Book of Durrow* was written, but perhaps we might more profitably ask by whom, and under what influences. If it was illuminated in Northumbria then it must have been by an Irish scribe whose mental images were formed by Anglo-Saxon and Pictish as well as by Irish art; if in Iona or Ireland then it must have been by a scribe who had spent time in England, and who was familiar with the exuberant animals of English jewellery. It was almost certainly produced at a scriptorium which had only recently acquired a Vulgate text of the Bible; the text is the Vulgate and the Gospels are arranged in the Vulgate order, though significantly the symbols given to the Gospels are the Old Latin symbols, not those of the Vulgate.

The *Book of Durrow* is the first of a series of splendid insular Gospel books. Some were definitely written in Northumbria: the *Book of Lindisfarne*, the *Codex Amiatinus*, the *Echternach Gospels*. The origin of others is less certain: the *Lichfield Gospels*, which lack the prefatory material of *Durrow* and which have a 'mixed' text (basically Vulgate but with considerable Old Latin adulteration), were at Llandeilo-fawr in South Wales during the late 8th and first half of the 9th centuries. This is a beautiful book which has never been adequately examined.

A panel from the Book of Durrow, written in the mid-7th century. It shows interlaced animals, a motif borrowed into Irish art from the Anglo-Saxons. The side-panels here are very like ornament in the royal treasure buried at Sutton Hoo in East

Anglia. The techniques of scriptoria in Ireland and Northumbria from this time on up to the Viking Age are so alike that manuscripts can often not be satisfactorily located, and are known as 'Insular'. (2)

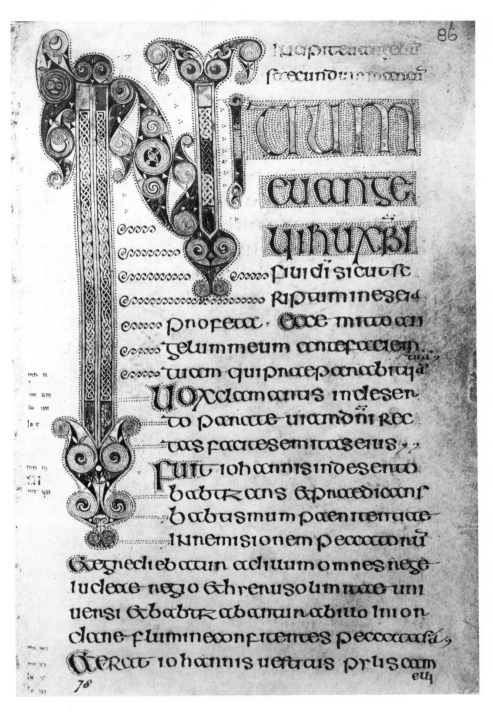

Part of an illuminated page from the Book of Durrow containing the opening of St Mark's Gospel. The words are so highly ornamented that it requires expertise to read them. The first letter combines I and N to begin the word INITIUM; the next two lines say EVANGELLII HESU CHRISTI (abbreviated) and the text then continues FILII DEI SICUT SCRIPTUM IN ESEIA PROPHETA: 'The beginning of the Gospel of Jesus Christ, the Son of God. As it is written in Isaias the Prophet. . . .' The interlace and spiral patterns are traditionally Celtic, going back to pre-Christian art. (3)

The *Book of Kells* shows that the community of artistic culture between Ireland, Scotland and Northumbria went on in the 8th and into the 9th century. It was presumably this book which was at Kells in 1007 when 'the great gospel of Columcille' was stolen and subsequently recovered, minus its shrine. Several features about it suggest an Irish origin. Similar designs, some of them rather rare in Ireland, occur on the crosses erected at Kells in the 9th and 10th centuries. Moreover, its text is a 'mixed' Irish type. Other features, however, are extraordinary in an Irish setting. It is lush with foliage patterns, which fit much better into a Northumbrian milieu than in Ireland, and its pages teem with human figures and little animals which,

though not absent from 8th-century Irish crosses, are more common in Pictish sculpture. So this manuscript also presents problems of localization.

The growing wealth and confidence of the Irish Church in the 8th century can be seen most clearly in its sculpture and jewellery. Relics and books were enshrined. The jewellery shows a variety of techniques, texture and colour: shining studs of millefiori glass, the matt texture of inlaid amber, twisted gold wire arranged in filigree panels, repoussé designs punched out from the inner surface, chip-carving usually executed by casting. Scrolls, spirals, trumpet-patterns, interlace, geometric patterns are all common decorative motifs. An object like the Ardagh Chalice is a triumph of virtuosity and

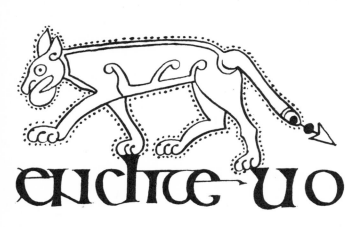

Recognizably the same animal peers at us from a Pictish stone from Ardross (above) and prowls between the lines of the Book of Kells (top). The question of the artistic sources of the Book of Kells is extremely complex, but parallels such as this show that there must have been influences from outside Ireland. (4, 5)

beauty. This piece also shows strong Anglo-Saxon influence. It must once have stood on the altar of some rich chapel, while the Moylough belt-shrine would have enclosed the relic in some monastic treasury; the Athlone crucifixion plaque may have been the cover of some book-shrine. The enshrining of relics is mentioned in the annals fairly frequently after about 700. Clearly the Church was growing in popularity, and the metal, jewels and the quality of the workmanship imply a rich institution. Some of the fine buckles which have survived may well have pinned the cloaks of ecclesiastics, for on the sculpture they are shown wearing them.

The splendid free-standing high crosses in western Ossory at Ahenny, Kilkieran, Killamery and Kilree are wheel-headed in design with bosses in the centre; most of them have bosses above, below, to left and right on the arms, as if the style had evolved from a metalwork cross in which the bosses represent studs clasping the ring to the main cross. Some of the bases have naturalistic scenes, while the shafts have key patterns, geometric motifs, spirals, animal, human and curvilinear interlace, complicated plaitwork, marigold patterns. Nearby at Tibberaghny is a stone with centaurs and fantastic animals as well as a leaping stag. All this represents tremendous elaboration of the simple stones of the preceding century – a variety, a complexity of design and a technical virtuosity comparable to those of manuscript art.

The same increase in wealth and power is reflected in the institutions of the Church. During the 8th century the annals mention churches allying with overlords to impose a type of ecclesiastical law, the saint's *cáin* (plural *cána*), usually in one province. These *cána* seem to be aimed at protecting clerics, Church property, women and children from violence, and they imposed penalties for violation. They were profitable to the Church and brought in taxes. We know that they were sometimes accompanied by the circuit of the saint's relic-shrine. The first of the *cána* was imposed in 697, and perhaps as time went on the financial aspect of the circuit became predominant: we may be sure that the profitability of the *cána* would ensure their enforcement whenever possible.

The annals of the 8th century afford a number of examples of inherited abbacies, of abbots succeeded by their sons, brothers, nephews, cousins. Clerical celibacy was not invariable, and it was customary for men to follow in their fathers' professions, so that 'Let the abbot's son enter the church', the advice in a 10th-century poem, seems to have been applied in some 8th-century communities. Secularization had proceeded so far in the later 8th century that monasteries occasionally went to war with each other. There seem to have been faction fights within monasteries (like that in Ferns between the abbot and the steward in 783) and major battles between monasteries. On one of these occasions (764) two hundred men of Durrow were killed. And in 807 the noblest of the *familia* of Cork were slain, which shows that monastic armies were not just composed of tenants. Such evidence suggests a Church which was now completely integrated into Irish society, so that some of its secular codes and values operated powerfully inside the monastery as well as outside.

In contrast to this secularization there were men leading an ascetic reform. One party called themselves *céli dé* (culdees), 'clients of God', the men who took God as their lord. These reformed monks were celibate. They gave time to prayer and ascetic exercises, and a number are called 'scribes', which probably means that they were leading figures in the monastic scriptoria. Towards the end of the 8th century some new houses of ascetics were founded, such as Finglas and Tallaght; sometimes groups of ascetics were maintained by major monasteries a short distance away from the old foundation. The spiritual revival within the Church affected the literary output. Men of learning began to take a renewed interest in the saints. The Martyrologies of Oengus and Tallaght (lists of saints arranged under each day of the year, one in verse) both belong to the culdee milieu, while the Old Irish Penitential and Table of Commutations also seem to have been inspired by the ascetic reform. But the constitution of the monastic order did not change, so that maintenance of the reform depended on the enthusiasm of particular monks, and by the end of the 10th century the tide of ascetic revival seems to have spent its force.

The Church in crisis

Viking raids began in 795, but it is clear from the annals that the years from 832 to about 870 saw the beginning of incursions of a larger scale leading to widespread dislocation.

The threat of violence was, of course, not a new one. Internal and intermonastic quarrels have already been noted. There were also attacks on monasteries from outside. In 735 Aed Róin was taken out of the monastery of Faughart to be killed. In 809 an abbot was killed in his own house beside the shrine of Patrick, and the Uí Néill overlord afterwards plundered Ulster to avenge the profanation of the shrine. But incidents like these would not seriously have affected the civilized life of the monastery. There are very few occasions mentioned in the annals before 832 when monasteries seem to have suffered wholesale attack, the sort of attack in which their treasures would be indiscriminately plundered and burned. The annalists clearly felt that the Norse effect on the Church was more devastating than any they had hitherto experienced, and they do not suggest any national effort in Ireland against the Vikings comparable to the one which Alfred and his descendants led in England in the later 9th and 10th centuries. Irish kings and overlords were fighting among themselves while Viking raids were going on, and attacks on churches by others than Vikings were still being recorded.

It has recently been argued that the destructive element in the Viking migrations has been grossly exaggerated, and that they were in the main peaceful settlers, pursuing commerce, and benefiting Irish metalwork by the introduction of silver. There is no doubt that the Viking effect on Ireland has been in some respects misunderstood, largely because the 12th-century tract *The War of the Irish with the Foreigners* misrepresents the period as a battle of the

Irish against the Vikings, culminating in the triumphant victory of Brian at Clontarf in 1014. But this is not what the annals say, and it is they that provide the contemporary evidence which historians need to take seriously. The annals tell us of war among the Irish kings, of war between Irish and Vikings, of Irish and Vikings fighting together against their own countrymen; but they suggest a far more troubled period for the monasteries during the years 832 to 870 than any hitherto, with Viking attack an ever-present threat, and status no longer a guarantee of security, for abbots and scribes might be taken off as prisoners. It may perhaps have been true that, other things being equal, the Vikings preferred peace to war (though if so they differed from the Irish aristocracy, who seem to have regarded war as a source of honour and possibly of economic gain). But they had to be fed, and they needed material for their trade; that is not only movables like metalwork but also human beings as slaves. The first generation of the settlement could hardly have been a peaceful one.

Recent work on the jewellery has shown that excellent brooches were still being made in Ireland in the second half of the 9th century, probably for the lay aristocracy. A few metalwork shrines were made in the 10th and perhaps the late 9th century, so some monasteries continued to invest in portable valuables. All the same, metalworkers who had previously executed orders under monastic patronage may now have sought the protection of secular lords. Kings would almost certainly have obtained Viking silver in the 9th century, perhaps by trade, certainly in war when after a successful battle spoils would be stripped from the dead. Some metal-workers had always worked under royal patronage. Monastic goldsmiths may have been itinerant – their equipment was portable – and if so in the 9th century they would take themselves to the best-defended forts. This interpretation of the archaeological evidence does not contradict the account which the annals give.

Not all monastic houses felt the Viking attacks equally. Some disappear from the records during the period of extreme Viking pressure. Tallaght, on the outskirts of Dublin, appears at 825 and 827, then no more until the entries start again in 868. Louth, about eight miles from the sea and uncomfortably near to the Viking centre on the coast at Annagassan, appears four times in the first three decades of the century; then the house was attacked in 832 and 840, and is not mentioned again during the 9th century. Bangor, situated on Belfast Lough, is mentioned in 839, then no more until 871, when the entries start again.

But others were luckier. Lusk was in an exceptionally exposed position, a short distance from the coast, with Lambay Island, one of the Viking haunts, just opposite. Yet the annals give us a steady sequence of ecclesiastical officials right through the period, though the oratory was burned once by Norsemen in 855. Monasterboice is only seven or eight miles from the coast, but the annals recall the natural death of one abbot in 846 and the drowning of another in 855, so the monastery here went on functioning. And there are seven entries (an unusually large number) between 832 and 870 for Slane, a house on the Boyne where the Vikings were very active. The obvious assumption is that these houses must have come to some agreement with the nearby Vikings, perhaps securing immunity in return for a food-rent. A lot must have depended on the diplomatic skill of the abbot, and perhaps on the military power of the nearest Irish king and on local alliances. Everywhere, however, the *cána*, those laws protecting Church property and noncombatants which begin in 697, come to an end in 842. Presumably it was no longer possible to enforce them.

A few of the great artistic productions of monastic scriptoria remain to be mentioned, but they are the last in a long tradition. The *Book of Armagh*, a manuscript of the New Testament with fine initials and Evangelist symbols, was written in and about the year 807: the fact that it was written at Armagh is proved by the Patrician material and by the inclusion of the *Liber Angeli*, a text of the late 7th or early 8th century, defining Armagh's legal claims. The *Rushworth Gospels*, less well executed, were illuminated by the scribe Mac Regol ('*Macregol dipincxit*'), a rather uncommon name borne by an abbot of Birr who died in 822. One cannot be sure when the *Gospels of MacDurnan* were written, but they belonged to Máel Brigte mac Tornáin, abbot of Armagh from 888 to 927. Their writing is very like that of the *Book of Armagh*, which suggests a date in the first few decades of the 9th century. However, a few of the forms used for abbreviations in this manuscript seem to fit better with later books, that is, after 850, so the *Gospels of MacDurnan* may well belong to the Viking period. Perhaps it was written by a scribe of Armagh trained in a very conservative tradition. After 850, Irish manuscripts decline in the quality of their illumination. Books were still written, but illumination was a skilled, expensive and lengthy process, and it looks as if these requisites were less easy to come by in the later 9th century. Perhaps it is true that the style was old and worn out; two hundred years is a long time for a fashion to be sustained: nevertheless it is surely more than a coincidence that the art declines so markedly with the onset of the major Viking attacks.

Sculpture, on the other hand, seems to have increased in output at this time, and that too was probably not an accident. It could well have been a deliberate act of policy by level-headed abbots, for monumental art was durable. Certainly in the 9th and 10th centuries sculpture was developing, and whereas the 8th-century Ahenny group of crosses bear abstract patterns on their shafts, the major part of the front and rear of the main shafts of these later crosses is taken up with figure sculpture, with an iconography based mainly on the Bible, both the Old Testament and the New, in particular on stories of David, and on the Gospels. Once the style had developed, the crossing at the front usually depicts the Crucifixion where Christ is flanked by the lance- and sponge-bearer, while the rear crossing bears the Last Judgment. On the shafts we see scenes such as Adam and Eve in the Garden of Eden; the Ark; David playing his harp, minding his sheep, fighting Goliath; Abraham preparing to sacrifice his son Isaac; the Virgin nursing the child Jesus with Joseph beside them; the arrival of the Magi; the flight into Egypt; Christ's baptism by John; the miracle of the loaves and fishes; His arrest in the garden; the soldiers asleep at the empty tomb; Paul and Anthony in the desert. These stones bear the message of God's revelation and redemption. Some are badly weathered, but some, like Muiredach's cross at Monasterboice, are remarkably clear and beautiful.

How this iconography developed and what are its sources of inspiration are rather puzzling. Though the David iconography turns up in 10th-century psalters, the crosses demonstrate very clearly that a monumental art can develop without a native art of fine illumination to provide its models. Did the sculptors have pattern-books which they passed round? Dr Henry suggests that Carolingian ivories were partly responsible for the new style, but there is no reason to believe that Carolingian ivories were circulating freely in Ireland, even though clerics were travelling to the Continent. There is 8th-century evidence that Irish sculptors were already in command of a naturalistic art, and the high crosses of the British Isles are *sui generis*, with distinct types in Ireland, Pictland and England. Perhaps the monastic reformers were eager to evolve a more popular and didactic art form, to which the administrators were glad to give financial support. Books were read by the few, crosses could be seen by the many.

It is thought that the round towers, so distinguishing a feature of the Irish landscape, developed during the Viking age. They are tall tapering funnels of stone, topped by a conical cap, with four large windows facing the cardinal points at the top, and a door well above ground level. The Clondalkin tower is 45 feet in circumference at the base and 84

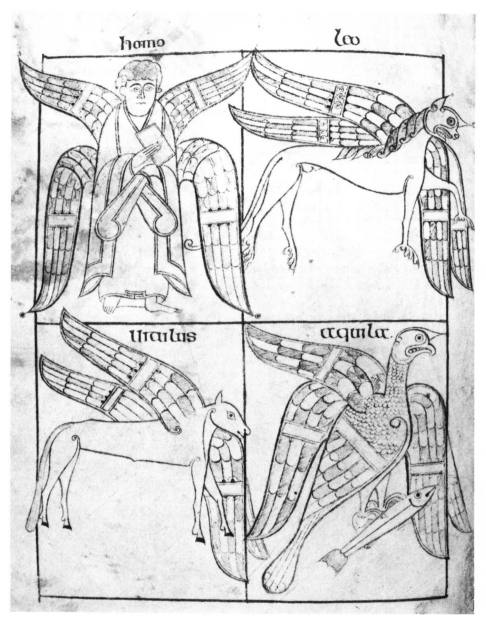

The four symbols of the Evangelists, a page from the Book of Armagh. It was written by Ferdomnach, at the dictation of Abbot Torbach, who died on 16 July 808. The end of the Gospel of Matthew was written on the Feast of Matthew, i.e. 21 September. And opposite the prophecy of the destruction of Jerusalem in St Mark's Gospel is the word 'Cellach', who was Abbot of Iona and who came to Ireland after his monastery was sacked by the Vikings in 806. It is therefore accepted that at least some of the book was written in 807. The Evangelist symbols are the Vulgate symbols: the Angel for Matthew, the Lion for Mark, the Ox for Luke, the Eagle for John. (6)

feet high. It originally had five floors, and the doorway used to be nearly 13 feet above ground level. These towers seem to have been used as bell-towers, look-outs, treasuries and places of refuge, and very probably evolved in response to the Viking attacks.

Literature and learning

Scholars belonging to the Irish Church began to make their imprint on European culture as early as the 7th century, although Irish monks had always regarded exile from their own land as a form of asceticism. At home, whatever his physical privations, the cleric was a person of consequence, commanding a high honour price. When he left his own land he abandoned his legal security and was dependent on God. Life became for him a roadway 'whereon none dwells, but walks', content with only 'a travelling allowance' without the security of home. Columbanus was the first of the famous Irish-

men to go to the Continent, and he founded houses at Annegray, Luxeuil and Bobbio, where he died in 615. The Ambrosian Library at Milan now contains manuscripts from Bobbio, some of which show strong Irish influence. St Gall, Columbanus' disciple, founded the house in Switzerland that bears his name, and here too illuminated manuscripts survive which are Irish in style.

Northern Europe saw several notable Irishmen in the 7th century. The most famous of these was Fursey, who went first to Burgh Castle in East Anglia, perhaps living inside the Roman shore fort which stands on the east side of Breydon Water about four miles from the sea. Later he moved on to the Continent, where the government of the Merovingian kingdoms was in the hands of 'mayors of the palace'. When Fursey died after founding the monastery of Lagny, Erchinoald, mayor of the palace in Neustria, obtained his body for the new church he had built at Péronne. Fursey's brother Foillán remained after him at Burgh Castle, then went on in 650 first to Péronne, then into Austrasia, where the widow and daughter of King Pepin had founded a double monastery at Nivelles. This house seems to have been under Irish influence, and Foillán founded a monastery of his own at Fosses, near Namur. Probably about 655 he was killed and Grimoald, mayor of the palace of Austrasia, played an important part in recovering his relics. A third brother, Ultán, after a stay at Burgh Castle, became abbot of Péronne where he was followed by another Irishman, Cellán, who died in 706. Péronne was known as Peronna Scottorum, and was a centre of Irish influence in the 7th and 8th centuries. In 779 the Irish annalist recorded the death of an abbot with an Irish name in the 'city of Fursey in Francia'.

The court circle was clearly in close touch with these Irishmen and with Ireland. In 656 Grimoald wanted to get rid of the young prince Dagobert and remove him from the throne. What was he to do with him? He had him tonsured and sent him to Ireland, where he remained for about twenty years. We can see the routes by which books from the Continent could have passed to Ireland.

Evidence for contact between Ireland and Spain in the 7th century is indirect but convincing. It rests mainly on the speed with which the works of Isidore of Seville became known in Ireland. Within a generation of Isidore's death the Irishman Laidcenn was quoting from him, and soon after, an Irish grammatical treatise uses several of Isidore's works. The name of St Finnian of Clonard, one of the great Irish monastic founders, occurs in a Visigothic abridgment of the Hieronymian *Martyrology* dating from about 800. The circulation of books does not necessarily mean direct contacts, for the books could have passed through Gaul to Ireland; but the Irish were great wanderers, and it is not impossible that some should have made their way to the coast of Galicia. We know that some travelled as far as Iceland in the pre-Viking Age.

Since there were Irishmen in Gaul (and even farther afield) in the 7th and 8th centuries, we should expect to find them in the schools of the Carolingian renaissance, where opportunities were plentiful for clever and ambitious men of learning. And we do. There are letters from the Englishman Alcuin, for some years at the end of the 8th century the head of the palace school, to the monks of Mayo and to Joseph his 'son', who seems to be the poet, Joseph the Irishman. An Irishman Clemens was associated with the palace school and Dicuil, the author of several treatises, including one on world geography derived from classical authors, was probably teaching in it early in the 9th century. The most famous Irishmen on the Continent were Sedulius Scottus, who was at Liège by the middle of

the century, and John Scottus Eriugena who became a teacher in the palace school of Charles the Bald.

These Irishmen brought a lively intellectual curiosity to the Carolingian renaissance, but everything suggests that the depth of their learning was acquired in Gaul. Here they met texts which were not available to them at home and they were able to learn Greek, through which they extended their knowledge. The Carolingian renaissance provided opportunities to stretch their intelligence which the schools at home could not. By the middle and third quarter of the 9th century conditions in monastic schools in Ireland were probably worse than they had been for some time – some monasteries were probably not able to maintain scribes in this period – and the most promising young scholars were no doubt glad to leave for the Continent.

The 9th and 10th centuries saw some major changes in monastic scholarship in Ireland. In the pre-Viking age most of the ecclesiastical literature was in Latin and the emphasis of the monastic schools had been on grammar and biblical exegesis, with some annalistic writing, canonical legislation and hagiography. Thus we have a straightforward 7th-century grammar book, the *Ars Malsachani*, and the *Hisperica Famina*, a master's exercises for teaching advanced students a difficult and ornate kind of Latin. There are scripture commentaries in Continental manuscripts where the author is unknown, but where the text suggests Irish influence. But we can see from the annals that the language of the scriptorium was changing during the early decades of the 9th century. In the 7th and 8th centuries the Annals of Ulster are mostly in Latin, though there are words and sometimes phrases and sentences in Irish. In the 9th century the amount of Irish increases. By the mid-830s most of the conventional-type obituary notices are in Latin, but most of the other entries are in Irish, a practice which continues. In the 9th and 10th centuries ecclesiastical literature was increasingly in Irish, and along with the change in the language comes a widening of interest in the work of monastic scholars.

Lyric poetry of the 9th and 10th centuries is often written in skilful and complicated metre, with alliteration, internal rhyme and end rhyme, yet with freshness and spontaneity of emotion. One cleric writes of his little hut in Túaim Inbir in Westmeath thatched by 'my darling, God of Heaven', a place with no enclosing wall, yet 'in which spears are not feared'; another wants to set up a tiny community of twelve young men and himself in a 'hidden hut in the wilderness', southward-looking, surrounded by trees and singing birds. Such poems present an idyllic picture of the hermit life, and suggest scholars on holiday from the scriptorium, seeing the world with a new awareness.

Much of the Irish literature of this period is by and for monastic scholars. They fitted their own native history into the world history provided by the Old Testament, synchronizing their heroes with the divine time-plan. The hold of antiquarian tradition on the minds of monastic scholars is very evident in the etymological glossary attributed to King Cormac, who died in 908. Irish tradition – pagan, heroic, Christian – tradition about gods and heroes, druids and poets and saints, was all proper knowledge for a 10th-century cleric.

We can see the combination of secular and Christian themes in the voyage tales and the saints' Lives. The voyage tales had begun before the Viking age arrived, and in the *Voyage of Bran* the secular character is clear enough: Bran is invited to the other world by a fairy woman. In the 9th- or 10th-century *Navigatio Brendani* (a text in Latin) the monastic element is prominent, the voyage being a *peregrinatio pro Christo*. Nevertheless here and in other (Irish) voyages, native traditions of the other world have been fused with the Christian idea of a search for the Land of Promise, and there is scope for fantasy. These stories provide some of the most delightful of all Irish literature. The saints are often lively and aggressive characters, performing miracles on behalf of their protégés with little regard for the morality of the situation. The Lives were often written to advertise the saint to a wide public, and it is the assumptions of secular society which prevail.

A new equilibrium

In the 10th and 11th centuries, the Vikings were firmly established in Dublin, Limerick, Waterford, Wexford and Cork. There was still fighting between Irish and Viking, but it was becoming limited and controlled. The two races were intermarrying, and the Vikings were adopting Christianity. This mingling of two cultures is proved not only by the annals but by archaeological evidence. Scandinavian art styles began to be adopted by Irish craftsmen. Croziers, book-shrines, bell-shrines and relic-shrines dating from the 10th and (in more abundance) from the 11th centuries show Scandinavian influence, like the Ringerike pattern on the shrine of the *Cathach* of St Columba, or the Urnes pattern on the shrine of St Patrick's Bell. One of the bronze trial-pieces found in the excavations at Dublin has a design of two intertwined animals strikingly similar to one of the panels of the *Cathach*, and it has even been suggested that the Hiberno-Scandinavian metal-workers of Dublin may have been producing objects for use elsewhere in the country. There is no

doubt that by the 10th and 11th centuries styles and sometimes objects were being exchanged between the Viking colonies and the Irish; but one Viking commodity which the Irish did not adopt was money. The Irish remained a society without a coinage.

Viking settlement probably had a major effect on the political structure of those parts of Ireland still in native hands. Petty rulers sank into insignificance and power became concentrated in the hands of a few great overlords. Minor kingdoms were unable to meet the forces ranged against them. Brian was the first king whose overlordship was recognized throughout Ireland.

The monasteries had to adjust to changed conditions. It seems likely that monasteries were now in close alliance with lay lords, so that they came to be attacked as if they were secular forces. Monastic officials were often laymen; the ascetic reform of the 9th century was a spent force. But the economic position of monasteries must have revived: schools were active, the monumental art of the scripture crosses reached its flowering in the 10th century, and in the 11th fine manuscripts and metalwork were produced.

In Armagh and Clonmacnoise, two of the greatest monasteries, we can see hereditary succession completely adopted as if the abbacy were a secular kingship. In the second half of the 10th century the Clann Sínaich came into power at Armagh, and abbots were succeeded by nephews, brothers or sons, none of whom was in major orders. In the mid-9th century the kin of Mac Cuinn na mBocht appear as monastic officials at Clonmacnoise, and the dynasty continues to play a major part in Clonmacnoise affairs until the 10th century. Some of these men were scribes or abbots, some were bishops or anchorites (i.e. they bore the title of asceticism), yet they were clearly not celibate.

It is the abbots of Armagh who emerge as the most powerful Church leaders in Ireland. This may be due to the bias of the sources, but all the same it is clear that Armagh was trying to substantiate claims which she had entertained from a very early period to an ecclesiastical suzerainty. In the 9th and 10th centuries Armagh had a 'steward' in Brega and some footing in the province of Munster (a 'unity' of twenty-four at the king of Cashel's table from the time of King Feidlimid). In 973 the abbot of Armagh went on a circuit of Munster to collect his tax there. Another abbot of Armagh went on a circuit of the Cenél Eógain in 993 when he 'conferred the degree of king' on Aed son of Domnall in the presence of Patrick's congregation. (A 'cemetery of the kings' is mentioned at Armagh in 935.) Brian came to Armagh on his circuit of Ireland and recognized the claims of the abbot of Armagh, as the scribe recorded in the *Book of Armagh* in the presence of Brian, *imperator Scotorum*. At times in the 10th century the abbot of Armagh also held control of the *paruchia* of Columcille. What had been claims in the 7th century were practical facts in the 10th and 11th.

It might have been in Armagh's interests had the overlordship of all Ireland remained in the hands of a single dynasty. But this did not happen. From Brian's death at Clontarf in 1014 until 1022 the most powerful king was Maél Sechnaill Uí Néill; later for a time Diarmait of South Leinster came to the fore, before the leadership passed back to the Uí Briain. From about 1114 to 1156 Tairdelbach Ua Conchobuir of Connacht was in the ascendant. A political history of this kind meant that ecclesiastical politics could have no very clear structure and had to proceed with a considerable degree of independence. The idea of ecclesiastical overlordship, as we have seen, was gaining ground. Provincial kingships had also evolved, so that a change to the European system of diocesan sees and metropolitancies had become a possibility.

Life in an Irish monastery
The monastic day was organized round the church services, the 'hours', starting with Matins in the small hours of the night and ending with Vespers as twilight fell (or, according to another text, with Compline, probably said by the monks in their cells before going to bed). A poem speaks of the sweet-sounding bell rung on a windy night to call the monk to his tryst with God. The monks living within the monastic enclosure attended the services, the *manaig* living outside came to church on Sundays.

But the life within different monasteries must have varied considerably. Small ascetic communities (of which Skellig Michael is the most striking example) spent much of their time in prayer, and the monks did the physical work needed to maintain life. In some sizable and important communities like Iona the monks also did the manual work of the monastery, but in most important Irish churches the physical work seems to have been done by the *manaig*.

The monasteries had to be self-supporting, keeping their cows for 'summer food' of butter, cheese and other varieties of milk products, growing vegetables. The staple of the 'winter food' was bread, for which the monastery grew grain. We hear frequently of barley; oats were suitable for a wet climate and wheat was the luxury crop. Big monasteries had their own water mills to grind the grain. In some houses meat was eaten. Flax provided the linen and sheep the wool for clothing: a long

tunic with a border, a cloak fastened by a brooch, and shoes. This was also the dress of the aristocracy. But clothing and hair styles varied. Some clerics dressed very simply in cloaks the colour of natural wool, while others wore bright colours. Hair styles were sometimes short, sometimes long and elaborately curled. Some clerics were clean-shaven, others had long beards and curled moustaches.

Some of the most dramatic sites today are those in remote places, often island sites to shut off the world; but most monasteries we hear about frequently in the annals were on or near main roads. Glendalough, for instance, which at first glance seems to be a settlement in a remote valley, is in fact near a junction of routes through the mountains, east through the Wicklow Gap, north by the Vartry River or by Lough Tay and Lough Dan, south by the Vale of Clara. Such monasteries grew. Already by 800 the poet Oengus was celebrating their vitality and popularity: Armagh with its 'choirs of scholars', 'the triumphant clamour of great Clonmacnoise', 'the thronged sanctuary' of Kildare and Glendalough. 'The little places settled by twos and threes are sanctuaries with throngs, with hundreds, with thousands.' Certainly the aerial photograph of Clonard bears out the claim of striking growth, for the little circle of trees, banks and ditches suggests the original monastery, while the traces of a much larger encircling ditch may denote the site as it was in the 10th century and later. By 800, and probably well before, some monasteries had become 'cities'.

When this happened, the monasteries were great estates, centres of population, not merely religious communities. Hospitality was one of the requirements of free society in Ireland, and the monasteries acted as guest houses in which clerics and laymen might stay. Some rules speak of a guest house and kitchen. The guest on arrival was offered hot water (the tub was heated by hot stones) and a meal: 'a clean house for the guests and a big fire, washing and bathing and a couch without sorrow'. We know from Bede that Anglo-Saxons, 'both nobles and commons', went to Ireland in the 7th century for study or to pursue the religious life and that 'the Irish welcomed them all gladly, gave them their daily food and also provided them with books to read and with instruction, without asking for any payment'. The distribution of charity to the needy in the locality was a social service which the monastery provided, so that even very ascetic houses gave away flitches of bacon and firkins of butter. The early Middle Ages had an extravagant non-egalitarian economy, but the Church gave back a considerable portion of its wealth in charity and social service. One 7th-century canon makes it clear that undesirable people were taking refuge in the monastic city and requires consecrated places to be

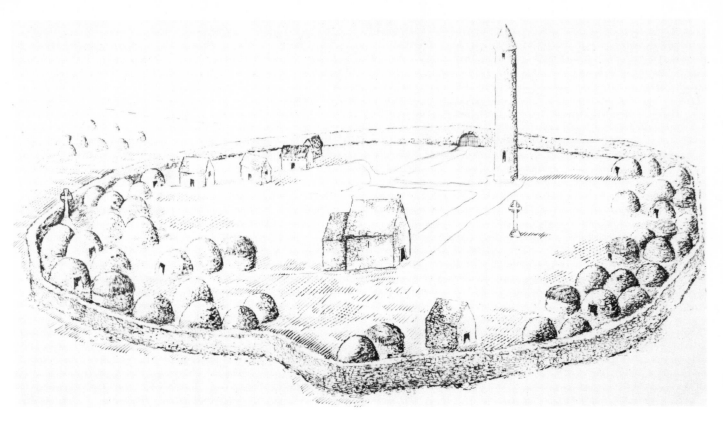

Conjectural reconstruction of a monastery, based on Kells as it may have been in the 12th century. The houses for manaig *(who did the agricultural work of the monastery) are outside the main enclosure. Cultivated fields and cattle are nearby. Buildings include church, round tower, scriptorium, school and workshops as well as dwelling houses. There would also have been a cemetery within the wall—an important feature since the burial fees paid by the lay population were a source of revenue for the monks. By 1100 there would probably have been a considerable settlement outside the wall. (7)*

cleansed of murderers, thieves, adulterers, perjurors, hawkers and *magi*.

A large monastery provided a school. Although the education it gave was mainly in Latin and the Scriptures, there is some evidence that it was sometimes attended by boys from lay society. The community was also a place of fosterage, for fosterage was a sensible institution in a society where a man might have children by several wives. The relations between ecclesiastical foster-fathers and their sons were often affectionate. Women's houses fostered young children; one of the best-known of the early Irish lyrics describes the babe Jesus as coming to be nursed by St Íte, not as a cleric or even a king's son, but Jesus King of Heaven.

Most of the early churches in Ireland were made of wood, small rectangular structures with small windows and steeply pitched gables and roofs covered with wooden shingles or thatch, with a door normally placed in the west end. Cogitosus' description of the church at Kildare implies a sizable building screened into three compartments, with a partition running across the church to separate off the area near the altar and the remaining space divided into two by a lengthwise partition. This church was hung with painted tablets, the altar was 'beautifully adorned' and the tombs of the founder,

Brigit, and the first bishop, Conláed, were 'surmounted by crowns of gold and silver'. No traces of interior decoration survive in existing stone churches and many are tiny; Gallarus, the date of which is debated, has internal measurements of 15 ft 3 ins. × 10 ft 2 ins. Some archaeologists think that wooden church-building went on until quite late, and that single-cell churches were not built in stone until perhaps the 10th century. Drystone beehive cells were used as dwellings by monks in stony areas, and those on Skellig Michael are still intact.

Craftsmen found patronage in the monasteries. Some were resident, but others may have been itinerant. There were obviously local 'schools', for the Ahenny group of monuments belongs to a particular style, as do the crosses at Fahan Mura and Carndonagh on the Inishowen peninsula in the north. We do not know where the jewellery was made, but crucibles and moulds were found in the excavation south of the cathedral of Armagh, and the author of the Tripartite Life of Patrick at the end of the 9th century thought it proper for Patrick to have metal-workers. Some monasteries show evidence of iron-working, and it seems likely that the iron implements in daily use were made by craftsmen resident in the monastic city. In the 7th-century *Life of Columba* it is the monks who melt the iron.

The Early Irish Church 69

The monastery thus had the natural resources of a self-sufficient economic unit. It was rich enough to support scholars and patronize craftsmen; it housed and protected treasures. Many of its oldest and most valued antiquities have been preserved because of their traditional connection with some powerful saint: the *Cathach*, the earliest Irish manuscript, was attributed to Columba and carried into battle to bring victory; the Moylough belt-shrine encloses a relic; Patrician documents were copied into the *Book of Armagh*. Clerics, lawyers and poets were familiar with each other, and clerics knew the heroic traditions. Ireland is rich in early historical texts because the Church became conscious of an Irish past and was eager to record it; she is rich in early treasures because the Church belonged to a heroic age and was striving for display. The medieval Church, learned families of the Middle Ages, scholar-collectors of the 16th and 17th centuries all contributed to preserve her inheritance.

3

THE LONG MIDDLE AGES

From the twelfth century to the Reformation

ROGER STALLEY

Bloody treason, murderous act,
  Not by women were designed,
Bells o'erthrown and churches sacked
  Speak not ill of womankind.

Bishop, King upon his throne,
  Primate skilled to loose and bind,
Sprung of woman every one!
  Speak not ill of womankind.

From *Against Blame of Woman* by Gerald FitzGerald,
Earl of Desmond, tr. by the Earl of Longford

One of the turning points of Irish history is the 12th century. Until then, in spite of the social and cultural changes brought about by the Viking settlement, Ireland had managed to retain almost complete independence both ecclesiastically and politically. But from the 1140s onward events conspired to bring the country much more definitely into the European mainstream and subordinate it to European authority. In 1142 the Cistercians founded their first house in Ireland at Mellifont, Co. Louth; in 1152 the Synod of Kells introduced a new framework of dioceses and bishops on the European pattern; and in 1169 Anglo–Norman knights entered Ireland at the invitation of the King of Leinster and embarked on a policy of conquest and expansion, recalling the invasion of England a century before.

The Cistercians, whose mother house was Cîteaux in France, had received a decisive impetus from the great reformer St Bernard. It was from his monastery at Clairvaux that the first Cistercian monks came to Ireland in 1142. Economically self-sufficient, they brought new land into cultivation, farming it with up-to-date methods that were usually more efficient than those of the lay landowners. Their early monasteries are plain, functional and remarkably standardized in plan and style. At Mellifont (opposite) the architect and the first monks were French. In this view we are looking through the ruins of the octagonal fountain house, where the monks washed before entering the refectory, across to the south side of the cloister. This fountain house (marked *g* on the plan on p. 82) was built later than the church, in about 1200, but still uses the Romanesque round arch. (1)

72

The old ways did not die, whatever innovations might come from abroad; even round towers went on being built. At Clonmacnoise the Nun's Church (upper left), founded in 1167, is the complete antithesis of Cistercian restraint, with its zigzag pattern, animal heads and (originally) bright colours. And at Timahoe the monks built a round tower in the 12th century that is hardly different from its 10th-century prototypes. (2,3)

The new bishops were not slow to assert their rights. On the 12th-century high cross at Dysert O'Dea (below left), the bishop is rather larger than the crucified Christ above him. (4)

Cormac's Chapel (right) on the Rock of Cashel is a unique combination of outside influences from England, France and possibly Germany. It was completed in 1134 by King Cormac McCarthy. (8)

St Molaise (far right) founded his monastery at Inishmurray, Co. Sligo, in the 6th century. It was a typically Celtic foundation, on a remote island in the Atlantic. This superb oak statue of the saint was probably made between 1250 and 1300. (9)

Snaky coils covering the top of the shrine of St Patrick's Bell (below) look to Viking art for inspiration. It was made at Armagh between 1094 and 1105. (5)

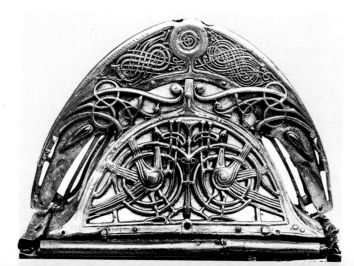

The strength and vigour of Irish Romanesque survived most fully in the lands west of the Shannon, where Anglo–Norman rule was slow to penetrate. The chancel arch of Tuam Cathedral, Co. Galway, with its strangely sculpted capitals (above), belongs to the years following 1184. Even more fantastic is the west front of Clonfert Cathedral, Co. Galway (right), where human heads are used as a grisly form of ornament in the spaces of a triangular pattern and in the tops of a narrow blank arcade. (6,7)

A chain of castles built by the Anglo–Norman lords was needed to hold Ireland in subjection after the first invasion of 1169. As in England, these changed as the conquest progressed. Wooden motte-and-bailey castles gave way to square stone keeps, and these in turn were surrounded by curtain walls with bastions. Trim Castle, Co. Meath, founded by Hugh de Lacy in 1172, is one of the most impressive. The three-storey keep, its walls 11

King Richard II came twice to Ireland, in 1394–5 and in 1399. Both expeditions aimed to halt the decline of English fortunes in the face of sustained Gaelic resistance. The ultimate problem was the impossibility of holding down an alien population by military force alone. As later monarchs were to realize, only col-onization could achieve permanent Anglicization. In 1399 Richard was obliged to return hurriedly to England to deal with Bolingbroke's rebellion (he is shown crossing the sea in this 15th-century miniature) and for over a hundred years English control continued to dwindle. (11)

feet thick, was finished about 1220, and it contained two main chambers. When Richard II visited Ireland he stayed at Trim and left there the son of his cousin Henry Bolingbroke—the boy who later became Henry V. (10)

'A filthy people wallowing in vice' was Gerald of Wales's jaundiced verdict on the Irish at the end of the 12th century. Below: two miniatures from a 13th-century manuscript of his book, illustrating Gerald's view of

For a fragment of the True Cross this cross-shaped reliquary (detail above) was made between 1122 and 1136 for Turlough O'Connor, High-King of Erin. The relic was set in the centre beneath a piece of translucent rock crystal, surrounded by gilt bronze panels and enamel discs. (12)

how kingship was conferred in Tyrconnel. On the right a white mare is killed, prior to boiling in a pot. On the left the king (in a bath) and his courtiers consume the flesh in a way that is certainly not over-refined. (13,14)

Splendid new churches on a scale never before seen in Ireland accompanied the Anglo–Norman conquest. In Dublin, Christ Church Cathedral was begun about 1186–90. The nave (below) dates from the early 13th century. The style is clearly that of the same period in England, and it seems certain that the master-mason was English. Even the stone was imported (from Dundry, outside Bristol). The cathedral nevertheless has special qualities of its own; particularly elegant is the way in which the triforium and clerestory are united by long vertical shafts of black marble. Christ Church was a monastic establishment, and apparently to escape from its restrictions Archbishop John Comyn began the equally grand St Patrick's, only a few hundred yards away. (15)

At Holy Cross, Co. Tipperary, the monks built a sumptuous shrine (above) for their relic during the 15th century. Planned between two chapels, it enabled the maximum number of pilgrims to venerate the piece of the True Cross. With its ribbed vault, twisted columns and fine workmanship it is like a small chapel, though in fact only a few feet across. (16)

The tracery of 15th-century windows and tombs in Ireland often looks back to a style current in England over a century earlier. Below: tomb-niche in the Franciscan friary of Kilconnell, Co. Galway. (17)

It was the friars rather than the regular priests and the bishops who dominated the rural west of Ireland, where English rule was weak or non-existent. Between 1400 and 1508 ninety friaries were founded, and their buildings constitute the major architectural achievement of 15th-century Ireland. Right: the Franciscan Rosserilly, Co. Galway, begun about 1498. A conspicuous feature of the friaries is the tall tower between nave and chancel. (18)

Tomb sculpture of the later Middle Ages is often naive but full of charm. Below: the donor kneels before an archbishop and Saints Peter and Paul on a tomb in the Dominican friary of Strade, Co. Mayo. (19)

Piers Butler, 8th Earl of Ormonde, lies with his Countess in Kilkenny Cathedral (below left). His head is protected by a keeled bascinet, and a pisane of mail covers his neck and shoulders. The main body armour is a coat of plates and below this is a mail habergeon. Such armour was common in Ireland at the time, although over a century out of date by English standards. At first sight this seems to be a parallel with Irish architecture, but the Butlers and other Irish lords were well aware of current fashions at the English court, and they seem deliberately to have retained these older methods. (20)

From the workshop of a sculptor named Rory O'Tunney comes this figure of St James the Less at Jerpoint, Co. Kilkenny. The left foot and the right side of the hair are unfinished. (21)

Rich with jewels, the crozier of Conor O'Dea, Bishop of Limerick, is the masterpiece of late medieval metalwork in Ireland. This detail shows part of the crook. Under elaborately chased canopies of gilded silver stand six tiny statues representing the Trinity, the Virgin Mary and four saints; visible on the left are St Patrick and St Peter with his two keys. Above them is a row of female saints engraved against an enamel background. The crozier was commissioned in 1418 and the goldsmith was probably Thomas O'Carryd. (22)

Monks singing mass: detail from a manuscript of the mid-14th century. The artist was English, but the commission came from Stephen de Derby, Prior of Christ Church, Dublin. Works like this exemplify the contrast between the English-controlled Pale, which was part of European culture, and the Gaelic areas outside, which were isolated and attached to their own past for inspiration. (23)

Chapter 3

*From the twelfth century
to the Reformation*

ROGER STALLEY

IT IS ONE OF THE MYSTERIES of early Irish society that the monasteries, which fostered so much learning and artistic splendour, should have shown so little interest in architecture. The patrons who commissioned such painstaking masterpieces as the *Book of Kells* were evidently content to live and worship in buildings of the utmost simplicity. In contrast, during the Middle Ages architecture assumed a far more conspicuous role. If the Early Christian period was the era of the metal-worker and painter, the Middle Ages was the epoch of the master mason, a time of ambitious building in stone – castles, cathedrals, monasteries, town walls and bridges. Moreover the social and political upheavals of the period are clearly manifest in changing styles and patterns of building. The great Anglo-Norman castles forcefully demonstrate the impact of the 1169–70 invasion, and the English style of 13th-century churches reflects the extent of subsequent immigration. The survival of hundreds of small tower houses is a brutal indication of the collapse of centralized authority in the 15th century. Albeit incomplete, architecture has thus bequeathed to us an image of Ireland's medieval past.

The watershed between the Early Christian and medieval world lies in the 12th century, when two major factors contributed to the transformation; the first was the reform of the Irish Church and the second was the invasion of Ireland by the Anglo-Normans in the years after 1169.

A reformed church

Long before the 12th century the peculiarities of the Celtic Church had attracted criticisms, and shortly before 1100 a movement for reform gathered momentum. In 1074 Lanfranc, Archbishop of Canterbury, wrote to Turlough O'Brien, High King of Ireland, urging him to rid his country of 'evil customs'. Lanfranc was horrified at the failure to apply Christian laws of marriage in Ireland. He was worried about the appointment of too many bishops who were not given defined dioceses. The

The city of Cork, as it was in the early 17th century. Many of the buildings are contemporary, but it is still surrounded by its strong medieval walls. The city stands on a narrow neck of land, with the River Lee on one side and the South Channel on the other. It can be traced back to a monastic settlement, of the 7th century. (1)

Christian sacraments were not being properly applied, and many priests were being consecrated in return for money, the all too prevalent medieval sin of simony.

Over the next hundred years a series of ecclesiastical synods was held in an attempt to correct these and other abuses, which eventually resulted in a complete reorganization of the Irish Church. Hitherto it was the monasteries which provided the basis of Christian teaching and worship, and it was the abbot, not the bishop, who had paramount authority. Normally the abbot was not even a consecrated priest, and his position depended on his role as *comarba* or heir of the founding saint. All too often, monasteries were regarded as family possessions by the *comarbas*, and the division between lay property and Church property was ill defined, to say the least. A notorious example was the ancient monastery at Armagh. Here the abbots inherited their office, and they were usually married and not ordained. In 1105 Cellach, a member of the hereditary family, temporarily removed the abuse by taking holy orders and working actively for reform. When he died in 1129 his kinsmen tried furiously to prevent the appointment of the saintly figure of Malachy, who was not a member of their family and was consequently regarded as an intruder.

Perhaps the most substantial achievement of the reformers was the introduction of a new framework of dioceses and bishops on the general European pattern. At the Synod of Kells in 1152 four archbishoprics were recognized, at Armagh, Cashel, Tuam and Dublin, and each was allotted specific dioceses. This structure of dioceses as the basis of ecclesiastical organization in Ireland gradually replaced the old monastic system, and it was the bishops, not the abbots, who now became the pre-

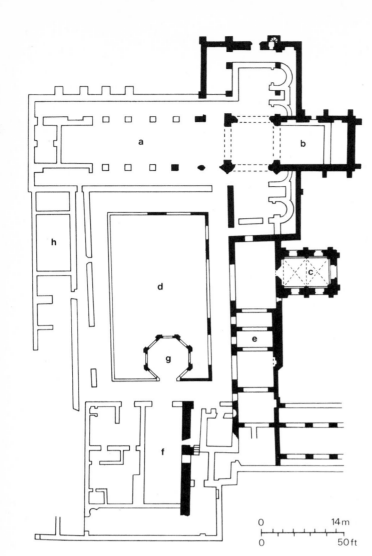

Plan of Mellifont, the first Cistercian abbey to be founded in Ireland. Begun in 1142, the church was consecrated in 1157. The layout of the monastery followed the standard plan used all over Europe: (a) nave of the church; (b) chancel; (c) chapter house; (d) cloisters; (e) dormitory range (over); (f) refectory; (g) fountain, for washing; (h) lay brothers' range. (2)

eminent Christian officials. Their enhanced authority was visually expressed on several of the high crosses of the period. At Dysert O'Dea we are left in no doubt about the prestige of the bishop who was presumably responsible for its erection. Beneath the figure of Christ crucified is the noticeably larger figure of the bishop himself, severe, stiff and solemnly impressive.

While the ancient monasteries lost their vitality and influence during the 12th century, new monastic orders were introduced from abroad by the reformers. The most prolific were the Canons Regular of St Augustine. The order had developed in the second half of the 11th century, and it was Malachy of Armagh who was instrumental in bringing them to Ireland. The canons followed a rule based on the writings of St Augustine of Hippo, but their exact way of life tended to vary from abbey to abbey. In Ireland many followed the rule practised in the

Augustinian house at Arrouaise in northern France. Although some completely new monasteries were founded for the Augustinians, they were frequently used to revitalize ancient foundations. Malachy, for example, established Augustinian canons at Bangor, and the reform was marked in 1140 by the construction of a splendid new church on Continental lines. St Bernard in his Life of the Irish saint explains how 'it seemed good to Malachy that a stone oratory should be erected at Bangor like those which he had seen constructed in other regions. And when he began to lay the foundations, the natives wondered, because in that land no such buildings were to be found.' Unfortunately this church no longer survives, but judging from the response of the locals it clearly represented a radical departure from tradition. Indeed Malachy was hotly opposed by one inhabitant who insisted that his large building was a needless frivolity, for he proclaimed, 'we are Irish not Gauls' (surely one of the first recorded protests against new building development!). Some Augustinian houses were founded in isolated places in the country and offered a strict semi-contemplative life almost indistinguishable from that of the Cistercian abbeys. Others served cathedrals, as at Christ Church in Dublin, where Augustinian canons were introduced by Archbishop Laurence O'Toole in 1163. After the invasion of 1169–70 many more Augustinian abbeys were founded by the Anglo-Normans as part of their settlement and colonization of the country.

It was also Malachy who brought the Cistercian order to Ireland. During his European journeys he had stayed at Clairvaux, which, under the formidable control of St Bernard, had become the most influential Cistercian monastery in Europe. Malachy was enormously impressed by the purity and simplicity of the Cistercian way of life which was particularly suited to the traditions of Ireland, where the early saints had been renowned for their asceticism. The first monastery was founded at Mellifont, just north of the Boyne, and it quickly prospered. Within twenty years, eleven more abbeys had been established, and after the Anglo-Norman invasion the total rose to almost forty. Not only did the Cistercians bring a new form of religious life but they also introduced a totally new concept of monastic architecture. Their churches, with separate aisles and transepts, were enormous in comparison to traditional Irish buildings. The domestic buildings of their monasteries were systematically planned around a rectangular cloister. Again this was a contrast to ancient Irish monasteries, where such buildings were normally made of wood and wattle, and were frequently scattered haphazardly arround the church. Impressive size and systematic planning made a significant contribution to the prestige of the Cistercians, and they were factors in explaining the swift and successful expansion of the order in Ireland.

The design of the original church at Mellifont was undoubtedly related to the early French houses of the order. A short square-ended presbytery, probably barrel-vaulted, and transepts with three small chapels opening off to the east, were typical of standard Cistercian planning. A contingent of French monks came to provide a firm nucleus, but French and Irish did not mix, and the friction became so serious that the French monks withdrew to Clairvaux. Despite this inauspicious beginning, work progressed steadily, and in 1157 the church was consecrated with lavish ceremony. Seventeen bishops were present and several Irish kings, including the High King Muircheartach Mac-Lochlain, who, in addition to land, presented the monastery with 'seven score cows and three score ounces of gold'. Devorgilla, wife of the King of Breifne, Tiernan O'Rourke, offered a golden chalice, together with cloths for the various altars within the church. The actual site of Mellifont lay within the kingdom of Oriel, and it was King Donough O' Carroll who was the chief benefactor of the abbey, providing most of the initial landed endowments.

Some of the Cistercian monasteries have been obliterated, but the ruins of about twenty are still impressive. Outstanding is the church at Boyle in Co. Roscommon which is easily recognizable as Cistercian. Its plan is typical of the order, and its builders used both pointed arches and pointed barrel vaults (in the presbytery and transept chapels), all features which ultimately derive from the early Cistercian abbeys in Burgundy. The rest of the design, however, is inspired by English architecture. Instead of the present rough grey stone, one must imagine walls covered with white plaster, creating an atmosphere of purity and perfection. The Cistercian statutes banning carved decoration and gold and silver ornaments are well known, but they were not always applied rigidly in Ireland. The piers at Baltinglass and Jerpoint, for example, are attractively carved with a variety of designs, both Irish and English in origin. At Boyle, the spirit of the order was flagrantly ignored about 1215–20 when a magnificent capital of dogs and cocks was used to decorate the nave, just the sort of thing which would have been anathema to St Bernard and the early Cistercian leaders.

The efficiency with which the Cistercians conducted their building enterprises was equally evident in other spheres. Each abbey was intended to be as self-sufficient as possible, producing its own crops and food, and the Cistercian monks quickly acquired a reputation as highly effective farmers.

Lands hitherto uncultivated were brought under the plough, and the systematic agricultural methods of the monks must have impressed the local Irish, whose farming tended to be pastoral rather than arable.

The continuing tradition

Despite the upheavals of the reform movement, and the innovations of the Cistercians, the ancient monasteries clung tenaciously to their old traditions. The painters who decorated the Gospel books, missals, commentaries and other religious texts continued to use familiar formulae, although some of the individual motifs were novel. An Irish ornamental initial, as in the Gospel books from Armagh or the Killiney book of hymns, was still entirely different in conception from one in an English or French manuscript of the period. The reluctance to experiment with grander buildings is equally surprising, in view of the large Cistercian churches which were now appearing. The traditional monasteries continued to build churches which were tiny in comparison, but quite why this was so is not clear. It is true the liturgy of Celtic monasticism remained simple, so that a huge space was not required for elaborate rituals. Even so there must have been occasions when services were conducted in extremely cramped conditions, with scarcely enough room to genuflect or swing a censer. Perhaps it was a worthy desire to avoid needless extravagance, or more probably the force of local tradition. Moreover, the general planning of monasteries still followed traditional lines, with a huge enclosing outer wall and an array of buildings scattered within. These included round towers, which were being constructed as enthusiastically as ever. One was built at Annaghdown as late as 1238. The 12th-century towers such as those at Timahoe and Ardmore are distinguished by their finely cut masonry and the frequent appearance of Romanesque decoration. The round tower at Clonmacnoise was also rebuilt during the period, after being struck by a 'thunderbolt' in 1138. This was a disaster continually inflicted on the towers, for their great height made them excellent lightning conductors!

The only conspicuous novelty in the buildings of the ancient monasteries was the delightful sculptural ornament used to decorate the doorways and arches. A magnificent example survives at Clonmacnoise, in the 'Nun's Church', founded in 1167 by Devorgilla who ten years before had bestowed gifts on Mellifont. The church consists of a simple rectangular nave, with a square chancel to the east, following the pattern of so many Irish Romanesque buildings. The west doorway is elaborately carved with four orders of arches, each with its own distinctive motifs, beading, chevron, animal heads and roll mouldings. The chancel arch is equally attractive and is distinguished by ambitious chevron designs, the individual stones deeply cut with great precision. Chevron appears to have originated in England, but the monster heads of the west door unquestionably derive from western France. This diversity of sources is a testimony to the widening horizons of the Irish Church during the period of reform. Yet despite this eclecticism, much of the design is distinctively Irish. Interlace and fret patterns appear, and the exceptionally shallow relief of some of the carving is typical of Irish Romanesque. In its original splendour, with the ornament picked out in paint, the Nun's Church must have been extravagant in its effect, a total antithesis to contemporary Cistercian thoughts on architecture.

The first dated church to receive elaborate sculpture was the chapel erected on the Rock of Cashel by King Cormac MacCarthy between 1127 and 1134. Cormac was a strong supporter of the Church reform movement, and he is known to have founded several new buildings; but of these, only the chapel at Cashel survives. When completed in 1134 it created a sensation, implied by the full references given in the Irish annals. It appears that the church was intended to serve a small community of Benedictine monks, some of whom may have been trained in the Schottenkirche at Regensburg. One of Cormac's own kinsmen, Christian, was in fact later to become abbot of Regensburg. Many writers have tried to point out German features in Cormac's Chapel, drawing attention to the two square towers flanking the chancel. They are certainly alien to Irish tradition, and without doubt they bear a general resemblance to the towers erected at Regensburg soon after 1110. But there is little else about the design which is German. The chief inspiration comes from England, not least the rib vault in the chancel and the ubiquitous chevron ornament. But one of the motifs on the chancel arch – a series of small human heads – has French connections, so that the range of sources for the chapel is bewilderingly varied. There are just two purely Irish features. One is the tiny scale of the building itself, and the other is a high pitched roof of stone. Thus Irish, French, English and possibly German ideas all played their part, but it is difficult to imagine how this extraordinary amalgamation was achieved. At least some foreign masons must have been present in the building team, and almost certainly there was an Englishman among them. Although Cormac's Chapel is unique, it set a fashion for elaborately carved doorways and chancel arches, providing the initial stimulus for Irish Romanesque stone sculpture.

In those lands swiftly conquered by the Anglo-Normans after 1169, Irish Romanesque did not long survive. But west of the Shannon the style continued until the early 13th century in a series of exotic works. Most famous is the fantastic doorway at Clonfert, with its seven orders of jambs and arches covered with an extraordinary medley of designs. One arch is decorated with sculptured bosses inspired by the 'Ahenny' group of high crosses carved four hundred years before, and there are plenty of traditional interlace patterns. English and western French motifs are also found among the ingredients, combined in a most ambitious and imaginative way.

Less famous than Clonfert is the cathedral at Tuam, where, the annals tell us in a succinct and dramatic statement, the church 'fell roof and stone' in 1184. After this disaster, the building was reconstructed and given a splendid array of carved ornament, some of it still as fresh as the day it left the mason's workshop. The best work is found on the three windows behind the high altar, where two themes predominate, classical foliage scrolls and a series of beasts enmeshed in a tight web of interlace, some elements of which suggest that the sculptor had Viking patterns before him. It is important to remember the strong Scandinavian presence in Ireland, for Dublin, Wexford, Waterford, Cork and Limerick were still essentially Viking cities. The inhabitants were the most active merchants in the country, and their continued links with Scandinavia explain the Viking elements in Irish Romanesque art, most notably the Urnes style which is reflected in stone sculpture, metalwork and, to a lesser extent, manuscript painting.

Urnes motifs are first clearly apparent in the metalwork of around 1100. The long snakes, with their rounded bodies and regular figure of eight coils, are a major theme on the shrine of St Patrick's Bell, made between 1094 and 1105, probably at Armagh. Tradition relates that the bell was used by St Patrick, and whether true or not, it was obviously an object of the utmost sanctity. The Irish reverence for bells, croziers and other relics of saints was a feature of the country noted by Gerald of Wales after his visits of 1183 and 1185. There was nothing uncommon about an awe for holy relics, but the Celtic interest in bells and croziers seems to have been without parallel. Once again this reflects the monastic character of the early Irish Church. A huge number of the Celtic saints were revered as founders of monasteries and it was as abbots that they were remembered, with bell and crozier in hand.

As well as bells, a magnificent series of croziers is displayed in the National Museum and a fine example is one from Clonmacnoise, made probably in the early 12th century. The basic wooden staff is completely lost from view beneath a covering of bronze, inlaid with silver and other ornaments.

84   *The Long Middle Ages*

Around the top of the crook is a line of beasts, cast in bronze, each biting the one ahead. Much of the surface of the crook is covered by ribbon-like interlace, exploiting a colourful technique which was used on several other objects of the period. Into a groove cut in the bronze, a thin strip of silver was laid, and further grooves either side were filled with black niello, so that black was contrasted with silver and gilded bronze. Clonmacnoise appears to have been an important centre of metalwork in the early 12th century, and there is evidence that families of lay craftsmen were attached to several of the great Irish monasteries.

One of the most distinguished of Irish metal-workers was Maelisu MacBratdan U Echan, the creator of the Cross of Cong. The long inscription on the cross indicates that it was made between 1122 and 1136, very probably in Roscommon. Its main purpose was to celebrate a tiny piece of the Holy Cross itself, and this fragment was mounted in the centre, beneath a piece of translucent rock crystal. The major ornament consists of panels of animal interlace, cast in gilt bronze. Once again there are strong Urnes overtones in the theme of the great beast, with its spiral hip and pointed eye, completely enmeshed in a mass of regular curving tendrils. But other features of the cross are entirely traditional, notably the discs of red and yellow champlevé enamel, and the filigree. Although the bronze casting is technically superb, the Cross of Cong still cannot compete with works of the golden age in terms of delicacy and minute precision. The same workshop also made the shrine of St Manchan from Lemanagher in Offaly, but with this the great series of Irish metalwork comes to an end, a final crescendo to the Early Christian tradition. It is curious that the series peters out in the 1130s, just when Irish patrons were turning their attention to the carving of their churches.

Among the inscriptions of the Cross of Cong is one which reads 'pray for Turlough O'Connor, for the king of Erin, for whom this shrine was made'. It was thus a royal commission and it was indeed Turlough himself who had obtained the relic of the True Cross between 1119 and 1123. Turlough was one of the most formidable of Irish kings, ruler of Connacht from 1106 and High King from 1121 until his death in 1156. Like all Irish kings he was on the move much of the time, but he visited Tuam with frequency, and was a benefactor of the monastery there.

As a ruler and warrior Turlough O'Connor was both energetic and ruthless, particularly when dealing with potential rivals. The kingdoms of Munster and Meath were divided to reduce their power and even his own son was blinded to prevent him usurping the throne. The fleet that he operated along the river and lakes of the Shannon is famous and he evidently established several fortresses in his territories. When he died in 1156 the high kingship passed from Connacht to Muircheartach MacLochlain of Ailech, the king who presided at the consecration of Mellifont. It would be wrong to suppose that either O'Connor or MacLochlain had total authority over the whole of Ireland. Most High Kings are described as ruling 'with opposition', and their reigns were usually a continual campaign to preserve as much authority as possible over the numerous sub-kings of the country. In addition to major kingdoms like Munster, Leinster, Connacht, Meath, Ailech, Oriel and Ulster it is reckoned there were between one and two hundred petty kings, not to mention the independent Norse towns. The political history of Ireland is thus fearfully complex, a shifting pattern of wars and alliances. Although the annals give an impression of incessant violence and discord, the picture was not quite so anarchic, for warfare was usually local and campaigns brief. But in 1166 an entirely new complexion came over Irish politics when the King of Leinster, outmanoeuvred by his enemies, sought aid from foreign allies.

The coming of the Anglo-Normans
When Dermot MacMurrough eventually persuaded Norman knights to come to his aid, he could scarcely have foreseen the immense repercussions of his action. The first group landed at Bannow Bay in Co. Wexford in May 1169, followed just over a year later by the far larger expedition of Richard FitzGilbert de Clare, generally known as Strong-bow. The military success of these forces was stunning. Waterford quickly fell, and a few months later Dublin was in their hands. Although the invasion had the approval of Henry II, the King was not directly involved in the early stages. The initial conquest was achieved largely through the campaigns of independent Norman adventurers, and it was this very independence which encouraged Henry II to visit the country himself in 1171, fearing that his great vassal, Strongbow, might be tempted to set up a rival Norman kingdom. During his stay, the King formalized what had been achieved so far, granting Leinster to Strongbow, and Meath to Hugh de Lacy, while retaining Dublin and other parts of the coast in royal control. From this foothold in the south and east of the country, the Normans gradually penetrated farther inland. Most spectacular was John de Courcy's daring raid into Ulster in 1177 which led to the establishment of his own principality there. The Norman advance, however, was not systematic, and the settlement of the country was relatively slow when compared to the occupation of England after 1066. By 1250 it is

The Long Middle Ages   85

An Irish foot-soldier of the time of Edward I. This is an unfriendly drawing from an English source, but the meagre clothing and large axe are authentic. (3)

estimated that three-quarters of Ireland was in their control. The Irish retained parts of north-west Ulster and south-west Munster, and further pockets of resistance remained in highland areas.

It is not difficult to find reasons for the Norman success. Their well armed knights had a devastating impact on the Irish armies, who were quite unfamiliar with this mode of warfare. Gerald of Wales explained how the Irish went 'naked and unarmed into battle', and although not literally true, he was stressing the enormous disparity between the two sides. The Irish wore no armour, and even when mounted had neither saddles nor stirrups so that in the tumult of fighting they had limited control over their arms and horses. The main weapon of the Irish soldier was an enormous axe, and although this was wielded with dexterity, it was inevitably a cumbersome instrument. In contrast the Norman knights were well defended with iron helmets and coats of mail. They charged in a disciplined array, attacking with both lances and swords. The knights were supported by skilled bowmen, whose arrows were more accurate and incisive than the equivalent Irish weapon, a stone sling. The Irish might have curbed the Norman onslaught more effectively had they used their numerical advantage. The fragmentary state of Irish politics meant that the invaders were rarely faced with combined armies from different Irish kingdoms.

Just as Norman tactics on the battlefield were unfamiliar, so too were their methods of consolidating victory. Irish warfare was rarely about seizing land and far more frequently involved seizing cattle. What the Irish kings faced after 1169 was something quite different from the traditional cattle raid, for the Normans had come to stay, and they secured their

gains with the construction of castles. The need for haste precluded the use of stone at first, and the invaders resorted to the expedient which had served them so well in England after 1066, the motte castle. These huge earthen mounds, defended by a ditch at the bottom and a wooden tower and palisade at the top, could be erected with great speed and provided an excellent refuge in face of attack. Vast numbers of such mottes punctuate the Irish countryside and they are a good indication of the extent of Norman settlement. Few are found west of the Shannon or west of the Bann, where colonization was much thinner than in the south and east. One of the most prolific motte builders was Hugh de Lacy. As part of his organization of Meath, he systematically erected them throughout his territory. It was he who built the first castle at Trim soon after 1172, and it was while directing similar operations at Durrow in 1186 that he was cut down by an Irishman, using that favoured Irish weapon, an axe.

With victory secure, the conquered lands were divided into fiefs, each subdivided among tenants, following the feudal pattern of Western Europe. The warriors were followed by a tide of immigrants from England, both tradesmen and farmers. One of the chief forces behind the invasion was a rising population in England and Wales and a resulting hunger for land. The conquest of Ireland thus led to a vast increase in the area brought under cultivation, and many scrubs and woodlands made way for ploughed fields. The wooded nature of Ireland is stressed by Gerald of Wales who explained that 'even to this day [c. 1185] the plains here are few in proportion to the woods'. In fact wood became a major export commodity. Irish timber was used for building the galleys of English kings and on one occasion the cathedral of Canterbury sent to Ireland for oak.

Anglo-Norman Ireland

We are fortunate to possess in the writings of Gerald of Wales a first-hand account of the impression that Ireland made on the early settlers. His attitude towards the natives is one of disdain, and there is no reason to suppose that his views were untypical. The Irish, he repeatedly asserts, were barbarous; they were wild and inhospitable, 'a filthy people wallowing in vice'. The abuse represents the reaction to a different civilization, for which the Anglo-Normans had little sympathy. What was different was necessarily inferior. The pastoral way of life, the tending of the herds, did not require the same physical toil involved in arable farming, and therefore the Irish were thought to be indolent. In architecture the contrasts were equally striking. The more mobile life-style of the Irish did not encourage the building of dwellings which would endure, so that apart from the celebrated palace of Dermot MacMurrough at Ferns, Irish kings rarely built houses or castles of stone. Wood and wattle were the normal materials, both in the countryside and in the Norse cities. During the recent excavations of Dublin, numerous such houses have been uncovered in the old Viking city, large sections well preserved in the damp soil. When Henry II spent Christmas at Dublin in 1171 he was tactful enough to accept the local tradition when building a palace for himself. This, we are told, was 'a wonderful structure of wattle-work' erected at Henry's request in the native style by the Irish kings and chieftains who had submitted to him.

Despite his general attitude of contempt, Gerald of Wales was prepared to acknowledge some Irish virtues. The clergy were in many points praiseworthy, though he felt they did not preach enough. He was fascinated by Irish illumination, giving an admirable description of the *Book of Kildare*, a manuscript which seems to have had much in common with the *Book of Kells*. Another Irish art he applauded was music, writing in his usual lofty manner: 'it is only in the case of musical instruments that I find any commendable diligence in this people. They seem to me to be incomparably more skilled in these than any other people that I have seen.' Irish society accorded high status to musicians, and one of the greatest must have been Aed, son of Donnsleibhe O Sochlachain, of Cong, who died in 1226. He was given a lengthy entry in the annals as 'a professor of singing and harp-making – who made, besides, an instrument for himself, the like of which had never been made before'. One other characteristic of Ireland noted by Gerald still makes its impact, the 'unceasing rain' and the ever-present overhanging of clouds and fog.

The Norman settlement of Ireland led to rapid economic expansion, and, as is so often the case, this was accompanied by a vast increase in the scale and quantity of building, both secular and ecclesiastical. After a few decades, many of the major castles were reconstructed as more durable fortresses in stone. An outstanding example was Trim, head of the lordship of Meath. The original motte castle here was destroyed by the Irish as early as 1173, but by 1220 an impressive stone castle stood in its place. At the centre lies a massive keep, in general arrangement similar to the numerous 12th-century Norman keeps of England. Trim, however, is unusual since it has rectangular chambers projecting from each face of the square core. The bailey extended over three acres, exceptionally large for an Irish castle. Numerous utility buildings were constructed within it to serve the needs of the lordship, and the whole was encircled by an outer wall with projecting mural towers. Much of this, as well as the two gateways, is

preserved, and provides an imposing testimony to Norman military strength in the first half of the 13th century.

While Trim provides an example of a castle which served as the headquarters of a great vassal of the Crown, Dublin Castle was the seat of the royal government itself. The king was represented in Ireland by the Justiciar and by the early years of the 13th century the administration was developing on the pattern of that in England, with a separate Council and Court of Exchequer. It was this government, based in Dublin, which gave Ireland a degree of political unity which it had never seen before. Some sort of castle existed as early as 1172, but in 1204 King John, aware that there was no suitable place in which to deposit the royal treasure, ordered the Justiciar 'to cause a castle to be constructed in Dublin for the uses of justice in the city, and if need be for the city's defence, with good dikes and strong walls'. The castle was totally remodelled in the 18th century, but the medieval plan consisted of a roughly rectangular outer wall flanked by cylindrical towers, with the administrative buildings arranged inside the bailey. There are numerous medieval references to repairs and additions to the castle, none more splendid than the great hall ordered by Henry III in 1243. The King, anticipating a visit to Ireland, which never materialized, sent exact specifications, including provision for a painting of himself and his Queen seated with their barons. With its fine proportions and polished marble columns, the hall was a sophisticated example of English secular Gothic, not unlike the surviving great hall of Winchester Castle. There was no question of Henry III, with his refined artistic taste, making any concession to Irish custom as his grandfather Henry II had done seventy-two years before.

During the course of the 13th century the keep and bailey castle, of which Trim is such a good example, was gradually replaced by a design in which defence was concentrated on the outer walls, allowing more freedom of planning within the bailey. The keep had always played an ambiguous role, serving as both ultimate defence and residential dwelling. In several castles the defensive characteristics of the keep were reduced to the extent that the building effectively became a great hall. The castle at Athenry, erected by Meiler de Bermingham soon after 1235, is a good example of this. The bailey is dominated by a building which at first sight appears to be a keep, but is in fact a residence with a fine first-storey hall.

In the castles of the second half of the century, this approach is increasingly apparent. Roscommon was erected in its present form between 1280 and 1285 by the Justiciar, as part of an effort to hold

Athenry Castle, from an 18th-century engraving. The tower in the middle is not a keep but the hall of the castle, raised on a vaulted basement. The main security against attack was provided by the outer walls. (4)

Connacht against the depredations of the O'Connors. It is derived from the concentric plans of the Edwardian castles in Wales, with a regular bailey, defended by semi-circular towers at the angles, and a twin-towered gatehouse. As English power waned during the 14th century, the authority of the Dublin government faded from Connacht and by 1340 Roscommon, which in 1285 must have seemed well-nigh impregnable, had fallen into the control of the O'Connors. Similar castles were built in the years around 1300 by Richard de Burgh, Earl of Ulster. Two of his fortresses, at Greencastle in Donegal, and Ballintubber in Roscommon, included towers of polygonal form, a fashion almost certainly derived from Edward I's splendid castle at Caernarvon in North Wales.

One result of the presence of a royal government in Dublin is the survival of documentary records relating to the administration of Ireland. Sadly these are not as complete as they were before 1922, when the Public Record Office in Dublin was destroyed. Apart from their importance for political history, these records occasionally preserve glimpses of life within the walls of an Anglo-Norman castle, giving details about the organization of building as well. About 1224, inventories were made of the equipment in the royal castles of Dublin and Athlone. These include items of furniture, as well as tools and weapons, though neither castle gives the impression of being well stocked. Athlone, which guarded the crucial crossing of the Shannon, possessed 'four coats of mail, two with and two without head pieces; nine iron hats; one helmet; two mangonels with 120 strings and slings; one cable; one crossbow with a wheel; 2,000 bolts' – not a particularly devastating array of arms! At Dublin three of the

main rooms had great chests for storage, but other items of furniture were minimal: six boards with trestles, and a footstool in the kitchen! It is hard to believe the inventory is complete, and some of the furnishings may have been regarded as fixtures and not included. The kitchen scarcely seems overstocked either. Listed are 'one cauldron; two platters; one tripod; one axe to cut wood with; 100 dishes'. The butlery contained five cups, five pitchers, and one new rope for the well. Other items of equipment in the castle were a great chain to guard the prisoners, and another for a drawbridge. There was also a workshop, with three great hammers, two pairs of pincers and an anvil. However incomplete, the inventories illustrate the needs of a great castle: military equipment, cooking facilities, workshops, prisons, etc.

One of the most valuable but rarely recognized achievements of the Normans was bridge building. The bridges constructed by the Irish before 1170 seem to have been fragile structures, normally of wood. Turlough O'Connor, for example, erected several bridges across the Shannon at Athlone, one of which was destroyed by lightning in 1131. A century later, the Normans tried to make this vital bridgehead more secure by using stone instead of timber. In 1233 the King asked that work on the castle at Rindown be suspended so that activity could be concentrated on the bridge. It was stated that it could be completed for eighty marks, fifty for the actual labour and thirty for the carriage of materials to the site. This relatively high cost for transport is typical of medieval building projects. Unfortunately the medieval bridge at Athlone has long since disappeared, but an even longer bridge across the Shannon at Limerick survived until 1840, and several depictions of it exist. It was constructed probably in the 14th century as a stone replacement for a timber predecessor and like many medieval bridges it was guarded by a gate tower at one end. The bridge itself had fourteen small arches with the usual pointed cutwaters facing upstream. The advantages of a reliable bridge hardly need to be stressed. Overland travel for merchants with their wares became considerably less arduous, and secure river crossings were of strategic military importance, which is why Henry III was so concerned about the bridge at Athlone.

Churches on a new scale

Far more noticeable than new bridges were the dramatic changes which occurred in church building after 1170. In areas controlled by the Normans, efforts were made to secure the appointment of Norman bishops, and by 1254 almost a third of the Irish dioceses were occupied by foreigners. The Normans displayed a predictable contempt for existing Irish architecture and many of the new prelates immediately began to reconstruct their cathedrals on a grander scale, aiming at the sort of magnificence to which they had been accustomed in England. New buildings appeared at Waterford, Ferns, Kildare, Dublin and Newtown Trim, to name the outstanding examples. Rebuilding was not, however, restricted to the Normans, and many Irish bishops sought to emulate the Norman architectural zeal. Most of the cathedrals, however, whether built at the behest of Norman or of Irish bishops, were small compared to those in England, and this is a frank reflection of the greater poverty of the Irish dioceses. The churches which come closest to their English models are the two cathedrals in Dublin.

The first Anglo-Norman Archbishop of Dublin was John Comyn, who was appointed in 1181. Comyn was an official at the court of Henry II and his appointment was overtly political, designed to secure royal control of the see. He probably took the initiative in rebuilding Christ Church Cathedral, for the style of work implies a start about 1186–90. Construction began in a Late Romanesque style derived from the west of England, though the design was clumsy and uninspired. Under Comyn's successors, work continued on the nave which, by contrast, is a masterpiece. It is built in the Early English style and the design relates so closely to contemporary work in England that there is no doubt that the master mason was himself English. Analysis of the sculpture suggests that he came from Worcestershire. In several respects the nave of Christ Church is typical of early Gothic in the west of England. The low massive piers recall those at Wells, and the complex mouldings of the soffits of the arches are characteristic of English architecture. The most significant aspect of the design is the way the triforium and clerestory are united, with black marble shafts linking the two stages. This stresses the verticality of the design, and it was one of the most sophisticated English schemes of the period. The proportions of the building are equally felicitous. The main string course is placed exactly half-way, and the vault was originally forty-eight and a half feet high, exactly three times the width of each bay. When complete about 1235, with the black marble shafts silhouetted against the golden-yellow stone from Dundry, the nave must have been handsome in effect, a marked contrast to its present atmosphere of gloom and grime.

Only a few hundred yards from Christ Church is the other medieval cathedral, St Patrick's. Two cathedrals in the same city is a bizarre situation, and calls for some explanation. When John Comyn became archbishop, he did not find the monastic character of Christ Church particularly appealing. With his worldly interests and responsibilities he had little time or desire for the monastic routine. Moreover, one suspects he inherited too many Irish monks for his liking. A further problem was Christ Church's position within the city, which restricted the jurisdiction of the archbishop. For these reasons in 1191 Comyn established a college of secular canons at St Patrick's outside the walls of Dublin, constructing a palace for himself nearby. The prebendaries of St Patrick's were solidly Anglo-Norman, and with greater freedom to act as he wished, Comyn must have found the atmosphere far more conducive to his taste. It is significant that prebends at St Patrick's were frequently held by officials in the royal government. It was not Comyn, however, who officially raised St Patrick's to cathedral status. This occurred about 1220 under Archbishop Henry de Loundres. For the next eighty years relations between the two cathedrals were, not surprisingly, tense, particularly when it came to electing the archbishops, a source of friction which was eventually resolved by an agreement in 1300.

Rivalry between the two cathedrals evidently extended to their building projects. The splendid nave of Christ Church was under construction at exactly the same time as the choir of St Patrick's. Both looked to England for their masons, and there are a few general similarities in style. Yet one gets the impression that the designs were deliberately intended to be different. Whereas Christ Church introduced its novel scheme of integration at triforium and clerestory level, St Patrick's kept the two stages firmly separate, following the normal pattern of English churches. A different team of masons was employed to carve the foliage capitals and there is little sign of any interchange among the work force.

The two Dublin cathedrals, with their rib vaults and elaborate elevations, were too grand to have much influence elsewhere in Ireland. Wooden roofs usually sufficed, and Irish Gothic was more a question of pointed arches and elaborate mouldings than a complex structural programme. Cathedrals, however, represent a mere fragment of the total amount of ecclesiastical building after 1170. The Anglo-Norman settlement led to the foundation of scores of new abbeys, embracing several different monastic orders. In Ulster, for example, John de Courcy established a Cistercian abbey at Inch in 1180, and his wife founded another at Grey in 1193; Benedictine monks were introduced at the cathedral of Downpatrick and more Benedictines were established at the priory of St Andrew in Ards. John de Courcy's other foundations included the Augustinian priory of Toberglorie on the outskirts of Downpatrick. Unlike previous Cistercian abbeys in Ireland, Inch and Grey were both founded from mother houses in England and this is apparent in their architecture. The early Gothic style employed, with its tall lancet windows, corresponds closely to English fashion at the close of the 12th century, and it is quite different from the style of earlier Cistercian abbeys in Ireland. In fact those houses founded by the Anglo-Normans after 1170 form a quite separate group from the Irish abbeys, a divide which went considerably deeper than architectural appearance.

By the mid-1220s the Cistercian order in Ireland was in a state of complete disarray, with some abbeys in open rebellion against the General Chapter. The causes of the conflict, known usually as the 'conspiracy of Mellifont', are complicated, but tension between Irish and Norman monks played a major part. Visitors sent by the General Chapter were inevitably French-speaking like the Normans. Consequently they were viewed with suspicion by the Irish houses, who naturally identified them with the Norman settlers. Stephen of Lexington, who conducted the visitation of 1228, was on several occasions in danger of losing his life, and some monasteries took desperate measures to oppose him. When he reached the monastery of Monasteranenagh he found that the monks had turned their buildings into a fortified castle, erecting a tower above the altar, and at Inislounaght he was confronted by an armed horde. Despite the force of the opposition, Stephen's mission achieved some success, and by the mid-1230s the worst of the trouble had subsided. The conflict between the two nations, however, continued to have serious implications for the Church in Ireland, and at the end of the 13th century, the Franciscan order was torn apart in an equally violent dispute.

In the early 14th century some of the finest Irish building was carried out by the friars. At this time the early simplicity of the friaries was giving way to more elaborate buildings, and at Athenry one can trace the process very clearly, since the Register of the friary is preserved. Around 1320 the choir was lengthened by twenty feet, and in the second quarter of the century a north transept or Lady Chapel was erected. This had a magnificent tracery window, employing curved triangular patterns, which suggest it was well up to date with English fashion. During the 1340s a belfry tower was under construction, a feature typical of the Irish friaries in the later Middle Ages. They are normally placed between the choir and the nave, and provide a striking accent to the cluster of buildings below. One of the finest friaries to survive is the Dominican house at Kilmallock. The church was begun soon after 1291 and planned with the normal aisleless choir. This is lit by a fine east window of five graduated lancets, the lateral windows containing simple switch line tracery. During the first half of the 14th century a large transept was added, as at

Athenry, and the south façade is filled with one of the earliest reticulated windows in Ireland. The advanced tracery patterns used in the Irish friaries between 1300 and 1350 imply that they were keeping in close touch with English styles of building.

Unlike the Cistercians, both orders of friars ministered to the religious and social needs of the local people, the Dominicans laying particular stress on the preaching of the Gospel. Consequently friaries were not normally erected in isolated rural sites, but as close to the lay-folk as possible, in cities and towns. This fact meant that friary architecture was to become a victim of industrial expansion in the 18th and 19th centuries. In England few buildings have survived, but in Ireland the situation was different. Since Gaelic society remained essentially rural, many later friaries were situated in the open countryside far from the nearest city, and consequently are well preserved. Many of those which were built in the Anglo-Norman towns have also survived so that Ireland possesses a collection of medieval friaries unique in Europe.

Far from expanding, many of the medieval towns of Ireland have scarcely retained their original size; and this is true of both Kilmallock and Athenry. In 1786 Mervyn Archdall described Kilmallock as 'formerly a town of great note, being walled, and the houses beautifully and elegantly built of hewn stone; it is now in ruins, yet has a greater share of magnificence even in that miserable state than any town in Ireland'. Kilmallock, like many Irish towns, was founded by the Normans. So too was Athenry, which grew up around the castle of Meiler de Bermingham soon after 1235. By 1241 the local population was sufficient to warrant the foundation of the Dominican priory. The town was later enclosed by a stone wall, and five of its flanking towers survive. This pattern of settlement was typical of scores of Irish towns between 1170 and 1300. One of the most successful was the 'Nova Villa Pontis' or New Ross, founded by William Marshal about 1200. Its position near the confluence of the River Barrow and River Nore made it an excellent port and for a time around 1280 it was the most prosperous town in Ireland. The ruins of the large parish church still evoke some of this mercantile prosperity and there were several other churches in the town, including a Franciscan friary.

English decline, Gaelic resurgence

The English colony reached its peak about 1250–75, to be followed in the 14th century by a period of decline. Its weaknesses were crudely exposed during the invasion of Ireland by Edward Bruce between 1315 and 1318. Although Bruce was eventually killed at the Battle of Faughart the effects of his invasion were disastrous. His troops wasted large areas of cultivated land, and this damage was exacerbated by a series of poor harvests. Many manors were abandoned, never to recover. Equally serious was the failure of the Dublin government to cope with the invasion at a military level. Resources were insufficient to maintain a large army in the field, and the Norman lords failed to unite with the government in thwarting the invasion. Indeed Bruce's attack revealed both an alarming degree of disloyalty among the settlers and the considerable power of the Gaelic chieftains.

Modern historians have stressed that the decline began long before the wars of 1315–18. During the later years of the 13th century, the resources of Ireland were drained away to support the English kings in their Welsh and Scottish campaigns. It has been estimated that £30,000 out of the £80,000 needed to build Edward I's Welsh castles came from Ireland, and during the wars themselves, Ireland supplied vast quantities of food to succour the royal army. If the resources of Ireland had been used to consolidate the English lordship, the Bruce invasion would not have presented so serious a threat. Equally important was the instability of the Dublin government itself, for which it was notoriously difficult to find honest and reliable officials. Finally it is clear that the whole impetus of colonization slowed down after about 1250. Outside Leinster, east Ulster and east Munster, the Norman population had remained sparse. Frank Mitchell has recently pointed out that these areas contain the best soil in Ireland and, once they were heavily colonized, Ireland became far less attractive for prospective immigrants. Thus Connacht, with its wide areas of mountain, bog and rocky terrain, was not settled with the same density as those lands occupied after the initial invasion. Geology and landscape helped to mould the course of Irish history, for it was precisely the less fertile areas, with few Anglo-Norman inhabitants, that provided the basis of the Gaelic resurgence.

These problems increased during the 14th century when many barons who inherited territory in Ireland were reluctant to reside there permanently. In 1380 the Statute of Absentees, one of several such measures, spoke of nobility who allowed their fortresses to decay and left their land 'without guard, rule and government', as a result of which the Irish enemies 'are increased and increasing and prevailing from day to day'. Indeed, far from further colonization, emigration took place. Before his expedition to Ireland in 1395, Richard II ordered the Irish living in England to return home, and this included not only nobility, but also huge numbers of craftsmen, artisans and labourers.

The weaknesses of the royal government in Ireland represent only one side of the question, for royal authority declined as Gaelic power increased. In 1261 the Normans had been expelled from southwest Munster, and in Connacht they suffered a serious defeat in 1270 at the Battle of Athenkip. The strenuous efforts required in this area to resist the O'Connors, with the construction of massive castles like that at Roscommon, is an indication of the vitality of the Irish kings. In 1318 the De Clare family, who had built the castle at Quin as part of their occupation of south Thomond, were routed at the Battle of Dysert O'Dea and expelled from the district. During the century, the political situation grew steadily worse for the Anglo-Normans, and by 1450 the area over which the Dublin government exercised direct authority had been reduced to the Pale, an area stretching about thirty miles north from Dublin, and about twenty miles inland.

The success of the Gaelic resurgence is often attributed to an improved fighting ability, in particular the power of the gallowglasses. Originating from the western isles of Scotland, these mercenary warriors gave the Irish armies a new strength and discipline. They were present in Ireland by 1258 and played a part in the Irish victory at Athenkip in 1270. Appropriate recognition of their value is found on tombs at Roscommon and Dungiven, where 15th-century sculptors have presented them as mourners or 'weeper' figures on the tomb chests. Each is well protected with a coat of mail, and pointed steel helmet, known as a bascinet. They carry swords or axes, though it was the axe which seems to have been their normal fighting weapon. It would, however, be wrong to overstress the role of the gallowglasses, for they were just one of several factors which contributed to the decline of the English colony.

The surviving records contain numerous appeals which were sent to the Crown, desperately asking for aid in the worsening situation. During the second half of the 14th century the English kings did make strenuous efforts to help, but there was little permanent improvement.

The climax to this more vigorous royal policy came in the reign of Richard II, when the King himself made two expeditions to Ireland, with the aim of recovering the lost parts of the lordship. His first expedition in 1394–95 appeared to be a splendid success, after the defeat of Art MacMurrough, King of Leinster, and the submission of most of the Irish chieftains. Again the success was ephemeral. Richard was forced to return to Ireland in 1399 and this time he failed to repress MacMurrough. With the news of Henry Bolingbroke's rebellion, the King made a hasty departure, and so ended the last serious attempt to stem the Gaelic revival.

On the second expedition of 1399, Richard II's

The Long Middle Ages 91

entourage included a French clerk, Jean Creton, who wrote a detailed account of what occurred. One of the manuscripts of Creton's text was lavishly illustrated by a Parisian painter between 1401 and 1405. This manuscript, now in the British Museum, was subsequently owned by the greatest bibliophile of the Middle Ages, Jean, duc de Berry, and, although not the most spectacular of his books, it is fascinating from an Irish point of view. Several miniatures are devoted to events in Ireland. The French painter was not familiar with Irish affairs, but he followed Creton's text with accuracy. For example one scene depicts a parley which took place between Art MacMurrough and Thomas, Earl of Gloucester. In the text, Creton explained:

> Between two woods, at some distance from the sea, I beheld Macmore [sic] and a body of the Irish, more than I can number, descend the mountain. He had a horse without housing or saddle, which was so fine and good that it had cost him, they said, four hundred cows; for there is little money in the country, wherefore their usual traffic is only cattle. In coming down it galloped so hard that, in my opinion, I never in all my life saw hare, deer, sheep or any other animal, I declare to you for a certainty, run with such speed as it did. In his hand he bore a great long dart, which he cast with much skill.

The spirit of Creton's words is admirably portrayed by the artist, who gives Art MacMurrough's charge down the mountain a terrific momentum. But he scarcely did justice to the King's famous horse, which looks exceedingly puny compared to the Earl of Gloucester's massive steed.

There are various reasons to explain the failure of royal policy in the second half of the 14th century. Although the armies which came to Ireland won some striking victories, what was required was a permanent military presence on a massive scale. Thus Richard II's victories in 1394–95 counted for little once he had left the country. Further colonization was also needed and Richard II fully appreciated this. After his successful reconquest of Leinster in 1395, he hoped to attract new settlers from England in order to consolidate control of the province, but the policy proved too optimistic. The need for new settlers was essential in view of the assimilation which had taken place between the original colonists and the native Irish. Intermarriage had led to the increasing use of the Irish language and the adoption of many Irish customs. An outstanding example of this was the third Earl of Desmond. Although he served on the King's Council and held royal office, his skill in the Irish language was such that he was described after his death in 1398 as 'a witty and ingenious composer of Irish poetry'. Many attempts were made to separate the two races from 1297 onwards, reaching a climax with the Statutes of Kilkenny in 1366, which aimed to prevent any further spread of Gaelic customs among the English. Marriage with the Irish was forbidden, and so too were Irish fashions in riding and dress. Only English was to be spoken by the settlers and they were to receive no Irish minstrels or entertainers. The Church was not excluded from the Statutes either, and no monastery or cathedral in the English areas was allowed to accept an Irishman into its community. One famous clause forbade 'the games which men call hurlings with great clubs at ball upon the ground, from which great evils and mains have arisen to the weakening and defence of the said land'. Most of the Statutes were impossible to enforce and consequently very limited in their effect.

Plague, violence and war

The decline of the English colony in the 14th century was accompanied by severe economic recession. The ravages of Edward Bruce made the livelihood of both merchant and farmer insecure. In 1334, for example, the priory of Selskar, Wexford, reported that all its lands and rents were destroyed by the war of MacMurrough and other Irish, and as a result the monks were about to abandon the priory and dwell in the countryside with their friends. Dozens of similar reports recur throughout the 14th century. With trade and agriculture already depressed came the Black Death in 1348. Inevitably the plague was most severe where the population was most dense, and this meant the Anglo-Norman towns. It is estimated that between a third and a half of the population died. Fourteen thousand are said to have died in Dublin within the first five months. In the country many manors lost their tenants, productivity declined and the settlers were spread even more thinly. A typical report was given by the dean and chapter of Cashel in 1351, when they claimed that their lands and rents had been 'all but totally destroyed by the King's Irish enemies and by the mortality of their tenants in the last plague'. The effects of the plague are strikingly evident in architecture, for the period 1350–1400 is the leanest in the Middle Ages. Many a skilled mason must have died, and the subsequent dearth of resources precluded any thoughts of ambitious building projects.

The political state of Ireland remained unsettled throughout the 15th century. The King's writ was directly effective only within the Pale, and royal authority beyond its boundaries depended on the loyalty of the three great Anglo-Irish lordships, those of Ormonde, Desmond and Kildare. The complexity of the situation is fully apparent in the

An illustration from Jean Creton's account of Richard II's Irish expedition of 1399. The text to which it refers is quoted opposite (p. 92). The contrast between English and Irish modes of warfare is fully evident, with Irish horsemen still disdaining the use of saddles and spurs. Although MacMurrough, charging downhill in the centre, appears to wear a coat of mail, he is thinly protected compared with his English opponents, clad in their impressive heavy armour. (5)

famous report of 1515 submitted to Henry VIII which spoke of 'more than 60 countryes, called regyons, in Ireland, inhabytyd with the Kinges Irishe enymyes' and 'more than 30 greate captaines of the Englyshe noble folke, that folowyth the same Irishe ordre'. Throughout the later Middle Ages there were in fact three nations in Ireland, the English, the Irish and the Middle Nation. The report stresses the independence of the various lords, who made war and peace for themselves, deriving their authority ultimately from the power of the sword. In the later 15th century the most influential figure in Ireland was the Earl of Kildare. Gerald Mor FitzGerald, 8th Earl from 1477 until his death in 1513, exercised immense power, owning vast estates and for long periods controlling the government in Dublin. Through his personal and family links, he was connected to many of the great Gaelic and Anglo-Irish lords and stood at the head of a network of loyalties stretching across the country. With Ireland fragmented into numerous semi-independent lordships, the politics of the period were inevitably confused. Local wars and feuds were frequent, though these tended to follow the pattern of the old-style cattle raids, rather than major pitched battles.

The dangerous and troubled state of the country produced one of the most distinctive features of the Irish landscape, the tower house. Many hundreds survive and it seems they were first built extensively in the Pale. For much of the 15th century, the government encouraged the nobility to build towers and castles and the most famous inducement was the £10 subsidy first offered in 1429 to gentry in Co. Louth. The Irish Parliament agreed that, since so much of the county was 'destroyed and wasted' by the Irish enemies and the English

rebels, £10 should be given to anyone building a tower within the next five years 'in length 20 feet, in breadth 16 feet, in height 40 feet'. The following year the offer was extended to the other three counties of the Pale, Kildare, Dublin and Meath. In 1431 Parliament took further measures to encourage the fortifications of Louth. Labourers were required to 'labour with their spades and shovels' for eight days in each of the next three years at certain specific sites. 'Freeholders and husbandmen having carts' were ordered to 'carry stones and sand' to these places and there were to be fines for disobedience. The statutes of the Irish Parliament repeatedly referred to castle-building in the Pale, and many specific castles are mentioned.

Numerous tower houses have survived within the Pale in various stages of ruin, but one of the best preserved is found at Roodstown in Co. Louth. It has lost its outer defences and subsidiary buildings, so the tower alone now stands starkly in the middle of a field. A pointed doorway leads into a vaulted basement, following the pattern of many such towers. A spiral staircase ascends to a fine first-floor chamber, which was well lit with large transomed windows. These have twin lights, each with a trefoiled ogee head, a hallmark of 15th-century work in Ireland. Above were two more floors, and at roof level there was a well-defended parapet and wall walk. Two turrets project from the tower, one containing the staircase, the other a garderobe. With various modifications, this type of tower was constructed in many parts of the country between 1400 and 1650.

Outside the Pale, tower houses are particularly common in the south-west, with over four hundred in Co. Limerick and 325 in Co. Cork. Here they clearly became the standard residence of any self-

Tower houses in the town of Carrickfergus, from a drawing of 1612 made in London by an artist who probably relied on descriptions (for a more accurate drawing of the town see p. 102). Hundreds of similar houses survive, though mostly in ruins. The door led into a basement, from which the living quarters were reached by a spiral staircase. Such an arrangement guaranteed a measure of safety if not of comfort. (6)

respecting Irish chieftain. With numbers so vast it is hard to generalize about their characteristics. Normally they are rectangular, though a few are round, like the attractive tower at Newtown in Co. Clare. One room per floor usually suffices, but some castles have a subsidiary chamber, as at Clara in Co. Kilkenny. This latter tower has a secret chamber, reached from above through a false garderobe seat, a grim reminder of the personal perils faced by the occupants of many such castles. The lower rooms tend to be dark, lit only by narrow arrow slits, but on the upper floors well off the ground it was safe to insert larger windows. Although there are many minor variations in the castles, it is surprising how similar they are in scale. With occasional exceptions, as at Bunratty, Blarney and Dunsoghly, the main chambers remained small, with few pretensions to grandeur. Staircases were steep and narrow, as any modern visitor knows to his cost, and it is hard to imagine how the ladies in their long dresses ascended with dignity. The elderly and infirm must have had enormous difficulties and no doubt there were many accidents like that which befell Turlough, prior of Lough Derg and rector of Derrymullan, who was killed in 1504 when he fell down a stair at Athboy. The lack of comfort in the Irish castles was noted by one foreign traveller in 1644 when he commented, 'to tell the truth, they are nothing but square towers or at least having such small apertures as to give no more light than there is in a prison. They have little furniture, and cover their room with rushes, of which they make their beds in summer, and straw in winter.'

The tower house was not designed to resist a long siege, but rather to give protection against sudden attack, and particularly against the cattle raid. For this reason the tower was normally surrounded by a bawn, into which the cattle could be driven for safety. It is rare for the bawn walls and their flanking towers to survive, but good examples remain at Derryhiveny and Fiddaun, in Galway, and Knockelly, in Tipperary. There are several early illustrations of complete towers and bawns, none more spectacular than the scene in *Pacata Hibernica* (1633) showing the siege of Glin Castle in Co. Limerick. Gunfire is being directed from all sides, with considerable accuracy to judge from the number of victims falling from the tower. A few of the larger castles could boast impressive halls of stone and the Earl of Desmond built a handsome example at Askeaton.

The feuds and violence of the 15th century forced many churches and monasteries to take defensive measures. Massive residential towers were often built for priests, and at Taghmon in Westmeath the whole church is fortified with a powerful western tower overshadowing the whole building. More remarkable are the two monasteries of Fore in Westmeath and Kells in Kilkenny. Fore was a Benedictine priory situated in dangerous marchlands just outside the Pale. In 1423 and 1428 its lands were raided by the 'Irish enemies', the O'Farrells and the O'Reillys. Two granges were burnt in the first raid, and in the second the cattle of the priory's tenants were stolen and the adjoining town attacked and burnt. As a result the prior began to build castles on the monastic lands, and robust towers were constructed at each end of the church. Kells Priory was an Augustinian house which experienced similar problems. At first sight it appears to be a huge medieval castle defended by an impressive array of curtain walls and flanking towers. The monastery itself is almost lost from view in an inner enclosure, and to the west of this is a vast outer bawn, guarded by five substantial towers. This great court was probably intended to defend not only the priory itself, but also the livestock of the priory, and its tenants. Whenever danger threatened or perhaps as a matter of routine every evening, the cattle would be herded into the enclosure.

Pilgrims and travellers

A fascinating description of Ireland in the later Middle Ages was given by a Spanish pilgrim to Lough Derg, the Count of Perilhos. He made his visit in 1397–98, and his text includes many observations on Irish life. Since Lough Derg is situated in Donegal, the count had to traverse the lands of O'Neill, King of Ulster. He was given repeated warnings by the English about the dangers of such a journey deep into Irish territory. The Archbishop of Armagh gave him a bodyguard as he set out from Dundalk, but the count explained: 'when I had ridden some five leagues, the said men dared not go further, since they were all great enemies; so that they remained on a hill, and I took leave and went forward'. In fact he was well treated by O'Neill and spent Christmas with him. He describes how the great lords were clothed in knee-length tunics, on top of which they wore 'great hooded cloaks'. The common people, however, 'go as they can, ill-clothed, but the principal of them wear cloaks of woollen plush; and they show all the shameful parts, the women as well as the men'. The Spanish visitor also made some interesting, though not wholly reliable, comments about food, which bring out the pastoral nature of Irish life: 'They sow no grain, and gather no wine, but their food is of beef, and the great lords drink milk, and they have excellent butter, since all their meats are of oxen and cows and good horses.' The Spaniard was evidently given a special treat when the King presented him with 'two little cakes as thin as wafers, and they bent like raw dough and they were of oats and earth, as black as coals, although they were tasty'. The King's court was far from refined, yet when eating he did have the medieval equivalent of a table napkin, for we are told, near him they put 'delicate grass to wipe his mouth'.

The purpose of the count's journey was a visit to one of the most celebrated places in Christendom, St Patrick's Purgatory in Lough Derg. Here was a cave said to lead into the depths of Hell. Those who spent a day inside experienced all manner of horrors, and, as one visitor explained, many 'come forth stupefied and raving'. Lough Derg attracted visitors from many parts of Europe, but the buildings on the island were of the utmost simplicity. Apart from a small stone church, there were two wooden houses for accommodation, plus three beehive cells dedicated to St Brigid, St Patrick and St Columba.

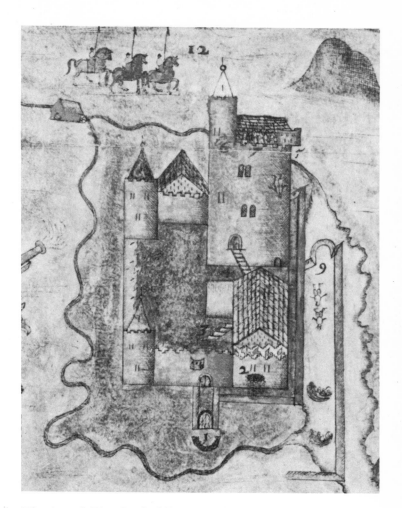

The siege of Glin Castle. The keep, which is virtually a tower house, is surrounded by an enclosed area for cattle called the bawn. In one corner stands a long low building which may have been a hall. (7)

Although this simplicity may seem surprising, no doubt it was thought inappropriate to glamorize the entrance to Hell. The cave was demolished in 1497 on the authority of Pope Alexander VI.

There were many other places of pilgrimage in Ireland. Crowds flocked to see the miraculous statue of Our Lady at Trim, the 'Idol of Trim' as it was later branded. It was housed in the Augustinian abbey, but all that is left of this famous building are the shattered remains of the great belfry tower. In the parish church at Trim is a hexagonal stone fragment with delightful sculpture of the Apostles, and it is just conceivable that this was connected to the shrine. The quality of carving is outstanding, with the details of faces, beards, clothes and attributes delicately portrayed. One of the finest collections of relics in Ireland was owned by Christ Church Cathedral, Dublin. These included the *Baculum Jesu*, a staff said to have been given by a hermit to St Patrick, the hermit having received it from Christ Himself.

More famous, however, was the shrine of the Holy Cross in the Cistercian abbey of that name. Until the 15th century Holy Cross was a relatively poor house, but for some reason its precious relic then began to attract enormous numbers of pilgrims. These visits were highly lucrative and there are many references to offerings presented 'by the faithful at the wood of the Holy Cross'. With the aid of these funds, major works of reconstruction were carried out during the century. Guest-houses were built for the pilgrims and the relic itself was given a sumptuous stone shrine in the south transept. This was designed in an ingenious way by opening out the wall which divides the two south transept chapels. Elegant arcades were constructed, resting on spiral fluted columns. The tiny structure was covered by an exquisite lierne vault, forming a miniature chapel. The outer walls below the arcade were adorned with a delicate frieze of arches and foliage. The craftsmanship in the shrine is the finest in Ireland at the time and the abbey obviously attracted top-quality masons to carry out the work.

The *peregrinatio* had been a frequent yearning of the early Irish monks, and the relish for foreign travel was not lost during the Middle Ages. Hundreds made the journey to Compostela to visit the shrine of St James, and a special hostel was founded in Dublin so that pilgrims could await fair winds for the sailing southwards. Irish tombs often portray St James in the guise of a pilgrim, with staff in hand and his famous emblem, the cockle shell. Among Irishmen who made the journey was James Rice, eight times mayor of Waterford between 1467 and 1488. English shrines were also visited, particularly that of St Thomas à Becket at Canterbury. Among the pilgrims there in 1449 was James, Earl of Ormond. But most prestige was attached to Rome and Jerusalem. One of Ireland's most inveterate pilgrims was Giolla-Chriost O'Fearadhaigh who in 1413 had already visited Rome and other shrines five times, and was then about to set out for Jerusalem. At a time when crossing the Irish Sea alone was often full of hazards, these were no mean feats of travel. Two other pilgrims to the Holy Land were Symon Semeonis and Hugh the illuminator, both Franciscan friars who set out from Clonmel in 1323. Hugh unfortunately died in Cairo before getting there, but Symon later wrote a fascinating account of his trip.

Despite familiarity with foreign monuments, Irish architects in the later Middle Ages were rarely directly influenced from abroad. The few links that did exist were with England and they are found chiefly in the Pale. One of the most knowledgeable masons available was employed by Sir Christopher Plunket between 1403 and 1445 to build a church beside his castle at Killeen. It is a long building without aisles, divided simply into nave and chancel. Impressive turrets flank the west façade, and a wooden rood loft crossed the east end of the nave in front of the chancel arch. Adjoining the

chancel is a residential tower for the priest, with a strongly fortified appearance. The most attractive aspect of the church is the fine detailing of the sedilia, doorways and windows. The tracery of the latter follows curvilinear patterns, but a few details are derived from English Perpendicular.

Outside the Pale, architects seem to have been only vaguely aware of contemporary English fashions and this is particularly true in the west. The contrast in styles is quite marked and reflects a deeper division within the organization of the Church. The Pale was divided into a network of parishes based on villages and manors as in England, though very few of these parish churches survive.

A return to the past

In contrast to this parochial organization, Christianity in Gaelic Ireland increasingly centred on the friaries. Between 1400 and 1508, ninety new friaries were founded, sixty-seven of them Franciscan. Since Irish society was rural many of these friaries are situated in isolated and remote places, far from the nearest modern town. In some respects this was almost a return to pre-12th-century times, with the monastery rather than the cathedral as the focus of Christian organization.

The Irish Church in the later Middle Ages became increasingly degenerate. There were many causes of abuse. The split between the two nations fractured Church organization. The archdiocese of Armagh, for example, was divided, and the archbishop, not daring to live in Armagh itself, usually resided in what for him was the safety of the Pale at Termonfeckin or Dromiskin. Discipline broke down, visitations could not be carried out. Appointments were frequently quite unsuitable and English holders of Irish benefices frequently failed to visit them. In 1432 four different men, all living in England, claimed to be bishop of Dromore. In the Gaelic areas the distinction between priests and laity became blurred. The clergy were reproved for looking like laymen, with long hair, moustaches and lay dress. They often married or lived openly with women. The worst result of this lack of celibacy was the inevitable presence of heirs. This led to the inheritance of clerical office, one of the serious abuses of the early Irish Church which had never been fully eradicated by the reform movement. Ecclesiastical property came to be regarded as a family possession, and this was especially so in the monasteries. In most Cistercian abbeys conventual life completely ceased and the income of the house was shared by the abbot and the few remaining monks. The architectural effects of this are still visible. Communal dormitories were abandoned and pleasant upper chambers fitted with fireplaces were often inserted above the transept chapels. This is apparent at Holy Cross, Kilcooly and Knockmoy, where the late style of the windows reveals the modifications. In 1498 there were only two monks at Kilcooly, and other houses had few more. In that year the abbot of Mellifont, in a despondent report, painted a dreadful picture of the Cistercian order in Ireland. Only at Mellifont and Dublin was the Cistercian habit still worn and the Cistercian rule of life observed.

Many cathedrals became ruinous, as essential repairs were neglected. An exception to this picture of decadence were the friars, whose vitality is reflected in their buildings, which form the major architectural achievement of 15th-century Ireland. Many friaries, like those at Quin, Rosserilly, Rosserk and Moyne, are exceptionally well preserved, lacking only their wooden roofs. Quin was founded in 1433 on the site of the earlier De Clare castle and the friars incorporated the ancient masonry in their building. The aisleless chancel is separated from the nave by an elegant tower, ninety feet high, and a large transept opens off to the south. A delightful cloister garth lies on the north side of the church, with the various domestic buildings grouped around. The barrel-vaulted cloister walk forms an integral part of the flanking buildings, unlike the arrangement in earlier monasteries, where the passageway projected into the central courtyard. Buttresses divide the cloister arcades into systematic bays, each with two arches resting on coupled shafts, the 'dumb bell' form so common in Ireland. Many shafts are given spiral flutings, and the bases and capitals have typical Irish mouldings of the period. The windows at Quin, however, are not very sophisticated. The tracery in the chancel has a switch line pattern, a type introduced to Ireland about 1300, and the west window is filled with two simple round-headed lancets.

The style of Quin provides an excellent illustration of the introspective nature of Irish 15th-century architecture. With little information about contemporary foreign building, masons looked to the past for their models. They revived the round arch, and used 14th-century tracery patterns, regardless of the context. Late Irish Gothic is thus a unique medley of previous forms, with a few doses of modern techniques. The magnificent tomb recess at Kilconnell, for example, is decorated with an elaborate geometrical pattern, which in England might date to about 1280–90. The mouldings immediately indicate that it is 15th-century work. On account of this deliberate revival, it is not always easy to date Irish architecture of the period. The reticulated windows at Kilmallock and Sligo friaries have erroneously been attributed to the 15th century, since they are so close to the east window at

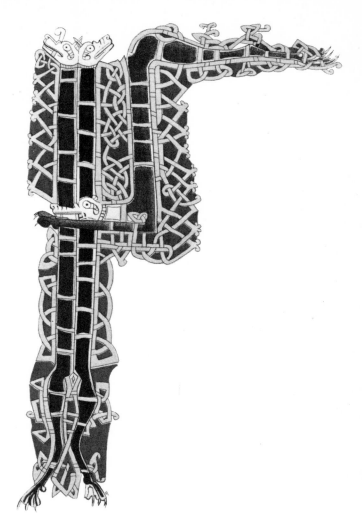

Illuminated initial from the Book of Ballymote, compiled in 1390 but looking back consciously to Celtic manuscripts of six hundred years earlier. The Book is a fine example of the Gaelic revival, for it includes a series of older texts, genealogies, histories, classical tales, law treatises, poems and even a tract on Ogham writing. (8)

Holy Cross. They are in fact fashionable designs of the first half of the 14th century, which the architect of Holy Cross chose to revive. Irish Gothic of the later Middle Ages is thus unpredictable and full of anachronisms. It defies the normal categories of style, producing unusual combinations, which are often refreshingly original.

The distinction between the Pale and the rest of Ireland was also noticeable in manuscript painting. Just as Gaelic masons looked to the past, so too did the artists. Many late medieval manuscripts are decorated with curious Celtic revival initials, usually grossly simplified. The *Book of Ballymote*, for example, compiled about 1390 at the residence of Tomaltach MacDonagh, Lord of Corann, has a whole series of coloured initials, with familiar Celtic animals. These beasts were relatively easy to copy from the early manuscripts but the complexities of interlace were way beyond the 15th-century painters, who were satisfied with the simplest of patterns.

The manuscripts owned by churches and monasteries in the Pale were very different in appearance. When Stephen de Darby, prior of Christ Church, Dublin, from 1349 to *c.* 1382, required a new psalter it was commissioned from one of the leading English workshops. The psalter, which is now in the Bodleian Library at Oxford, has a number of superb miniatures, painted by an artist who was familiar with Italian painting of the Trecento. In the initial to Psalm 97, *Cantate Domino*, the solid block-like forms of the singing monks, and the way they are overlapped to give a sense of depth, recall the techniques of Giotto, whose work the artist knew. These tentative steps towards naturalism are the direct antithesis of the abstract tastes soon to be revived by the Gaelic artists.

There was no equivalent revival of early styles in metalwork. Whereas a painter could copy previous designs without too much difficulty, after a gap of three hundred years the painstaking methods of the Early Christian goldsmith were completely forgotten. When medieval craftsmen repaired earlier objects, their work was usually clumsy, as on the Moylough belt-shrine. Most metal-workers followed general European fashions, using a debased Gothic figure style. Among the most proficient works are the crozier and mitre commissioned in 1418 for Conor O'Dea, Bishop of Limerick. The richly jewelled mitre carries the name of the artist, Thomas O'Carryd, who was presumably a local Limerick goldsmith. The crozier is the finest piece of late medieval metalwork in Ireland. Its basic material is gilded silver, and it is decorated with various floral and foliage designs. The base of the crook is furnished with six cast images of the Trinity, the Virgin Mary and four saints. Above are further saints, this time engraved against a coloured enamel background, and in the curve of the crook the scene of the Annunciation is portrayed. As John Hunt pointed out, the crook which signifies the bishop's pastoral office rises from a pinnacled tower filled with saints, who form the very foundation of the Christian Church and the bishop's authority. Although no other surviving works can compare with the Limerick crozier, many formerly existed.

More enduring than metalwork is the series of attractively carved tombs which survive from the later Middle Ages. They were produced by a number of different workshops, which developed a distinctively Irish style. The initial stimulus came from the Pale with monuments for such families as the Plunkets, but it was in the neighbourhood of Kilkenny and Cashel that the style was fully evolved. The hands of the various workshops have been carefully analysed by Dr Rae, and among the most prolific is that which he termed the 'Ormonde School'. This group of masons produced tombs for the Butler family, Earls of Ormonde, who were commemorated in the collegiate church at Gowran and in the cathedral of Kilkenny.

The sides of tombs like that of James Butler in Kilkenny Cathedral are lined with sculptures of the Apostles, each standing within a niche. The use of Apostles as 'weepers' was uncommon in 15th-century Europe, but they became a regular feature in Ireland. Those carved by the Ormonde artists are particularly engaging. They clutch identifying attributes and offer happy smiles. Their drapery is robustly carved in firm bold pleats, revealing a strong sense of pattern. One of the Ormonde masons may have journeyed north-west to Mayo to carve the magnificent tomb at Strade. Instead of the normal Apostles, the programme on this tomb surround includes the three Magi, plus the donor kneeling before an archbishop, and Saints Peter and Paul. The choice of figures is strange and they could represent places of pilgrimage visited by the deceased – Cologne (the Magi), Canterbury (Archbishop Thomas à Becket) and Rome (St Peter and St Paul). The tomb at Strade embodies many of the qualities of late medieval sculpture in Ireland. It may lack sophistication, but the carving is technically precise, the forms bold and rhythmic, the general effect full of charm.

No effigy survives at Strade and it is therefore fortunate that the patron was depicted on the side. He must have been a wealthy local lord, but exactly who remains unclear. Instead of military dress he wears a trim tunic and hood, and around his belt hangs a peculiar object, which has defied identification. The figure provides a convincing image of a prosperous Irish baron, wearing normal daily clothes and not weighed down by cumbersome armour. The great lords of the Middle Ages might have wished to be remembered as resplendent figures clad in military dress, but armour was brought out only for special occasions. It was scarcely suitable attire for striding up and down the staircase of an Irish castle.

The smiling faces which adorn these monuments evoke a society of serenity and happiness, providing an antidote to the documentary records with their continual reports of violence, feuds and raids. Most information about medieval Ireland tends to come from the English side and inevitably a very black image was painted of lands beyond the Pale. But the revival of both architecture and sculpture in the 15th century implies conditions of relative stability and economic prosperity. Even a tower house could not be built in a couple of weeks, for stone had to be quarried, transported and dressed. While Irish lords felt that life was sufficiently insecure to require such defences, the situation was not so chaotic that elaborate building became impossible.

4
THE END OF THE OLD ORDER

From the Reformation to the Jacobite defeat

BRIAN DE BREFFNY

This night sees Eire desolate,
Her chiefs are cast out of their state;
Her men, her maidens weep to see
Her desolate that should peopled be.

Her chiefs are gone. There's none to bear
Her cross or lift her from despair;
The grieving lords take ship. With these
Our very souls pass overseas.

From *This night sees Eire desolate*
by Aindrais MacMarcuis tr. by Robin Flower

The iron rule of England tightened its grip upon Ireland during the reign of Elizabeth I. When her father, Henry VIII, had inherited the title of Lord of Ireland in 1509 English authority had been limited to a few square miles round Dublin. In 1520 Henry began a sustained campaign to subjugate the Irish. The break with Rome added religious to civil discord—discord which was only partially resolved by Mary Tudor's restoration of Catholicism. With the accession of Elizabeth the situation deteriorated again. The Pope absolved the Irish of their allegiance to the sovereign, who retaliated by attempting to colonize Ireland with Protestants who were to own the land and keep the native Irish in permanent subjection. It was a policy whose repercussions are still being felt.

The first attempt to colonize Ulster, under Sir Thomas Smith, failed. The second was led by Walter Devereux, 1st Earl of Essex (opposite), a man of considerable talents but ruthless in pursuit of his aims. The Queen granted him lands in Co. Antrim and loaned him £10,000, with which he waged a determined war against his unwilling subjects. His treacherous capture of Sir Brian MacPhelim O'Neill and the massacre of four hundred people on Rathlin Island were long remembered with hatred. But in the end he had to admit defeat and died in Dublin in 1576 a disappointed man. (1)

A DÑ 1572
ÆSVÆ 32

VIRTVTIS·COMES·INVIDIA·

HONI·SOIT·QVI·MAL·Y·PENSE

To Elizabeth Ireland was a danger. Permanently disaffected and rebellious, devoted to the Roman Church, it represented a door through which her enemies could attack England. She was therefore doubly determined to assert her rights. The circular drawing (above left) is a design by Nicholas Hilliard for her Great Seal of Ireland. The record of her attempts to conquer the country consists largely of failures, but the campaign of Charles Blount, Lord Mountjoy (above), stands out for its success. In 1601 he defeated first an Irish army under Hugh O'Neill and then a Spanish one under Don Juan de Aguila. (2,3)

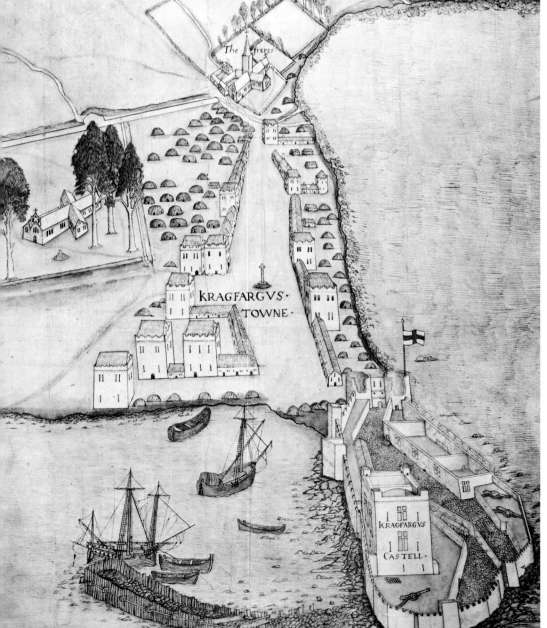

Over Carrickfergus (left), Co. Antrim, the English flag flies resolutely. This was traditionally an English stronghold, with a castle going back to the 12th century. In the reign of Elizabeth, when this drawing was made, it was one of the only two real towns in Ulster (the other was Newry; Belfast was only a village). Several tower houses are shown, and in the distance is the friary, standing as usual on the outskirts. (4)

The native Irish struck visitors from abroad as primitive and barbarian. There are a number of vivid written descriptions but few authentic visual records. On this page are reproduced three drawings of the late 16th century which have some claim to have been made from life. One group (above left) includes a woman, with a long cloak and hair partly hanging loose, partly rolled up in a linen coil with a hat on top, and a young bagpiper, reminding us that the instrument is indigenous to the Irish as well as to the Scots. All have bare feet. So do the soldiers shown in the group below. The shaggy cloaks, shirts tucked in at the waist, short jackets and long hair all agree with the literary evidence. They carry the same type of sword with a large ring at the end of the hilt while the man on the right brandishes a long dagger. Above right: a foot-soldier from the charter of Queen Elizabeth to the City of Dublin. He is dressed in a totally featureless costume which is hard to believe, but carries a convincing pike and a sword resembling those of the rest. (5–7)

DRAVN AFTER THE QVICKE

CHARLEMOVNT

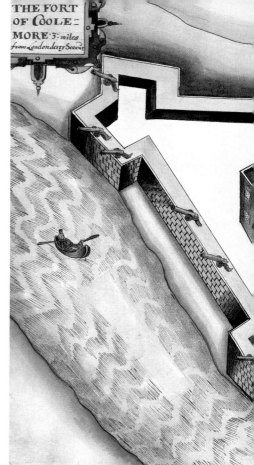

THE FORT OF COOLE=MORE 3 miles from Londonderry Seaward

Eneskillin Castell

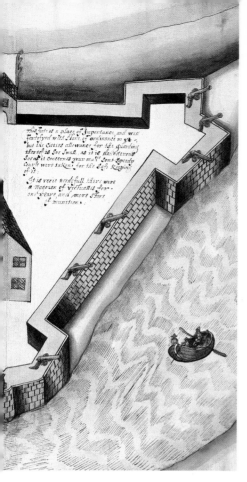

Simmering discontent marked the reigns of the first two Stuarts in Ireland. Above left: Sir Toby Caulfield's Charlemont, Co. Tyrone, in 1624. A typical Jacobean mansion is surrounded by star-shaped artillery ramparts. (8)

Culmore Fort commanded the estuary of the River Foyle and the maritime approach to Derry. Around 1624, Sir George Carew inspected it and made recommendations (above) for its greater security. (9)

The siege of Enniskillen (left) was only one episode in a long history of rebellion and feud. In February 1594 the English governor of Connacht took the castle from the local chief Hugh Maguire. (10)

Sir Thomas Lee (right), an English officer, is depicted in this portrait painted in 1594 wearing a glorified version of the costume and accessories of an Irish kerne. The bare feet and legs, the round shield, the long spear held with the forefinger by a loop, all belong to the Irish tradition, but the short skirt is bedizened to show his rank. Lee acquired an estate at Castlemartin, Co. Kildare. His wife, 'a mere Irish', interpreted for him in negotiations. He was executed for treason in 1601. (11)

A new wave of violence struck Ireland in the 1640s. Political confusion in England gave the Irish their opportunity. The Catholic Confederacy (May 1642), virtually a declaration of independence, was followed by a bloody insurrection in which the Protestants suffered severely. The end came in 1649 with the reconquest of Ireland by Cromwell. After Charles II's restoration conditions eased slightly, but in 1681 the Catholic Primate, Oliver Plunkett (below left), was accused of involvement in the 'Popish Plot', brought to London and executed. He was in fact innocent and in 1975 was canonized as a martyr for his faith. At the head of the King's government was the Duke of Ormonde (below right), one of the ancient Butler family, born a Catholic but raised as a Protestant. His tolerance and wisdom partially defused an explosive situation. (12,13)

The last chance for Catholic Ireland to assert its right to exist came when James II was ousted from the English throne by the Protestant party, who installed William and Mary. With the support of Louis XIV, but not of the Pope, James landed at Kinsale (below) in March 1689. In this drawing the King's boat is announced by trumpeters, and priests on the shore stretch out their arms to welcome him. (14)

At the Battle of the Boyne—1 July 1690—William III's forces defeated those of James and dashed all hopes of Irish independence for more than a century. The battle (above) was not a major one in terms of losses, nor was it the last, but James gave up the struggle and fled to France, eventually followed by many of his Irish supporters. Below: the exiled King being received by Louis XIV at St-Germain-en-Laye. (15,16)

The foundations of the Ascendancy had been laid by the early 17th century. Adam Loftus, the first Provost of Trinity College and Archbishop of Armagh, came from Yorkshire. One of his treasures was the Loftus Cup (left), made in 1593 from the Great Seal of Ireland, which Loftus had melted down. His nephew, also called Adam, became Chancellor in his turn. He is seen here (above) with his hand laid patronizingly on the Chancellor's purse. Below: Richard Boyle, the most successful of the English adventurers. He amassed a fortune in Ireland, founded towns, churches and almshouses and became the first Earl of Cork. (17–19)

Chapter 4

From the Reformation to the Jacobite defeat

BRIAN DE BREFFNY

'For God, King and Country' — crown, cross and harp, holy dove and flaming heart: the seal of the Catholic Confederacy, proclaimed in 1642, brings together the religious and political symbols of the Catholic party in Ireland, loyal to Charles I. Other Irish Catholics refused to support the King even in the face of a common enemy, Cromwell. (1)

WHEN, IN APRIL 1509, Henry VIII succeeded his father as King of England and Lord of Ireland, practically the only region of Ireland where the royal writ could be enforced was the Pale, which then stretched from Dundalk on the north to Dalkey on the south and no farther into the Leinster hinterland than Kells, Kilcock, Naas, the Bridge of Kilcullen and Ballymore Eustace. Within these limits the King's authority was exercised by a Lord Deputy. Gerald FitzGerald, 8th Earl of Kildare, had followed his father in this office and held it for the best part of more than three decades until his death in 1513 when his son Gerald succeeded him. Ruling in the King's name, these 'Geraldine' earls established their power so effectively that inside their territories they were really kings in all but name.

Outside the Pale

But who held sway over the rest of Ireland? In Munster the earls of Desmond, another branch of the FitzGerald family, ruled a vast palatinate, over half a million acres, virtually as feudal sovereigns, with an intricate network of both Gaelic and Hiberno-Norman vassals. Their banqueting hall and the detached audience chamber of Newcastle West, Co. Limerick, where they held court, testify, even in their present ruinous state, to the grandeur of the Desmond establishment. The numerous buildings were surrounded by orchards and an extensive garden. At Askeaton, in the same county, they had another important castle with an adjacent banqueting hall.

Between the territory of the Desmond Fitz-Geralds and the Kildare FitzGeralds lay the palatinate of another powerful Hiberno-Norman dynasty, the Butlers, earls of Ormonde. They controlled what is now Co. Tipperary and much of Co. Kilkenny.

Most of the rest of Ireland was in the hands of the Irish chiefs and their clans, who continued to live according to their ancient laws and customs. The great Hiberno-Norman lords lived in their castles, mostly built or extensively improved in the preceding century; their more substantial feudatories inhabited the tower houses, usually of four stories, which were still built in the 16th century in the bleak traditional style, devoid of decoration, scant of comfort and ill lit.

Foreigners were astonished at the primitive living conditions and customs of the Irish chiefs, who appeared to them barbaric and extraordinary. There was little in the Irish world which appealed to outsiders; the Irish aquavitae, usquebaugh (from the Irish *uisqe beatha*, water of life) – now called whiskey – was considered by some to be excellent. The comely fair-skinned freckled women, with long golden tresses braided or knotted, were admired. Of things Irish the foreigners most prized the falcons, the sparrowhawk, the swift slender greyhounds and the wiry-coated wolfhounds which were the gifts usually chosen to be sent from Ireland to foreign potentates. The principal exports were hides, sheepskins, martens' and other pelts, fish, timber, woven rugs and some linen yarn. The largest single import was wine from Spain and France of which thousands of tuns came in yearly; iron, arms and ammunition were also regular imports.

Rich in cattle, reckless in the hunt, prompt to donate gold and jewels from their coffers to the Church, proud, rancorous, independent, recalcitrant, amorous, lustful, devout, superstitious, hospitable, loving fighting and loving poetry, the Irish chiefs lived roughly, an outdoor life, disdainful of alien manners and fashion, not so much resistant

Irish manners in 1581, a woodcut from John Derrick's hostile but popular 'Image of Irelande'. Chiefs did in fact normally dine in the open air. On the left two men slaughter an ox and roast it in its hide. A friar preaches during the meal while the bard and the harper provide lighter entertainment. On the right two men near the fire prepare to defecate. (2)

to change as inconsiderate of it. Habitually the chief, his family and cohorts dined *al fresco* despite the inclement climate, sometimes under a bower of rushes, using a table and benches made of ferns; at night they slept on rushes on the ground. Consequently for them campaign life was little different from home life and they took to the woods and hills with ease when necessary, to wage guerrilla warfare. Nor did their diet have many refinements: herbs, shamrock, watercress, berries and esculent roots eaten raw, simple milk products, oatcakes, whey, broth and sometimes barely cooked, unseasoned venison, mutton, or beef were the fare which strangers found execrable, although apparently it suited those who were used to it, for they were described as hardy, sinewy and fleet. The Irish clansmen and the villeins lived in primeval windowless huts of rushes or of rushes and mud, with scant clothing, a few rags under an ample woollen mantle.

When Hugh Oge O'Donnell, the ruler of Tyrconnel, appeared at the English court on his way back to Donegal from a leisurely pilgrimage to Rome, he received great honour from Henry VIII. The unusual mien of this liege chief and the outlandish garb and obscure language of his party, with their saffron-coloured smocks, narrow trews, rug-like fringed russet mantles, their moustaches, and their hair worn in long, thick, matted fringes over their eyes, must have aroused considerable comment and curiosity at the Tudor court.

In 1520 Thomas Howard, Earl of Surrey, was appointed Lord Lieutenant. The King's instructions were to achieve the complete submission of Ireland to the Crown by diplomatic means; in Henry's own words '... by sober waies, politique driftes and amiable persuasions', avoiding 'rigorous dealings, comminations, or any other inforcement by strength or violence'. He explained explicitly that he wanted only the lawful allegiance due to him and not to deprive anyone else of his just rights.

It did not take Surrey long in Ireland to conclude that sober ways, politic drifts and amiable persuasions would be of no avail in bringing the country to heel. His first victorious incursions into the hinterland were quickly reversed and the treaties he managed to arrange were lightly taken and speedily broken; at the same time the King baulked at the considerable cost to the English treasury of the military operations in Ireland. In 1521 Surrey sent the King his pondered advice for the conquest of Ireland, that it would 'never be brought to good order and due subjection except by conquest ... one way is if Your Grace will one year set on hand to win one country and another year another ... till all at length be won'. Then, Surrey urged, '... unless Your Grace send inhabitants of your own natural subjects to inhabit such countries as shall be won, all your charges should be but wastefully spent'. Here was the basis of future English policy in Ireland taken up by the later Tudor and Stuart monarchs and Oliver Cromwell, the genesis of the change in the physiognomy of the Irish which is still evident due to the importation of settlers to colonize the island, loyal English and Scots who could, as Surrey put it, 'set the Irish to Labour on the land'. At the time, Henry VIII was unwilling to finance the campaign which called for an army of several thousand; Surrey was released and returned to England.

Plots continued to proliferate. The 11th Earl of Desmond, who conducted himself like an independent ruling prince, after his intrigues with the King of France began negotiations with Charles V. Accused of treason, he died in 1529. Kildare, suspect for having failed to apprehend Desmond, was summoned to England and detained in prison there. His son Thomas, Lord Offaly (called Silken Thomas for the fringes on his follower's helmets), believing a rumour that his father had been executed, mounted an open rebellion.

'No more Christianity . . .'

In 1525 the new Deputy, Kildare, reported: 'the late Bishop of Leighlin was heinously murdered by the Abbot of Duiske's son, being the Earl of Ormonde's nigh kinsman for that intent the said Abbot might have enjoyed that bishopric . . .' and added 'all the churches for the most part within the said counties of Kilkenny and Tipperary are in such extreme decay . . . no divine service is kept there . . . if the King's Grace do not see for the hasty remedy of the same, there is like to be no more Christianity there than in the midst of Turkey'. In fact, all over Ireland church buildings were in disrepair; Clonmacnoise Cathedral, for example, was roofless and only the bare walls stood of the cathedrals of Ross and Ardagh.

Undoubtedly ecclesiastical discipline was lax in Ireland as it was in other European countries, and the defective administrative structure of the Church obstructed the remedy of abuses. Hereditary control of some ecclesiastical offices still obtained in Connacht and Ulster and was tolerated. At least two 16th-century bishops were also secular chiefs, embroiled in feuds and skirmishes. A number of bishops contracted secular marriages or raised families with concubines, and no social stigma was attached to their offspring. This laxity in matrimonial matters was also prevalent among the laity, who frequently contracted secular marriages which could subsequently be disclaimed with ease. This led to cases which bordered on polygamy; Ulick Burke, 1st Earl of Clanrickarde, was survived at his death in 1543 by two rival wives, and his son Richard, the 2nd Earl, had at one time five living wives.

The rather unusual view of sexual continence which existed in Ireland is evident in the obituary of the principal compiler of the Annals of Ulster in 1498; he held the office of dean, and was a canon of Clogher and of Armagh and the father of a dozen children; but his necrologer extolled him as 'a gem of purity and a turtle-dove of chastity'. Indiscipline was rife in most of the religious orders, with the Cistercians to the fore in disintegration and deterioration. The irregularities generally were exacerbated by the absenteeism of English clerics appointed to benefices in the Pale and the port cities.

Wolsey's claim that his jurisdiction as papal legate included Ireland was rejected by many of the Irish prelates on the grounds that his Bull of appointment from Pope Leo X in 1520 specified only 'in Regno Angliae'. Therefore they applied directly to Rome for dispensations by sending 'Rome runners', a practice which greatly exercised Wolsey who was keen to abolish direct intercourse between Ireland and Rome.

Despite the abuses, the irregularities, the promiscuity and the problems of communication, the faith

In 1521 Dürer met and sketched a party of Irish soldiers and their attendants. The latter wear the typical mantle or 'shag rug' and under that a jacket, belted at the waist. (3)

of the people was vital, largely owing to the zealous activity of the mendicant orders. The Imperial ambassador in London reported to Charles V that the Irish feared, obeyed and adored the friars to such an extent that the Lords would even submit to corporal punishment at their hands.

The crisis of the Reformation

In 1534, the archbishops of York and Canterbury had declared in Henry VIII's favour that 'the Pope has no greater jurisdiction conferred on him by God in Holy Scriptures in the Kingdom of England than any other foreign bishop'. In the same year the English Parliament passed the Act of Supremacy. It ruled that 'the King shall be taken, accepted and reputed the only supreme Head in earth of the Church of England'.

In Ireland, Piers Butler lost no time in making it known where he stood. 'The Bishop of Rome's provisions and usurped jurisdiction have been the chief cause of the desolation and decay in Ireland . . .', he declared in 1534, accusing the Pope of having given ecclesiastical preferment in Ireland to 'vile and vicious persons, unlearned, . . . murderers, thieves and of other detestable disposition'. This stand probably helped him get back his title of Earl of Ormonde in 1537; in any case the Hiberno-Norman earls had always resented being deprived of the power to control lucrative Irish benefices by the papal appointment of foreigners.

The Irish Parliament managed to pass the Act in 1536 declaring the King Supreme Head of the Irish Church and recognizing Anne Boleyn as Queen of England (although by the time news of the passing of this Act reached London, Anne Boleyn had been beheaded and the King's new wife Jane Seymour was Queen). As no doctrinal or moral issues were

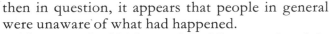

The forelock or glibe and the long moustache became symbols of Irish national identity. Various English edicts forbade them but were widely disobeyed, as this 17th-century woodcut shows. (5)

According to the biased Derrick, the friar in this woodcut is absolving a noble 'from all his former sin and bids him plague the prince's friends, if heaven he mind to win!' Catholic priests did encourage rebellion against the heretic Queen Elizabeth. (4)

then in question, it appears that people in general were unaware of what had happened.

The new Archbishop of Dublin, appointed in 1536, was George Browne, a former Augustinian friar who had performed the wedding ceremony of Henry and Anne. Archbishop Browne was no ideologist; he might be best described as a fellow-traveller of the Reformation party and he managed to survive their downfall, and later even his own immediate dismissal by Queen Mary I, until the encumbrance of a wife and family cost him his see. Soon after his arrival Browne became aware of the difficulties of establishing the royal authority in Ireland; he too advocated colonization by companies of soldiers and impecunious English gentlemen 'of good discretion' to keep the Irish in check in Wicklow, Kildare and south Co. Dublin. The military campaign was constantly hampered by lack of money. At Cashel, in the summer of 1536, the army refused to march against Conor O'Brien of Thomond, who had been intriguing with the Emperor, until they received their arrears of pay.

Meanwhile the cultural campaign against the native language, costume and habits was prosecuted hopefully. The citizens of Galway received a royal injunction in 1536 requiring them 'to shave their lips, let their hair grow over their ears ... wear caps ... wear the English dress ... shoot with the long bow ... leave unlawful games ... learn English'. The following year an Act of Parliament was passed for the English Order, Habit and Language. It forbade cutting or shaving the hair above the ears, glibes, moustaches, any shirts, smocks, kerchiefs, bibs or caps of saffron-coloured linen, shirts or smocks of over seven yards of cloth for men, and for women

skirts or coats tucked up or embroidered or laid with 'usker' (Irish *usgar*, a jewel or ornament) after the Irish fashion, and, finally, Irish mantles. The proscriptions appear to have been widely disregarded despite the threat of fines and confiscation of the garments, for fifty years later the authorities were still inveighing against the Irish hair style and costume, and travellers in the next century continued to remark on the gathered linen smocks or tunics with abundant full pleats, the close-fitting hose and fringed mantles of the men and the unusual appearance of the women, who favoured a headdress of many yards of linen wound turban-like but broad and flat on top like a large Cheddar cheese, or in some parts in the west plucked up like a mitre. The women also wore the fringed mantles, usually in a dark colour but sometimes dyed yellow, red or green; the richest wore gold collars set with precious stones, but there were commoner ones set with gaudy painted glass. Rings and bracelets were fashionable and usually a crucifix hung from the fancy collar.

Big changes began quietly with the order for the dissolution of five large Cistercian abbeys, Baltinglass, Bective, Dunbrody, Graiguenamanagh and Tintern, in 1536; the abbots were granted a pension and the estates soon passed to new owners. In 1537 other religious houses, all in Leinster, were named for suppression. As the confiscations continued Lord Deputy Grey, a moderate, urged that six should be allowed to survive, including the Cistercian houses of St Mary's Abbey, in Dublin, and Jerpoint, and the nunnery at Grace Dieu, because in default of common inns in Ireland they served as lodgings when needed for the King's Council and also because they educated young men and women virtuously in the English language. These houses were suppressed nevertheless and in the following decades, as the Crown's authority was asserted over the whole island, eventually all the monasteries and nunneries were sequestered and their valuable properties distributed. The subservient officers of the Crown were well rewarded; as well as Bective, Alen, for instance, got St Wolstan's in Co. Kildare which remained with his descendants for over two centuries. The Dublin Corporation was sweetened with the grant of All Hallows Priory. When the suppressions reached the Gaelic regions the chiefs were not averse to receiving sequestered monastic properties.

It is difficult to determine to what extent the destruction of shrines was motivated by a genuine reforming zeal to eradicate superstition and idolatry and to what extent by the desire to acquire the valuable treasures of the shrines, the gifts of pilgrims accumulated over the years. In 1538 Archbishop Browne wrote to Cromwell, 'there goeth a common brewte amongst the Irishmen that I intend to pluck down Our Lady of Trim with other places of pilgrimages, as the Holy Cross and such like; which indeed I never attempted, although my conscience would right well serve me to oppose such idols'. Later that year Lord Deputy Grey heard Masses at Trim and knelt in devotion before the statue of the Virgin; but before another year had passed Browne had the famous statue burned and its treasure of gold, silver and jewels was confiscated. Other precious statues like that of the crucified Christ in the Augustinian priory at Ballyboggan, Co. Meath, were destroyed. As news of the destruction of relics in the Pale reached the remoter areas, many sacred objects were hidden, often by the families who were their hereditary guardians. Several came to light in the 19th century in the possession of the descendants of their earlier custodians; undoubtedly a number are still buried beneath the soil, hidden and forgotten. On Browne's orders Ireland's most revered relic, the *Baculum Jesu*, was burned outside Christ Church Cathedral; inside the cathedral the statues were eventually replaced by gilt-framed panels inscribed with the Credo, the Paternoster and the Ten Commandments, in the English language.

Browne went on a tour to preach the King's supremacy and denounce the usurped authority of the Pope; he distributed copies of the King's English translation of the Paternoster, the Ave Maria, the Ten Commandments and the Articles of Faith. Several bishops did take the Oath of Supremacy and abjured the Pope's authority. Emboldened by his successes Browne triumphantly proclaimed his intention of travelling throughout the country to repeat this performance as far as

English could be understood, and in the Gaelic regions with the help of an interpreter.

Another move towards consolidating the authority of the Crown was the policy of surrender and re-grant whereby the Irish chiefs were urged to surrender their estates to the Crown in order to receive them back immediately under a formal royal grant. To sweeten this procedure some of the major chiefs were offered hereditary peerages and thus Con O'Neill became the Earl of Tyrone, Morrogh O'Brien the Earl of Thomond and Ulick MacWilliam Burke the Earl of Clanrickarde.

Pope Paul III wrote to Con O'Neill in April 1541 addressing him as 'Prince of Ulster', expressing his grief at the impiety and destruction which the King's cruelty had provoked in Ireland, deploring that 'the honour of God is trodden down by that man'; but the Pope rejoiced that O'Neill was the defender of the Roman Catholic Church and religion and exhorted all the Irish to persevere in the faith of their fathers. Nevertheless the next year, while a Jesuit mission sent by the Pope landed in Ulster, Con O'Neill put on his robes of state in the Queen's closet at Greenwich to receive from the King with due pomp the title of Earl of Tyrone. In return he submitted to the King, swore fealty to him, promised to forsake utterly the name of O'Neill, to put his lands to tillage and husbandry and build houses for the husbandmen, to adopt English habits for himself and his heirs, speaking English to the best of their knowledge. It was not perhaps an auspicious start when the newly-made Earl thanked the King in Irish, his speech being translated into English by a priest who accompanied him.

The Gaelic clansmen were far from pleased to see their clan lands transformed into a personal estate for the then chief and his male heirs by primogeniture, thus alienating their own complex and ancient rights in the lands and extinguishing the practice of tanistry. Meanwhile, among the Hiberno-Normans, the Geraldines, smarting under the harsh punishments they had received, brooded revenge. Lord Deputy Grey was eventually dismissed and arrested, suspected of favouring the league which supported his nephew the infant Earl of Kildare, in exile in France.

For all the various discontented and the enemies of the Crown, the papal banner increasingly became a rallying point, thus beginning that long association of Irish nationalism with Rome and with England's enemies on the Continent, the ultimate effects of which are still with us. By the end of the 16th century the devotion of the majority of the Irish to the Holy See and to the Pope's person became one of passionate attachment; it was nurtured principally by the ubiquitous and unsuppress-

able Franciscans who were therefore described in reports to London as 'false and crafty bloodsuckers ... leaders of the opposition'.

During the reign of the boy King Edward VI who succeeded Henry VIII, the Reformation party, no longer hampered by rigid royal orthodoxy, were able to promote doctrinal and liturgical changes. In Ireland the authorities attempted to suppress the Mass. The English Prayer Book was introduced and on Easter Day of 1551 the English liturgy was read for the first time in Ireland in Christ Church Cathedral, Dublin.

Catholicism restored

The successor of Edward VI was his half-sister, Mary I, the daughter of Catherine of Aragon. She was a devout Catholic, anxious to heal the breach with Rome and restore the Mass, but she made no attempt to restore the monastic properties, nor to relinquish her title of Queen of Ireland. Eventually Pope Paul IV, bowing diplomatically before a *fait accompli*, by the first Bull of his reign in 1554 elevated Ireland into a kingdom and granted Mary and her husband Philip the titles of King and Queen of Ireland. Mary's Irish policy was in the tradition established by her father, to quash all resistance to the Crown and to anglicize the inhabitants. In ecclesiastical matters she decreed a return to the old faith; freedom to attend Mass was reintroduced in Ireland and celibacy for the clergy re-established. A number of the bishops who had taken the Oath of

Supremacy managed nevertheless to retain their sees, even some who had promulgated doctrinal changes. Despite his previous activities, even Browne clung to his throne for a while. Surprisingly he was among the bishops who consecrated the new Archbishop of Cashel appointed by the Pope in 1553; but the sly and ambitious Browne was saddled with a wife and children. It appears that he attempted to repudiate Mrs Browne, but he was deprived of his see and returned to England. Some of the most politic prelates like Hugh Corren achieved careers which rival that of the Vicar of Bray, surviving reform, counter-reform and reform. The last bishop in Ireland recognized by both the Pope and the Crown was Eoghain O'Hart, Bishop of Achonry, who died in 1603.

One of the prominent reform bishops who did not survive Mary's counter-reform purge was John Bale, a one-time Carmelite and, as the married Bishop of Ossory, a zealous promoter of Lutheran principles; he had caused all the statues and relics in St Canice's Cathedral at Kilkenny to be broken. Bale was the author of morality plays by which he attempted to instruct the populace, having them performed by boys at the Kilkenny market cross: God's promises under the old law, St John the Baptist's preachings, Christ's temptation in the wilderness, were some of the subjects. When Bale was absent the clergy rang the bells, brought out the hidden copes, candlesticks, crucifixes, censers and holy-water stoups and made a gorgeous procession chanting 'Sancta Maria, Ora pro nobis'. With the

Counter-Reformation the unpopular Bale was forced to flee for his life. He went to Dublin, whence, disguised as a mason, he managed to leave the country. In Kilkenny the clergy re-erected the altars in St Canice's and set up images again.

The boys who acted in Bishop Bale's morality plays were probably scholars of the grammar school, at the west end of the cathedral churchyard, founded in 1538 by the 8th Earl of Ormonde and his Countess. By an Act of Parliament of 1537 Henry VIII had ordered the establishment of an English-speaking school in every parish in Ireland. Later in Elizabeth's reign, in 1570, an Act of Parliament set up a Protestant school in each diocese with a master who was an Englishman or of English birth. About a dozen of these free diocesan schools survived until the latter part of the 19th century.

In the Gaelic system youths destined for the priesthood were instructed in the monasteries, which may also have accepted some secular students. Certainly Lord Deputy Grey's reference to the education of boys and girls in monasteries and a nunnery of the Pale implies that this was the case there. An inventory of the library of the Franciscan Observant house at Youghal, Co. Cork, of 1523 which survives shows that it contained liturgical, philosophical and theological works and volumes of canon law as well as a printed Bible and the sermons of such 15th-century preachers popular in Italy as Roberto Caracciolo and Leonardo da Udine. *Meditatione vitae Christi*, another theological work by an Italian author, circulated in an Irish translation, *Smaointe beatha Chríost*. The families of jurists, physicians, harpists and poets taught and trained their own boys privately in their art or craft in family schools. Every Irish family of consequence had its anthology compiled by its bards to record its history and prowess. The lay poets also turned to poems of courtly love and to religious themes, usually in a spirit of exuberant laudation. It was customary for chiefs to invite poets, professors and learned men to assemblies where they competed for prizes.

Although there was no university in the country the preliminary instruction available to youths was sufficient to enable those few who sought further education abroad to gain admission to English or Continental universities. After the Reformation the Irish had to make arrangements for schooling as best they could. The closing of the monasteries and the collapse of the Gaelic social system contributed to a deterioration in education generally, but at the end of the century Sir John Dowdall reported to Burghley that in all the towns there were schools where the sons of noblemen and gentlemen were taught by schoolmasters (whom he deemed 'superstitious and idolatrous') and overseen by priests. Dowdall considered these schools nests of cor-

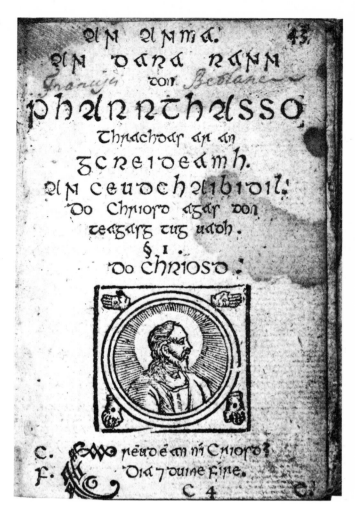

Pages from the Paradise of the Soul *by the Franciscan Anthony Gernon, 1645. This elementary catechism in Irish was printed at Louvain where the Irish Franciscans set up a printing press to help foster the old faith and the Counter-Reformation among the people in Ireland. 'In order that there be nothing on earth necessary for your spiritual life unknown to you, we will set forth all the knowledge which is meet for you to know' states the author. The first of the simple questions and answers is: Q. What is Christ? A. True God and true man. (7)*

ruption and civil disobedience. Certainly the Irish language and culture and the Catholic faith were fostered in these independent schools. The conditions were often far from satisfactory; Campion, describing such a school a few years after Dowdall's report, wrote 'some ten in one chamber grovelling upon couches of straw, their books at their noses, themselves lying flat prostrate'.

Sir Edward Bellingham, an able and energetic soldier appointed Lord Deputy in 1548, enlarged the Pale by thrusting westwards into the territories of the O'Connors Faly and the O'Mores, Offaly and Leix, and established forts to help in holding the conquered lands. Under Mary I the recommended policy of colonization was implemented; Fort Protector, the garrison in Leix, was renamed Maryborough for the Queen and the garrison established at Daingean in Offaly was named Philipstown for her Spanish consort. The Irish inhabitants were pushed back west of these forts; the territory was shired, Offaly becoming King's Co. and Leix, Queen's; the lands were leased to Englishmen at attractive rents. The grantees, who included officers and soldiers of the military campaign, were obliged to maintain armed men ready for service to the Crown when required. Some Irish who collaborated with the English and were therefore termed 'loyal Irish' were rewarded with grants of land inheritable by primogeniture. The new settlers were incessantly and mercilessly harassed and attacked by the displaced Irish to the west but some of them hung on nevertheless. The descendants of William Vicars who was at Maryborough in 1560, for example, became established gentry in the vicinity and held lands in Co. Leix down to the end of the 19th century.

Rebellion and repression: Ireland under Elizabeth
With the accession of Mary's Protestant half-sister Elizabeth, the religious situation in Ireland hardened again. In 1570 Pope Pius V issued a Bull formally absolving all the Irish of allegiance to Elizabeth; this undoubtedly gave an impetus to insurrection. Elizabeth's position was weak: her brother-in-law Philip, King of Spain (whom the Pope recognized as King of Ireland), and her kinswoman the Catholic Mary, Queen of Scots, the next heir in line, both represented a threat to her security. Rebellious Ireland, predominantly Catholic, looked to France and Spain for help in opposing the English. Elizabeth therefore charged her generals to prosecute the conquest and subjugation of Ireland with determination and she encouraged the colonization of Ireland as she did that of Virginia across the Atlantic.

In 1560 the Irish Parliament passed the Elizabethan Church Settlement with an all-embracing Oath of Supremacy obligatory for all the office-holders in the country, and the Act of Uniformity of Common Prayer which re-established Edward VI's Book of Common Prayer and prescribed penalties for those not using it. It was widely believed in Ireland that these laws were placed on the statute roll by some trick. This may be true as the Irish Lower House had a big Catholic majority.

Between 1565 and 1567 a series of battles between rivals for the O'Neill chieftainship in Ulster led to the abolition of the sovereignty of the O'Neills by an Act of Attainder (1569) and the first serious attempt at the colonization of Ulster. The man chosen to direct this was Sir Thomas Smith, a scholarly man, one-time Provost of Eton, who received a grant of the Ards, near Belfast. He envisaged his colonial enterprise in Ireland as that of an ancient Roman bringing civilization to barbarous lands, and he planned military backing and protection for his settlers. But at this point he was sent to France as

Elizabeth's ambassador, so the colonization was supervised by his son, who bungled it. The military protection was inadequate, the O'Neills of Clandeboy attacked the Ards, burning as they went; Smith junior was murdered by an Irishman in his own household; and the unhappy colonists fled. Undaunted, Sir Thomas planned a second colony around a fortified town to be called Elizabetha, but as he was unable to reduce the O'Neills of Clandeboy and make the Ards safe to begin this venture, it never came to fruition.

Nevertheless, this was a time when many adventurous Englishmen and Spaniards were excited by the get-rich-quick prospects of colonization abroad. Immediately after Smith's failure the Earl of Essex attempted to colonize Ulster. The Queen granted him a vast amount of land in Co. Antrim and loaned him £10,000 on mortgage to finance his venture. Essex, at first truculently confident, soon found that plans on paper were not so easily concluded in unfamiliar country. He might, however, have been successful in subduing Ulster, for he was ruthless and able, but the Queen did not understand his problems and failed to back him up with the military and financial support he required. She was petulant about the length and cost of the military campaign and eventually ended it; disgruntled, Essex died in Dublin in 1576. In the course of his efforts to subdue the inhabitants of Antrim he added to the store of anti-English resentments. In the course of a merry and peaceable feast he apprehended Sir Brian MacPhelim O'Neill at Belfast (then a village), had two hundred of O'Neill's men murdered and sent Sir Brian and his wife to Dublin to be killed and quartered. At Rathlin Island, after an attack in which Francis Drake took part, the four hundred people sheltering there, including the womenfolk and children of the MacDonnells, were all massacred. When events in Munster caused the English to turn their attention to the south-west, the men of Ulster, thirsty for revenge, regathered their strength.

During the first decade of Elizabeth's reign there was constant friction between the new colonists and the dispossessed Irish. The English grip slowly tightened. In 1570 an English presidency was established at Munster, with a Lord President and council. But the Irish landowners were looking for support from abroad. Pope Pius IV had sent a Limerick-born Jesuit to Ireland to foster the formation of a league for the defence of the Catholic faith; then Pope Gregory XIII finally came through with some tangible help and sanctioned a papal expeditionary force in 1578. The following year James Fitzmaurice, a cousin of the Earl of Desmond, returned from Rome and landed at Dingle, Co. Kerry, where he made a proclamation of war: 'This war is undertaken for the defence of the

Catholic religion against the heretics. Pope Gregory XIII hath chosen us for general captain in this same war ... We fight not against the lawful sceptre and honourable throne of England but against a tyrant which refuseth to hear Christ speaking by his vicar.' It was a convenient excuse for another Desmond rebellion. James Fitzmaurice perished in a skirmish with the Burkes before the papal expedition arrived; the Earl of Desmond then led the rebellion, sacked Youghal and marched on Cork. Part of the papal expeditionary force had been dispersed en route but six hundred men in five vessels, Spaniards and Italians with six thousand muskets, landed with the Catholic Bishop of Killaloe at Smerwick, Co. Kerry, in 1580. They were besieged by the English in Dunamoir Fort and on surrendering unconditionally all six hundred were slain by Walter Ralegh and his men on the instructions of the Lord Deputy.

Although the Pope granted a plenary indulgence to all who took up arms against Elizabeth, no other help arrived from Rome or Spain despite the appeals of the Earl of Desmond for reinforcements. The outlawed Earl held out for three years, waging guerrilla warfare until he was killed in 1583 in a quarrel over cattle-raiding in the hills of Kerry. Dermot O'Hurley, the Catholic Archbishop of Cashel, who had plotted with Pope Gregory XIII in Rome, was apprehended and executed in Dublin in 1584. The Desmond power was broken, the vast lands of their suppressed palatinate were confiscated and surveyed; over half a million acres were divided up into lots of four, six, eight and twelve thousand acres each and granted to English adventurers. The undertakers were encouraged to settle on their lands bringing yeomen farmers, husbandmen, servants, farm stock, ploughs and implements, and they were enjoined to exclude the 'mere Irish'. Many of these first Munster settlers were wiped out by the rebellion at the end of the century, many others fled from it, but a few stubbornly made roots and the once-alien names of some of the Elizabethan settlers survive today among their descendants in Kerry, Limerick and Cork.

The suppression of the Desmond rebellions left plenty of hard feelings among the 'mere Irish' who remembered the consequent ghastly privations, the ferocious massacre of the papal force at Smerwick and instances like the brutal slaughter of the monks of Monasternenagh Abbey in Co. Limerick, put to the sword around the altar by Sir Nicholas Malby and his troops. The Irish retaliated by murdering settlers whenever a convenient occasion arose so that resentments festered on both sides and attitudes hardened.

The poet Edmund Spenser, who had been present at the Smerwick massacre as the Lord Deputy's

Heading of a page in the Council Book of the town of Galway, 1632. The scribe's use of Celtic interlace decoration shows that this style survived for centuries. Prominent among the names of the burgesses are Blake, ffrench, Lynch and Martin, four mercantile families of Norman origin, part of the so-called 'tribes of Galway'. (8)

secretary, was a settler in Co. Cork. He was so exasperated by the Irish that he even considered a final solution of getting rid of all of them, but discarded it. He found Ireland 'a most beautiful and sweet country as any is under heaven' and Munster 'a most rich and plentiful country, full of corn and cattle' but, like most of the settlers, he heartily despised the native Irish, whom he found impossible and incorrigible. He described the cloak worn by most of the Irish people as 'a fit home for an outlaw, a meet bed for a rebel and an apt cloak for a thief'. In his A View of the State of Ireland he drew a vivid picture of the terrible desolation wrought by the Desmond rebellions, wretched starving people who looked like the 'anatomies of death' reduced in their desperation to eating dead carrions. Like many other disillusioned adventurers the poet fled to England when his residence, Kilcolman Castle, was burned in the rebellion of 1598.

A presidency like that of Munster was also established in Connacht with its seat at Athlone. Galway was then a small but prosperous walled

town with fair stone houses; the old Irish were excluded from living in the town which was inhabited by the so-called 'tribes of Galway', hibernicized families of Norman origin like the Lynches, Joyces, Blakes, Frenches, Skerrets and Bodkins, or of Gaelic origin but long integrated with the others, like the Kirwans. The Galway families were mainly merchants trading with Spain. The English set about taming the Burkes and the Berminghams and subduing the Irish families who held the rural areas of Connacht, the O'Flahertys in Galway, the O'Connors in Sligo and Roscommon, the O'Malleys in Mayo and the O'Rorkes in Breffni, now Leitrim.

The ruler of Breffni, one of the principal opponents of the Crown in Connacht, was executed for treason in London in 1591 and his lands parcelled out. O'Rorke, who asked to be hanged with a halter of withy according to the Irish custom, was met on his way to the gallows by Myler M'Grath, the Protestant Archbishop of Cashel. M'Grath, who had himself once been Catholic, attempted to make O'Rorke recant but the chief scorned and reviled the prelate for his own apostasy and treachery.

In the uneasy peace of the 1590s the Composition of Connacht was organized; commissioners travelled through the province assessing the size of land holdings, fixing the rents and establishing the dues to the Crown. The towns were fortified and sheriffs installed.

As well as the English settlers with colonial dreams, some industrious Protestant Walloons and Flemings came to Ireland in Elizabeth's reign. Forty Dutch families, for example, settled at Swords, Co.

Dublin, where they engaged in making diaper and tick and worked excellent leather. There were Flemish painters, too, working in Ireland; one of them painted two of the O'Briens in 1577, probably the earliest surviving oil portraits executed in the country. Dublin boasted all the usual trade guilds of the time: goldsmiths, vintners, cordwainers, tailors, barbers, coopers, glovers, skinners, butchers, bakers. At Kilkenny, there was a tapestry manufactory established in the 1530s by the 8th Earl and Countess of Ormonde, who brought skilled weavers from the Continent to introduce their art to the local people.

Hugh O'Neill, grandson of Con, 1st Earl of Tyrone, was sent by Lord Deputy Sidney to England to be educated and anglicized. He returned to Ireland an apparently loyal subject of the Crown, fought with the English against the Irish in Antrim and in the Desmond wars. The Queen, convinced of his allegiance, made him Earl of Tyrone. However, in 1595 O'Neill accepted to lead a northern rebel confederacy which had been formed by the O'Donnell with the help of the Catholic Primate. Assembling a sizable army of well-armed men, including many mercenaries, he made use of his knowledge of English military tactics in training them. At the Battle of the Yellow Ford on the River Callan, O'Neill's army defeated and routed the English force of four thousand infantry and cavalry.

The ageing Queen, highly exercised, dispatched Essex, son of the Earl mentioned earlier, to Ireland to quash the northern rebellion. He landed in 1599 with a force, at least on paper, of sixteen thousand foot soldiers and over a thousand cavalry; but it was soon diminished because instead of proceeding at once to Ulster, Essex tried first to cope with the border chiefs who were threatening the Pale. He was routed by the O'Mores and the O'Connors in Leix and by the O'Byrnes and the O'Tooles in Wicklow. Meanwhile O'Donnell and O'Rorke had caught and beheaded the Governor of Connacht. Essex returned to London, to rash, foolhardy rebellion, and death.

Had the Spaniards landed an army in Ireland at this crucial moment of English disadvantage they might well have been victorious; but the Spanish were undoubtedly discouraged. Memories of the Armada's fate were still fresh, when about three thousand Spaniards had perished by drowning and two thousand more were slain after swimming to the shores of Antrim, Donegal, Sligo, Mayo and Kerry. One redoubtable Irishman alone, Melaghlin M'Cabb, killed eighty Spanish survivors with his gallowglass axe. At best they were stripped and robbed. Some Irish chiefs did help the Queen's enemies but the reports of the Spaniards who contrived finally to return to Spain, like Captain de Cuellar, did little to help the cause of the Irish, whom they described as savages.

In 1600, the Pope, Clement VIII, as obliging as his predecessors in issuing Bulls for the Irish, proclaimed one granting to all those who followed and assisted O'Neill 'our beloved son, styled Earl of Tyrone . . . and captain-general of the Catholic army . . . plenary pardon and remission of all sins as usually granted to those setting out to the war against the Turks for the recovery of the Holy Land'. Finally, Philip III of Spain yielded to the entreaties of O'Neill's envoy Mateo de Oveido, the Spanish Franciscan Archbishop of Dublin, and sent a sizable Armada to Ireland. But the timing was bad; Elizabeth's new commander, Mountjoy, had beaten O'Neill in the Battle of Benburb and engineered treaties with some of the Irish chiefs. Some of the Spanish vessels were forced by stormy weather to turn back to Spain. O'Neill had insisted that the Spaniards should land in the north-west or the north but Don Juan del Aguila decided it was more prudent to disembark his depleted force of 4,800 men in the south rather than attempting to navigate that treacherous west coast. He landed them at Kinsale where they were besieged by Mountjoy. The northern earls were obliged to cross the entire country hastily with their army of about eight thousand men. The Irish were poorly co-ordinated and their battle strategy was betrayed to the English by Brian Oge MacMahon. They were routed by Mountjoy's disciplined army and after a hundred days in Ireland the Spaniards were obliged to sue for terms. Hugh O'Donnell left for Spain on one of the returning Spanish boats and died there.

Four years later his successor, with O'Neill and other Ulster notables, followed him into exile and their lands were confiscated. O'Cahan of Derry died in the Tower of London. The lands of the O'Doherty, the Maguire and the O'Reilly also passed into the hands of the Crown. It was the end of the old order.

Festering discontent: Ireland under the Stuarts

The accession of James I, King of Scotland, England and Ireland, in 1603, united the crowns of the three kingdoms. It also marked a renewed effort at colonization. The Plantation of Ulster was put under way. Its architects were able to profit from previous failures. Lots of two thousand acres went to undertakers who were required to build a strong castle and bawn; lots of fifteen hundred acres for servitors carried the requirement to build a stone or brick house with a bawn; those who received a lot of a thousand acres were obliged only to build a bawn. Ulster then had virtually no towns save Newry, where the first purpose-built Protestant church in Ireland had already been erected in 1578, and Carrickfergus. Twenty-three new towns were planned and laid out on a grid pattern with a central square or diamond for the public buildings. Roads were built to link these new towns, which included Belfast and Derry. This latter place, efficiently settled along with Coleraine, by the London Companies, Vintners, Drapers, Mercers and others, was renamed Londonderry; a Protestant cathedral was built there in 1628 in a style reminiscent of London City parish churches.

The thrifty, hardy Scots were encouraged to settle in Ulster and they did so in such numbers that by 1640 there were about forty thousand of them, mostly Presbyterian in their religious tenets. In the next century many of their descendants, the so-called Scots-Irish, emigrated to North America because as their numbers had increased there was not enough land or work for their needs; from those that remained descend the bulk of the Protestant population of Ulster today.

The houses built by the Companies were usually like contemporary English domestic buildings. Some were battlemented and semi-fortified as the need required; all were enclosed by a protective bawn. The new magnates built Jacobean mansions of which there are but scant remains. Sir Arthur Chichester's tall turretted Joymount (1610) at Carrickfergus and Sir Toby Caulfield's stylish Charlemont (1622–24) in Co. Tyrone have both vanished. Some had Scottish features like the distinctive angle turrets on strongly moulded corbel-courses and with conical candle-snuffer roofs like that of Sir James Balfour's castle at Lisnaskea (1618) or Malcolm Hamilton's Monea Castle (1618–19),

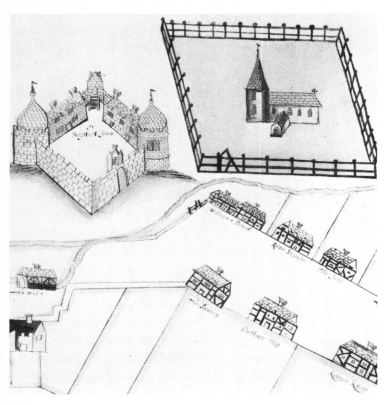

The Plantation of Ulster under James I was a continuation of Elizabeth's policy of colonization. It involved the foundation of new planned towns, some of which were developed by the London Livery Companies. This neat row of dwellings was part of the Vintners' estate at Bellaghy, Co. Derry. (10)

both in Co. Fermanagh and both now ruinous. These turrets survive intact, however, on James Shaw's castle at Ballygalley (1625) in Co. Antrim. Sir James Hamilton's building at Killyleagh (*c.* 1624–26) also survives, incorporated in extensive later additions. Sir Basil Brooke, who obtained the confiscated O'Donnell property, enlarged and renovated the castle at Donegal about 1623; along with other refinements he inserted the elaborate and ornate armorial Jacobean chimneypiece which has survived.

Possibly the finest of the Jacobean mansions built in Ireland was Portumna, in Co. Galway, still impressive though now only a shell, built in 1618 by Richard Burke, Earl of Clanrickarde. Necessarily these mansions were at least semi-fortified, with machicolations and firing-holes.

Norreys, who was Lord President of Munster, built himself a castle on the lands he acquired at Mallow, Co. Cork. Richard Boyle, the most outstanding and successful of the adventurers, created 1st Earl of Cork in 1620, laid out the town of Bandon in Co. Cork, which remained for centuries a Protestant stronghold, and built the Protestant church of Kilbrogan there in 1610. At Lismore, his seat, he repaired the ancient Cathedral of St Carthage for the use of the Protestant diocese and in the town of Youghal, where he also had a residence, he

built the almshouses which have survived, rare examples of early 17th-century buildings in Ireland.

Many Irish merchants and gentlemen had conformed outwardly to the Established Church for convenience while remaining loyal, privately, to the old faith, and sending their womenfolk and children to the Mass. The Jesuits spearheaded a counter-reform which flourished during the first forty years of the 17th century. One of them, Henry Fitzsimon, the son of a Dublin alderman, was active in reconverting the gentry of the Pale and celebrated Mass openly in 1596 in the capital before congregations of four to five hundred, with torch-bearing priests wearing vestments, and harpists and lute-players. He was arraigned before Archbishop Loftus and spent several years in prison, where he reconverted some of the inmates and the head warder.

Those Irish who nourished hopes that James I, the son of the unfortunate Catholic Queen of Scots, would be lenient to Catholics were quickly disillusioned. In 1604 the Presidency of Munster banned all 'Jesuits, priests and seminarists', accusing them of leading the people into sedition. A royal proclamation the next year ordered 'all Jesuits, seminary priests or other priests whatsoever made and ordained by any authority derived or pretended to derive from the See of Rome' to quit the kingdom of Ireland within five months. The recalcitrant southern mercantile towns had their commercial privileges curtailed by the Crown. Despite, or because of, the restrictions, resistance stiffened. The exiles were busy in the Irish cause abroad wherever possible; the clandestine traffic of priests, and students for the priesthood, flourished.

At Louvain the Franciscans set up a type-press to print books in Irish and from 1611 their catechisms in the native tongue circulated widely in Ireland. Some monasteries were repaired and, in the remoter areas, quietly reinhabited by the religious with the connivance of the owners.

The foundation-stone of Trinity College, the University of Dublin, established by Queen Elizabeth at the instance of the Primate, Henry Ussher, had been laid in 1593. The first Provost, Adam Loftus from Yorkshire, had come to Ireland as chaplain to the Viceroy and rose to be Archbishop of Armagh and of Dublin, Lord Keeper of the Great Seal, and Lord High Chancellor of Ireland as well. His excessive acquisitiveness was such that it was said that his right arm and hand had grown longer than his left from years of grasping and snatching. Loftus had twenty children and his descendants became pillars of the new Protestant aristocracy for three centuries, knights, earls and marquesses; and the name is still found in Ireland today.

Although Trinity was controlled by the Estab-

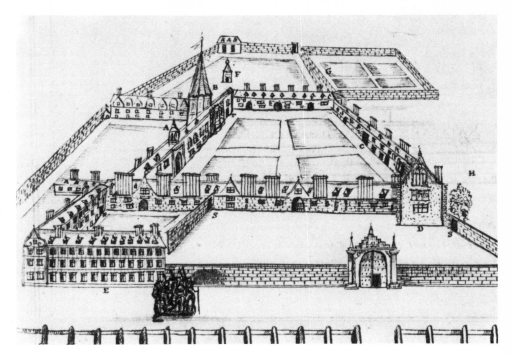

Trinity College, Dublin, founded in 1593 by Queen Elizabeth I, provided Ireland with a trained Protestant priesthood, so that soon Protestant clerics such as Archbishop James Ussher (who entered the college at its foundation and graduated MA in 1601) were as well versed in theology and Irish as their Catholic rivals. The eminent 17th-century Franciscan Luke Wadding referred to Ussher as 'the pseudoprimate' but admired and praised his learning. (11)

lished Church, a number of Catholic lay students were educated there during the first half-century of its existence. The Protestants in Ireland had suffered from the low calibre of the clergy who came over from England, for it was difficult to attract superior men to dangerous and uncomfortable Irish benefices which were not even lucrative. In 1598 it had been reported that some of the clergy had not even one word of Latin. Now, however, well-instructed clerics began to emerge from Trinity, versed not only in theology and the classics but also in the Irish language, which was taught there.

The discontent of the dispossessed and disadvantaged Irish festered. It went hand in hand with nationalism and with a passionate attachment to the old faith. So, within forty years of the siege of Kinsale, the settlers and the government had to face not this time an invasion, but a ferocious insurrection in 1641. It started in Ulster and spread rapidly through the island as the Irish rose in fury to reclaim their patrimony and position, falling on the settlers, murdering them, ransacking their goods and even desecrating their graves. Many old scores were savagely settled. Terrified settlers who fled to England with awful reports of assault, child murder, manglings, brainings and gory massacres, fanned the flames of anti-Irish, anti-Catholic feelings there. England itself was drifting towards civil war; the King, Charles I, was confronted by the mounting opposition of the Puritan Parliamentarians.

In all, several thousand settlers were murdered in Ireland. The violence and the rapid spread of the rebellion caused the virtual collapse of the English administration outside Dublin. At Kilkenny, where the rebels had ripped Bibles to shreds and stripped

Protestant clergymen naked in St Canice's Cathedral, the Catholics repossessed themselves of the cathedral. When their bishops met there in synod in May 1642 they concerted with Catholic nobles and military leaders and decided to set up a provisional government. A General Assembly convened; it established the Catholic Confederacy which, while confirming its allegiance to the monarch, refuted any claim to legislative power in Ireland by an English parliament. The influence of its ideologist, Patrick Darcy, on whose *Model of Civil Government* the Confederates' Declaration of Independence was based, may be discerned in the development of American constitutional and political ideas in the next century when the American colonists conceded their allegiance to the Crown but refuted the authority of the English Parliament over them as the Irish Confederates had done.

The Catholic Confederacy was formally recognized as the legal government of Ireland by France, Spain and the Holy See, but it was divided internally into two factions. One, principally of the old Irish of Gaelic extraction, really viewed King and Parliament only as a lesser and a greater evil respectively. Objectively it must be admitted that as far as their interests went they were right. This faction grew increasingly adamant in its refusal to support a heretic king even against a common enemy. The papal nuncio, Archbishop Giovanni Battista Rinuccini, who arrived from Italy with gorgeous ecclesiastical apparel, spent four years in Ireland and became the leader of this faction. His ultramontanism was obnoxious to the Earl of Ormonde, the leader of the other faction, which was composed mostly of Hiberno-Norman aristocracy

The End of the Old Order 121

Tracts such as this, published in 1647, exaggerating the atrocities committed by Irish insurgents against the settlers, fanned the flames of Protestant feeling in England, and helped to provoke the even worse cruelties of Cromwell's conquest in 1649. (12)

and Catholic Palesmen, traditionally loyal to the Crown. In a desperate welter of intrigue, conflicting loyalties, distrust, intransigence, incomprehension, deception, excommunication and interdictions, the Catholic bishops, nobles, gentry and people were divided among themselves in a theological as well as a civil war. United they might well have withstood the Parliamentarians, but divided they were all grimly defeated.

From Drogheda to the Boyne

The reconquest of Ireland was carried out by the most efficient army in Europe, led by the ablest soldier, a man of rigid Puritan principles and iron determination. Cromwell's appalling cruelty at Drogheda, which he took in 1649, was a foretaste of his merciless intentions. Even in a time and country where brutality was no rarity Cromwell's ruthlessness was extraordinary. Thousands of Irish were butchered at Drogheda, many in St Peter's Church where they sought sanctuary; a few wretched survivors were deported to the West Indies to be slaves. The barbarity was soon repeated at Wexford where over two thousand among priests, religious, soldiers and townspeople were slaughtered. When Kilkenny fell to the Cromwellians the eighty-year-

old Catholic Bishop David Rothe, the author of *Analecta*, was stripped and humiliated. Throughout the country, churches were desecrated, sacred books and pictures destroyed, priests hunted down and banished. Those who contrived to remain disguised themselves as labourers or herdsmen. Cromwell felt himself anointed to smite the Catholics, whom he considered idolaters, as the God of the Israelites had destroyed their idolatrous enemies.

In 1653, the victorious English Parliament passed an Act which confiscated *all* land in Ireland; grants, deeds and patents became worthless papers overnight. Ten counties, Antrim, Armagh, Down, King's (Offaly), Limerick, Meath, Queen's (Leix), Tipperary, Waterford and Westmeath, were then set for distribution among English adventurers and soldiers. Land in Ireland was subscribed for by 1,360 adventurers; an eleventh county, Louth, was allotted as an additional security for them. Four counties, Carlow, Cork, Dublin and Kildare, were reserved for disposal by the government to pay its debts, save two baronies in Dublin and one in Cork which were earmarked to raise the money to liquidate the arrears due to maimed English soldiers and soldiers' widows. In 1654 another four counties, Donegal, Leitrim, Longford and Wicklow, had to be assigned to raise the arrears still due to the military. The crushing campaign had been costly, the debenture holders who had helped to finance it had to be paid off and the officers of 1649 pressed for their pay, long overdue. All but four of the remaining counties were additional security for the army; the four, Clare, Galway, Mayo and Roscommon, all west of the Shannon, in Connacht, were reserved for a sinister purpose. The former Catholic landowners of the rest of Ireland were listed and systematically transplanted from their former homes to the degradation of this Irish 'reserve' which was surrounded by a mile-wide belt settled by English military. About two thousand families were thus forcibly moved, some being followed by their former tenants and workers.

After Cromwell's death and the restoration of the monarchy, the government of the new King, Charles II, was faced on his return from exile with a massive problem in Ireland: whom to oust? whom to pardon? whom to reward, and how? In the 1660s the Commissioners of the Acts of Settlement meted out a justice that was convenient to an impoverished government. Those Catholics who managed to have themselves qualified as 'Innocent Papists' were restored to at least part of their patrimony. Many Cromwellians were pardoned and allowed to retain their spoils and form the backbone of a loyal Protestant ascendancy. The same Earl of Ormonde who had fallen out with Rinuccini and remained a

Fol: 159

Cromwell's attack on Drogheda in 1649, a contemporary wooduct. The massacre which followed was part of a deliberate policy of terrorizing the population. It succeeded in this but the bitterness it aroused outlived any political advantage. (13)

faithful Royalist became the Duke of Ormonde and ruled Ireland for the King as his viceroy. Ormonde, born a Catholic and raised as a Protestant by government order, was a convinced member of the Established Church; but he was an intelligent, tolerant and unbigoted man.

The Catholic Irish were still the victims of discrimination, of the government policy to maintain a pro-English Protestant ascendancy, and of such unfair restrictions as a new tax imposed on the householders of the principal towns, mostly Catholics, for the support of the Protestant clergy. All schoolmasters were supposed to take the oath of allegiance and supremacy but a number of Catholic schools flourished, albeit inadequately housed, and in several, like that of the Jesuit Father Stephen Gelosse near New Ross, Co. Wexford, which in 1669 had 120 Catholic and Protestant scholars, youths of both religions studied together. No attempt was made to interfere with Catholic worship. Certainly all was not forgotten, far less forgiven, but the Viceroy's policy of 'live and let live' permeated the country, and it did seem to many that a peaceable coexistence might be achieved.

Wary landlords in the rural areas preferred to remain in their semi-fortified tower houses despite the discomfort of those medieval buildings, preferring the protection of the bawn wall, the slit windows, firing-holes and machicolations, in case of further trouble, to the gracious style of a classical mansion. The bolder and more optimistic built new

unfortified residences, of which examples can be cited in many different parts of the country. The handsome Beaulieu in Co. Louth, built by the Marshal of the Army about 1662 with brick dressings, dormers, fine interior wood-carving and cantilevered eaves carried on carved Baroque consoles, survives, still inhabited by descendants of its first owner. Eyrecourt, in Co. Galway, a house of about the same date, is a ruin; its magnificently carved staircase with elaborate finials was sold to a museum in America when the house was dismantled. Ballintober, in Co. Cork, reminiscent of a château in France, with wings 'en echelon' and fine formal gardens, has vanished; the pink-brick classical Carolean mansion of the Mathew family at Thomastown, Co. Tipperary, was engulfed in later additions, now all a ruin. Of the Kilruddery, Co. Wicklow, of Charles II's time, the formal gardens with twin canals survive and attest to the presence of style and grace in living that came to Ireland in the years when Ormonde was viceroy. At Burton Hall, in Co. Cork, another splendid house of the period which has vanished, the Percivals lived in fashionable luxury among rich velvet and silk hangings, furniture inlaid with tortoise-shell and ivory, and paintings of classical subjects. Few 17th-century country houses have survived; Richhill, Co. Armagh, is one exception; Waringstown in Co. Down, and the more modest Turret at Ballingarry in Co. Limerick, are others; these have curvilinear gables, but the last two have undergone alterations

The End of the Old Order 123

KNAVE

4 3

Tyrconel arming ye Papists in Ireland.

This English playing card of about 1689 casts James II's Viceroy, the Earl of Tyrconnell, as the Knave. When James was expelled from England Tyrconnell held Ireland for the Catholic cause. Macaulay called him 'lying Dick Talbot . . . Bully, Bravo, Pimp, Sycophant, Hypocrite . . .' A more charitable writer commented: 'Whatever were his faults he had the rare merit of sincere attachment to an unfortunate Master'. (14)

over the years. The demolition or conversion of so many houses of the late Stuart period and the absence now of much of the artistic production of that time, can give an erroneous impression that little or none ever existed, which appears to be quite incorrect.

Under Ormonde's brilliant patronage viceregal society in Ireland enjoyed for twenty-five years some of the gaiety, artistic activity and style that characterized Restoration England. The Viceroy attracted to Ireland the English painter James Gandy who came over in 1661; a former pupil of Van Dyck, he energetically copied the works of his master and painted portraits. Several of his works embellished the Ormonde castle at Kilkenny, which had a notable collection of paintings and tapestries. The Duke remodelled the medieval building to give it the appearance of a French château. Not far from the town the Duchess built Dunmore, a fashionable brick mansion. The building activity on and about the Ormonde estates was rivalled by the intensive

building in the capital, where the Viceroy promoted and encouraged the expansion of the city, applauded by an eager corporation. Dublin, not least among the mercantile towns, was enjoying an increase in the export trade. Yearly up to twenty thousand ounces of silver were assayed there and the silversmiths produced plate of excellent quality and design. The Guild of Dublin Cutlers, Painter-Steyners and Stationers (the Guild of St Luke) founded in Dublin in 1670 gave official recognition to artists. The College of Physicians was founded in 1667. In the new development of St Michan's parish across the river a new church was built, and several hundred houses erected for people of some substance. In the old city, the medieval parish churches like St Audoen's were repaired or, like St Werburgh's, St Bride's, St John's and St Peter's, rebuilt, often with more haste than care. In the frenzy of building, one new church, St Andrew's, was so jerry-built that it was not long before it collapsed. The topographical artist Francis Place (1647–1728), who was probably brought over from England by the Viceroy, has left some views which record Dublin in Ormonde's day. Other artists were attracted from England by the opportunities in Dublin; the most successful was Thomas Pooley, a prolific portraitist who had many clients at about twenty pounds per canvas. His closest rival in Dublin was Gaspar Smitz from Germany or Holland who was also active in the 1680s. John Michael Wright the elder, a court painter to Charles II, painted portraits in Ireland in 1679–80, although it is not known whether his portrait of Sir Neill O'Neill as an *Irish Chieftain*, rather surprisingly shown with Japanese armour at his feet, was actually painted in Ireland or not.

Another English virtuoso, Sir William Robinson, was the leading architect in Ireland. He designed the finest 17th-century building in the country, the elegant Royal Hospital at Kilmainham, Dublin, commissioned by Charles II in 1679 at Ormonde's suggestion, to accommodate disabled soldiers and veterans. Built in the classical style, it has florid Carolean plasterwork and some fine wood-carving by James Tabary, one of the refugee Huguenot artisans whose activity and skill added much to the artistic output of Dublin craftsmen.

The prosperity of Dublin and the gaiety of its society were not reflected throughout the country. The harpists played, but often only to accompany mournful and patriotic songs which reminded the Irish of what they had lost. The people engaged in their favourite pastime of dancing, and enjoyed relaxed conditions; but events such as the execution of the Catholic Primate, St Oliver Plunket, in 1681 for his supposed part in the 'Popish Plot', re-awakened old grievances and seriously damaged

Irish-English and Catholic-Protestant relations.

Then with the death of Charles II in 1685, the Irish found themselves for the first time since the death of Mary Tudor subject to a Catholic monarch, for James II was an avowed member of the Church of Rome. At once he appointed a Catholic as his viceroy in Ireland, Richard Talbot, Earl of Tyrconnell.

The Viceroy raised a Catholic army in Ireland to support the King; but this only added to his unpopularity in England, where anti-Catholic sentiment was considerable and anti-Irish feeling strong. In 1688 James had to flee to France. His Protestant daughter and son-in-law, Mary and William, succeeded to his throne; but in Ireland the Viceroy held the whole country, save the towns of Enniskillen and Derry, for James. Backed by Louis XIV, James landed in Ireland at Kinsale in March of 1689. These were heady days for the Irish and the future looked very bright if not entirely clear. A Catholic Parliament reversed the Act of Settlement and passed an Act confiscating almost all Protestant property. For the first time a Catholic was appointed Provost of Trinity College. A Catholic university was established at Kilkenny.

The triumph was shortlived. The Irish were at long last, virtually for the first time ever, united among themselves under a Catholic monarch. However, alliances on the Continent had changed. James's enemy, his son-in-law William, was in alliance with the Emperor, to whom he gave assurances of his intention to treat the Catholics well if he defeated James in Ireland. James was supported by France. The Holy See had worked for over a century for a Catholic king in Ireland, but now that there was one the Pope was not on his side. Because of his quarrel with France, the Pope, Alexander VIII, was aligned with the Emperor and the Protestant hero 'Good King Willy' against France and the Catholic, James.

Just as the city leaders in Derry weakened and decided to surrender, the apprentice boys defiantly slammed the city gate and the Protestant population determinedly held on in the besieged town until they were relieved by the English fleet, in July 1689. The pluck of the Derry apprentices is still commemorated by the Protestant majority in Ulster, for whose ancestors King William III, who arrived in Ireland the next year, 1690, was a delivering hero. William and his able general, Schomberg, with a force of 36,000 including many Danes, Germans and Dutch, superior in numbers and in training to James's army, defeated the Irish at the Battle of the Boyne in July 1690. James, never a sticker, readier to flee than to fight, returned to France; but his army continued to fight for the now divided country. The Irish were again defeated by William's army under

his Dutch general, Ginkel, at Aughrim in Co. Galway in July 1691 and in October of the same year General Sarsfield was obliged to surrender Limerick on terms to William's besieging forces.

As part of the terms of surrender the King promised the Catholics protection from religious persecution and the same limited religious freedom that they had enjoyed in the reign of Charles II. To placate Protestant opinion in England the King subsequently shamelessly repudiated these terms just as he broke his promises to the Emperor not to mistreat the Catholics, and his promises to the Irish before the Battle of Aughrim that Catholics would, under his rule, have a share in government, freedom of worship, and restoration of their estates and of one-half of all the churches in the country.

The Penal Laws: a century of oppression

As soon as William III was free of his obligations to his Catholic allies on the Continent, with whose support and the consequent tacit support of the Pope he had taken Ireland, he sanctioned the enactment of the Penal Laws, passed between 1702 and 1715. Over a million acres were confiscated and the harshest restrictions ever were imposed on the Catholic population. All the Catholic hierarchy were ordered into exile under pain of imprisonment or deportation. The religious orders were similarly banished and forbidden to return. Diocesan parish priests had to register and provide sureties for their loyal and obedient behaviour. Catholics were barred from public office, from Parliament, from the university, the Bench and the Bar; they were totally disenfranchised and even forbidden to teach in or keep schools. Severe restrictions were imposed on land tenure so that a Catholic who changed his religion could claim all the family estate to the exclusion of his father and brothers, and a few were tempted to do this. Protestant 'Discoverers' who reported on Catholic neighbours whom they could find in breach of the Penal Laws were awarded their property in return; a number of despicable men enriched themselves by this method. Kinder Protestants and converts of convenience held property in trust for their disabled Catholic friends and kindred.

About one-half of the officers and soldiers of the Jacobite army, ten thousand men or so, with, or followed by, their dependents, left for the Continent after their defeat at Aughrim and the surrender of Limerick. James II was to end his days in exile at St-Germain-en-Laye under the protection of Louis XIV, surrounded by a court in exile, composed largely of his Irish émigré subjects. Many settled permanently in France, where their descendants rose to fame like MacMahon, Duke of Magenta and

Marshal of France, or Henry Clarke, Duke of Feltre and Minister of War. Many fought in the Irish Brigades on the Continent in the service of France and Spain or as mercenary officers and soldiers where Catholics were welcome in Austria and in Russia, so that O'Rorkes can be found in Russia to this day, Taafes, Hegertys and O'Donnells in Austria, Walshes and Dillons in France, Murphys, Butlers, Kindelans and O'Briens in Spain and O'Neills in Portugal, to name but a few. Irish communities flourished in Liège, Nantes, Bordeaux, Oporto, Lisbon, Madrid and Cadiz, where a number of merchants were established.

The Penal Laws forced many proud and ambitious Irish to leave the country in the decades after the Jacobite defeat, to escape oppression, humiliation and servility. These young men, the 'Wild Geese', debarred from the professions and the army, and landless, sought a career and a place in society abroad. Perhaps the most successful was Ambrose O'Higgins who claimed descent from a dispossessed landowning family in Co. Sligo but left them in reduced circumstances in Co. Meath. He went to South America and rose to be Viceroy of Chile.

The departure of many of the best elements among the Irish and the severe restrictions imposed on those that remained left the settler families free to enjoy the fruits of the conquest, to profit from their privileges and to create their own society. Irish pride in that society is bound to be slightly ambiguous, since it depended directly on an alien and oppressive regime and the great majority of the Irish people were excluded from it. Gaelic culture went underground, and not until the 19th century did it re-emerge as a living force, as we shall see in a later chapter. But before that we must look in detail at what is by any standard one of Ireland's most splendid periods, that of the Protestant Ascendancy.

5

THE NEW CULTURE

Domestic Life and the Arts, 1680-1830
ROSEMARY FFOLLIOTT

Painting and Sculpture
ANNE CROOKSHANK

Hers were the fruits of a family tree :
A china clock, the Church's calendar,
Gardeners polite, governesses plenty,
And incomes waiting to be married for.

From *The Woman of the House* by Richard Murphy

Peace and prosperity came to Ireland in the 18th century. If it was peace at the price of harsh and unequal laws and prosperity only for a minority, the country was at least spared the anarchy of the 16th century and the hideous massacres of the 17th. The long Middle Ages were at last over.

The Penal Laws which followed William's victory at the Boyne meant the eclipse of one Ireland (Gaelic-speaking, Catholic and ancient) and the rise to prominence of another (English-speaking, Protestant and relatively recent). But the division was not clear-cut, since intermarriage occurred and the Protestant ranks were by no means unified. Moreover, as the century wore on the Penal Laws relaxed and some Catholics found it possible to gain wealth and influence. Above all, it is misleading to see one side as truly Irish and the other as alien. Both had a right to the name, and one of the most significant themes of 18th century Irish history is the growth of a national consciousness that united both. By the 1780s a middle-class Irish Protestant might well feel that he had more in common with an Irish Catholic than

with an English Protestant. Protestant Irishmen of English descent like Robert Emmett and later Parnell emerged as the most fervent of Irish patriots.

Socially and artistically, Ireland took its place again in the mainstream of European culture, a place which it had not occupied for nearly a thousand years. Dublin grew into one of the most perfect of Georgian cities. Architecture, painting and sculpture all flourished, but perhaps even more outstanding were the arts of domestic life for the town houses and country estates of the landed gentry—furniture, stucco, textiles, silver and glass—which reached a peak of sophistication.

The family shown opposite is that of John Foster, the last Speaker of the Irish House of Commons. It is 1786, and he leans against the portico of his seat, Oriel Temple (built in a demesne of 1,000 acres in Co. Louth), with his wife, née Margaret Burgh. She was created Baroness Oriel in 1790. The girl and two boys are their children. The artist, John James Barralet, was born, and practised, in Ireland, but emigrated to America a few years after this picture was painted. (1)

128

Architectural fashions were late in reaching Ireland. When William van der Hagen painted his view of Waterford in 1736 almost every house still had 17th-century Dutch gables, and only the arcaded Exchange in the centre is at all up-to-date. Yet they had all been rebuilt since 1699. (2)

The Cosby family home, Stradbally, Co. Leix (below), shows the old and new side by side. In the 1720s or 30s the right-hand block, with its pediment, was grafted on to the older house. The estate granted to Francis Cosby in 1592 was still in the possession of his descendants in 1977. (3)

Carton, Co. Kildare (below), forfeited by the Viceroy Tyrconnell, was bought by Lord Kildare. Between 1703 and 1711 he added a new Palladian façade and wings to the old house, still visible behind. This view is by Van der Hagen, and shows the home as it was before 1738, amid its formal gardens. (6)

The new Dublin was the most obvious sign of restored political stability. From about 1700 an impressive programme of church and public building in the classical style began to give a new character to the city. This first phase culminated in Leinster House (left), designed in 1744 by Richard Castle for the Earl of Kildare. (4)

Trinity College Library was begun in 1712 to the designs of Thomas Burgh, though the interior dates largely from the 1720s. The College went on growing throughout the century, acquiring its monumental façade to College Green between 1752 and 1760. (5)

On the great estates the gentry abandoned their uncomfortable old houses for lavish new mansions. Ireland lacked great country houses of the 16th and 17th centuries, so that the Palladian architecture of the 18th formed a particularly unified and consistent series.

Powerscourt (left) was another work of Richard Castle, the most influential architect of the first half of the century. Set amid the splendid scenery of Co. Wicklow, its effect was one of dramatic grandeur. Sir Richard Wingfield came into the property in 1608, and the house seen here incorporated part of an older one of that date at the back. The central block has recently been destroyed by fire. (7)

Mount Ievers Court, Co. Clare (below left), is an example of the less ambitious country mansion. It was designed and built for Col. Henry Ivers JP in the 1730s by Dublin mason-architects named Rothery. Only the main façade is dignified with stone; the garden front, seen here, is built in more economical red brick. Instead of the present picturesque fields and woods, formal gardens originally surrounded it. (8)

Castletown, Co. Kildare, was the house which set the style for Irish Palladianism. Begun in 1719, it was widely admired and imitated. It was built for 'Speaker' Conolly, who rose from modest origins in Co. Donegal to be the richest man in Ireland. His architect was the Italian Alessandro Galilei. Castletown's plan follows the Palladian model fairly closely, but the elevation is remarkably severe. Like Carton, it consists of a large central block with wings connected by quadrant galleries. (9)

Inside these houses the life-style was relaxed and elegant. Class division was not rigid, and successful merchants could enter the ranks of the gentry without undue difficulty.

The Conolly family lived at Castletown until 1965. Tom Conolly, the Speaker's great-nephew, inherited it in 1754, and a vivid record of life there in his time is provided by the paintings of Robert Healy; they include this one (detail above) of Conolly and his friends hunting. (10)

The Batesons settled in Ulster from Lancashire. Thomas Bateson acquired the lands of Orangefield, Co. Down, and after his marriage in 1747 to the widow of a wealthy Dublin merchant, he purchased another large estate in Derry. This group by Philip Hussey (left), painted in 1762, includes Mrs Bateson, her daughter and three sons. The self-possessed eldest, also Thomas, is ten years old. (11)

At the top of the social tree were the Dukes of Leinster (formerly Earls of Kildare), whose demesne was at Carton. The lake was made in the 1760s. A painting (left) by Thomas Roberts shows the second Duke and his Duchess entering a boat to cross over it. (12)

A satirical view of Irish manners is provided by certain paintings by Herbert Pugh. *Lord Granard having his wig powdered* (right) has a touch of Hogarth. The family was of Scottish descent and settled in Co. Longford in 1620. (15)

The men cultivated an image of prowess in the field of sports and it is rare to find a full-length portrait that does not include a dog. Mr Windham Quin of Adare, Co. Limerick (above) was MP for Kilmallock from 1769 to 1776. The painting is by Stephen Slaughter, an Englishman who worked in Ireland in the 1730s and 1740s, influencing Irish artists like Philip Hussey. (13)

The ladies followed the London fashions—five to seven years late. Families were large but women in general suffered fewer restrictions than in England. These girls at the harpsichord, painted by James Latham about 1740, are probably connections of the Leslie family of Tarbert House, Co. Kerry. The music is by Handel, a reminder of his popularity in Ireland. (14)

The provincial cities looked to Dublin as their model but could never equal her. The artist Nathaniel Grogan was a native of Cork and his views of the city show a mixture of the ambitious and the humble, the old and the new. Here Lord Barrymore's coach and pair leaves Cork by the North Gate. (16)

Dublin Castle, by contrast, was the magnet to which Irish society was drawn. A contemporary painting of a ball in the Castle in 1731 is naive in style but expressive of some magnificence. The ballroom, described in a letter as 'finely ordered with paintings and obelisks', had been decorated by the architect Edward Lovett Pearce. In the centre, opening the ceremony, is the Viceroy, the Duke of Dorset, and his Duchess. (17)

Daughter of the house: Miss Sarah Cosby, later Lady Farnham (above), was the daughter of Mr. Pole Cosby of Stradbally Hall, Co. Leix (see pl. 3). This charming portrait is by James Latham and dates from about 1745. Latham, born in Co. Tipperary, studied at Antwerp, but seems to have spent most of his working life in Ireland. His mastery of drapery and lively handling of texture make him the best resident Irish painter of the whole century. (18)

Of strong Protestant opinions but licentious habits, Charles Coote belonged to a family founded by an English Captain of Foot who fought at Kinsale and settled in Ireland. Created Earl of Bellamont in 1767, he was given the Knighthood of the Bath 'in testimony of his good and laudable service in suppressing tumultuous and illegal insurrection in the northern parts of Ireland'. A splendidly Baroque portrait (right) by Sir Joshua Reynolds shows him in the robes of that order, and manages to convey at the same time both the 'refinement' and 'dazzling polish' which some of his contemporaries saw in him, and the 'disgusting pomposity' which was what impressed others. (19)

The Rococo brilliance of Irish plasterwork in the mid-18th century surpasses that of England. Above: part of the hall of No. 20 Lower Dominick Street, Dublin, by Robert West. Above right: the figure of Faith from the Rotunda Hospital Chapel, by Bartholomew Cramillion. (20,21)

Bantry House, Co. Cork (opposite), was built about 1750 but enlarged in 1845 by the 2nd Earl of Bantry to accommodate his collection of works of art. The dining room shown here boasts fine Irish Chippendale furniture and splendid portraits of George III and Queen Charlotte in even more splendid frames. (26)

The minor arts of the first half of the 18th century bear witness to the flowering of Irish talent that the long peace of the Ascendency brought forth. Above left: a quilt embroidered in Belfast, signed and dated by 'Martha Lennox, 1712'. Centre: a coffee pot, with a dog stalking a pheasant through its luxuriant arabesques. Right: goblet

made for Archbishop Cobbe about 1745, engraved to the memory of King William and Queen Mary 'and perpetual disappointment to the Pope, the Pretender and all enemies of the Protestant religion'. Below: panel for the organ-loft of St Michan's, Dublin, probably carved by John Houghton about 1725. (22–25)

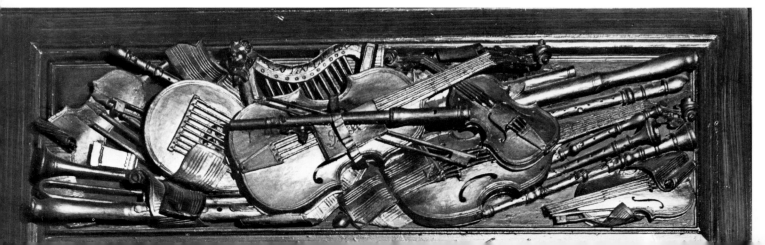

Dublin's renewal continued throughout the century, until by 1800 there was little to be seen that was more than a hundred years old. The public buildings, the palatial houses of the wealthy, the wide streets, elegant squares and terraces and even many humbler dwellings of the artisan class all reflect a consistently high level of taste and accomplishment. The engravings of James Malton give an excellent idea of its appearance—this one (below) shows Capel Street, one of the two thorough-fares leading over the Liffey—but do not exclude social criticism: while the well-dressed visit the lottery office the poor beg in vain. (27)

National pride came into sharp focus with the Volunteer Corps, formed in 1778 to meet the threat of a French invasion. The movement spread rapidly, demonstrating a certain solidarity between all religions. In this detail from a large painting by Francis Wheatley (right), Lord Aldborough reviews the local Volunteers, who appear in the background on the left. In the carriages are members of his family and household. Belan, Co. Kildare, the house in the distance, was designed by Richard Castle and built in 1743. (28)

Architects from abroad were invited to Ireland by sympathetic patrons. Most of those who came stayed for only short periods, but James Gandon, a pupil of Sir William Chambers, arrived in 1781 and remained for the

Sir William Chambers never crossed the Irish Sea, but he designed what is perhaps Dublin's most perfect building, Lord Charlemont's Casino, Marino, Clontarf, begun in 1759. It cost £60,000. (30)

rest of his life, designing the three major public buildings of Neo-Classical Dublin, the Custom House, the Four Courts and the Kings' Inns. The Custom House (above), built between 1781 and 1791, is a work in the grand

James Gandon by William Cuming and Tilly Kettle: in the background are the Four Courts on the left and the Custom House on the right. The plans are of the Four Courts, commissioned in 1785. (31)

manner, its long façade cleanly articulated by central portico and end pavilions. The high dome on its drum dominates the seaward side of the city, and contrasts with the shallow dome of the Four Courts further west. (29)

Charlemont House, on the north side of Rutland (now Parnell) Square, was the town house of Lord Charlemont, and again he chose Chambers as his architect. In this view (below) it is the end house on the left, set back

The keystones of the Custom House are grotesque heads representing the rivers of Ireland (above: the River Bann). The sculptor was Edward Smyth, who collaborated on several of Gandon's buildings. (32)

behind the others. Rutland Square was laid out behind the Rotunda in the 1750s, with the idea that the profits from its pleasure gardens should support the hospital. (33)

Neo-Classicism rejected the artificialities of Rococo, concentrating on dignity, simplicity and truth. The fountainhead was of course Rome, and it was there that Robert Fagan, the son of a baker from Cork who settled in London, went to live. Fascinated by ancient civilization (he excavated at Selinunte in Sicily), he made a prosperous career painting Irish and English visitors, buying, selling and occasionally smuggling works of art, and became British Consul General in Palermo. This self-portrait with his second wife Lodovica Flajani was painted in Rome about 1803. Her topless costume can be documented in contemporary fashion, but the way her hand rests on her husband's shoulder and the extreme pallor of her colouring, almost approaching marble, make it likely that he is portraying her as his muse. (34)

Before the fragments of Antiquity the artist could only feel insignificant. James Barry, in a revealing and characteristic self-portrait (right), is holding his own painting *Cyclops and Satyrs*, but behind his head is the giant foot of a huge statue. Here Neo-Classicism is already half-way to Romanticism. (36)

Political events provided themes of heroic dignity in the last decade of the century, when rebellion, sparked off by the French Revolution, flared up in several parts of the country. Thomas Robinson's *Battle of Ballinahinch* (below) shows a clash which occurred in Co. Down on 13 June 1798 between an Irish contingent led by Henry Munro and Government forces under General Nugent. Robinson's painting, though based on eye-witness accounts, is firmly on the side of the Government. (35)

The art of the miniature gained in popularity in the latter part of the century, and there was a special fondness for painting them on ivory. John Comerford's portrait of an old man—possibly Charles Farran—is soberly realistic. The artist was born in Kilkenny and settled in Dublin about 1802. He gave up full-length portraiture to concentrate on the more lucrative miniatures. (37).

145

A wider world beckoned the patrons as well as the artists of the New Culture. Many gentleman went on the Grand Tour, collecting antiques and works of art for their seats in Ireland. Frederick Augustus Hervey, Earl of Bristol and Bishop of Derry (the 'Earl Bishop' after whom are named numerous Hotel Bristols on the Continent) was the most indefatigable traveller of them all. In this portrait by Hugh Douglas Hamilton he sits on the Janiculum Hill, the splendours of Rome spread out beneath him. (38)

The peer: John van Nost's tomb effigy of Charles Moore, 1st Earl of Charleville (1711–1764) is at Tullamore, Co. Offaly. Van Nost, who came to Ireland about 1749, spans the transition between Rococo and the more classical restraint that followed it. (39)

The sculptor: Christopher Hewetson was born in Kilkenny and probably trained under Van Nost before leaving Ireland to settle in Rome. In this portrait by his friend Anton Raphael Mengs he is seen working on a bust of Gavin Hamilton. (40)

In Rome connoisseurs could order work from artists as celebrated as Canova. An intriguing group portrait, also by Hugh Douglas Hamilton (above), shows him with his own *Cupid and Psyche*, carved for Col. John Campbell, and Campbell's friend the Irish painter Henry Tresham.

Hamilton lived in Rome for many years. He eventually went back to Ireland in 1791 and wrote to Canova ten years later complaining of attacks of *nervi* and of the fact that there was nobody in Dublin with whom he could talk about art. (41)

The Pope: Clement XIV by Hewetson. Hewtson rose to be one of the most fashionable sculptors in Rome, living there for over thirty years, but he continued to sign his work 'Christophorus Hewetson Hibernus'. Clement was Pope from 1769 to 1774. (42)

The Dean: posthumous portrait bust of Jonathan Swift by Van Nost. Swift, the greatest genius of the New Culture, was born in Dublin in 1667 and died there in 1745. Tied to Ireland against his will, he was yet a champion of the Irish. (43)

Bookbinding: 'The Gentleman and Citizen's Almanack', 1779, with intricate foliage sprays finely tooled on leather. (44)

Carving: Detail of the pulpit sculpted with heads of the four Evangelists by Richard Stewart for the Church of St. Werburgh, Dublin. (45)

Mirror chandelier made in Ireland between 1785 and 1790. (46)

Goblin mask on a mahogany side table; masks were a special feature of Irish furniture. (47)

Irish Delft bowl with basketwork sides, decorated by Peter Shee of Dublin between 1752 and 1757. (48)

Lion mask from another table, its vigorous flowing lines held in check by classical volutes. (49)

Decanter (left) engraved 'Ireland for Ever' with Irish harp and shamrock, c. 1800. (50)

Silver dish-ring (often called a potato-ring): it protected the table from hot dishes; this one is by David Peter of Dublin, 1763. (51)

Tea-caddy of silver, by Matthew West of Dublin, 1773. The hinged lid is surmounted by a finial of ivory dyed green. The owner's crest or arms were usually engraved on such objects. (52)

Chapter 5

THE NEW CULTURE

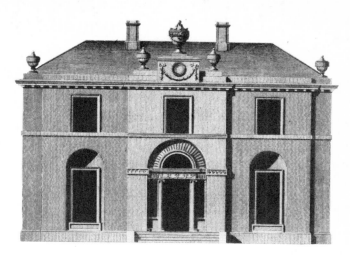

THE FINAL CRUSHING OF THE OLD GAELIC society by the Battle of the Boyne and its aftermath produced a vacuum into which the New Culture of the settlers moved quickly and inevitably. Since the Restoration these two societies had existed side by side, that of the newcomers dominant but not wholly unchallenged. Now the old order was gone and the newcomers stood alone.

Many of them were not such newcomers, either. Descendants of Elizabethan soldiers were now three generations Irish-born and it was the grandsons of Cromwellian soldiers who were the up and coming men. New arrivals were the Huguenot refugees and those who had followed William of Orange, but they were not numerous.

The description 'Anglo-Irish', so freely and indiscriminately applied to the holders of this New Culture, is an invention of the 20th century.

Richard Morrison's 'Useful and Ornamental Designs' of 1793 illustrates the way in which a European style, Neo-Classicism, could be adapted with perfect success to the economic needs of Ireland. (1)

Moreover it defies definition. It cannot be defined by race, for the settlers were soon intermarried with the Old English, Welsh, Scots, French and Gaels to a startling degree; nor can it be defined solely by religion, for it not only covered such nonconformists as Quakers and French Church, but a substantial number of settlers married Irish Catholics and left descendants who kept to the old faith; it is hard to define it by money, since the settlers came in all economic ranks, from peers to labourers. It is, in fact, a foolish description, best forgotten, and its most apt definition may well be Brendan Behan's – 'a Protestant with a horse'.

Domestic Life and the Arts, 1680–1830

ROSEMARY FFOLLIOTT

The opening years of the 18th century were characterized by quiet consolidation. There was a growing sense of security, a belief that a long overdue period of peace had come at last, a conviction further strengthened by the squashing of the Jacobite rising in Scotland in 1715. The lands forfeited by the losers of the Boyne were sold by the government to selected purchasers and provided a welcome chance for the ambitious to increase their property and invest available funds. Trade improved steadily and by the 1720s was in fair shape. The country was settling down.

Palladian essay 1700–40

The first obvious signs of stability were in Dublin where in 1703 Bishop Marsh founded his notable Library near St Patrick's Cathedral. Designed by Sir William Robinson, its red brick exterior is now beautifully mellowed: inside, the oak bookshelves

are arranged so as to form private studies into which readers could be locked to deter any light-fingered intentions. In 1704 Robinson's successor as Surveyor General, Thomas Burgh, designed the large Royal Barracks with its arcaded courtyard where eight regiments (four of foot, four of horse) could be lodged. In 1712 he embarked on the great Library for Trinity College, which was not completed until 1732. Like the Barracks it too had an arcaded ground floor, later closed in to increase storage space.

In 1707 a programme of extensive city church-building was begun, there having been hardly any churches erected for a hundred years and remarkably few repairs done to those in existence. Now, inside a decade, no less than seven churches were rebuilt within the inner city, all of the new, galleried type which persisted throughout the century. Public buildings were also in progress, starting with the Foundling Hospital in James's Street, then Steevens Hospital. The poor of Dublin were acutely poor and this was the impetus for a great wave of 18th-century charity building in the capital.

In the provincial towns and cities public building was also in progress. Cork acquired two churches (Christchurch and St Anne Shandon), Skiddy's Almshouses and a Custom House. The country gentry, who had not yet felt the lure of Dublin, were building houses for themselves in their local towns. Many of these have vanished but enough survive to show their quality – houses such as the Uniacke mansion in Youghal, the somewhat later house built in Roscrea by the Damers, and Kildrought House in the street of Celbridge, compare favourably with some of the surviving country seats of the same period. This was the age of the carpenter-joiner: houses were fitted with handsome timber staircases and panelled window-seats; walls were ornamented with wainscot in preference to plaster-work, thereby increasing dramatically their chances of destruction by fire. Such a house was Shannongrove, Co. Limerick, built in 1709 and, by the standards of twenty years later, relatively small. The reputation of the Irish gentry at this time was for a marked lack of interest in houses. Only a few sizable houses were built – Stackallen, Co. Meath (1716); Saunders Grove, Co. Wicklow (1716); Castle Durrow, Co. Leix (begun 1713); Buncrana, Co. Donegal (1716); and Killarney, Co. Kerry (c. 1726) were among the more notable. The lack of interest extended to the interiors, for inventories show that the contents of houses were meagre, with little or nothing by way of curtains or carpets, and furniture of oak, yew or deal, walnut being only for the rich. Although mahogany had come into use in wealthy households by the late 1720s, oak remained the staple wood of the middling gentry right up to the 1760s. A great deal of simple oak furniture must have existed, but the strange fact is that when the contents of numerous country houses were dispersed between 1930 and 1960 they included remarkably little oak furniture. Regarded in England as virtually indestructible, it apparently fell victim to the Irish attitude to 'that ould thing', age being inducive of contempt instead of respect.

Early 18th-century Ireland was surprisingly literate. Merchants, gentry and their womenfolk were well able to read and write. Books were printed and imported, bought and read and – in Dublin at least – handsomely bound. They feature regularly in wills and inventories, and the existence in the provinces of early 18th-century armorial bookplates (including some belonging to women) presupposes a sufficient collection to make them worthwhile. Before 'Alexander the Coppersmith' was published

in Cork in 1737, 273 persons subscribed to the issue, the bulk of them businessfolk in the city. The Irish middle classes regarded illiteracy as disgraceful and took good care to avoid it, except for the Presbyterian farmers of Ulster, who were less fussy. This middle-class literacy owed nothing to Trinity College, still the preserve of the well-to-do and of prospective clergy.

Money, always short below the top income group in Ireland, was extremely scarce in the first half of the century. The ambitious of the middle class were determinedly trying to make money: landowners would move from land to trade and back again with no loss of social position and usually a considerable increase in funds. A desirable bride was a merchant's daughter whose dowry (with luck) might be given in hard cash instead of being arranged as an annual charge on land, which would probably remain unpaid to become a cause of litigation. The settlers, to a great extent, married locally amongst themselves; this seems to have been caused less by religious than by economic differences. Except in Connacht, there was no sizable Catholic middle class of a standing similar to their own with whom they could intermarry. Those Gaelic families who had changed their religion and hence preserved their economic position, were fully acceptable matrimonially and the lower economic ranks of the settlers – who were numerous – married freely into their Gaelic equivalents, irrespective of religion; the descendants of some were Protestants and of others Catholics in no discernible pattern. In Connacht, where due to Cromwell's activities there was a substantial, educated, landowning and merchant Gaelic Catholic population, intermarriage and fraternization with the Protestant settlers was on a regular basis. This province devised an amicable arrangement whereby the sons followed their father's faith and the daughters their mother's, which seems to have avoided much dispute. In Ulster, owing to the different system of landholding imposed by the Plantation, there was a meagre middle class, the population being roughly divided into great Anglican landlords, small Presbyterian farmers and Catholic labourers. There was not one city with a really flourishing culture in the whole province: up to 1757 Belfast was a backwater, entirely owned by the feeble-minded 4th Earl of Donegall; Londonderry, although a port and a city, never achieved the cultural impetus of Cork, Limerick, Waterford or Galway; and the other towns remained nonentities. The result was that the rich of Ulster – the Conollys and the Caulfeilds – gravitated to Dublin.

William Conolly, from Donegal, Speaker of the Irish House of Commons and reputedly the wealthiest man in the island, was – as his name shows – of Gaelic origin. Nonetheless he was in the forefront when it came to establishing the New Culture. The building of his great Palladian mansion at Castletown, Co. Kildare, was the most important single event in the development of the 18th-century Irish life-style of the rich. Begun in 1719, it revolutionized Irish architecture by its introduction of Palladian principles, notably the twin pavilions linked to the main house by colonnaded curtain walls. Here, for the first time, Italian elegance stood against a grey Irish sky. The curious came to look and marvelled at what they saw: the first real idea that a grand house was a highly desirable asset was born.

Not only did William Conolly commission Castletown but in 1728, during his term of office as Speaker, Edward Lovett Pearce (who had worked at Castletown and succeeded Burgh as Surveyor General) was engaged to design a new Parliament House for Dublin. The Dublin Parliament, sitting much more frequently than in the past, was already growing in power and importance, and Pearce's *tour de force* brought it into further prominence. Although since added to and enlarged (first by Gandon, then by Francis Johnston), much of Pearce's building still stands and since 1802 has housed the Bank of Ireland. There was a psychological importance in this new Parliament House: it set a seal on the belief that peace and stability had come.

In a short career of only eleven years Pearce did much architectural work of importance – country houses such as Bellamont Forest, Co. Cavan, terrace houses such as those in Henrietta Street, Dublin (an area developed as his first great speculation by Luke Gardiner), town mansions in places as far removed as Boyle, Co. Roscommon, and Cashel, Co. Tipperary, suburban seats like Drumcondra House near Dublin, theatres such as that in Aungier Street, Dublin, and probably the Theatre Royal in Cork. His work was heavy, handsome and very good, decorated internally either by fine wainscot (as at Drumcondra) or stucco-work with Baroque tendencies (as in Henrietta Street) and elaborate, compartmented ceilings. In his time he was a giant. His time was that of Jonathan Swift, Dean of St Patrick's, of Thomas Prior, Samuel Madden, Bishop George Berkeley; a time when the Dublin Society was founded and when there was a relatively small but very choice literary and intellectual circle flourishing amid the social grandeur of Dublin.

Pearce's premature death in 1733 was less of a disaster than it might have been had there not been a worthy heir to his architectural abilities. The German-born Richard Castle (Cassels) had come to Ireland in 1728 to work on Castle Hume, Co. Fermanagh, and remained working on the Newry Canal, which was begun in 1731 and opened in 1742,

the first inland canal in the two kingdoms. He was well fitted to take over Pearce's practice in private works. His output was enormous and he popularized the Palladian principles first demonstrated at Castletown. The rich fell for Palladianism: it suited them exactly now that they had decided to turn their attention to house-building. Up to the 1730s only a tiny minority had felt any such urge: the majority demonstrated their wealth by their gorgeous clothes, their lavish entertainments, their horses and their hard drinking instead of by the elegance or appointments of their establishments. Castle changed this. Great Palladian houses arose both in Dublin and through the countryside – Powerscourt and Russborough in Co. Wicklow; Westport House, Co. Mayo; Hazlewood, Co. Sligo; Ballyhaise, Co. Cavan; and Kildare (later Leinster) House and Clanwilliam House in Dublin are all known to be of his design, and many other fine country residences built about the same period may be as well. Dublin acquired numerous cut-stone mansions: suddenly it became the fashion for the nobility to have a splendid house and they revelled in the novelty, vying with each other if not by building a new house then by re-modelling an existing one, as Castle was engaged to do at Carton, Co. Kildare. There was no veneration of the past: 18th-century Ireland looked with bored eyes on the stout Norman fortresses, on the decaying cagework houses in the towns, on the converted (or, worse still, unconverted) tower houses into which so many of the country gentry were still uncomfortably crammed. Should such properties chance to fall vacant there was no rush to occupy them: a new house was the smart thing to have. A few families who retained ancestral strongholds did continue to inhabit them, with due alteration. Cases in point were Kilkenny Castle; Donamon, Co. Roscommon; Curraghmore, Co. Waterford; and Rathfarnham, Malahide, and Howth, all in Co. Dublin. In most instances the alterations were extensive, the old indestructible keep being nearly submerged under new buildings; in rare instances, such as Donamon and Rathfarnham, the minimum was done and that not until the second half of the century.

To surround and embellish the great Palladian houses, extensive garden works were undertaken. Continuing the tradition of the 17th century, terraces and gravelled spaces were levelled, waterworks devised and trees planted. The usual layout was a series of separate walled or hedged gardens adjoining the house, some in full view of its windows, the walls being partly for shelter, partly to prevent pilfering of produce. Less positive divisions were effected by tree-lined radial walks. Avenues were straight, either aligned on the front door or approaching the façade at right angles. Even the

The Conolly Folly at Castletown had two purposes. One was to close the vista at the end of the main axis of the house. The other was to provide employment during the exceptionally hard winter of 1739. It was commissioned by Speaker Conolly's widow and designed by Richard Castle. (2)

grandest architects did not scorn to design pigeon-houses, ornamental gates, obelisks and eye-catchers. The big formal garden at Powerscourt, though not completed until Victorian times, was projected when the house was built, the terraces and Triton pond, on which the whole scheme focuses, being constructed at the same time as the house. Like house-building, gardening was fashionable and from the marriage of the two came the craze for follies. This appealed particularly to the Irish and took many forms – a Classical temple at Drum-condra (designed by Pearce), a 140-feet-high obelisk at Castletown, the highest and most elaborate obelisk in the two kingdoms, built to give employment during the hard winter of 1739 (designed by Castle), corkscrew barns, triumphal arches, shell-houses, bone-houses, grottoes, columns, cones, towers and fake ruins. The passion for follies continued unabated into the mid-19th century and was carried to remarkable and ingenious lengths, until Robert Watson of Larch Hill, Co. Meath, was constructing a fox's earth for his own use in a future incarnation! However, with the possible exception of Kilronan Castle, Co. Roscommon, the mania does seem to have stopped short of the fake hermitages, inhabited by unshaven, unwashed hermits, that were installed in England.

The interiors of the Palladian mini-palaces were imposing. Castle specialized in a large, rather heavy, flagged entrance hall which set the tone for the house. Excellent woodwork was installed and handsome stucco-work, gradually becoming lighter than in Pearce's day and steadily tending towards a new style of figure-work with allegorical and mythological subjects, sometimes even incorporating family portraits into the design. This elaborate figure-work was first introduced by the Italian Francini brothers, who in the 1730s were employed at Castletown by Speaker Conolly's grand-nephew and heir, at Carton by the Earl of Kildare, and later at Riverstown by Bishop Browne. Not much true Baroque stucco-work was done in Ireland, but the Francini's dining-room (now the saloon) at Carton, with its magnificent coved ceiling, does verge on the Baroque. Baroque influence also appears in the massive pedimented chimneypieces, mainly of Italian marble, which were outstanding features of these houses. Sadly, even before the end of the century a substantial number had been replaced by others in the Adam style.

The furniture was plain, and mainly of walnut, though mahogany was just coming into use by the 1720s. A touch of the exotic was supplied by the many 'japanned' (i.e. lacquered) pieces which included cabinets and tables as well as more humble items such as bellows and screens. Chairs often had caned or upholstered seats, the latter perhaps covered in silk or needlework, described as 'Turkey'. This was home-made by the ladies, working silk and wool in gros point, petit point or more rarely cross-stitch; surviving examples show that a very high standard was achieved. To present-day minds one of the strange features of the household arrangements was the negligible difference in the furnishing of a reception room and a bedchamber. Beds were everywhere. In 1736 Killeen Castle, Co. Meath, had a bed in every apartment (including the lobby) except the kitchen, dining-room and tea-room. The Scarlet Room seems to have been a sort of drawing-room, yet it too had its bed. Even as late as 1758 the inventory of Robert Fayle, a prosperous Quaker farmer in north Offaly, shows that he kept a bed in his 'parlour'.

Requirements for soft furnishings stimulated local industry. All through the 18th century Ireland was busy in the textile trade, despite the slump in woollen weaving during the early 1720s, against which Dean Swift fought so fiercely. In the 1730s imposing tapestries were being woven in Dublin, geared to local interest by depicting such subjects as the Battle of the Boyne and the Siege of Derry.

Clockmakers had been at work since the previous century, and the trade now spread to provincial centres like Cork. It remained closely allied to the goldsmith's trade, many goldsmiths being also clockmakers. The best early 18th-century longcase clocks were either of walnut or 'japanned', with flat tops to their hoods; bracket clocks were also made in plenty but did not survive so well. As trade increased so did the clockmakers until by the 1780s they were to be found in little towns like Nenagh and Monaghan.

Lead glass had been made in Dublin since the 1690s, and from at least 1729 until 1740 there was a flint glass manufactory at Gurteens near Waterford. Though much must have been made, little of this early glass has survived, with the possible exception of goblets engraved with toasts to and equestrian portraits of William III, although even these cannot be positively dated earlier than about 1745. In 1735 Joseph Martin of Fleet Street, Dublin, advertised that he was the only 'person in the Kingdom' employed 'carving glasswares', so obviously the bulk of glass was unengraved. In 1736 Killeen Castle possessed several 'sconces with glass branches', 'drinking glasses', a 'glass jug and decanter' and 'water glasses with servers', and that glass was available to the middling gentry is shown by the 1751 inventory of Mrs Neptune Blood of Co. Clare, who had 'decanters and other glasses' to the value of 18s. and $13\frac{1}{2}$ dozen empty bottles, assessed at 13s. 6d.

Handsomely framed looking-glasses were supplied by the Dublin firm of Booker for at least eighty years of the 18th century: it is uncertain whether their mirror plates were made locally or imported from Normandy. The splendid frames were certainly made in Dublin where there were excellent carvers and gilders.

Silver – known as plate – was being worked in all the chief towns, including Kinsale. In marked contrast to London, the Huguenot population of Dublin played a very minor part in the Goldsmiths' guild and were far from being its most notable craftsmen, who seem instead to have been of Scottish origin. Early 18th-century designs, made in heavy gauge metal, were severely plain, perhaps relieved by a border either gadrooned or with a scroll decoration, the whole emphasis being on good basic lines and an expanse of plain surface. This provided scope for the engraving of flamboyant armorial bearings similar to those used for bookplates. Some simple, serviceable church plate was made at this period – patens, chalices and flagons. Domestic piece silver included wine cisterns, sauce-boats, coffee-pots, chocolate pots, small tea-pots (though about 1730 silver ones were very widely replaced by china versions), tankards, beakers, two-handled cups (those with harp-shaped handles being peculiar to Ireland), bowls, castors, candlesticks, snuffers, salvers (often mounted on an applied foot)

and strawberry dishes. A selection of saucepans in assorted sizes, tea-kettles (incorporating a spirit lamp) and hot-water jugs were also made. For the less affluent, such utilitarian objects were, of course, supplied in pewter or brass. Cutlery differed little from that in England, consisting mainly of spoons, ladles, strainers and, from the 1730s, sugar nippers. Forks of the three-pronged and four-pronged variety, though in use, seem to have been scarce.

In the early 1730s cream jugs and cream boats made their appearance; helmet-shaped cream jugs mounted on a single foot were made only in Ireland, and a three-footed version was introduced as early as 1736–37. By the late 1730s some decorative chasing was being used with scrolls and diaper designs as well as human masks on foot knuckles, foreshadowing the delights of the Rococo soon to come.

Rococo heyday 1740–70

If the first forty years of the 18th century were a tentative experiment, the following thirty years were exuberant in their fulfilment. The young, confident New Culture had found its feet.

Economic results had been encouraging. Though ever scarce, money was circulating, and into areas it had never penetrated before. Roads had been laid out and were relatively good: after 1760 they were further improved under the charge of the Grand Juries. A network of important fairs had been established, leading to much-improved commerce, and also a network of race-meetings which produced a similar result. There was a brisk linen trade between Ulster and Dublin, and trade of all kinds plied between the ports. The gentry's venture into business had paid off, leaving them with enhanced capital, much of which found its way into the land. The same easy movement between land and trade continued as hitherto with no social stigma attached. Higher education was available to clever but poor boys (many of whom became clergymen or schoolmasters) through the award of sizarships at Trinity College. This too was a period when a substantial number of fairly impecunious people graced the peerage, and their close relatives were to be found in almost every walk of life. Social rank depended on money rather than on origin or occupation: if a man made money he moved up because he could afford to live on a grander scale; if he lost money he moved down because he could no longer maintain the pace. The Registry of Deeds frequently chronicles the rise though not the descent: a man who starts as a 'tallow-chandler' or 'cabinet-maker' will presently turn into a 'merchant' and before too long become a 'gent' and, having made sufficient money, may even end up as 'Esq.'. Having made money in trade, the regular practice was to invest it in land since banks were, rightly, regarded as a risk and there was no stock market. This produced close links between land and town, further fostered by the fact that the bulk of such landlords as had a Dublin mansion still lived for a considerable part of the year on their country estates. Regular absenteeism was not yet a problem: only the very rich felt the lure of London – lesser fry preferring to be big fishes in the smaller pool of Dublin – and it was likewise only the very rich who could afford to disport themselves on the Continent. In consequence most of the Irish landlords stayed in their own island, to the great advantage of all.

The Penal Laws were at their most severe in the middle of the century, far more, of course, on paper than in practice, but still severe enough. To their credit, many Protestant gentry and merchants went to considerable lengths to help their Catholic neighbours overcome difficulties with land and business. When the land restrictions were lifted in the 1770s it became clear that a proportion of Catholics, particularly in Connacht, had contrived to retain some property, mostly by such co-operation. As opposed to this decent dealing, there were others who operated the infamous system of 'Protestant Discovery' whereby the 'discoverer' could legally seize a Catholic's land. Such 'discoverers' were not in general favourably regarded: it was held to be a dirty trick. Penal Laws notwithstanding, Catholics were in trade, including such crafts as clock-making, cabinet-making and stucco-work, though only rarely as goldsmiths. Their work, of course, fell into line with the prevailing New Culture.

At this period England and Ireland were linked and yet strangely separated. In general, only the sons of the very richest peers were sent to English schools; the remainder of the boys were educated in Ireland, some at well-known schools such as Kilkenny, Armagh, Midleton or Drogheda, others by being boarded as pupils with a clergyman (often a curate) who needed to eke out his stipend; a few had private tutors. In towns boys might attend either a school or a parson as day scholars. Between the ages of about fifteen to eighteen, if they were to receive further education, they went to Trinity College, which provided a sort of 'old school tie' in the way the public schools did in England. Budding barristers had to eat their dinners at one of the London Inns of Court, and medical students (if aspiring to something better than apprenticeship to the local apothecary) went to the universities at Glasgow, Edinburgh or Leiden; but these were the main educational destinations abroad. Only a few students attended English universities, and an even smaller number made a Continental Grand Tour. Those who did, like the future 1st Earls of Milltown and of Charlemont and the Earl Bishop of Derry,

brought back not only new ideas but a wealth of paintings and statuary.

Daughters were mostly educated at home, but to a reasonably high standard. All middle-class girls could write (though their spelling was erratic) and the women bore the burden of family correspondence. Initially, teaching was provided by mother, aunt or elder sister, more rarely by a governess. In the larger towns there were 'seminaries', both boarding and day, for the instruction of young ladies. It is difficult to assess how many girls from the age of ten onwards actually attended these establishments. What is not in doubt is the ability of the women. They were a notable breed. Below the economic class of such ladies as Speaker Conolly's widow, who pursued ambitious building schemes, many a merchant's unmarried daughter set up and ran a profitable school or a millinery or haberdashery or mantua-making business. It was customary for a wife to be appointed executrix of her husband's will and guardian of their children. In innumerable cases the widow took over her late husband's business or land and ran it successfully until their eldest son came of age. Bankruptcies among female-run businesses were extremely rare, for the women were both cautious and competent. Right into the mid-19th century they seem to have suffered fewer social restrictions and frustrations than in England, and were busy rather than ornamental. Those of country-gentry class managed their large households, often without a regular housekeeper, superintended the garden (and in many cases worked hard in it themselves), produced large broods of children (up to twenty-one is on record), doctored the neighbouring poor, nursed the sick of their own family and in addition led an active social life and took an interest in horses. Gentry and merchant girls were seldom married under seventeen years of age; twenty-five was common and over thirty not at all rare. Marriage between cousins was frequent, partly from propinquity, partly from considerations of property. In general marriages seem to have been arranged, though at times only to the extent of throwing a suitable pair together socially and hoping for the best. In most cases the girl appears to have had the right of veto, and some matches were genuinely devised by the couple, irrespective of family intentions. Since divorce could only be had with difficulty (and much social disgrace), mutually agreed separation was a more practical solution to domestic discords, though it did not permit remarriage. The practice of a married pair addressing each other as Mr and Mrs, which was so widespread in England, was not adopted in Ireland, probably because so many of them, being nearly or distantly related, had known each other as Tom and Betsy since childhood and would have felt exceedingly foolish had they started calling each other Mr and Mrs Bennett, as they do in Jane Austen. Terms of considerable friendship and close companionship seem to have been the rule with married couples of the middle class, possibly cemented by the mutual sorrows endured through the appalling rate of infant mortality. Relationships with children were usually good, inevitably sometimes strained between father and sons, habitually affectionate between mother and daughters, while sisters frequently retained close friendships despite marriages and the raising of children. Dogs were numerous and highly indulged: the character in Somerville and Ross's late 19th-century novel *Some Experiences of an Irish R.M.* who remarked that the house was rotten with dogs was describing a state of affairs that had lasted many generations. Almost every full-length portrait from the 18th century includes a faithful canine. Fashions in clothes lagged about five to seven years behind those of England up to 1790, when they suddenly drew level.

Family feuds were nasty when they arose. All originated over money, more specifically land charges (mortgages, annuities, marriage settlements) which remained unpaid, and which were taken to court but often not fully resolved and persisted for years as festering sores. Though cash might be scarce for other purposes, it was never stinted for litigation, of which the Irish were so exceedingly fond that an impoverished lawyer was virtually unknown. To become an attorney was the quickest way to prosperity, as many a younger son discovered. Illegitimate offspring were not uncommon and though their status varied they inevitably took their father's surname and frequently his religion. Many bastards were recognized, educated at their father's expense and received legacies under his will. Some even succeeded to the bulk of his property, usually when he had no legitimate heirs. In such instances they were wholly acceptable socially and both sexes would marry into the local gentry, another example of the economic origin of the social yardstick. If bastards were left in reduced circumstances they married accordingly. On the other hand a middle-class girl who produced an illegitimate child was thereafter totally unacceptable socially, with the result that remarkably few of them made this mistake, though chaperonage was never strict.

Visitors always exclaimed over the vast quantities of food and drink – especially claret – consumed by the gentry, seemingly grossly in excess of their means. There was regular and extensive smuggling along the south and west coasts, to which the local gentry not only turned a blind eye but which they actively encouraged. This partly accounted for the

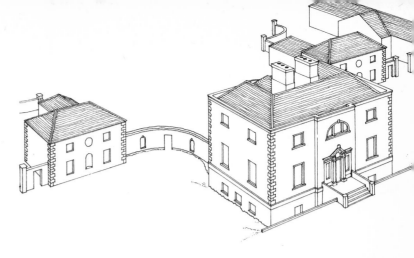

Colganstown, Newcastle, Co. Dublin. Built probably in the 1760s, this elaborately laid out farm-house follows a Palladian plan, with curved walls uniting the central block and the outbuildings. On the opposite side, the staircase is contained in a shallow bow. The interiors have rich stucco decoration. (3)

availability of cheap claret. No doubt this contributed to the high death-rate for middle-aged males: the women, who presumably ate less and certainly drank little, lived on average much longer despite the dangers of childbirth.

During this mid-century period the average gentleman had no great incentive to build a house. While there was much building in the cities and some in the towns, there was a lack of any master architect and the prevailing country-house style remained Palladian, out of reach of the mass of the gentry. A few, acting as their own architect, working from pattern books or copying a neighbour, did attempt houses, often with strange, mixed results, architecturally improbable but sometimes not without a certain naive charm. The architects Bindon, Clements, Ducart and their contemporaries did produce some small adaptations of Palladian ideas, but such houses were the exception, not the rule. The Sardinian Ducart, who was the most skilful of these, built some country houses of fine quality – Castletown Cox, Co. Kilkenny, and Kilshannig, Co. Cork, being among his best. The former, built about 1767, is held to be his masterpiece; it has splendid Rococo ceilings by the Waterford stuccodore, Patrick Osborne, whereas at Kilshannig, dating from a couple of years earlier, the plaster-work is by the Francini brothers, still active after nearly three decades in Ireland. Though Ducart delighted a sensitive minority, he failed to establish a widespread clientele. He also experimented with Baroque designs, as did John Roberts. While individual results were good – those of Roberts at Curraghmore very good indeed – no real enthusiasm was kindled for the style. The bulk of the gentry remained housed as before, many of the lesser fry in two-storied thatched houses, others in converted tower houses, while only an adventurous few risked a Palladian adaptation.

Radical and universal change in the immediate surrounds of houses appeared in the 1750s with the vogue for landscape gardening. Out went straight avenues, radial walks and formal parterres in view from the windows. In their place were laid out tree-dotted parks; avenues were re-routed to take long tours through these parks; lakes were formed or enlarged, and streams diverted. That Irish park planting was extraordinarily beautiful is obvious from what survives. It was all in hardwood – beech, oak, chestnut and elm being the most common.

Household goods were steadily improving: mahogany had come into general use for furniture, silver was being bought (often, like land, as an investment) and Dublin-made delft was doing good business. The delft factory was greatly expanded by Henry Delamain during the 1750s and some of its products, such as plates with open-work sides, tureens, baskets, sauce boats and pierced flower holders, were relatively ambitious. Decoration on plates included armorials (to special order), Chinese-type designs and rural scenes. These were dispatched for sale in towns as distant from the capital as Cork.

The provincial cities were booming. There was much public building – churches, mayoralty houses, custom houses and the like – though the great outbreak of court-house building did not come until after the Union. Limerick acquired an elegant Custom House by Ducart, Belfast an arcaded Market House, Kilkenny an arcaded Tholsel with a cupola and Dunlavin a remarkable combined Court and Market House. Handsome squares and terraces of houses were laid out in Limerick, Cork and Kilkenny, their interiors decorated with stucco-work in the latest Rococo taste. Inns were numerous and universally held to be bad, though travel was commonplace, to judge by the regularity with which luggage for the road was listed in inventories. Stage-coaches now ran on the main thoroughfares and post-chaises could be hired – at a price.

Touring companies of players from the Dublin theatres moved through the provinces, usually carefully timing their arrival to include the week of the local races. They performed a wide variety of plays, most of which are now forgotten, the chief exceptions being *The Beggar's Opera* and Shakespeare. Provincial newspapers made their appearance in the late 1730s in Belfast, in the 1740s in Limerick, in the 1750s in Cork, in the 1760s in Kilkenny and Waterford and in the 1770s in Tralee and Ennis. Many were short-lived; several survived indefinitely. Newspapers provided a fine means of advertisement of commodities for sale, and their importance in this field was even greater than in the dissemination of news, very little Irish news being printed in any case.

But the provincial cities paled in comparison with Dublin, acknowledged as the second city of the two kingdoms. Rococo's heyday was also that of Dublin, which was experiencing for the first time the true joys of a capital city. During a Parliamentary session – which was also the social season – it was full to bursting. Those who did not own a town house took lodgings and all available lodgings were habitually let. Part of Dublin's social success stemmed from the abysmal poverty of its poor, to allieviate which Dr Bartholomew Mosse organized his Rotunda Charity, a pleasure garden and Assembly Rooms which were favourably compared with those of Vauxhall in London. They enjoyed excellent patronage, and presented illuminations, entertainments and concerts (and in the 1770s operas), the money from receipts being applied to the Rotunda Lying-In Hospital, opened in 1757.

Dublin had grown steadily into a centre of good music: at the 'Musick Hall' in Crow Street, opened in 1731, was staged Handel's opera *Acis and Galatea* in 1734. In 1741–42 the composer visited Dublin and *The Messiah* had its first performance in the new Music Hall in Fishamble Street. The tradition continued, fostered by Lord Mornington (father of the future Duke of Wellington) and his 'Musical Academy', until in the 1760s Italian-type opera was being sung. Several theatres were offering a wide variety of plays, securing both local talent and leading actors from England.

Trinity College built its West Front in 1759 and then employed John Smyth to design an elegant Provost's House. He was the architect for two new churches (St Thomas's and St Catherine's) and also re-modelled the interior of St Werburgh's.

Dublin, in fact, was a boom city, full of exciting ideas, high living, much business, much pleasure, rakes, bucks, expensive whores and, beneath it all, desperate poverty. It was ripe for speculators, who multiplied exceedingly in the wake of Luke Gardiner as great new streets and squares were laid out. In 1757 the first Commissioners for making Wide and Convenient Streets were appointed, on the occasion of the construction of Parliament Street. This body, with greatly extended powers and manned by persons of remarkable taste and discernment, remained extremely influential until the Union. In 1762 John Ensor designed Merrion Square for Lord Fitzwilliam and the development of the south city followed quickly. The exteriors of the houses were plain, the individual mansions and public buildings faced with cut stone, the street terraces faced with brick in a style that survived, with only minor modifications, into Victorian times. But if the outsides were simple the insides were not. Nowhere was the exuberance of mid-18th-century Dublin more vividly displayed than in its

156   *The New Culture*

The Rotunda Lying-In Hospital, founded by Dr Bartholomew Mosse in 1751, was the first maternity hospital in the whole British Isles. Mosse's aim was to alleviate some of the appalling poverty in Dublin by using the profits from the adjoining Assembly Rooms and pleasure gardens to pay for the hospital. These proved extremely popular, and this satirical print shows them still frequented by the rich and fashionable in 1790. (4)

plaster-work. Out of favour were the handsome but heavy compartmented ceilings that had adorned Pearce's houses and Castle's early efforts. In the hands of the French Bartholomew Cramillion and of the Irish Robert West the new ideas first introduced by the Italian Francini brothers were brilliantly developed. Cramillion favoured the trend towards Baroque: his masterpiece is the small chapel of the Rotunda Hospital, designed by Castle to the order of Dr Mosse. The numerous figures are modelled in full relief: slender arms and hands reach out from the ceiling, flying putti hold up plaster curtains to form an altarpiece, while large personifications of Faith and Hope sit above the cornice, overflowing it just enough to break the rigidity of its line. One can only imagine it was a (wholesome) shock to the Low Church Irish gentry: clearly its grace went unappreciated, for it was never even remotely imitated.

Robert West, a Dubliner, was the great stuccodore of the period. He rejected the Baroque concept in favour of the vigorous, asymmetrical, naturalistic and highly inventive designs now loosely called Rococo (a term then unknown) and of which he proved himself a master. Birds were his speciality and became his trademark, but he also made lavish use of flowers and musical instruments. His eye was unerring. Designs which are entirely asymmetrical provide unrivalled visual satisfaction. His two best houses are thought to be 86 Stephen's Green and 20 Dominick Street. In the latter, the work on the walls of the staircase and staircase gallery is outstanding: fully modelled exotic birds crane forward from their perches on plaster consoles, caryatids emphasize the curves of the coved ceiling, while fruit and foliage swirl in a riotous profusion, almost as if emulating the dizzy whirl of the society for which they were executed. West's hand can also be seen in country houses near Dublin, such as Malahide Castle and the now ruinous Kinure Park. While working for the Cobbes at Newbridge near Donabate he even ventured into the parish church, incorporating the arms, motto and swan crest of the Cobbes into Rococo foliage on the ceiling of their private gallery. West had plenty of imitators throughout the country, where some excellent work is to be found, some of it so indistinguishable from his own that it may even be his, as at Florence Court, Co. Fermanagh, but unhappily, every indifferent bird is now ascribed to his hand. While the provincial stuccodores lacked his artistry they could turn out charming work which would be more highly regarded had it not to stand comparison with that of West himself.

Much of his work was soon lost. Its day was short, for within a mere twenty years fashion had turned whole-heartedly to the geometrical precision of Neo-Classicism and, in Dublin particularly, the outmoded, swirling Rococo work was pulled down to make way for the cool elegance wrought by Michael Stapleton and his fellow stuccodores. This was a major tragedy, for good as the Neo-Classical stucco-work is, it never attained the brilliance of the Irish Rococo. Fortunately provincial alterations were less drastic, and decoration like that of Francini's Kilshannig survived intact.

Next, perhaps, to plaster-work, the mid-century vigour is most evident in furniture, where the style now known as 'Irish Chippendale', but more truly Irish Baroque, was at its height. Some splendid pieces were made, all in dark mahogany from the West Indies (with which Ireland did a brisk trade), many showing the same taste for swirling and interlaced foliage as in the stucco-work. This was used mainly on the deep frieze of tables, which were boldly carved, sometimes pierced right through: backgrounds to the designs were frequently lightly punched, producing a stippled effect, and there was much ornamental use of masks, mostly those of lions but occasionally of goblins. Some are definitely caricatures, some 'straight' carving. It is tempting to trace a derivation from the Celtic work of the past. The choicest pieces seem to have been cabinets and tables, especially side-tables, which were sometimes topped with marble instead of mahogany, tea-tables and gaming tables. Settees, either with double or triple backs, and chairs, both arm and single, were also made in quantity, arm-ends being regularly finished with animal masks or birds' heads. Bottle-stands, wine-coolers, plate buckets and longcase clocks were also in production, the lions' masks even finding their way into the hoods of the clocks.

Dublin craftsmen obviously worked from and skilfully adapted the pattern books issued in England by Thomas Chippendale and others: instances are known when they copied a design for a chimneypiece, neatly substituting a grotesque mask for the suggested centre cartouche. Provincial cabinet-makers followed the trend in simpler terms, often producing an elegance of line and economy of emphasis that are very striking. Some pieces of this kind have hardly any carving, the elaborate lion's-paw foot being replaced by an uncarved pad-foot, and the knees of the cabriole legs being gracefully turned with, at most, a single acanthus leaf as ornamentation. Dining tables were of the type called hunting tables, with plain legs and long side flaps that could be let down so that the table could be carried out of doors for a meet. Another speciality was the half-moon-shaped claret table whose open centre was fitted with a net into which carousing gentlemen could toss their empty bottles. Many provincial pieces were much smaller than those of the Dublin masters, a consideration obviously dictated by the cramped conditions in which so many of the country gentry lived. Cabinet-makers were to be found in all the lesser towns and did prosperous local business; oak was now thoroughly out of fashion (the wood being impossible to work in the Chippendale manner) and more and more of the medium-sized houses were being refurnished in mahogany. The hardy oak now began to meet its unrecorded end, often starting with banishment to the nursery or servants' quarters.

Complementing this dark, handsome, somewhat solid furniture went the glorious swirling lightness of the Rococo gilt-framed looking-glasses. Both pier-glasses and overmantels were made, some of the most fanciful being carefully based on Thomas Johnson's published designs.

Soft furnishings had come into more general use. Between 1752 and 1757 linens printed from metal plates were produced at Drumcondra and between 1758 and 1760 printing of fabrics from copper plates was done at Templeogue. In 1758 a factory for linen and cotton printing was established at Leixlip by Samuel Dixon, formerly of Capel Street, Dublin. Though this factory long outlived him, Dixon's real claim to fame lies elsewhere. Between 1748 and 1755 he produced three series of a dozen embossed pictures, the first set showing bunches of flowers, the other two groups of birds, all mounted in japanned frames. Sold in Dublin and Cork, they were immensely popular, enjoying the highest patronage. He engaged good craftsmen; three of his apprentice painters became competent mini-aturists, and his colourful pictures have been much sought by collectors. Inevitably he had his imitators, about whom he complained bitterly, and some of whose wares have long masqueraded as his own.

Another minor art that was in its heyday was bookbinding. Good bookbinding had been done in Ireland since the Restoration, but from the 1730s there were really first-class binders at work in Dublin whose speciality was, at first, a 'Persian carpet' type of design and later, in the 1750s, elaborate featherwork tooling and subsequently intricate foliage sprays surrounding a Baroque-type centre motif. True Rococo does not seem to have occurred in Irish bindings. The best work was done for the government (binding the Journals of the two Houses of Parliament) and for Trinity College, but a few private patrons did employ these craftsmen, particularly the Earl of Moira who formed a large collection of books in the 1750s.

Glass continued to be made in Dublin, and in 1751 the Round Glass-House in Mary's Lane described itself as the only manufacturer of glass in the kingdom. Its advertised output was immensely varied, ranging from everyday claret and burgundy glasses, decanters and jelly glasses through hall lanthorns for as many as four candles, 'glass branches' and 'gardevins', through apothecaries' bottles and babies' sucking bottles to weather-glasses. Glasses were also supplied cut or engraved 'with a Vine Border, Toasts or any flourish whatsoever' (including armorials to special order). This was the heyday of the engraved Williamite glasses and of elaborate constructions such as a pyramid of three salvers. Such refinements were only for the rich: the middle classes were still restricted to necessities, like James Uppington of Mallow who in 1769 had only 'half a dozen of wine glasses and a decanter'.

Although Rococo had become the prevailing style for London silver by 1720, the Irish capital lagged behind by at least twenty years. The fashion seeped in by about 1746 to reach its full glory by the early 1750s. The stark simplicity of the heavy-gauge earlier pieces was replaced by light-gauge metal in ornate, asymmetrical, naturalistic designs, mainly in repoussé work but also in flat chasing. Indeed the Irish lust for alteration and modernization – so visible in their periodic attacks on their houses – also affected silver, and many a simple old piece went back to the silversmith to receive Rococo decoration to bring it up to date. The results were dubious, for the pieces thus tampered with never attained the quality of the true Rococo. A marked feature of the new style was the cast feet in the form of lions' masks applied to creamiers, sauce-boats and sugar bowls and cast birds'-head spouts applied to coffee-pots. These were stock lines, sold in bulk to the craftsmen workers. The repoussé designs on bowls and cream jugs not only included escallops and marine creatures, as found in similar English designs, but added a whole range of more homely fauna and buildings, mingled with pears, roses and blackberries. Some of the best farmyard scenes are on the open-work sides of dish rings. Dish rings had a short career in England early in the century and were completely out of fashion there when they became the rage in Ireland. Apparently made only in Dublin, their purpose was to protect a table-top from damage by the hot dish or bowl, which was, accordingly, placed on top of the silver ring. Rococo scrolls and foliage link a delightful assortment of rural objects – cottage, churches, castles, swans, ducks, pigs, sheep, poultry and cattle, not to mention milkmaids, spinners, shepherds, sportsmen and the stray lion or fox. The variety is enchanting.

Apart from dish rings, the main items in production were cream jugs, sauce-boats, coffee-pots and three-legged sugar bowls. Some creamiers had human masks on their foot knuckles instead of those of lions, a variant especially popular in Cork, whose silver production was at its height and where excellent work was being done. Epergnes, though made, were large and expensive and only for the very wealthy. In Dublin a new style of candlestick was developed, formed from twisting scrolls, an idea imported from France and possibly attributable to Huguenot journeymen working for some of the big silversmiths. Coasters were introduced in the mid-century and received the usual Rococo decoration: like dish rings they seem to have been made only in Dublin and most are of a higher walled type than was current in England. Wine funnels also came into use, at first very small but gradually being made in larger sizes; in the 1770s they were supplied complete with a matching silver tray.

Cutlery remained discreet, continuing the earlier tradition of strainers (for use with punch), scoops,

ladles and rat-tailed spoons, though knives were made with the new Rococo scroll-work on the ends of their handles. An innovation was a type of scroll-work sugar nippers, shaped like scissors.

Neo-Classical finale 1770–1830

By the 1780s a radical change had come over Irish taste, due to the acceptance of Neo-Classical ideas. These were based on a clear appreciation of the art forms of Greece and Rome, coupled with an intense desire to apply these forms correctly, a desire that had never really troubled the Palladian mind. At its most pure – as in Lord Charlemont's Casino – it was quite unsuited to the Irish gentleman's purse: when slightly debased it proved extraordinarily popular. For this reason, though the surviving face of Georgian Ireland is overwhelmingly Neo-Classical, the trend was slow to take root. It flourished in England all through the 1760s, while in Ireland Ducart and his like were still turning out Palladian buildings. A few English architects such as Robert Adam and Sir William Chambers sent over Neo-Classical designs to Irish clients. The most influential of these was Lord Charlemont, on whose behalf Chambers designed first a Dublin mansion in Rutland Square and then the Casino in the grounds of his suburban seat at Marino. The Casino, begun in 1759, took a decade to complete, by which time it had cost a shattering £60,000. Small, yet of great beauty and perfection, it was undoubtedly the best building so far seen in Ireland. Not unnaturally, the expense discouraged its admirers and only a very few risked a Neo-Classical house. Rather more acceptable in the 1770s was the style of Gothic Revival which was running concurrently with Neo-Classicism in England. A couple of large houses were actually built in Ulster with one Gothic and one Neo-Classical façade – an amazing mixture. Gothic Revival was also used, rather successfully, to smarten up existing houses, including medieval tower houses like Leap Castle, Co. Offaly. Later, by the 1790s, it tended to lose the field to its rival, only to stage a vigorous come-back in the first twenty years of the 19th century, when nearly forty important castles were built, not to mention innumerable smaller ventures and Gothic details applied to mills, gate-lodges and estate cottages.

The closing thirty years of the 18th century were the only ones in which politics played any vital role. The American War of Independence was followed with an interest and sympathy that underlined the similarity between that colony's situation and Ireland's. In 1778 Luke Gardiner's Relief Bill brought the first measure of Catholic Emancipation, and the same year produced a threat of French invasion which scared Ulster into forming Volunteer Corps, a movement which spread quickly

Neo-Gothic taste began to appear in Ireland as early as in England. Francis Johnston, one of the most successful Neo-Classical architects, designed this charming Gothic three-decker pulpit. (5)

throughout the island. The government eyed it with distaste but felt unable to suppress it, supported as it was by three leaders of the Irish Parliament – Charlemont, Grattan and Flood. In 1782, with the Dublin streets packed with Volunteers, Grattan's call for legislative independence was passed without any opposition.

The sixteen years of 'Grattan's Parliament' up to the 1798 Rising were the final triumph of the century. Trade and industry were encouraged by a series of bounties and preferential tariffs; not only was there a real sense of nationhood but a number of important projects were carried out, including the construction of a canal system, much favoured for passenger traffic as well as for goods. Theatres flourished both in Dublin and the provinces, and Irish literary work burgeoned likewise. Since Swift's international success with *Gulliver's Travels* in 1726 (immediately translated into French) there had been a hiatus. Now there was a sudden flowering, mostly in the form of work by Irishmen living in England. Oliver Goldsmith followed his *Vicar of Wakefield* (1766) and his *Deserted Village* (1770) with the immensely successful play, *She Stoops to Conquer*, in 1773. This was produced in theatres all over the two kingdoms and is of course still produced today. In 1775 Richard Brinsley Sheridan capped it with *The Rivals*, then in 1778 *The School for Scandal* and in 1779 *The Critic*, all of which had splendid success. As the century closed Maria Edgeworth published *Castle Rackrent*, to be followed in 1812 by *The Absentee* and in 1817 by

Ormond, the first novels of Irish life and the precursors of many to come. Opera, too, broke new ground, for in 1777 the first season of true Italian opera was held in Fishamble Street, succeeded in 1781 by another at Smock Alley.

Though the 1780s were politically quiet a new spirit was abroad. The French Revolution was watched with interest, sympathy and that touch of apprehension bestowed on anything French other than wine. Now, even more than heretofore, Dublin was the acknowledged second city of the British Isles and aware of it. In the 1790s its population was probably about 170,000, out of the island's total population of about 4.5 million. A competition to design the new Royal Exchange, organized in 1768–69 and won by an Englishman, Thomas Cooley, had inaugurated a new epoch of public building. In 1781 the efforts of Lord Carlow (later Earl of Portarlington) and John Beresford induced another English architect, James Gandon, a former pupil of Chambers's, to settle in Dublin. Certainly the capital needed the services of such a man and it was indeed fortunate that they were secured and retained for more than twenty years. In general English architects did not care to visit Ireland and, with the exception of Cooley and Gandon, still less did they care for actually living there. Adam and Chambers never braved the Irish Sea; James Wyatt and later John Nash paid fleeting visits; but Gandon came, worked steadily until he retired in 1808 and then still remained at Lucan, occasionally designing villa-type houses for friends until his death in 1823. He was the ultimate master on whom fell the mantle of Pearce and Castle.

It was during his reign that central Dublin took on its guise of a Neo-Classical city. His own work was almost entirely in the field of public buildings, as he designed few private houses (he started Emo Park for Lord Portarlington, and built the crescent in Beresford Place, opposite his Custom House, but his designs for the new southern stretch of Sackville Street were rejected). Though he did a little provincial work, such as a Court House and gaol for Waterford and a church at Coolbanagher, Co. Leix, all his great creations are in Dublin. First came the new Custom House, begun in 1781 on a site down-river from the existing city and thereby opening the way for Dublin's extension eastward. This was followed by alterations to Pearce's Parliament House, by the Military Infirmary in Phoenix Park, old Carlisle Bridge (now possible after the transfer of the Custom House to its new position), the Four Courts and the King's Inns, all in the Neo-Classical manner of which he was so brilliant an exponent.

The Wide Streets Commissioners, who were then exceptionally active and politically powerful, carried out their brief with startling success, extending the city towards the new Custom House. To both north and south of the river were built squares and long streets of terraced brick houses. These were often developed by individual contractors in blocks of two or three lots, yet achieving a marvellous unity without sameness, enhanced by brass door-furniture and decorative wrought ironwork – railings, lantern-holders and the like. The work did not go unappreciated by its beholders. Daly's Club House in the recently widened Dame Street was described in 1791 as 'the most superb gambling house in the world'. Begun in 1789, it was completed within two years. While Gandon was not directly responsible for all this, the presence of so great an architect cannot have failed to stimulate his contemporaries, who, beyond all dispute, produced a city of rare quality. Great town mansions were still being built, among them Powerscourt House in William Street, Belvedere House, Clonmell House, Ely House and finally Aldborough House, the last of its breed.

A whole range of lesser architects were in practice in addition to Gandon and Cooley, among them Thomas Ivory, George Ensor, Michael Stapleton (who, like Robert West, was both stuccodore and architect), Richard Morrison and, a little later, the brothers Richard and Francis Johnston and Gandon's pupil, Henry Aaron Baker. Such men were of a new generation who understood Neo-Classicism and how to apply it in a manner suited to Ireland – not at the £60,000 outlay on an exquisite casino but offering, as Richard Morrison did, a 'Villa or Country House' with a handsome frontispiece in Bath or Portland stone for a trifling £1,100. This was essentially the sort of box-house which soon became the standard residence of the country gentry and clergy. The less affluent, so long deprived of anything that combined a degree of fashion with their economic needs, seized on the Neo-Classical box as the answer to their troubles, which indeed it was. Most tower houses, thatched houses, and early 18th-century houses, were abandoned or demolished. In their place (often on their exact site) arose a nice, manageable box-house, usually two-, sometimes three-storied, over basement, one room each side of the front door, the latter embellished with a graceful leaded fanlight. Inside, a gently graded staircase turning beneath a tall round-headed window at the back of the house rose from the entrance hall. The outlook was still across a stretch of park – large or small according to means – with a walled garden for fruit and vegetables hidden away at a distance, often a very inconvenient distance, the entire premises being enclosed by a demesne wall, approached by front and back gates. Gateways were frequently in a style different from that of the actual house – say a Gothic entrance to a Neo-Classical

mansion – and it was not unknown for the gateway to be more imposing than the house itself. Gate-lodges were always provided, some of them of great charm, Gothic Revival or Neo-Classical in miniature. Coade stone ornaments were imported from England in quantity, both for the adornment of demesnes and of buildings: features such as a Coade stone keystone may be found inserted quite casually above a stable door. In more remote areas, however, traditional styles persisted: for instance at Dunmurry, Co. Antrim, a charming Presbyterian church with Gibbsian details then fifty years out of date was built as late as 1779.

The rich, of course, continued to build grandly: this was the era of such houses as Ballyscullion, Co. Derry; Avondale, Co. Wicklow; Caledon House, Co. Tyrone; Townley Hall, Co. Louth; and Lyons House, Co. Kildare. Existing houses were also adapted in a lavish manner, both externally and in respect of interior decoration. The lovely Rococo stucco-work fell from favour (and from ceilings) in an orgy of Neo-Classical renovation. Wyatt, who had a considerable Irish country-house practice – his designs included Mount Kennedy, Co. Wicklow; Castle Coole, Co. Fermanagh; and Abbeyleix – produced many interior schemes for incorporation into extant houses, such as Westport, Curraghmore and the Bishop of Meath's palace at Ardbraccan. His outlook was not restricted to the Neo-Classical: he was also the leading Gothic architect of his day, which style he used at Slane Castle in Co. Meath, the first really large Irish venture into this mode. Its true masters, however, proved to be Francis Johnston and Richard Morrison whose talents promoted Gothic Revival into its intense popularity early in the 19th century.

The new fashion in plaster-work introduced by Robert Adam's pattern books was characterized by low relief, strict symmetry and classical motifs. Birds lost their place to urns, human figures were chastely confined to oval medallions and the free-hand swirls of foliage gave way to carefully regulated husk chains and swags of flowers. Michael Stapleton, who was the greatest Irish exponent of this idiom, occasionally placed musical instrument trophies among the otherwise Classical objects, perhaps in affectionate remembrance of his old friend, Robert West. There was a short vogue for using the plaster-work as a frame for grisailles either in medallions or alcoves, but this was soon found inconvenient, as occupying too much wall space, and abandoned.

Numerous good stuccodores were at work during this period, not only rivalling Stapleton in Dublin but active in all the provincial cities. Where documentation is lacking, it is generally impossible to differentiate between their work, as all were competent and the rigours of design left little scope for individual touches. For his public works Gandon employed Edward Smyth, who was both sculptor and stuccodore, and who is famous for his fourteen riverine heads on the ground-floor keystones of the Custom House.

Provincial towns were not slow to follow in Dublin's wake. Cork, too, had its Wide Streets Commissioners and laid out new streets and its Mardyke; Limerick continued to extend its brick terraces; Kilkenny acquired a fine Deanery near the old Palace and a particularly handsome house for the use of Kilkenny College, while Grace's Castle was rebuilt as a court house. Waterford was not only building fine terraces but Ireland's best 18th-century church, designed by John Roberts when he was over sixty. He had already done excellent Baroque work in the forecourt at Curraghmore: now he produced a fanciful yet very fine Neo-Classical cathedral for his native city. A decade later he was responsible for the Waterford Assembly Rooms and later still, aged eighty but undaunted, he designed the Catholic cathedral, without repeating himself. Many smaller towns, of the size of Monaghan, Tullamore, Portarlington or Midleton, built cut-stone market houses in their centres. During the 1780s Roger Mulholland remodelled much of Belfast for its landlord, the 5th Earl of Donegall, but before that the city had achieved a handsome Poor House in 1774 and St Anne's Church in 1776. Francis Johnston, succeeding Cooley in 1784, did extensive work in his native Armagh, both in the form of public buildings and of terrace houses under the patronage of Archbishop Robinson. It was the era of the improving landlord, such men as Lord de Vesci, who laid out the town of Abbeyleix, or Denham Jephson who brought Mallow to its peak of prosperity as a spa and social centre.

Neo-Classicism invaded everything. Adam-style chimneypieces all too frequently replaced the pedimented Baroque ones of the previous generation. In Ireland one strain of these developed a distinctive form of centre plaque, descended from the Rococo 'farmyard' style and wholly at variance with strict Neo-Classical principles, and yet these plaques are the most attractive of the period. Subjects range from pastoral scenes – a piping shepherd, a shepherd reclining amid his flock, a rustic hitching horses to a plough – to musical trophies to fantastic adaptations of Classical themes, such as a blindfolded putto asleep in front of a large and improbable house. The best are to be found in the provinces, where the old tradition died hard. Abraham Hargrave, the gifted Cork architect who continued to work in a semi-Palladian manner up to 1800, put a superb one into the drawing-room at Castle Hyde; others are in such houses as Mount

Juliet, Co. Kilkenny, and Ardbraccan, Co. Meath. They provide a fantasy and variety quite lacking in the habitual Adam chimneypiece.

As with chimneypieces, so with furniture: Baroque was no longer fashionable – too dark, too heavy, too asymmetrical, too fanciful, it was entirely outmoded. A much paler mahogany was imported and extensive use made of satinwood, rosewood, fruit woods, veneering, inlaying, cross-banding. Legs became straight and slender, often reeded or poised on neat little spade feet. The pattern books of the English Sheraton and Hepplewhite were avidly studied and faithfully reproduced, even down to such minor items as banjo-shaped barometers, very fine examples of which were made in Dublin. With one marked exception, the extremely well-made Irish furniture of the period fell tidily into line with that in England. The exception was the mahogany 'Cork chair'. This, while following the general shape of a Sheraton-style dining chair, is unique in that it has a narrow gallery below the upper rail and a double crosspiece in its centre back bearing a medallion with a lion's mask. The legs are tapered and reeded, the size of chair varies from small to quite large, and they were made in sets of at least a dozen. Oddly, armed carvers seem to be extremely rare. Made only in Cork, these chairs show a clear descent from the earlier Baroque type and are certainly the most interesting Irish furniture produced towards the end of the century.

Like furniture, Neo-Classical silver tended to follow English patterns to a degree unknown at the time of Rococo. Dish rings were still made, but with grille sides or engraved bands of symmetrical decoration, wholly lacking the vigour and individuality of the 'farmyard' variety. Tea-pots (silver ones having come back into fashion), coffee-pots and urns were all produced in Classical forms; coasters and trays had pierced sides or galleries and were decorated with elegant, formal bright cut engraving. Small tea caddies, often elaborately engraved, were introduced, and so were decanter labels. One of the few distinctively Irish pieces was the piggin, a little cream-pail with either a single upright for handle or else a swing handle. Butter dishes, vase-shaped creamiers and swing-handled sugar bowls also tended to be Irish specialities. But the real glory of the time was cutlery. Hitherto plain and serviceable, it blossomed into most beautifully shaped and balanced spoons and ladles with pointed tops, all lavishly engraved in the new bright cut manner, which was even extended to such mundane items as meat skewers. Such work was by no means confined to Dublin: Limerick excelled in a bright cut design topped by three Prince of Wales feathers, while Cork favoured a form of feather-edging on the handle, though both cities also produced the more

162   *The New Culture*

usual patterns. Unfortunately, shortly after 1800 the plain fiddle-pattern became the rage for spoon handles and the pretty bright cutting fell into disuse. The Union did nothing to encourage Irish silver. Though quantities continued to be made, its design followed that of England ever more closely and this was currently poor, suffering from the fussy ornateness of Regency taste. The Cork silversmiths held out the longest, producing pieces in the traditional style up to about 1820, but in the end even they succumbed.

One of the chief beneficiaries of the partial Free Trade measures of 1780 was glass-making, which remained heavily taxed in England. Long established in Dublin, the industry had spread to Belfast in the 1770s and to Cork and Waterford by 1783. In Dublin the 1780s saw the production of a design that is regarded as peculiarly Irish – an oval mirror in front of which hung a small glass chandelier. The mirror frames were composed of rectangular faceted glass 'jewels', silvered on the back, and set side by side, either with rich blue 'jewels' alternating with flat sections of opal glass, or with a continuous row of clear 'jewels'. Many such mirrors now survive lacking their chandelier.

The founding of the Cork Glass Company and of the Penrose brothers' enterprise in Waterford marked the great expansion of Irish glass production. For the first three years the Penroses employed a Worcestershire glass-maker, John Hill, and his workmen. When Hill left, after a disagreement, he bequeathed the recipe for compounding glass to his friend Gatchell, one of Penrose's clerks, who eventually took over the whole firm. Though some mould-blown glass was made with the factory name on its bottom, most Irish glass is unmarked, which renders identification difficult. Several peculiarly Irish shapes and designs were developed, two of the most notable being the boat-shaped or circular fruit bowls with either a deeply cut trefoil rim or a turned-over rim, and mounted on a domed foot. Others were covered bowls and small jars with a button finial, barrel-shaped decanters with mushroom stoppers and thick neck rings (habitually two in Belfast, three in Munster) and tall claret jugs with elaborate diamond cutting – further testimony to the continued large and widespread consumption of claret. The Union in 1800 was celebrated by decanters and wine glasses delicately engraved with the emblems of rose, thistle and shamrock. A great deal of the best of the Waterford and Cork glass was produced in the twenty years following the Union, Cork production being increased by the establishment of a second factory in 1815, the Waterloo Glass Company. Many shapes that had been made in silver were now made in glass – fluted plates, piggins, candlesticks, covered butter-coolers and Classical

The Volunteer movement was commemorated in some attractive textiles produced by the Leixlip factory in 1782. Known as 'Volunteer Furniture', the design is based on a review held in Phoenix Park, Dublin, in June 1781. (6)

urns with pointed finials. With so much in production, the use of glass became widespread among the middle classes in a way it had never been before, and may even have provided an inexpensive substitute for silver, since for example in 1812 a Waterford butter-cooler cost a modest 12s. 6d. On the whole the engraving at this period was inferior to the cutting, which was lavish and sometimes possibly overdone. Considerable care was taken at Waterford to ensure a clear glass, the blue tinge to be found in the products of other factories being regarded as quite unsatisfactory.

The Volunteer movement had unexpected repercussions in textiles for in 1782 the so-called 'Volunteer Furniture' was produced by the Leixlip factory founded by Dixon. These printed fabrics, in chintz colours, depicted such items as soldiers, cannon and Lord Charlemont as commander-in-chief, and were the delight of the patriotic for both hangings and upholstery. Since about 1760 the rich had been importing exquisite Chinese wallpapers, it being fashionable to have at least one room decorated in this manner. Wallpapers were also made in Ireland from at least 1740, supplemented by others imported from England and, in the early 19th century, by French scenic papers. Not that such refinements ever became universal. Mrs Daniel Conner, describing the house of her grandfather, John Longfield, JP, at Longueville near Mallow during the first decade of the 19th century, recalled that 'off the breakfast parlour was a large dining room very scantily furnished. (Curtains that did not reach the ground and *no* drapery.) A carpet just the size of the dining table. A spindled legged side board and chairs and a large four leaved screen covered with silk, or what I think was called Taffita, a thin silk material stamped with Figures of Butterflies, Chinese scenery etc. . . . The entire house was most scantily furnished . . .'.

From the 1790s politics began once more to dominate social life. In 1793, again under threat of French invasion, local regiments of militia were raised which remained in being, more or less, until after Waterloo. In 1798 came the disastrous Rising, partly engineered by such liberally-minded scions of the New Culture as Lord Edward FitzGerald, Theobald Wolfe Tone and Arthur Conner (who called himself O'Connor for good measure). Crushed after a year of destruction, it provided a ready-made excuse for hurrying through the Act of Union, which by dint of extensive bribery took effect in 1801. If the Rising was a disaster, the Union was even worse, though the full implication of its effects was masked until the end of the Napoleonic War. The war led to much increased prosperity: money could be earned by all classes by service in army, navy or militia; the forces had to be clothed, fed, armed and repaired, thereby providing great employment; grain was being shipped to blockaded England and millers grew rich, new mills (some of them amusingly castellated) sprouting all over Leinster. It was on the indirect proceeds of the wars that the middling gentry built their Neo-Classical box-houses and the rich employed Francis Johnston and the English John Nash to build great castles – Charleville, Co. Offaly (begun 1801); Killeen, Co. Meath (1802); Markree, Co. Sligo (1803); Kil-

lymoon, Co. Tyrone (1803); and Glenmore, Co. Wicklow (1804). But peace brought tragedy in its train.

The army strength was reduced, the militia disbanded. Parliament had left Dublin for Westminster, taking most of the rich with it. The middle-income men, who could not afford long sojourns in London, abandoned politics: the great mansions of Dublin fell vacant, to be taken over by professional and merchant classes grown prosperous in the war. Lack of Treasury support had already hampered the completion of works begun by the Wide Streets Commissioners in their attempt to shift the city eastwards. The last two great Dublin churches of the Establishment were begun during the war, St George's in 1802 and the Chapel Royal in 1807. A few of the big landlords, heartbroken like Lord Rosse, limped home to the country, there to make a new start improving their local town or village: mostly they followed the gay life to London and became absentees, with the worst results. The sons of the gentry had no local militia to join: if they wanted to see service they went perforce into the regular army. The 'old school tie' became important and boys began to be sent to English schools and universities, which led to many of them marrying English wives and introducing the ruinous theory that trade must be eschewed by a gentleman. Architecture, silver, furniture, even thought, were filtered through with Englishness in a way they had never been before. The New Culture shrivelled in the chill of the English wind: it died unrecorded, unlamented and unrecognized for what it was, yet leaving behind a great and beautiful capital, four lovely cities – Limerick, Cork, Waterford and Armagh – countless country houses and a wealth of silver, glass and furniture as memorials to the glory that had been Georgian Ireland.

Painting and Sculpture

ANNE CROOKSHANK

To understand the development of painting and sculpture in Ireland during the 18th century, we must retrace our steps and look at the situation following the Battle of the Boyne and the Jacobite exodus.

In the last decade of the 17th century only a few painters of merit were working in Ireland. One was an emigré from Holland or Germany, Gaspar Smitz, who worked both in England and Ireland, where he died in 1707. Not only did he paint portraits, subject pictures and still-lives but he worked as a restorer and possibly as an artist's colourman and was the

first recorded teacher of painting in Ireland. He probably taught Garret Morphey (*fl.* 1680–1716), whose early work closely resembles Smitz's portraits. Morphey, who emerges as the first known native Irish painter, has a remarkably sophisticated style. His knowledge of contemporary painting both in England and on the Continent was considerable and his links with Netherlandish painters are particularly interesting. His small whole-lengths set in landscapes derive from the work of the Netchers, Gaspar and Constantine, and Adrian van der Werff. He had a very large practice based at first on the older Catholic families and after 1690 on the newer Protestant gentry as well. It is unfortunate that most of his sitters were highly conservative and wanted conventional half-lengths; but even these he managed to enliven with landscape backgrounds and always by his fine lace painting and rich, velvety colours. In his use of details such as urns and cupids as well as in the poses of his sitters such as Baron Bellew, who reclines on the grass in the pose which links with the concept of melancholia in English Jacobean painting, Morphey introduced the use of symbolism into Irish painting.

Portraits and sitters

While Garret Morphey was enjoying his success in Dublin, another Irish artist, Charles Jervas (c. 1675–1739), was studying in Kneller's Academy in London in 1694/95 and travelling to Rome in 1699 where he remained for ten years until he settled in London. There he became the friend of Alexander Pope and moved in the highest literary and social circles, being appointed Principal Painter to the King in 1723. However, he did not neglect his native land and returned regularly for visits lasting months, even years, so that Pope could write in a letter on 9 July 1716 'Your Acquaintance on this side the sea are under terrible Apprehensions, from your long stay in *Ireland* . . . Everybody Here has great need of you. Many Faces have died forever from want of your Pencil, and blooming Ladies have wither'd in expecting your return . . . Come then, and having peopled *Ireland* with a World of beautiful shadows come to us . . .' The realism of his best portraits, usually of his friends, was direct; it should have appealed to the Irish gentry, but his portraits are rarer in Ireland than might be expected. Possibly the simplicity with which he handled clothes, and the plainness of his backgrounds, reduced his popularity even though until late in his life he had no real rival in the country. It was not until the 1720s and the 1730s that there was a real increase of interest in fine housing and in the arts generally and no doubt up to then only a few people were interested in pictures. From 1734, when he first visited Ireland, the English artist Stephen Slaughter (1697–1765) seems to have been extremely popular; the emphasis he lays on accessories and clothes is marked. Portraits like his *Henrietta O'Brien* of 1746 have great charm and reflect a knowledge of French Rococo which he must have acquired in his long stay in Paris and Flanders in the 1720s.

A more important artist was James Latham (1696–1747). Nothing is known about his early career except that he came of a Tipperary family and presumably studied first in Ireland, because by the time he became a student in Antwerp in 1724 he was twenty-seven and must already have been an accomplished painter. It is unfortunate that none of his early work has yet been identified. There is no mention of him in Vertue's *Notebooks* which suggests that any visit he may have made to England is likely to have been short; apart from Highmore there would have been little to interest him in London in the 1720s, as Hogarth had not started to paint the life-size portraits with which Latham's work has been confused and which he probably never saw. From about 1730 till his death Latham was the most sought-after painter in Ireland and he sustained a remarkably high standard. He seems never to have painted anything but portraits but he had considerable variety within his range, from magnificent costume pieces like *Sir James Cottar* or the *Earl of Inchiquin* to the intimacy of the Leslie girls at the harpsichord or the charm of his sophisticated children. He painted a number of double portraits and at least one family group. His success must surely have been because he painted so well, had such a sure handling of tone, and lively brushwork. Although his whole-length portraits tend to be dull he was very successful with half-lengths, where he achieved great vivacity through his beautiful painting of such simple items as a brown coat with silver lace, or even the curls of a white wig. This painterly quality which raises his work far above the merely competent, makes him unquestionably the best resident Irish painter of the 18th century; it also suggests that his visit to Antwerp was preceded or followed by a stay in Paris where he would most easily have seen and learnt to value the importance of brilliant painting. His quality was recognized by contemporaries, although none of them attempted to follow in his footsteps. Phillip Hussey (1713–83), a prolific and sound painter of the mid-century, is said to have owned a Latham which he valued a lot; but he was more influenced in his early days by Slaughter, whom he may well have known, for they were both working for the Inchiquin O'Briens in 1746. His late works have a high finish with great attention to detail. It is probable, but not proven, that late in his life he painted several large group portraits of families living near Belfast; these are too stiff to be called conversation pieces, but they have great charm with their precise settings and beautifully painted costumes.

The only painter who does show the influence of Latham in his work is Thomas Frye (1710–62), who went to live in England in the mid 1730s, possibly because there was still too little work in Ireland to keep two painters fully occupied. Frye had a remarkable career in England, where he became involved in the founding of the Bow porcelain factory. His oil paintings are not numerous but they have something of Latham's direct poses and silvery tonality. With the exception of Edward Luttrell (*fl.* 1673–1723), who was painting pastels on copper from the late 17th century, Frye was the earliest of a long and distinguished line of Irish pastellists. He must have developed his interest in pastel independently, but most users of this medium had been students of Robert West and James Mannin at the Dublin Society's schools, founded in the mid-1740s. Established through the influence of men like Bishop Berkeley, Samuel Madden and Thomas Prior, they aimed only to give basic teaching in design and were not primarily a 'fine art' establishment; even later in the century they do not appear to have taught oil painting. Students stayed for about two years and were then apprenticed to a suitable master so that pupils went on to become silversmiths, stuccodores, etc. as well as painters and sculptors. The high quality of the applied arts in Ireland in the second half of the 18th century can certainly be attributed to the excellence of this school. Both West and Mannin were said to have studied in Paris; and besides teaching design they held life classes.

Frye also excelled in mezzotint engraving. His own fame in this lies chiefly in his imaginary heads and candlelit figures; but the art reached its apogee in the field of portraiture. It was dominated by a number of great Irish craftsmen of whom the first was John Brooks of Dublin (*fl.* 1730–56), who learnt the art in London in 1740, probably from John Faber; on his return to Dublin he had as a pupil the great James McArdell (1728/29–65) who went to London with Brooks in 1746, and lived there until his death, although he retained commercial links with Ireland. His ability to interpret an artist's work in black and white has never been surpassed and he was, in the words graved on his tombstone, 'the most eminent in his Art in his time'. McArdell's own pupil, James Watson, continued his series of splendid prints after Reynolds and sustained the reputation of his countrymen in this art to the end of the century.

It is unfortunate that Robert Healy (*fl.* 1765–71) had a very short career, for his beautiful grisaille pastels of the Conolly family and their friends at Carton are among the finest and most unusual paintings created in Ireland in the century. His charming picture of the Duke of Wellington's mother, Lady Mornington, feeding her peacocks at Dangan, is typical of his small whole-lengths of ladies, usually in outdoor dress. However, the best-known Irish pastellist is Hugh Douglas Hamilton, born about 1793, whose small oval portraits are a feature of most Irish country houses, and also of many in England because he worked in London from about 1764 to 1778. He had studied, as had Healy, under Robert West in the Dublin Society's schools.

Though the oval format is the most usual for his pastels he also exhibited small whole-lengths, portrait groups and even subject pictures in the Society of Artists in London. Hamilton appears to have occasionally painted in oil, but he was still working in pastel during his twelve-year stay in Italy. While in Rome he became a friend of the two great Neo-Classical sculptors Flaxman and Canova and their influence changed his style considerably. On his return to Ireland he painted in oils, and the fluffy prettiness of his early work changed to a more severe clarity of outline; a number of his half-lengths even show the sitter in profile, which together with the use of a low range of colours, browns and silvers, achieves a sculptural quality quite different from the more realistic style of his Irish contemporaries. Between his return from Italy and his death in 1808, Hamilton executed portraits of many leading Irishmen of the day including Lord Edward FitzGerald and the barrister John Philpot Curran.

Painting the Irish landscape

As in England, landscape painting developed very late in Ireland and only has a continous existence from the 1720s when a Dutch artist, Willem van der Hagen, settled in Ireland. In both countries the development of landscape painting relates to the new interest shown in the countryside; in Ireland it was coincident with the interest in landscaping and country-house building on the part of the new affluent Protestant gentry. Van der Hagen, who remained in Ireland until his death in 1745, painted topographical landscapes and decorative scenes. In 1728 he was commissioned to paint a series of views of the ports of Ireland; surviving pictures of Waterford and Derry are no doubt connected with this commission. In the view of Waterford the artist introduces genre figures, a boy coursing a hare, people playing with a kite, which enliven the scene. From the way such figures are introduced into Irish landscapes in the 1740s they were obviously much admired. The topographical views which represent work contemporary with Van der Hagen are of country houses and their parks; though they have great naïve charm their lack of knowledge of drawing and perspective is total. The change which can be seen in the work of the next generation in artists like Anthony Chearnley and Joseph Tudor is surely due to the influence of Van der Hagen. Chearnley, a gentleman amateur associated with the growing antiquarian movement, was also an engraver; several of his landscapes, including his view of Kinsale, were illustrated in Smith's Histories of Waterford and of Cork published in 1745 and 1750. Joseph Tudor may have been more closely connected with Van der Hagen, for he also worked as a decorative artist as well as a landscape painter, but there is no actual evidence of their association. He seems to have succeeded Van der Hagen as the artist employed by Dublin Castle for the decorations needed for important social events such as the ball given for the King's birthday. Van der Hagen had done murals in a number of houses, at Beaulieu, Co. Louth, and Curraghmore, Co. Waterford, and for the Christmas family in the same county, where he painted grisailles of Classical gods and goddesses. Tudor, who never seems to have worked for private commissions, did paint scenery for the theatre at Smock Alley, as Van der Hagen had done before him. He is best remembered now for the engravings after his views of Dublin, but a newly discovered landscape of the Boyne Obelisk proves him to have been a fine painter. Another scene painter for Smock Alley, John Lewis, appointed in 1750, strangely enough in his spare time painted not landscapes but portraits. These vary greatly in style and quality, from elegantly painted Rococo ladies with roses tucked into their bosoms, to more broadly handled male portraits like the playwright John Brooke and the producer Thomas Sheridan at their desks.

The tradition of scene painting was carried on by Robert Carver (*fl.*1750–91), who succeeded Lewis at Smock Alley in 1754 and went on later to London where he worked at Drury Lane and Covent Garden. His landscapes are usually imaginary, rather dull Claudian works; the same applies to his pupil Edmund Garvey's (d.1813), although his landscapes normally have the interest of being topographical views.

The Dublin Society gave a premium for landscape painting in 1747 to George Barret, a Dublin draper's son. His earliest known views are of the demesne at Powerscourt and the Dargle valley. Despite the difference in their style – for Barret was always less prosaic – he was following in Van der Hagen's footsteps, as the Dutchman's last recorded work was a view of Powerscourt waterfall done in 1745. Barret developed an interest in wild nature; he was one of the earliest painters in the British Isles to exploit mountain scenery; but to make money he also painted numerous rather boring topographical views of country houses. He left Ireland in 1763 and spent the remainder of his career in Britain where he was painting, in North Wales in 1764 and later in the Lake District and the lowlands of Scotland, landscapes which, with their feeling for the atmosphere of isolated mist-covered hills and rushing peat-streams, are in the vanguard of the Romantic movement. In 1777 he painted a room for his friend William Locke of Norbury with mountain landscape views which give the effect that one is sitting in the open air; the ceiling is painted as sky

seen through an opening in trellis work, the overmantel (which is lost) was surrounded by a trellis covered with honeysuckle and roses. Cipriani painted imitation stone figures between the windows, which open on to a lawn sweeping down to a valley; beyond there is a wooded landscape. The room must have been an enchanting conceit when it was fresh and Barret's mountains complemented the actual scenery. It is one of the finest of such 18th-century decorative rooms and one of the earliest to be entirely devoted to landscape.

There seems to be no reason for Barret, who became a founder member of the Royal Academy, to have spent his career in England, as apparently landscape painting was by the second half of the century a profitable trade in Ireland. William Ashford (1746–1824), a young man from Birmingham, came over in 1764 to work in a minor position in the Board of Ordnance; he stayed to become the principal Irish landscape painter and the first President of the new Royal Hibernian Academy in 1824. Ashford mostly painted the parks of country houses, or pleasant farmlands, which he peopled with gentlemen and industrious farmers. His earliest paintings show the influence of Dutch art and unlike most of his contemporaries he does not seem to have painted Classical landscapes at all. Ashford's prosperous vistas are beautifully handled, nearly always depicting a sunlit scene. His rivals were the Roberts brothers, Thomas (*c.* 1749–78) and Sautelle; Sautelle, the younger, after his brother's death in 1778 took his Christian name also and became known as Thomas Sautelle Roberts. Both brothers were educated at the Dublin Society's schools, Thomas becoming a pupil in 1763. In his short career he painted a number of landscapes, varying from the topographical series of Carton, to views where his beautifully controlled distances are extraordinarily effective; the scenes, probably imaginary, are based on the Wicklow Mountains. Thomas Roberts used a minute technique with very small brush-strokes, employed with good effect on his foreground vegetation. He was clearly in demand for his country-house views and did a series of houses near Lough Erne, as well as Dartrey and Carton, but he had a much greater feeling for natural scenery than Ashford and clearly enjoyed country pastimes like hunting. He introduced round towers and Gothic ruins into his work and, had he lived longer, might well have developed the romantic elements in Irish landscape. He visited England in 1775, when he painted two landscapes for Sir Watkin Williams Wynne; otherwise little is known about his life. Thomas Sautelle Roberts (*c.*1760–1826), who had trained in the Dublin Society's architectural school, started as an imitator of his brother's style; then about the turn of the century he exhibited a number of romantic landscapes painted with vigorous brushwork which were a marked advance on his earlier work. Like most other landscape painters he worked for the engravers of views and he started, but never completed, a series of 'Illustrations of the Chief Cities, Rivers and Picturesque scenery of the Kingdom of Ireland'. The younger Roberts also painted a number of horse pictures though, strangely, this type of work never became popular with Irish painters.

Another painter who worked extensively for the print makers was Jonathan Fisher (d. 1809), best remembered for his splendid views of Killarney, the Mourne Mountains and Strangford Lough. With William Sadler (c. 1782–1832), landscape took on a slightly different air; his small panels have the quality of journalism, they so often represent contemporary drama like fires, military raids or wrecks. Thomas Robinson, who died in 1810, painted one extremely interesting work of this type, his *Battle of Ballinahinch* of 1798; but he is more usually known as a portrait painter in Belfast.

In the mid-century several Irish painters left to make their careers in England where opportunities for portrait painters were greater and where at least lip-service was paid to the idea of subject pictures, which were hardly considered at all in Ireland. Of these expatriate painters, the best-known are Nathanial Hone and James Barry. Two more opposed characters could not be found, their only common feature being their quarrelsome natures. Hone, who disliked the Classical tradition and fashionable adulation of Italy, never travelled farther than Paris; Barry, on the other hand, was a true disciple of Reynolds, and a friend of Burke, to whom the value of the Ancients and the great painters of the Italian Renaissance and Seicento was all-important. Hone (1718–84) was in England by 1742, when he married an heiress and worked at first as an enamel miniaturist. By 1760 he had established himself as an oil painter, and he became a founder member of the Royal Academy in 1768. Largely because of his dislike of Reynolds, he fought with the Academy. So, in 1774, he held a one-man show, a very great rarity at the time, as a deliberate defiance of what he felt to be his ill-treatment by that body. Though he painted a number of portraits with Classical motifs he is at his best in works of an informal character, like the portrait of his son painting, which shows his skill in the use of light and shade.

A larger stage

James Barry (1741–1806), the son of a builder in Cork, tried from the beginning to make a career painting subject pictures. When only twenty-two he painted his *Saint Patrick Baptizing the King of Cashel*, for which he was awarded a prize by the Dublin Society; and he attracted the attention of Edmund Burke who brought him to London in 1764 and paid for his visit to Italy, which remained the most overpowering influence on his career. He was also much influenced by Burke's *A Philosophical Enquiry into the Origin of Our Ideas of the Sublime and the Beautiful*, published in 1756, which was of great theoretical importance in the development of the arts in the later 18th century. Apparently partly written when Burke was a student at Trinity College, Dublin, this work raises the interesting question, to which no answer can yet be given, about the quantity, quality and accessibility of works of art in Ireland in the mid-century. There must have been far more for people to see then than there is today, after nearly two centuries of sales and of emigration of the rich as well as the poor, since the Act of Union of 1801. When Barry was young in Cork there must surely have been more than engravings for him to see, more than the works of the Cork landscape painter John Butts, whom Barry recognized as his first guide and inspiration, something more to fire his imagination. Burke too must have seen actual pictures in some quantity in private houses even if their quality and attributions would not necessarily be acceptable today. One notable collection was that of the well-travelled and learned Protestant Bishop of Cork, Robert Clayton, who, according to Lord Orrery, ate, drank and slept in Taste and had 'Pictures by Carlo Morat, Music by Corelli and Castles in the Air by Vitruvius'.

Barry had very doctrinaire attitudes to the arts, but his work was clearly appreciated by his fellows: from 1782 to 97 he was Professor of Painting at the Royal Academy. His greatest works are the murals he painted between 1777 and 1783 in the Great Room of the Society of Arts in London on the subject of the Progress of Human Culture; they contain passages of real grandeur as well as bathos and remain the most important paintings of their kind done in the British Isles in the 18th century. Barry despised portrait painting; but those few portraits which he did undertake all have a sincerity and solemnity which is wholly convincing. His poses and settings are usually connected with the antique; his double portrait of himself and his friend and patron Burke as *Ulysses and a Companion fleeing from the Cave of Polyphemus* is one example. He was also impressed by the sublimity of Shakespeare and painted two versions of *The Death of Cordelia* as well as other Shakespearean subjects.

The economic necessity to travel in search of work drove Thomas Hickey (1741–1824), a Dublin confectioner's son, to travel to the East, where he lived mainly in India from 1784 to his death, with a brief return to the British Isles in the 1790s. Earlier he had divided his time between Ireland and England and, as befits a student of the Dublin Society's schools, his earliest works were in chalk. Later he became known for his charming conversation pieces and his portraits both of Indians and of the British in India. Robert Fagan, who was actually born in London in 1767, the son of a prosperous Irish Catholic baker from Cork, was usually described as an Irishman by his contemporaries. He spent most of his adult life in Italy where he varied work as a brilliant Neo-Classical portrait painter with archaeology, dealing in and smuggling antiquities and works of art, and a diplomatic career as British Consul General; he died in Rome in 1816. Another expatriate, Martin Archer Shee (1769–1850), worked almost entirely in England where he achieved prominence, became President of the Royal Academy in 1830, and was knighted. He had started, however, at the Dublin Society's schools and was a fine pastellist, although it is for his oils that he is now remembered. Shee's grand manner is rather turgid, but he was capable of a simpler and more informal style particularly for his child portraiture. He retained a great interest in the Irish art scene and was much involved in the complicated negotiations which finally resulted in the foundation, in 1823, of the Royal Hibernian Academy, of which his only pupil, Martin Cregan (1788–1870), a prolific but uninspiring portrait painter, was President from 1832 to 1865.

Robert Hunter (*fl.* 1748–*c.* 1803) was a Dublin portrait painter who, although he lacked the quality of his contemporaries who went to live in England, enjoyed the greatest patronage in Ireland in the third quarter of the century. Very little is known about his career, and little work is known by him after the 1780s; he is not recorded as visiting England but he was clearly aware of the work of English portraitists like Reynolds, Gainsborough, Francis Cotes, Devis and Alan Ramsay, whose work he could have seen in many great Irish houses. He had the facility to imitate their styles and no doubt did this to suit his patrons' wishes, so that there is great variety in his work. He was at his best in his male portraits where he posed his sitters in the open air, and successfully gives them an informal atmosphere as they take their dogs out shooting. There was a whole series of lesser men working at the same time as Hunter, particularly in the provinces where in the north, for example, an artist like Joseph Wilson made a considerable career for himself. Wilson may have attended the Dungannon convention in 1782 as he painted so many gentlemen in their Volunteer uniforms about that time.

While Irish artists went to work abroad, a number of English and even American artists visited and worked in Ireland in the late 18th century when Dublin society was in its high-flown heyday. Francis Wheatley was in Ireland between 1779 and 1783, Tilly Kettle briefly about 1783, and George Chinnery was in Dublin for a few years. More influential, however, on Irish painting was the visit of Gilbert Stuart who spent a few very successful years in Dublin in 1787–93; his highly accomplished style influenced many local painters such as William Cuming (1769–1852) and John Comerford (1770–1832). Comerford, a native of Kilkenny, began his career as a portraitist there; he later turned to miniature painting, a very popular genre which reached its height in Ireland with the work of Horace Hone (1756–1825), and counted some skilled provincial practitioners such as Sampson Twogood Roche (*c.* 1759–1847), a deaf and dumb miniaturist from Youghal who worked for the south Munster gentry and also at Bath. Adam Buck (1759–1833) and Alexander Pope (1763–1835), who were both miniaturists at this time, also painted small whole-length watercolour and crayon portraits which were popular, no doubt, for their economy as well as for their charm.

The rebirth of sculpture

Sculpture as an art unconnected with decorative carving for buildings developed very late in Ireland. This is strange, as free-standing sculpture of the early high cross type was still being executed in the early 17th century, when a number of commemorative crosses were put up, for example, in Co. Meath. The dominant Protestant religion on the whole frowned on memorial sculpture; however, in the early 17th century there were a great many tombs with life-size or near life-size figures modelled in plaster, very few of which survive. The few free-standing statues erected in the Restoration to early Georgian period were sculpted by foreigners. A sculptor like William Kidwell, who made his career in Ireland from 1711 until his death in 1735, spent most of his time on chimneypieces and architectural ornaments; however, he occasionally had work of a more exciting nature and sculpted the fine Baroque tomb of Sir Donal O'Brien in the church of Kilnasoolagh parish, Newmarket on Fergus, Co. Clare: Sir Donal reclines on a mattress, attended by weeping cherubs, some of whom draw up the curtain so that we may see him.

There is much fine wood-carving from the end of the 17th and the early 18th centuries, probably by Irishmen, especially in the organ lofts of Dublin city churches such as St Mary's and St Michan's and in architectural details such as overdoors. John Houghton carved the handsome picture frames for St Patrick's Deanery and Trinity College. This tradition was continued by John Kelly, whose exquisite floral swags for overdoors and mantelpieces in houses in Parnell Square and elsewhere show craftsmanship of the highest order. Although carvers like Robert Stewart in the Chapel Royal of Dublin Castle and in St Werburgh's and Richard Cranfield in the Provost's House, Trinity College, show great skill and quality, it is with Kelly's work that the high point of Irish 18th-century wood-carving was reached.

John van Nost the younger (c. 1712–80) was the principal sculptor in Ireland from his arrival from England about 1749 until his death. His practice, both varied and considerable, included commissions for public monuments like the *George II* for Essex Bridge, the statues of Mars and Justice on the gates of Dublin Castle, and memorial work such as the splendid Baroque tomb of Judge Gore in Tashinny church and the more restrained monument to Thomas Prior in Christ Church Cathedral, Dublin. Van Nost was also famous for his vigorous, realistic portrait busts; Mrs Delany said of them 'he takes as strong a likeness as ever I saw taken in marble, his price is forty guineas for the model and bust'. He was employed too in making garden statuary, and busts of famous men for decorating libraries and niches in houses. This sculptor's importance for Ireland was not only his actual work, which because of its quality set a high standard and was readily accessible in public places, but because the Dublin Society apprenticed students to him and therefore he influenced the next generation of sculptors. Of his immediate pupils, one, Patrick Cunningham, did some notable busts, including the famous Dean Swift in St Patrick's Cathedral; but he died young and little of his work is known. An artist who worked with Van Nost in the Rotunda Hospital and who may also have been his pupil was Christopher Hewetson, born in Kilkenny about 1739 and who settled in Rome after 1765. There he achieved fame as one of the finest statuaries of his day; he received commissions from Pope Clement XIV, from visiting notabilities, from Trinity College, Dublin, for the Baldwin Memorial and from the Elector of Hanover for a statue of Leibnitz.

The most famous sculptor resident in Ireland in the last decades of the 18th century was Edward Smyth, a pupil of Vierpyl, the Anglo-Flemish decorative carver brought to Ireland by Lord Charlemont and responsible for much of the superb craftsmanship on the Casino, and on other buildings such as the City Hall, where he was assisted by

Smyth. Smyth's career was closely linked with that of James Gandon, the architect who engaged him to carve decorative work including the famous keystone heads, coats of arms and some of the statues on the Custom House, as well as similar work for the Four Courts, the House of Lords entrance to the Parliament House (now the Bank of Ireland), and the King's Inns. Gandon also used Smyth in all these buildings for the skyline statuary for which his dramatic style was particularly well suited; his whole-length figures, like the Charles Lucas in the City Hall and the Duke of Buckingham in St Patrick's Cathedral, show his ability to create vivid and impressive figures. Many of Smyth's portrait busts were done in collaboration with his son John, who also worked with him in the Chapel Royal and whose career shows him to have been the reverse of his father, better as the creator of tomb statuary, at which his father failed notably, but weaker in creating the expressive silhouette so important for great public buildings.

The early 19th century shows an increase in pictorial memorials of the type introduced by Van Nost but now sentimentalized by artists like Thomas Kirk, who was also influenced by Flaxman. His style varies from the Neo-Classical sensibility of *The Parting Glance* (a tomb monument in Monaghan church to the first Lady Rossmore), to the realism of the charity child in the Abbott tomb in Christ Church, Dublin. Like all his contemporaries Kirk sculpted many portrait busts which rarely reach that boring pomposity which characterizes so much of Christopher Moore's images of his fellow countrymen done in Regency London. Many Irish sculptors were then working in England, mostly as assistants to more affluent English artists. The Geogahan family were the most important of these: no less than four of them worked for Nollekens, Westmacott and Flaxman; only one, Sebastian, achieved individual identity. The first quarter of the 19th century saw the battle of the styles develop in Irish sculpture as well as architecture; this is best exemplified by Peter Turnerelli (1774–1839) of Belfast, who achieved considerable international fame and whose surviving works in Ireland show him to have worked in the Italian Renaissance manner as well as in the Gothic. Turnerelli's principal commissions in Ireland were for the pro-Cathedral of St Mary in Dublin and with this new patronage his work leads into the new Ireland which emerged after Catholic Emancipation in 1829.

6

THE DISTRESSED SOCIETY

The struggle for emancipation and independence, 1801-1918

GEARÓID Ó TUATHAIGH

And one read black where the other read white, his hope

The other man's damnation:

Up the Rebels, To Hell with the Pope.

And God Save – as you prefer – the King or Ireland

The land of scholars and saints:

Scholars and saints my eye, the land of ambush,

Purblind manifestoes, never-ending complaints,

The born martyr and the gallant ninny;

The grocer drunk with the drum,

The land-owner shot in his bed, the angry voices

Piercing the broken fanlight in the slum,

The shawled woman weeping at the garish altar.

From *Autumn Journal* by Louis MacNeice

The forces, both conservative and dynamic, which made of the 19th century one of the most eventful and tragic epochs in Irish history, were complex in their origins and in their impact. The Union of 1800 was itself clear evidence that the Ascendancy Protestant landowning class no longer had the capacity to exercise direct political control through its own parliament. During the 19th century, as the advance of democracy brought the long-submerged Catholic masses on to the political stage, the ideas and interests of the 18th-century patricians and their heirs came under strong and sustained attack. Simultaneously, the growth of a centralized bureaucratic state struck at the roots of the aristocracy's control of local government and administration. Above all else, however, the economic position of the landowning Ascendancy was undermined by a complex combination of economic crises, agrarian agitation and state intervention. In short, those who in 1800 were the 'men of no property' (or very little property), were by 1900 poised to establish their own state. It was a remarkable story of struggle and survival.

But the way to victory led through desperate suffering. The first half of the century saw the condition of the small farmers, cottiers and labourers deteriorating. Grain prices and high rents forced those at the bottom of the

social ladder to live on potatoes. When the potato blight struck in 1845 they had no defence. Disaster on a scale scarcely imaginable in England took hold on Ireland and for five years hardly relaxed its grip. Between 1841 and 1851 the population fell by twenty per cent.

The alternative to death was emigration. One and a half million Irish men and women emigrated between 1845 and 1851, and the exodus, once started, was not quickly stemmed; by 1914 another five million had followed them. Most of them went to America, and we shall see what happened to them in Chapter 8. Liverpool was their usual port of embarkation; during those years the sight of Irish families laden with their entire earthly possessions became commonplace there. Not a great deal of sympathy was expended on them, and such commentaries as have survived are not always immune from sentimentality. A painting by Erskine Nichol (opposite) is typical of its time, 1871. A middle-aged emigrant stands ready to board, his face sombre but not despondent. Two boys have intercepted him hoping to make a few pence. One of them offers to polish his shoes. To the left a young man points west and tries to cheer his wife with the promise of success in the New World. And in the background the ships—one with a giant paddle-wheel—are busy loading their cargo. (1)

172

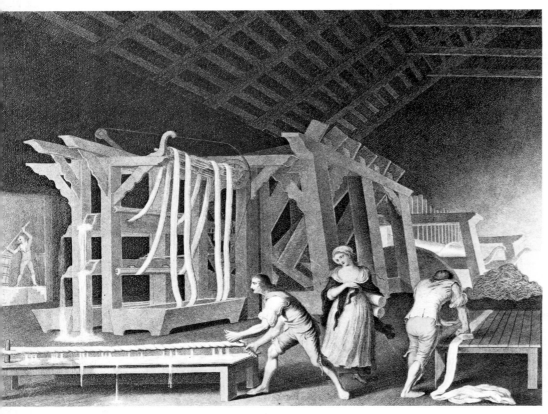

Ireland before the famine was not a place of unrelieved gloom. Some parts of the country were benefiting from industrial progress, while in the more remote areas the traditional festivals and amusements remained vigorously alive. In the early part of the century linen was an important export; its production centred on eastern Ulster, where up-to-date techniques of spinning, bleaching (above) and weaving were in use. Above right and below: two survivals from ancient Ireland—*The Blind Piper*, painted by J. P. Haverty in the middle of the century, and *The Festival of the Seven Churches, Glendalogh*, by Joseph Peacock, 1813; this celebration, held every year on June 3, eventually led to such disorders that it was suppressed by the Catholic authorities in 1862. (2–4)

Many tenant farmers led comfortable lives, especially if they held favourable long-term leases on tolerably large holdings. This *Kitchen Interior* by J. G. Mulvany belongs to the early 19th century and is particularly informative on the tools and furniture one would expect to see in such a house. The family is well-dressed and well-fed and conditions are clean if austere. By 1845 this standard of living was enjoyed by a minority of rural dwellers; only about thirty per cent of tenants had holdings of more than twenty acres. (5)

Travel was expensive and slow at the start of the 19th century. Most country people had never been far from their villages. But in 1815 an enterprising Italian, Charles Bianconi, set up a network using long carriages drawn by four horses. Forty years later (below), on the eve of the railway age in Ireland, they were still the best form of transport. (6)

The realities of life in the Irish countryside are naively portrayed in these pages from a sketchbook from Yougal, Co. Cork. Already by that date the main item of peasant diet was the potato, easy to grow, with a high yield and highly nutritious. It was all too easy to become wholly dependent upon it, with the result that when the crop failed there was nothing to put in its place. Selling the pig (below) was a desperate and temporary solution. The other crop shown in these drawings is probably kelp. (7–11)

After the famine—eviction. The years 1877 to 1879 were again marked by bad harvests. Many landlords refused to reduce rents and a confrontation rapidly developed which came to be called the Land War. The tenants, clinging to their homes, would either passively barricade themselves in or actively defend themselves with stones and, occasionally, boiling water. This family (above) was photographed probably in the late 1880s. They have been turned out of their cottage and the door is nailed up to prevent them returning. Right: the battering ram was used to force an entry and to make houses uninhabitable if the landlord so wished. (12,13)

The coming of photography in the second half of the 19th century gives us suddenly a new and vivid insight into the lives of ordinary people.

Cutting turf: turf, or peat, is produced by decaying vegetation under pressure in waterlogged conditions, and is therefore found in the form of bogs. The old method was to dig it out in slabs three or four feet long by means of specially shaped spades called 'slanes'. The slabs were then stacked to dry, a process that took about six weeks (in its natural state peat contains up to ninety per cent water), and then piled up round the edge of the pit for transportation. It burns with a red smoky flame and gives off a strong smell. (14)

Puck Fair, at Killorglin, Co. Kerry, was an annual market for the sale of goats—later of cattle in general. Its strangest feature was the erection of a high scaffold and the enthronement of a goat, who remained there for the three days of the fair, August 10–12. (15)

Fisherman, Co. Donegal: he carries a coracle, one of the most primitive forms of boat, made from a wooden or reed frame covered with canvas or animal skin. Fishing at this basic level was usually done with two coracles, each man holding a corner of the net in one hand and paddling with the other. (16)

Spinning remained a home occupation in many country areas, especially in connection with tweed making. This scene was taken at Cliffony, Co. Sligo. The vat at the back may contain dye and next to it are two carding combs. Both the girl and the old woman on the right are barefooted. (17)

Harvesting: an old woman, who has perhaps been tying up the sheaves, sits down to a midday meal of potatoes and buttermilk. Before the famine, and for some time after, grain was grown to be sold, not eaten. (18)

Grinding corn at Inishmurry, Co. Sligo: there can hardly be a more primitive method of grinding than the hand-quern. Grain is poured into the hole in the middle, and the upper stone turned with a handle. (19)

The Easter Rising of 1916 was the act of a clandestine minority of republicans within the nationalist movement. Lacking wide popular support and effective help from Germany, the insurgents holding the Dublin Post Office (above) and other public buildings surrendered after a week's siege. The Rising shifted the centre of gravity of Irish nationalism from Home Rule to a more separatist nationalism, but it also strengthened the fears and the resolution of the unionists (20)

In the North the polarization of opinion between nationalist and unionist elements had already reached the threshold of civil war. This demonstration at Portadown, Co. Armagh in 1912, clearly indicates the unionist resolution that 'Ulster would fight' if Home Rule became a reality. The spectre of partition loomed large on the Irish political horizon. (21)

Chapter 6

The struggle for emancipation and independence, 1809–1918

GEARÓID Ó TUATHAIGH

The Triple Alliance of Famine, Eviction and Coercion march through a desolated Ireland. This was how the 'Weekly Freeman' saw the state of the country in 1885. (1)

THE PENAL LAWS had been enacted to keep the Catholic majority in a permanent state of subjection. Already by the mid-18th century their harshness had been greatly mitigated. By 1800 the greater part of the code had been either repealed or allowed to lapse. Catholics could now own land; in law all but the highest levels of the state were open to them. Since 1793 Catholic owners in the counties of freeholds worth 40s. or more per year had the vote. There had never been any serious obstacle to Catholics doing well in trade, and an influential Catholic bourgeoisie (professional and commercial) had emerged in the cities and towns.

The Protestant community in the 18th century was no monolith, either in interest or circumstance. Presbyterians found themselves subject to almost as many restrictions as Catholics. Moreover, a rising tide of Protestant colonial nationalism, gathering force under the stimulus of American experience, resulted in an increasing number of Protestants asserting their 'Irishness', and seeing their interests as separate from, and perhaps opposed to, those of their co-religionists in Britain. The Volunteer movement of the 1770s was a product of this Protestant patriotism, and by 1782 the Irish colonial parliament enjoyed a considerable measure of independence.

Under the impact of the French Revolution many Protestants (particularly Presbyterians) and Catholics espoused republican views, and eventually conspired, in the United Irishmen, to establish an Irish republic by force. However, the failure of the French to send adequate help in time, the mixture of conciliation and repression through which Pitt sought to defuse the republican threat of the 1790s and above all the inability of the republican gospel to triumph over sectarian bitterness and agrarian violence, all contributed to the failure of the 1798 rebellion. The violence of the rebellion frightened the propertied classes into the camp of those who had longed for the security and protection of a Union with Britain. Pitt was also convinced of the necessity of an immediate Union. And so it was that the Act which created the United Kingdom of Great Britain and Ireland became law on 1 January 1801.

To offer an overview of the long span of time from 1801 to 1918 is a daunting task. There are few generalizations which one can make which do not immediately suggest a host of exceptions. Yet it seems to me that there are certain definite trends which can be isolated. At the time of the Union the Protestant colonial Ascendancy owned most of the land of Ireland, and the Big House symbolically dominated the rural village. They had a total monopoly of political power at parliamentary level and in local government, and their Church was the Established Church of the land. In supporting the Act of Union they placed their trust in the imperial parliament to protect their position of privilege. At one level, the history of the 19th century in Ireland is intelligible as the chronicle of betrayal of that trust. In Emancipation, disestablishment and the gradual but irreversible advance of democracy in the 19th century the bulwarks of privilege fell one after another. With the challenge of the land war the colonial landlord class lost its last commanding height, and there ensued what one noted historian has described as 'the euthanasia of the aristocracy'.

The victors of the land struggle, and indeed the victors of the 19th century in general, were the Catholic tenant-farmers and petit-bourgeois elements in town and country. The famine and emigration decimated the rural proletariat, the land war liquidated the landed aristocracy. Throughout

Some of the atrocities which occurred during the '98 rebellion gave little evidence that the message of the United Irishmen (a Union between Irishmen irrespective of creed) had been widely accepted. Those who advocated the Union in 1800 were not slow to pillory the advocates of the United Irish Gospel. (2)

four-fifths of the island the Catholic tenant-farmers were the new masters. Their values were the dominant values, their politics the dominant politics, their Church the dominant Church. They were poised to establish a state of their own. It was an impressive victory.

In the north-east part of the island the story was different. Here an alliance of Protestant landowners and industrial magnates presided over a popular Unionism which encompassed all social classes and which found triumphant expression in the Orange Order. It too was poised to establish its own state. But within that state there would be a sizable non-Unionist population which shared the values of the majority of the island, and which could not accept an enforced ideological exile in the northern Orange state. These conflicting views did not augur well for the stability of the future Irish states.

Town and country 1800–45

Between 1791 and 1841 the population of Ireland increased from about 4·7 million to just over 8 million, of whom about two-thirds depended on the land. In a European context there was nothing exceptional about this increase, but what made it

disturbing was that the rate was highest in the small-farmer, cottier and labouring classes. And it was exactly these classes which, from the last quarter of the 18th century, were becoming dependent on the potato as the main component of their diet.

The potato is a highly nutritional root; it enables a whole family to survive on a small plot of land; and, in a country of expanding tillage (as was Ireland from the late 18th century), it was suitable for healthy crop-rotation and for feeding a necessary labour force at minimum expense. While grain prices remained high, up to the end of the Napoleonic War, many landlords were not opposed to subdivision and the proliferation of smallholders or cottiers. But competition for such holdings meant that the tenants' labour and their cash crop went on rent, and they were left to survive on potatoes. The grain was largely exported to Britain at boom prices. The landlords, through increased rents, did well. So did the comfortable tenant-farmers and the middlemen, especially those who held favourable leases settled in terms of low prices; but little of this profit went to the smallholders.

Nor was the picture much more hopeful in industry. Some sectors of Irish manufacture had expanded during the late 18th century in response to demand at home and in the export market, which was, to an ever-increasing extent, the British market (by 1800, 85 per cent of Irish exports went to Britain, while 78 per cent of all Irish imports came from Britain). The outstanding product was linen, which in 1798 accounted for 58 per cent of total Irish exports. The centre of the linen industry was in east Ulster, but it was spread throughout wide areas of the country. Brewing and distilling, having undergone changes in organization and production methods, were also geared for expansion and for export. Certain other industries (e.g. sugar refining and silk) depended on imported raw materials, and their viability in the immediate post-Union years depended on heavy tariff protection from more efficient competitors.

But from the third decade of the 19th century, with the removal of the protective tariffs from all Irish manufacturers, Irish industry felt the cold winds of competition. Some industries, such as brewing and linen manufacture, proved capable of meeting the challenge to some extent by introducing new techniques of production. For others, however, the story was not so happy. The growing disparity in price between some Irish goods and the cheaper competing products of a rapidly industrializing Britain brought crisis, collapse and unemployment to inefficient Irish industries. Silk, leather and glass suffered. There was widespread distress among the weavers, especially in the smaller provincial towns. In Bandon, Co. Cork, the number of weavers fell

Pattern for handwoven damask cloth, drawn between 1790 and 1820 for Coulson of Lisburn. Linen was one of Ireland's major exports, owing its popularity largely to its elaborate patterns. (3)

from about 2,000 in 1815 to 150 in 1840. In 1841 there were still over 700,000 textile workers listed in the census, but the value of their labour was depreciating and with it their living standards. Only part-time farming, or at least access to a potato plot, kept many of them from starvation.

Tradesmen in provincial towns enjoyed mixed fortunes, especially where their trades were not yet affected by mechanization, or where remoteness from the main centres of wholesale and retail distribution gave temporary protection from competition. In 1846, for example, Ennis, Co. Clare, with a population of over 9,500, had 16 grocers, 22 drapers, 16 bakers, 5 pawnbrokers, 14 blacksmiths, 5 leather-sellers, 5 painters, 4 milliners, 2 straw-bonnet makers, 7 tailors, corn and butter dealers, butchers, masons, wheel-wrights and 19 publicans. The coming of the railways in the second half of the century brought new challenges to some of these tradesmen and retailers throughout the towns of Ireland.

Close to the soil

With the slump in agricultural prices which followed Waterloo, the prudent and comfortable classes of rural Ireland tightened their belts. On the Dublin market the annual average price of wheat slumped from 17s. 6d per hundredweight in the period 1812–15 to just 11s. 6d during 1821–25. There was a shift in investment to livestock,

especially when the arrival of the packet-steamer in the late 1820s made it cheap and convenient to transport live cattle from Ireland to England in a short time, with little deterioration in condition, and at a comfortable profit.

The rural poor continued to increase in number, and, as they did, their economic and social condition worsened. By the mid-1840s the potato was the staple food of as much as 30 per cent of the population, and was a key element in the diet of a much larger number. In coastal areas potatoes and herrings was the regulation dish. By 1845 about one-sixth of the total cultivated acreage of Ireland was under potatoes. Moreover, increasingly in the years before 1845 the type of potato most cultivated was the prolific but inferior-quality *lumper*. In the decades from 1815 to 1845 the struggling cottier or smallholder found that even the sale of the pig (the peasant's insurance against a poor crop or a rent increase) did not always suffice to enable him to keep his holding. Partial failures of the potato crop brought deep distress in many areas in 1817, 1821 and throughout the 1830s.

In 1845 the great majority of landholders (over 70 per cent) occupied holdings of less than twenty acres. About 14 per cent had holdings of less than one acre. As with all national statistics, these figures mask certain marked regional differences. In Ulster, a small holding did not necessarily mean poverty, since many farmers also worked in the linen industry. In much of Leinster, especially in the south-east, there existed a comfortable class of smallholder, working good land most efficiently. In the Midlands, east Munster and parts of east Connacht there was a high quota of large holdings, commercially farmed, and a large number of cottiers and landless labourers. Along the poorer land of the west coast, subdivision was general, the land was poor and there was a chronic incidence of deep poverty.

It was chiefly among the poor cultivators in the west that tourists (and Royal Commissions) found the hordes of children and adults clad in rags and living in primitive mud cabins built on the side of a mountain or in the cutaway of a bog. The worst of these mud cabins had little or no furniture, no chimney or windows; a fire in the centre of the clay floor emitted smoke through the entrance, and the hastily constructed thatch was often wet and soggy. For those fortunate enough to own a pig or fowl, all sheltered under the same roof, and cesspools were often alarmingly close to the cabins. Such miserable hovels were not entirely confined to the western parts of the country. In 1841 some 40 per cent of Irish houses were one-room mud cabins, while a further 37 per cent had between two and four rooms. As late as 1861 there were still 580,000 mud

The Distressed Society 183

As late as the 1860s there were over half a million mud cabins in Ireland. About 90,000 of them had only one room, occupied by an average of eleven people, plus whatever animals they possessed. (4)

cabins occupied in Ireland, of which about 90,000 had only one room. It was generally in the smallest of these that the greatest overcrowding occurred and there was an average of eleven persons per one-roomed cabin. In the 1860s in Co. Sligo the cabin of a by no means poor tenant-farmer measured twelve feet by twenty-four; in which lived the farmer and his wife, four daughters and one son. The household had three cows, two calves, a horse, two pigs and poultry. 'The pigs dwelt beneath the beds, the people in them, and the poultry in the rafters above.' Conditions, however, were below average in the western counties. In general the accommodation of the rural labourers and cottiers improved throughout the country in the post-famine decades.

Naturally, the houses of the more prosperous tenant-farmers were more comfortable and better furnished, even in the poorest areas. Visitors to a pleasant house in west Galway belonging to 'the better class' in 1843 found 'no upper storey; but there was a room branching to the right, and another to the left, of the "kitchen parlour and hall" – the sleeping rooms of the family, decently furnished'. The furniture included a roughly made elm chair, three- or four-legged stools, and on either side of the chimney there was a stone seat; a quern for grinding corn, wooden drinking cups, a primitive gridiron to 'broil the red herrings', a candlestick, a dresser 'well garnished with plates', a saddle hung upon a peg, a pair of oddly shaped tongs to place the turf on the fire, a churn, a rafter to hang clothes upon, a salt-box, 'the iron-pot, of course, and the crook fastened up the chimney, to hang the pot upon', and a wheel for wool and a wheel for flax. 'The inhabitants of the cottage consisted of the father, mother, grand-

mother and seven children', and the family had the services of a barefoot 'waiting wench'. A cupboard in the wall was converted into a hen-roost for half a dozen 'laying hens'. 'This cottage . . . may be taken as a model of the better class . . . The roof was sound, the windows were whole . . . the stagnant pool was at a respectable distance; the pig had his separate apartment; and there was a stable for the cow and horse.'

Comfortable farmers on the rich land of the east and south lived in still greater comfort. By the early 19th century many of them were converting to slate roofs, their houses were larger and better furnished than the 'comfortable cottage', and the outhouses were on a grander scale. They usually had servants' quarters, as well as family accommodation. We know that one at least could afford to spend twelve guineas a year for private tuition for his children. This latter example, it must be said, comes from the top level of farmer in prosperous Leinster, in a home where 'no day ever passed . . . that we had not a goose, turkey, pair of ducks, or a couple of fat fowl for dinner'. The poorer small-farmer's diet might include milk, oatmeal, wheaten bread and, of course, potatoes, with the possibility of meat on rare occasions. For the cottier and labourer the potato diet (sometimes with milk) was the rule, and only at Christmas was there the possibility of meat.

The pre-famine rural hierarchy was also evident in differences in dress. The comfortable farmer had knee-breeches, waistcoat, shirt and cravat, tailcoat, woollen stockings and strong boots; his wife had shifts, petticoats, skirt, bodice and a cloak. She also wore shoes. For the lower levels of rural society the clothes, though of the same cut generally, were more threadbare (and in shorter supply) and patched. Shoes were not usually to be seen on women or children of the small-farmer class and under, and the labourer who owned an overcoat was the exception.

Work and wages

The wages of labourers in pre-famine Ireland varied enormously from place to place, and at different times of the year. In Co. Cork, for example, in the 1830s, male agricultural labourers earned from 4d to 8d per day in ordinary times, rising to between 10d and 1s. 2d per day at harvest time and during potato planting and digging. Women might earn 5d or 6d a day in planting potatoes or in binding grain. Some labourers and cottiers received little or no money payment, but could remit rent through labour, or might be fed and housed and given access to a potato plot. But the chronic over-supply of the labour market in the pre-famine decades left the majority of the labourers in a permanently precarious state of under-employment and poverty.

In the west, where conditions were worst, many labourers sought a solution through seasonal migration. The migrant labourer or *spailpin* went from the poorer to richer lands (of Leinster and Munster), and in the case of western migrants there was already a well-established traffic of seasonal labourers to England and Scotland in the pre-famine decades. In addition to the personal indignity of the hiring-fair, the hard work demanded of him and the miserable lodgings provided for him, the migrant labourer often encountered a rough welcome from the local labourers of the areas to which he journeyed.

Not all casual labour was involved in agriculture. A much-prized source of employment was the public works sponsored by the government in times of distress, and by the county grand juries at other times. The government schemes had the advantage of generally higher average wages, which also were usually paid more promptly. In 1834 in Galway several hundred casual labourers were employed at 10d a day on the construction of the new dock (though work and pay were suspended when it rained). A sample of food prices in Galway in the summer of this year may give an idea of the standard of living prospects of the lower classes:

beef	5d per pound
lamb	4s. per quarter
pork	2d a pound
a turkey	2s.
a goose	2s.
a couple of fowl	1s.
mutton	6d per pound
eggs	4d per dozen
butter	1s. per pound
a good cod fish	1s. 6d
potatoes	$3\frac{1}{2}$d per stone (14 pounds)

The most inflated rents were probably those being paid under the conacre system, whereby the lessor prepared a plot and let it for a single crop. In the 1840s annual rents of up to £10 or £12 per acre were being paid for conacre plots, though there were wide differences in various parts of the country. It is certain, however, that rents and prices pressed hard on the cottier and casual labourer in the pre-famine years. The domestic servant was often better off, if only on the grounds of greater security in basic food and lodgings. By the 1840s a manservant, fed and housed, might receive between £6 and £10 a year in wages. The female servant could hardly hope for more than £5.

The majority of the poorer peasants seldom moved outside their own area in pre-famine days, and those who did usually went on foot. Travel by the extensive network of inland waterways which Ireland possessed by the second quarter of the 19th century was both slow and very expensive. After 1815, through the entrepreneurship of an Italian immigrant, Charles Bianconi, the greater part of the country was provided with an efficient and reasonably cheap system of road transport on long horse-drawn cars. Yet, though Bianconi's cars were cheaper than the mail coaches, they were still too dear for the poorer classes. For example, in 1843 a return journey between Ennis and Limerick cost 2s. 6d by coach and 1s. by car. In fact Bianconi provided a regular and economic transport system for the comfortable tenant-farmer and urban middle class. Ireland had to wait for the railway age before the democratization of transport services could begin.

Violence

During the first half of the 19th century violence was never very far from the surface of everyday life in rural Ireland. The bitter competition for access to land, the sole means of subsistence for the majority, led to the growth of agrarian secret societies from the second half of the 18th century. These societies were generally composed of cottiers, labourers and struggling farmers, who felt threatened by rising rents, enclosures of commonage, conversions of tillage land to grass, or other heavy exactions of taxes, tithes or clerical dues. Their methods were quite violent; they threatened landlords' agents and bailiffs, besides burning hay, ploughing up grassland and maiming cattle. The agrarian societies were spread throughout the country, but in the early 19th century they were particularly strong in the counties of Munster and south Leinster, where land was good, rents high and the willingness of the landlords to resist subdivision greatest. Tipperary was particularly notorious for agrarian violence. In the north-east the conflicts of these secret societies had, by the late 18th century, settled into a sectarian mould, especially in the border areas of south and mid-Ulster where the relative strength of Protestant and Catholic tenants was fairly evenly balanced. Here, the Protestant Orangemen and the Catholic Defenders met fire with fire. Elsewhere, the societies had such colourful names as Caravats, Shanavests, Whitefeet, Terryalts and Rockites. In their grievances and organization the societies were usually local and largely non-political. The only significant exception to this rule was the society of Ribbonmen, which had political aims and seems to have had the outline of an organization (with liaison between different areas and a committee structure at local level). The Ribbonmen was more an urban than a rural society, with clerks, schoolmasters and artisans prominent among its members. Its oaths were often derived from the egalitarian republican tradition of the 1790s, and members called for the freedom of Ireland and for full civil and religious liberties for all.

The activities of the agrarian secret societies usually took place under cover of darkness. Not so with the faction fights, which were public spectacles of violence. On the fair day in the market place, or at race-meetings, these factions (led by faction leaders trailing their coats in challenge to rivals) met and battered each other with fists, sticks and more lethal weapons. The *casus belli* might be a land dispute, a family feud, a personal insult, or a rivalry between parishes or townlands. Very often it was sheer bravado, the product of too much drink.

In the second quarter of the 19th century a determined effort was made from several directions to curb the activities of all these violent groups. The Catholic bishops and priests came out strongly and consistently against secret societies. The Bishop of Kildare and Leighlin, Dr Doyle (more commonly known as JKL), put the official Church view clearly: 'Beloved brethren, I tell you in truth that these associations are opposed to all your interests both temporal and eternal, that the oath which binds them is illegal, sacrilegious and unjust, and if it is observed it will be a bond of iniquity.' Priests who condemned the societies very often had their church windows broken in retaliation. Political leaders, and especially the colossus of the period, Daniel O'Connell, exhorted the people to reject and abandon the secret societies. O'Connell did more than merely exhort, of course. He redirected popular energies into constitutional politics, as a means of getting popular grievances redressed. His direction of 'mass politics' did much to weaken the influence of the secret societies. From a different direction, the gradual introduction of a centralized and efficient police force in Ireland (beginning with Peel's reforms in 1814 and culminating in Drummond's in 1836) had the effect of reducing the incidence of faction fighting and seriously weakening the agrarian societies.

The towns were by no means free of 'organized' violence. Apart from the recognized and respectable trade unions, there were also less scrupulous 'combinations' of urban workers (skilled and unskilled) who had their own ways of dissuading rural labourers from crowding into an already over-supplied urban labour market.

In general, such violence was probably decreasing in the immediate pre-famine years. Nevertheless, the tradition of violence and 'direct action' by clandestine societies outlived the famine. Ribbonmen formed a direct link with the oath-bound Irish Republican Brotherhood (or Fenian movement) after 1858. The tradition of rough justice in settling agrarian disputes was very much in evidence during the land war in the late 19th century, and Parnell openly acknowledged the tradition when he warned the government of the day that if he himself were imprisoned the rule of Captain Moonlight would again hold sway among the land agitators.

Leisure, learning and the Churches

Talk of violence and of a relatively deprived material culture should not lead us to conclude that life for the masses in pre-famine Ireland was a cycle of unrelieved sadness and pain. On the contrary, there was great variety of popular entertainment. Popular poetry and story-telling, survivals of a once majestic Gaelic civilization, still had meaning and an audience in rural communities. The rich lore of ancient mythology, and the more ephemeral verses on everyday happenings, bore witness to riches of imagination and spirit which mocked the material poverty in which they were caged. Story-telling and versifying were, in fact, public acts. So also were music-making and dancing, where class and condition were for a time forgotten in the exhilaration of life and merriment. The blind harper, O'Carolan, had his wealthy patron; the blind poet Raftery was a household name throughout much of Connacht in his own time, and for long afterwards. Pipers and fiddlers were welcome at any door, and the travelling music teacher or dancing master could maintain himself by teaching the children of the well-to-do farmers.

The great days of the life-cycle were celebrated in style. Indeed, entertainment was generally so riotous at wakes (with singing, dancing, food, snuff and plenty of drink, not to speak of cards and other games) that the clergy were constantly preaching against the profane excess of Irish wake amusements. In fact, as we shall see, the Catholic Church did not hold total, or indeed, decisive sway over the habits and morals of the poorer classes in many parts of the country in early 19th-century Ireland. In the sporting line, horse-racing was a most popular sport among all classes of rural society. Along the west coast, regattas (races of currachs or *naomhoga*) were quite popular. And then, of course, there was hurling, the most distinctive native sport. In 1808 an observer had this to say of hurling in Co. Clare:

The hurling matches, called goals, are very injurious to the morals and industry of the younger classes; after performing feats of activity that would astonish a bread and cheese Englishman, they too often adjourn to the whiskey house, both men and women, and spend the night in dancing, singing and drinking until perhaps morning, and too often quarrels and broken heads are the effects of this enebriety; matches are often made between the partners at the dance; but it frequently happens that they do not wait for the priest's blessing, and the fair one must apply to a magistrate, who generally obliges the faithless Strephon to make a honest woman out of her.

Local pattern days – days dedicated to the local saint – were not only occasions of devotion, but also days of merriment. Even events such as harvesting or turf-cutting were often followed by merrymaking.

One aspect of these festivities which visitors invariably noted and which gave concern to the priests and the more sober members of society was the heavy drinking indulged in by the Irish peasantry. A great deal of the drink consumed was *poitín*, or illicitly distilled whiskey, although beer and labelled whiskey were relatively cheap. The improved efficiency of the excise men in the 1830s reduced the trade in *poitín*, and the temperance campaign of Father Mathew had considerable success in reducing the general level of alcohol consumption.

In the battle against the evils of drink and violence enlightened opinion in the early 19th century placed considerable trust in the benefits of education and the influence of the Churches. By 1800 there were many agencies involved in the elementary education of the masses in Ireland. The majority received their education in the hedge schools, so-called because of the custom of holding classes in the open air in fine weather. During bad weather a shed or barn was generally provided by the farmer with whom the schoolmaster happened to be lodging. The quality of teaching in the hedge schools varied enormously, according to the qualifications and dedication of the teacher and the expectations of the parents. Most parents wanted the boys educated for specific jobs as clerks, storekeepers or, for the more ambitious, in preparation for the seminary. Accordingly the curriculum usually centred on the three R's, with occasional smatterings of Latin and Greek. Although some schoolmasters were undoubtedly well versed in native learning and folklore, it was a general policy in the hedge schools to suppress the native language and learning among the children, and to replace it with English. English was the language of jobs and progress and social mobility, and Irish-speaking parents (very often monolinguals) were anxious that their children should have English rather than Irish as a vernacular, in order to improve their life chances. Teachers, on the instruction of parents, often kept a tally-stick on which a notch was cut every time a pupil spoke Irish. At the end of the day the pupil was punished *pro rata* with the number of notches. It is difficult to comprehend the psychological consequences (individual and collective) of this frightful method of forced linguistic change.

By the 1820s an estimated half-million children (of whom four-fifths were Catholics) were availing themselves of hedge-school education; but already the system was in decline. Since the late 18th century there had been a steady growth in the provision of Catholic education by religious orders. The first priority had been the training of priests, and by the early 19th century not only was there a national seminary at Maynooth, founded in 1795, but there were also seminaries in Carlow, Kilkenny, Killarney and other dioceses. The new teaching and charitable orders like Nano Nagle's Presentation Sisters and Edmond Rice's Christian Brothers and many others were expanding their activities in this period. The state itself gave some assistance to several educational societies under the direction of the Established Church. But their impact on the Catholic masses was not numerically significant.

By the late 1820s the time was ripe for a new departure, and in 1831 the Whigs announced the establishment of a National Board of Education to administer a centralized system of nondenominational education. The new system had its faults and its teething problems. It was opposed and largely boycotted by the Established Church; it ran into strong opposition from a section of Catholic opinion on the grounds of its anti-national and irreligious bias, and it was somewhat bureaucratic and under-financed in administration. But it did succeed in drawing into the net of elementary education many poor children who were hitherto outside that net. It quickly absorbed the hedge-school population. It undoubtedly played its part, alongside the denominational schools, in greatly reducing the illiteracy rate during the 19th century. In 1841 some 47 per cent of the population claimed to be able to read; by 1911 the figure was 88 per cent.

At secondary level the efforts of the teaching orders made an impact on only a section of the middle classes. The establishment of nondenominational university colleges at Cork, Galway and Belfast in 1845 by Peel had an even more limited impact on the population at large – though it did allow the clerical interest an abundance of field days in denouncing the 'godless colleges'.

In the spiritual domain the Catholic Church was the Church of about four-fifths of the population in the pre-famine years, and it was the Church of the vast majority of the poor. By the early 19th century its work of reconstruction after the crises and disruption of the Penal Code era was well under way. Several major seminaries had been established and further diocesan schools were being built. There was considerable work to be done in reorganizing diocesan and parochial boundaries to accord with demographic changes. As the manpower supply improved this was accompanied from the 1830s onwards by a sustained effort in church-building.

The Catholic Church was supported by voluntary contribution. The Established Church in Ireland came in for much criticism in pre-famine Ireland, not only from Catholics and nonconformists but also from reforming Anglicans. While it contained many men of undoubted piety and heroic charity, it was nevertheless over-wealthy and overstocked by the 1830s. By 1833, for example, it had 4 archbishops, 18 bishops and 2,000 clergymen and enjoyed a gross annual income of between £800,000 and £1 million. Through tithes, and through vestry cess, a tax levied for the upkeep of ecclesiastical property, the population at large had to maintain this minority Church. There was heavy absenteeism, and income differentials among the clerical hierarchy were too great. In 1833 a considerable pruning and reorganization of the Established Church took place, and in 1838 tithe was commuted to a charge on rent. Both of these measures benefited the Church in its mission, which was mainly, but not exclusively, directed towards the landed gentry and professional classes.

The major nonconformist group was the Presbyterians, heavily concentrated in east Ulster. They were strongly represented in the small farmer and business classes and among textile operatives. A tendency towards recurring splits on doctrinal matters was partially arrested in 1840 with the establishment of the General Assembly of the Presbyterian Church of Ireland. Though Presbyterians (like other nonconformists) resented Anglican privileges, from the 1820s onwards there was a tendency for all Protestants to see the differences between themselves as of far less importance than their common antipathy to the machinations of Rome.

The 'Modern Hercules', Daniel O'Connell, rescues the fair maiden Hibernia from the oppressions of the English army, church and government with his club, Repeal; a cartoon of 1843. (5)

The struggle for Emancipation

Political and religious consciousness were inextricable in Ireland and, as we have seen, in spite of the concessions that had been made since 1793 the post-Union Protestant Ascendancy class was still firmly in control. For middle-class Catholics the political demand of the early 19th century, as it had been for some decades before, was for full civil and political rights. They wanted equality of opportunity to participate fully in the civil and political life of the country. It was far from being a revolutionary demand.

So far as the mass of the people was concerned political life in the early 19th century merely involved an occasional turn at the hustings to vote for the landlord. Among the Irish-speaking peasants political consciousness had somewhat atrophied in a totally unrealistic obsession with the messianic role of a deliverer (Bonnie Prince Charlie or even Napoleon) who would come over the water and restore the Catholic religion and native learning to their rightful place. The essential features of this consciousness were its sense of deprivation, its nostalgic defeatism and its basic passivity in contemporary political life. The transformation of this consciousness to an assertive, optimistic and challenging attitude was in large measure the work of one man, Daniel O'Connell. Born of Catholic gentry stock, and one of the most popular and formidable lawyers in the country by the second decade of the 19th century, O'Connell typified in some ways the characteristics of his class. He was of Gaelic background, but during the 18th century his ancestors had adopted the English language, had accepted the political settlement of the Hanoverian succession, and had concentrated on doing as well as they could within the system. They had always sought acceptance, not revolution. O'Connell had been educated on the Continent and at Lincoln's Inn in London. He was very widely read, had proclaimed himself a follower of Bentham, and was that *rara avis* in early 19th-century Europe, a sincere Catholic and a convinced liberal. His experience of the French Revolution strengthened his opposition to violence as a means of effecting political change. He believed in the invincibility of public opinion when properly mobilized.

Armed with this faith, he organized during the 1820s a great mass movement for the carrying of Catholic Emancipation, i.e. the removal of the remaining civil and political disabilities on Catholics, most notably the right to enter Parliament. Under the leadership of the Catholic middle classes (especially the lawyers) and the priests, the Catholic masses were mobilized by O'Connell and educated in all the techniques of pacific political agitation. Petitions were signed, the 40s. freehold votes were cashed in at election time for pro-Emancipation pledges from candidates, a fighting fund was set up and through subscriptions of 1d a month the mass of the people became involved and identified with the cause. All popular grievances were given an airing by O'Connell, and through sheer force of personality he raised the level of popular expectations of political exertion. In 1829 the campaign succeeded in its immediate objective when Wellington and Peel (against their own and the King's deepest convictions) carried Emancipation through Parliament. But Emancipation carried a sting in the tail; the 40s. freeholders were disenfranchised. The victory of 1829 was of immediate benefit only to that section of the Catholic middle classes (like O'Connell himself) whose political ambition could now be satisfied by a seat in Parliament. But it would be wrong to dismiss Emancipation so simply or so cynically. It had important psychological significance for a people among whom the habit of defeat had cut through to the bone. A victory had been won, the Ascendancy had been forced to yield. O'Connell had taught the peasants self-discipline and self-reliance; he had instilled into them the will to win, and had convinced them that they could win. It was no mean achievement.

In the later 1830s the Whigs carried out a number of generally welcome reforms in Ireland. Municipal government had been reformed in the interests of efficiency; reforms were carried out in the police system and in the administration of justice. More contentiously, the English Poor Law system, based on the workhouse, was transplanted to Ireland in 1839, at a time when a Royal Commission estimated that about 600,000 labourers were unemployed for thirty weeks in the year. The workhouse system was designed to meet the needs of 'normal poverty'; but who was to say what was 'normal poverty' in pre-famine Ireland?

O'Connell's second great popular campaign, for the Repeal of the Act of Union, was not successful. Unlike Emancipation, Repeal had no British friends. After a false start in the early 1830s, O'Connell returned to the Repeal cause in 1841 when his implacable political foe, Peel, returned to power. To his well-tried bag of political tricks O'Connell added some new tactics in the Repeal agitation. He held a series of monster meetings at historic sites, such as Tara. He was supported by a group of young romantic nationalists, later called the 'Young Irelanders', including Charles Gavan Duffy, Thomas Davis and John Mitchel. The Young Irelanders founded a newspaper, the *Nation*, which enjoyed enormous influence. But, when the government refused to budge, O'Connell sought a compromise. The Young Ireland purists, outraged, broke with him, and, with little support and under

the spur of famine at home and revolution abroad, lurched into a rebellion on behalf of an Irish republic in 1848. The result, predictably in a famine-stricken land, was a fiasco. The previous year O'Connell himself had died on a pilgrimage to Rome. Repeal was buried with him. Politics seemed irrelevant in a land of famine and death.

The famine

In 1845 calamity, in the form of a potato blight, struck Ireland. Some of the crop was saved that year. The blight struck again in 1846. The following year it was less severe; but due to the fact that seeds had been eaten or not planted at all in 1846, the year 1847 was a black year for the potato-eaters. The blight struck again in 1848 and was accompanied by a poor grain harvest. In 1849 the severity of the blight had weakened and by 1850 it was clear that it was on the wane.

These were harrowing years of death, disease and emigration for the poorer classes, those who depended on the potato for their food. The workhouse system was over-run; private charity was a drop in the ocean, and even the massive programme of state aid (public works, soup kitchens and imported Indian meal) was less than adequate to deal with the crisis. In August 1847, for example, some three million people were in receipt of daily rations from the soup kitchens, the vast majority of them gratis. A question which continues to puzzle and anger is, why did people starve while food was being exported from the country? With the exception of a short interval in the winter of 1846–47 there was no absolute shortage of food in Ireland during the famine. It was not a question of absolute food shortage but rather of distribution, involving not only communications and transport, but also the very basic concepts of property.

The consequences of the famine for Irish society were many and complex. The population fell by about 20 per cent between 1841 and 1851. During the famine years of 1845–51 about one and a half million emigrated, while famine mortality (mostly diseases such as typhus, relapsing fever and dropsy, together with an outbreak of cholera in 1849) accounted for a further 800,000. While no area totally escaped, the counties hardest hit were those of the west and south-west, where dependence on the potato was greatest, subdivision most acute and the retail network least developed. Furthermore, the fall in population was not a temporary lapse. Between 1848 and 1914 close on five and a half million emigrated. This haemorrhage, together with a decline in the marriage and birth rates, explains why, despite a relatively low normal death rate, the population of Ireland fell from 6·6 million in 1851 to 4·4 million in 1911.

The Distressed Society 189

Bare figures, however, only tell part of the story. The famine and its aftermath transformed the class structure of rural Ireland. The labourers, cottiers and smaller farmers were the chief victims of the famine and of the emigration of the next half-century. The following table, taken from Professor Lee's excellent study, shows the pattern:

acres:	LABOURERS	COTTIERS (under 5)	FARMERS (5–15)	FARMERS (over 15)
1845	700,000	300,000	310,000	277,000
1851	500,000	88,000	192,000	290,000
1910	300,000	62,000	154,000	304,000

The class balance of Irish rural society was radically changed. The relative weight of the *prudent* classes (i.e. the farmers who were against sub-division and delayed marriage until encouraged by the prospect of security of inheritance) was greater in post-famine Ireland than it had been before 1850. The surviving post-famine labourers and cottiers tended more and more to conform to the now very definite norms of caution and prudence. The dowry and the fixed match, already common among comfortable farmers before the famine, dominated the rural marriage scene after 1850.

The famine had a traumatic effect on the attitudes of the Irish peasantry. Many folk-customs and pastimes lapsed, never to be revived. The famine also transformed the linguistic map of the country. In 1800 Irish was the language of about half of the population, and by 1845 there were probably 4 million Irish speakers in the country. Six years later it was spoken by less than 25 per cent of the population, and only about 5 per cent were monolingual Irish speakers; and during the rest of the century the language continued its retreat to the communities of the Atlantic seaboard. The long-term factors involved in this linguistic change are easily listed. English was the dominant language of politics, the courts and the market place. Already by the early 19th century the Catholic gentry and middle classes had abandoned Irish for the language of success and of upward social mobility. The lower classes were following this example as fast as they could, as is evident from the hedge-school system. In the years after 1800 the increasing influence of English-speaking priests trained in Maynooth, O'Connellite mass politics, the state elementary education system, and the popularity of the *Nation* newspaper, all tended to accelerate the shift to English. Due to the rapid population increase among the poorer classes and in the poorer regions the *absolute* number of Irish speakers continued to rise up to 1845. But the famine and emigration decimated these classes, and from 1851 onwards the size of the Irish-speaking population began its long cycle of contraction.

The bitter memories of food being exported while people starved were turned to political advantage by those who followed John Mitchel's example in laying the blame for the famine at the door of the British government. This view and this bitterness were particularly strong among the famine and post-famine Irish who emigrated to the USA. The folk-memory of the famine was transmitted through successive generations of Irish-Americans, and was to make them a powerful base of support for all Irish movements which sought to break the connection with England. Within a generation of the famine the growth of the Fenian movement, in America and in Ireland, testified to the potentially explosive political legacy of the famine.

After the famine

In economic terms the period from 1850 to 1877 was, with one serious slump, a period of general prosperity for Irish agriculture. Agricultural prices were high and all classes shared in the general prosperity. The continued contraction of the pool of

By the winter of 1846–47 two crops of the potato had failed. Cold and lack of food made the population an easy prey to epidemics of typhus and cholera. At the funeral of two children at Skibbereen, January 1847, there is no money even for coffins. (6)

'Where is this to end?' asks Erin. 'In forty years I have lost, through the operation of no natural law, more than three millions of my sons and daughters, and they, the young and the strong, leaving behind the old and the infirm, to weep and to die.' (7)

labourers (due to emigration) meant that those who remained could demand higher wages and better conditions. By the 1860s farm labourers' wages had increased by about 80 per cent from their pre-famine level. In agricultural output the livestock sector, which had been expanding since Waterloo, assumed the dominant role in the agricultural economy after 1860, when tillage at last began to decline. Total tillage acreage fell from 4·3 million acres in 1861 to 2·3 million in 1910. Cattle numbers increased from 2·7 million in 1848 to 5 million by 1914, and there was expansion also in sheep and poultry numbers over the long term.

It was a prosperous time for the agricultural community, and this was reflected in general improvements of diet and dress, in improved housing, and in rising consumption of such 'luxuries' as tea and snuff. A significant contribution to rural incomes was made by emigrants' remittances to those left at home.

Considerable changes were brought about by the coming of the railways. From a mere 475 miles of track in 1850 the Irish railway network advanced to 2,000 miles in 1872 and by 1914 it had 3,500 miles of track. The impact of the railway was felt in many areas of Irish life. In trade it brought into the national retail network areas which had hitherto not been penetrated by the larger producers and wholesalers of Dublin and the other large towns. However, the major share (55 per cent) of railway receipts in the later 19th century came from passenger traffic. The most important contribution of the railway was that it enabled classes which had hitherto not travelled very much (if at all) in the country to so do so cheaply and speedily. Between 1860 and 1910 the number of *third class* passengers on the railways increased from 5 million to 25

million. Trips to seaside resorts became possible for the working-class in town and country. The concept of time and punctuality took on a new significance in many towns and villages throughout the country. A considerable labour force was employed in running the service, from porters to clerks, with good wages and relatively attractive working conditions. A number of splendidly solid hotels at the major termini gave a certain style and excitement to rail travel, and even the more modest stations were very often delightful additions to the architecture of the countryside.

The supply of railway clerkships was but one aspect of a more general development of the 19th century, namely the growth in numbers of the white-collar and professional elements in the major towns and cities. Irish towns enjoyed mixed fortunes during the 19th century. In industrial terms the only success story was Belfast, the population of which grew from 100,000 to 400,000 in the sixty years after the famine. The linen industry had laid the foundation for Belfast's industrial growth and when from the 1860s onwards the growing stature of shipbuilding and its auxiliary industries captured world markets for Belfast, it was clearly Ireland's only industrial city. Suburban housing for the middle classes contrasted with the congested and unhealthy houses of the industrial labour force in central Belfast. To make matters even worse the rural immigrants who formed a great part of Belfast's proletariat carried their racial and sectarian passions into the city, resulting in riots and violence at regular intervals from the 1850s onwards. Elsewhere in the country the towns which came best out of the 19th century were those which were administrative or market centres.

The growing penetration of the state into the life

of the community during the century was reflected in the public buildings of many country towns – a courthouse, a workhouse, a hospital, a police barracks, a couple of schools, a post office, a railway station and a bank. Terraced houses and neat gardens were white-collar comforts. Working-class housing in the towns was often rather poor, though it improved gradually in the latter half of the century. In general the population of most Irish towns, having undergone an influx of rural paupers during the famine years, remained fairly static in the second half of the century. However, largely due to rural exodus (and to Belfast's growth) the percentage of the population living in towns increased from 15 per cent in 1841 to 35 per cent in 1914.

Dublin's growth in the later 19th century was much less spectacular than and of a different character from Belfast's. In fact the population of Dublin rose by only 50,000 (from 250,000 to 300,000) during 1850–1914. The city's industrial base was rather narrow (brewing, distilling and biscuits were its main components) but it was a major commercial and administrative centre. If the city was short of industrialists it was more than well stocked with professional and white-collar elements. In terms of income, by the early 20th century the professional classes were very well paid indeed. Lawyers' incomes probably averaged about £1,000 a year, as against an average of £100 for a skilled worker, and as little as £6 a year for a female domestic servant living in. Not surprisingly, even the more modest middle-class families could afford a domestic help, and by 1891 there were 23,726 of these in Dublin and its suburbs. The expansion of suburban living in Dublin was accompanied by a chronic congestion of the poorer classes in unsanitary tenement lodgings in the centre city area. As Professor Cullen notes, 'Outside the slum districts, and especially in the townships beyond the canals, a large, prosperous and expanding middle-class existed.'

Fenianism and the land war

In political life the mid-Victorian period witnessed a major struggle between Fenian republicanism and moderate Catholic nationalism within the nationalist camp, punctuated at regular intervals by explosions of Orange triumphalism in the northeast with resulting riot and disorder. The 1857 Belfast riots were particularly vicious evidence of racial prejudice. The Fenians, or Irish Republican Brotherhood, was a secret oath-bound society dedicated to the overthrow of the English government of Ireland by force. It was founded in 1858 by veterans of the Young Ireland rising of 1848 who were determined to erase the memory of that fiasco. The leaders were all, to some extent, disciples of the

Nation of the 1840s. They were of mixed social origin – John O'Mahoney sprang from an established landed family in Co. Cork; James Stephens was a civil engineer; John Devoy, a cottier's son; O'Donovan Rosa, a grocer; John O'Leary and Charles Kickham, both shopkeepers' sons. But the general character of the movement was decidedly working-class and lower-middle-class. Farm labourers, small farmers, artisans in the towns and cities, shop-boys in Dublin, Cork and other large towns – these were the backbone of the Fenian rank and file in Ireland. A significant number of Ribbonmen and other small groups were absorbed into the movement, and the Fenians had considerable success in penetrating and establishing Fenian 'cells' within the British army. The Fenians could count on massive support from Irish immigrants in English towns and, especially in the USA, immigrants anxious to retain group identity and to avenge the shame of the famine. Indeed, in financial and organizational terms the American support was crucial. Numerically the Fenian movement was the best-supported clandestine separatist movement in Irish history. By 1865 it was estimated that some 80,000 Fenians had been enrolled in Ireland and Britain. In 1861, the massive funeral of Terence Bellew McManus (an 1848 veteran) showed a wide latent sympathy for the Fenians. A short-term agricultural crisis between 1860 and 1863 helped to swell the ranks still further.

However, the organization suffered from serious defects. Stephens, the chief organizer in Ireland, had supped with Europe's revolutionaries in Paris and had learned much from their proven inexpertise in planning revolution. There was constant misunderstanding and friction between the Irish and the American wings of the movement. The government had many spies in the movement. The Fenians established a newspaper, not entirely what one might expect from a clandestine oath-bound society. Eventually in 1867 the long-awaited rebellion went off at half-cock in bad weather. The leaders and a sizable number of their followers were sentenced to long periods of penal servitude.

But the Fenian legacy was significant, indeed crucial, for the subsequent history of Ireland. In the first place, despite all the dissensions and difficulties of the next half-century, the organization survived to play a central role in the rebellion of 1916. But its significance does not stop there. It brought into revolutionary political activity (in organization and consciousness) social classes and regions of the country which had hitherto been confined to the margins of Irish political life. Moreover, it was the first significant political movement in nationalist Ireland which did not depend on the support of the Catholic clergy. Indeed, the most bitter opponents of the Fenians were the Catholic bishops, led by Cullen and Moriarty. Furthermore, though its main objective was the uncomplicated one of breaking the connection with England, there was a social reformist bias in the movement which O'Connellite nationalism had lacked and which harked back to the republican egalitarianism of the 1790s. Ironically, however, the major immediate consequence of the Fenian rising (and of the subsequent Fenian campaign in English towns) was Gladstone's decision to pacify Ireland by legislating on those very issues which had been pressed by the main opponents of the Fenians, the Catholic moderate nationalists under Cullen's inspiration. Thus, the Established Church was disestablished in 1869, a Land Act was passed in 1870 which aimed at reducing discontent among farmers and an abortive attempt was made to deal with Irish university education in a way acceptable to all parties. By the late 1870s, however, Ireland was engulfed in a crisis which went far beyond the reach of Gladstonian palliatives.

In 1874 a world-wide industrial boom came to an end. British industry began to flood the Irish market with cheap surplus stock and prices fell. This dumping coincided with new techniques in production in certain areas (e.g. nail-making), which threatened Irish craftsmen. Irish industry was rocked: many workers were paid off as industries closed down. Skilled craftsmen found themselves sliding into the casual labour market. It was a time of crisis in the cities and towns. In the countryside the situation was still more alarming. Starting in 1877 there were three successive bad harvests, that of 1879 being particularly so. In the west the failure of the potato and oats crops brought many communities to the edge of famine. In an unprecedented development low yields were accompanied by falling prices, due to the arrival in Europe of grain imports by ocean steamer from the vast new wheatlands of North America. The late 1870s and early 1880s saw a combined industrial and agricultural crisis, with widespread distress in town and countryside.

The response of the peasantry to this crisis demonstrates very clearly the change in attitudes which had taken place since the great famine. If the horrors of famine did not return to the west in 1879 this was only partly due to an improved relief programme and to conditions of communication better than those which had existed in the mid-'forties. In fact the change was due to a combination of several factors. Higher literacy levels and sharper political consciousness (due in large measure to Fenian influence) were two important factors. The high quality of local leadership was also important, as was the fact that an inflated force of unemployed was idle in the countryside due to a fall-off in demand for immigrant labour in America and Britain during the slump. Above all else, however, the major determinant of changed attitudes was the experience (however limited) of rising prosperity during the previous twenty-five years. Even the poorer peasants were determined that the gains which had been made since 1850 should not be sacrificed.

The result of these changed attitudes was the land war of 1879–82. Starting in the west with radical demands not only for rent reductions but also for land redistribution, the land agitation as it spread became dominated by tenant-farmers whose demands crystallized around the three F's – fair rents, fixity of tenure and freedom of sale. The early leaders in the west were local men (many of them Fenians), but from an early stage a prominent role was played by an extraordinary one-armed ticket-of-leave Fenian named Michael Davitt. Davitt was born in Mayo, and was forced to go with his parents to Lancashire where he lost an arm in a factory accident. He worked hard to gain a cautious backing for the land agitation from some of the Fenian elders, and in 1879 founded the Land League, the body which directed the land war. The most unlikely hero of the land war, however, was the young Home Rule MP who decided to place himself at the head of the land agitation and to lead the campaign at Westminster. Charles Stewart Parnell was a patrician, an Anglo-Irish landowner with estates in Co. Wicklow. He was an aloof, solitary and essentially lonely man. His personality reflected a complex mixture of shyness and arrogance. Elected MP for Meath in 1875, his defiance of the rules of the House of Commons and his unconcealed anti-English sentiments earned him the admiration of the Fenians, and his timely intervention in late 1879 put him at the head of the land agitation.

The years 1879–82 were turbulent and dramatic ones for rural Ireland. Tenants refused to pay high rents and asked for reductions, landlords refused and tried to evict, tenants resisted eviction. Violence and outrage increased, and the weapon of social ostracization used against one offending landlord added a word to the English language – boycott. The government tried to quieten the country by coercion. There were bitter scenes in the Commons as the Parnellites were expelled for causing disorder. Some MPs, including Parnell, did time in jail. The struggle was a victory for the tenant-farmers. The decisive turning point was the Land Act of 1881 which established a land court to determine 'fair rents'. In 1882 an Arrears Act effectively cleared the rent arrears of the previous three years. The land court made average reductions in rent of 20 per cent, and in 1887 there was further downward revision of

Gladstone's Land Act of 1881 was an attempt to solve the problem of the tenant-farmers and to end evictions and violence. It largely succeeded, but was seen by its opponents as appeasement to the Land League. (8)

rents. Parnell had said of the 1881 Act that 'while it has not abolished landlordism, it will make landlordism intolerable for the landlords'. It was a shrewd verdict and a true one. If agitation and adverse price movements could cause perpetual rent revisions, then no landlord could budget with any certainty of future income. Many landlords saw this early and sought favourable terms to sell out. In a succession of land purchase acts – from Ashbourne's in 1885 to Wyndham's in 1903 – the state made credit available to entice the landlords to sell and the tenants to buy. It took time to get the terms right. So long as revised rents seemed likely to remain below the level of repayments which purchase loans would entail, the tenants, quite reasonably, were reluctant to buy. But with Wyndham's Act of 1903 the terms finally came right for the tenant and the landlord. A few extra pushes to some landlords and the change-over took place. By 1917 two-thirds of all Irish farmers were owners of their farms. A remarkable social revolution had taken place.

Not all the demands of 1879 were met by the changes of 1881–1903. In the west, where the land war had begun, there remained a problem which neither rents nor purchase schemes could solve, namely the contrast between minute holdings and large ranches. The demand of the western smallholders for the break-up and redistribution of grazier land was not satisfied by the land 'revolution' of 1879–1903. It remained on the agenda for future settlement.

With considerable rent reductions and rising agricultural prices in the 1890s, the condition and comforts of the farming community improved after 1890. There was significant accumulation of capital.

Between 1890 and 1913 bank deposits almost doubled, from £33 million to £60 million. Improved housing, more varied and more plentiful creature comforts, and a steady if unspectacular rise in the numbers proceeding to secondary education were further signs of this prosperity. At a lower level, the condition of the farm labourers was also bettered in this period. In an ever-dwindling labour force wages rose from 7s. per week in 1870 to 11s. per week in 1914. Moreover, from the early 1880s a spate of legislation obliged first the Poor Law Boards and after 1898 the County Councils heavily to subsidize improved dwellings for labourers. Even in the congested districts of the west living standards rose considerably after 1890. Heavy emigration from the late 1870s relieved pressure on scarce resources. The establishment of the Congested Districts Board in 1891 heralded an imaginative programme of state aid in the western counties (e.g. improved infrastructure, cottage industry, fisheries, agricultural methods, land purchase, redistribution and reclamation). Again, between 1883 and 1896 a programme of state-aided light railways opened up the remote coastal areas of the west to traffic (tourist and local), and greatly expanded the retail network. Bicycles became popular, and cheap household utensils became a feature of even the poorest country homes.

The situation in the towns and cities was much less satisfactory. True, the pick-up in agricultural prosperity in the 1890s was reflected in the trade of the towns. But the pool of unskilled labour was very large, especially in the bigger towns, and it was increasing as craftsmen became redundant. Unskilled casual labour was especially vulnerable to cyclical slumps and booms in demand. This was obvious from the houses of the working class, especially in Dublin. By the early years of the 20th century Dublin's tenement slums were among the worst in Europe. Congestion and appalling sanitation and hygiene resulted in Dublin's crude death rate being well above the national average. Rents of unfurnished tenement rooms were from 1s. 6d per week, while for the luxury of a furnished room one might expect to pay 4s. per week. In view of the wretched conditions of many of the poorer classes, it is not surprising that the early 20th century saw the rise of a strong and militant trade union and labour movement among the unskilled workers of Belfast, Dublin and other major cities and towns. The leading figures of this movement were James Larkin and James Connolly. Larkin, of Liverpool-Irish immigrant stock, was a big man, a wonderful orator and a colourful personality. A trade unionist of syndicalist views, Larkin arrived in Belfast in 1907 to organize unskilled dockland labour. A year later he transferred to Dublin, where he founded the Irish

Transport and General Workers' Union. In a few short years the union's membership rose to 10,000. Many employers disliked Larkin and all he stood for. Some refused to recognize his union. In 1913 Larkin challenged the most powerful employer in Dublin, William Martin Murphy, on the issue of union recognition. A strike and lock-out followed, and other employers took Murphy's example. There was violence, loss of life and severe hardship for the strikers and their families before the strike ended in early 1914 with a victory for the employers, for the time being at any rate. Larkin emigrated to America and his place as head of the labour movement in Dublin was taken by James Connolly. Connolly, a revolutionary socialist, was also of immigrant stock, in his case from Edinburgh. In 1896 he had founded the Irish Socialist Republican party in Dublin, but shortly after doing so he emigrated to the USA. He returned to become ITGWU organizer in Belfast in 1911; and on Larkin's departure for America, Connolly was the leading labour figure in Dublin. In 1913 he founded the Irish Citizen Army, the nucleus of the force through which the workers' republic would be established. The rapidly changing political situation in 1914 soon gave Connolly a chance to use his workers' army.

Home Rule and the 'de-anglicization of Ireland'

In political affairs the period of great social change during the land struggle of the late 19th and early 20th centuries coincided with the ascendancy of the Home Rule party in Ireland. The demand for Irish Home Rule (i.e. some kind of subordinate parliament in Dublin) arose immediately from discontent with Gladstone's Irish policy during 1868–74; and the movement's first leader was Isaac Butt, an established Protestant lawyer and formerly an ardent Conservative. The movement could depend on exploiting the resilient, if unheroic, moderate nationalist sentiment, an earlier version of which had powered O'Connell's Repeal campaign. But it was the combination of the economic difficulties of the late 1870s and early 1880s (especially the agrarian crisis), and the superb political opportunism of Parnell, which made the Home Rule movement a formidable political force in Ireland and at Westminster. After the Reform Act of 1884 (which extended the county franchise and changed constituency boundaries) the Home Rule party won eighty-five seats in Ireland in the general election of 1885. This impressive performance gave the Home Rulers the balance of power at Westminster between the Conservatives and Liberals, and in 1886 Gladstone announced his own and the Liberal party's conversion to Home Rule. Gladstone's act split his own party and put the anti-Home-Rule Conservatives and Unionists into power for almost

In the general election of 1885 Parnell's Home Rule party won eighty-five seats. At last, it seemed, Erin was to be delivered from Castle Coercion. In fact, the movement collapsed because of the hardening resistance in Ulster and Parnell's fall from power. (9)

twenty uninterrupted years. The Liberal Home Rule Bill of 1886 was defeated in Parliament, as was Gladstone's second Home Rule Bill in 1893. Gladstone's act was decisive, however, in ensuring that after 1886 Home Rule remained a basic part of the Liberal creed, despite the fact that some of Gladstone's successors (and many rank and file Liberals) were singularly less enthusiastic about the Irish nationalist claim than Gladstone himself had been.

In Ireland, however, the spectacular electoral breakthrough of 1886 was in many ways a false dawn for Home Rule. In the first place it was significant that, as Home Rule consolidated its electoral hold on nationalist Ireland during the 1880s, opinion among the Protestant Unionists also hardened; and especially in the north-east it became increasingly militant in its total opposition to Home Rule. In electoral strength, the Unionists were firmly entrenched in the north-east. In short, there was a bitter polarization of nationalist and Unionist opinion on the question of Home Rule, so much so indeed that, as early as the 1880s, there were influential voices calling for 'special treatment' for the Ulster Unionists (the only Unionist group whose geographical cohesion made them a formidable political force) in any Home Rule settlement.

The second major blow to Home Rule after 1886 was the Parnell divorce scandal and its repercussions. When Parnell was cited in a divorce case in 1890 the Home Rule party which he had created was bitterly divided on the question of his continued leadership of the party. The majority voted against him, but Parnell refused to accept the verdict of the parliamentary party and carried the fight to the platforms in Ireland. Parnell's tragic death in 1891 left sad and bitter divisions in the Home Rule ranks, within the parliamentary party and in the country. Indeed throughout the 1890s the Home Rule party was constantly consumed by bitter feuding (on policy and personality grounds) between rival factions. These divisions began to heal with the reuniting of the party factions in 1900 under the leadership of John Redmond. He had been among the pro-Parnellite minority in 1891; but his style was conciliatory, and he was intelligent, sincere and an able parliamentary performer. He and his fellow Home Rulers could only mark time during the long period of Conservative government, and when eventually the Liberals returned to office in 1906 their majority was sufficiently large for them to be able to ignore the Redmondite pressure and to keep Home Rule in abeyance. In 1910 this situation was changed; in the general elections the Liberal majority was reduced and the Home Rulers were again in the classic balance-of-power position in the Commons. The result was predictable. Asquith pressed ahead with a Home Rule Bill and since the 1911 Act now set clear limits to the delaying power of the House of Lords, it seemed inevitable that Home Rule would at last be on the statute book by 1914. The Home Rulers at last seemed within sight of the promised land.

The sustained electoral support for Home Rule in the period 1880–1914 did not necessarily mean that this precise measure of devolutionary self-government represented the limit of Irish nationalist ambitions. Home Rule was simply the most coherent and most attainable political objective on offer to the nationalist population of that time. But, as Parnell shrewdly reminded his listeners:

'No man has the right to set a boundary to the onward march of a nation. No man has the right to say "thus far shalt thou go and no further".' This probably summed up the attitude of many ordinary Home Rule supporters, while to the 'left' of Home Rule there were less elastic versions of the Irish separatist claim.

Certainly, in the last twenty years of the 19th century there were several societies or movements active in Ireland which saw in Home Rule a kind of nationalism manqué, and which saw more to the Irish national identity than mere devolutionary self-government. Most of these societies or groups were more concerned with the cultural than with the political predicament of Ireland. Briefly, these societies were all, in their different ways, alarmed at the seemingly inexorable assimilation of Irish culture (in all its ramifications) to that of England. In speech, dress, institutions, manners, aspirations, ideas; in short, in the mental make-up of the people the process of anglicization seemed to be proceeding apace. Davis's cultural nationalism seemed buried without trace: as Yeats put it, 'Romantic Ireland's dead and gone / It's with O'Leary in the grave.' The new cultural separatists (for such they were) determined to renew the battle to preserve the Irish 'identity'. Already in 1883 the Gaelic Athletic Association had been founded to encourage and organize the playing of native games and to 'outlaw' cricket, soccer, rugby and other foreign games as belonging to the English garrison culture. In D. P. Moran (a talented journalist) the new men found a good publicist. His writings in the *Leader* from 1900 onwards castigated the West Britons who were aping English ways, and proclaimed the gospel of Irish Ireland – with a strong emphasis on the need to defend the Irish language. The language was also the object of the most outstanding, and arguably the most revolutionary, Irish cultural movement of the late 19th century – the Gaelic League.

The Gaelic League was founded in 1893 by, among others, Douglas Hyde, the son of a Protestant rector, Eoin MacNeill, a professor of history, and Father Eoin O'Growney. Its policy is well summed up in Hyde's phrase, 'the de-anglicization of Ireland'. The key to this social and cultural revolution lay in the Irish language, which alone enabled the Irish people 'to render the present a rational continuation of the past'. It was Hyde's thesis that 'The moment Ireland broke with her Gaelic past she fell away hopelessly from all intellectual and artistic effort. She lost her musical instruments, she lost her music, she lost her games, she lost her language and popular literature, and with the language she lost her intellectuality.' The restoration of the language, it was argued, would lead to a cultural renaissance which could express itself in every aspect of natural life. Hyde's thesis had several weaknesses: he often confused anglicization with more general European features of modernization in social and economic life; he often simplified the complexities involved in the process of linguistic change. But undoubtedly the League exercised an enormous, indeed revolutionary, influence on key aspects of Irish life between 1893 and 1916. In the practical sphere, through propaganda and pressure it succeeded in gaining legal recognition for the language at all levels of the educational system, from primary to university. Its publications laid the basis for a new vernacular literature in Irish. Through its travelling teachers, its local language classes, its summer colleges in Irish-speaking areas, its summer *feiseanna* (open-air gatherings where competitions were held in dancing, singing, story-telling and recitation of poetry), and its *céilithe* (evening sessions of native dancing and music) – through all of this diverse programme the League attracted wide support as an educational-cum-entertainment movement. By the early 20th century the League had an active membership of over 50,000, not to speak of more casual supporters. Most important of all, however, was the decisive change in attitude that it brought about. The debate on the nature of Irish nationalism was totally transformed; dimensions were added which found no mention in Home Rule politics. A spate of new groups joined the debate.

In the literary field, as we shall see in the next chapter, the leaders of the Anglo-Irish literary revival – Yeats, Lady Gregory, A E, George Moore – shared much common ground, and many personal friendships, with Hyde and the Gaelic League. True, there were significant differences of opinion between the groups on the nature of literature, the feasibility of providing an Irish national literature in English and on general questions of art. But both groups stressed the heroic past of Ireland, as portrayed in its ancient literature, both groups drew inspiration from Irish history and mythology, both groups were in revolt against the values of petit-bourgeois Home Rule county councillors.

The road to rebellion

The foundation of Sinn Fein by Arthur Griffith in 1905 marks a further boundary in the extension of the national debate. Griffith, a first-class journalist, was himself a separatist, but his belief in the impossibility of successful military challenge to the British Empire prompted him to offer an alternative and more realistic policy. Sinn Fein recommended the Dual Monarchy formula which since 1867 had regulated relations between Austria and Hungary as a suitable arrangement for Ireland and Britain. Griffith not only called for the abstention of Irish M Ps from Westminster and for the setting up, *de facto*, of an Irish parliament in Dublin, but he also put forward detailed proposals for economic development in Ireland. The details of Griffith's policy are less important than the fact that Sinn Fein represented an alternative to Home Rule.

Despite Hyde's determination to keep the movement non-political, the Gaelic League, no less than the other movements mentioned, was objectively separatist in its political impact. That is to say, it emphasized the separateness and distinctiveness of Ireland's 'genius' in ways which were bound to have political implications. This is abundantly clear from the way in which the League led to the revival of the oath-bound Irish Republican Brotherhood in the early 20th century. The I R B, the custodian of the Fenian separatist tradition, had been badly buffeted since the débâcle of 1867 by internal disagreements on policy and personality issues, so that by the end of the 19th century it appeared to be fated to an ignominious and unsung death. However, in the early 20th century the I R B had a transfusion of new recruits, many of them disciples of the Gaelic League. Idealistic young men like Patrick Pearse, schoolmaster, writer and educationalist, joined with the veteran Fenian Tom Clarke in reviving the moribund I R B. If by 1916 the Fenian phoenix was ready to rise from the ashes, it is hardly fanciful to say that it was the Gaelic League and its offshoots that fanned the dying embers back to life.

Yet despite the revolutionary potential of these various movements they were very definitely minority movements in the early Edwardian era, and so far as Irish political life was concerned they may fairly be described as fringe movements. What brought them to the centre of the stage was the Home Rule crisis which exploded on the political scene in 1912 and which was to lead eventually to the rebellion of 1916 and to the extinction of the Home Rule party two years later.

The crisis occurred because of the refusal of the Ulster Unionists to accept the decision of the Westminster Parliament to grant Home Rule to Ireland. The claim that Home Rule meant Rome Rule had long been the stock Unionist reply to nationalist demands, even before the phrase 'Home Rule' had been coined. The economy of Belfast and the north-east was closely tied to the fortunes of the British Empire – shipbuilding, engineering and linen were all export industries. Ulster Unionists claimed that an Irish parliament in Dublin with economic powers would put the prosperity of the industrialized north-east in jeopardy. Behind this economic argument against Home Rule lay more primitive racial and religious prejudices which had hardened during the 19th century.

By 1912, when it seemed that a Home Rule victory was inevitable, the Ulster Unionists began to mobilize their forces to resist the act. They were led, most ably and unscrupulously, by Sir Edward Carson, a brilliant Dublin Tory lawyer, and James Craig, a shrewd and very wealthy Ulster distiller. Originally, the Unionists hoped to use the 'Ulster question' to veto a Home Rule settlement for the whole island, but before long the idea of separate treatment for Ulster began to be canvassed widely. In January 1913 an Ulster Volunteer Force was formed to resist Home Rule, and it soon had 100,000 recruits. From this point on, the pace of events quickened. The Conservative party, led by Bonar Law, supported the Ulster Unionists in their defiance of the will of Parliament. A provisional government of Ulster was set up, backed by the UVF. Asquith seemed paralysed by the Ulster challenge, and in November 1913 the Irish Volunteers were formed in the South in answer to the Ulster Force. Formed at the instigation of Eoin MacNeill, the southern Volunteers were soon infiltrated by IRB members, and an alarmed John Redmond felt obliged to put Home Rule members onto the coordinating committee of the Volunteers. Not to be outdone, the Irish labour movement under James Connolly set up its own Irish Citizen Army. In short, there were five armies in Ireland in early 1914 – the UVF, the IRB, the Irish Volunteers, the Irish Citizen Army and the British army itself. The latter force gave Asquith cause for alarm in early 1914 when a group of officers gave notice that they would have no part in 'coercing' Ulster into a Home Rule Ireland. When the Ulster Volunteers and Irish Volunteers both imported arms the stage was set for confrontation.

At this point World War I intervened. The Ulster Volunteers were incorporated into the British army en masse. When John Redmond called on all Irishmen to do likewise the Irish Volunteers split: the majority went with Redmond while a minority (about 11,000), led by Pearse and MacNeill, seceded and retained the name Irish Volunteers. Within this compact force the IRB had a decisive influence, and the supreme council of the IRB had already decided to stage an insurrection in Ireland before the end of the war. Independently, James Connolly had also decided that the Citizen Army would strike a blow

for a workers' republic in Ireland during the war. Both these strands came together in the Easter Rising of 1916. Confusion and indecision at command level and the failure of promised German aid (in arms) to materialize resulted in a poor turn-out in Easter week 1916. The insurgents proclaimed an Irish Republic and held out in certain public buildings in Dublin for a week against overwhelming military odds. At the end of the week the centre of Dublin was badly battered and the insurgents surrendered to avoid further loss of life.

The insurgents had little popular support for their act during Easter week 1916. In fact, public response among ordinary Dubliners (many of whom had relatives in the British army in Europe) varied between puzzled curiosity and open hostility. But when the government, in an attempt to 'teach a lesson' to would-be rebels, executed the leaders of the insurrection and imprisoned hundreds more, public attitudes began to change. The government had inaccurately called the insurrection the 'Sinn Fein rebellion', and Sinn Fein was now transformed into a republican separatist political movement. The shift in public attitudes towards the rebels might never have made a decisive political impact if the government had not decided to impose conscription in Ireland in 1918. The Sinn Fein party, now led by Eamon de Valera, one of the surviving leaders of 1916, was the beneficiary of the anti-conscription campaign throughout the country. In December 1918, under a new and expanded electorate, the Home Rule party was decimated and Sinn Fein won seventy-three seats. The Unionists held firm in the north-east but throughout the rest of the country a major political change had taken place. Yeats's verdict on 1916 was that all was 'changed, changed utterly'. Certainly the 1918 election showed that the centre of gravity of Irish nationalist opinion had shifted decisively to the left. It remained to be seen, however, whether much else had been changed by the 'episode at Easter'.

7
THE CELTIC REVIVAL

Literature and the Theatre
PHILLIP L. MARCUS

The Visual Arts
JEANNE SHEEHY

O brave young men, my love, my pride, my promise,

'Tis on you my hopes are set,

In manliness, in kindliness, in justice,

To make Erin a nation yet.

From *Lament for the Death of Thomas Davis* by Samuel Ferguson

'Raising the taste and cultivating the nationality of Ireland' were the declared aims of the Young Ireland movement in the 1840s. Such a union of art and nationalism was of course not peculiar to Ireland. All over Europe the Romantic movement had inspired artists and writers to look not to Greece and Rome but to their own past for meaningful subjects. For architecture this meant a revival of Romanesque and Gothic; for painting a choice of themes from barbarian or medieval history. In Ireland, attention naturally focused on the age of the Celts and Celtic Christianity, the last period when Ireland could be said to have been truly herself, untinged by influences from England or the Continent. The movement also had explicit political overtones, since the cause of Irish nationalism was the cause of independence.

William Butler Yeats, a great poet and the most significant figure to emerge from the Celtic Revival, was intensely committed to the idea of Ireland and Irish culture. Subscribing to John O'Leary's maxim that

'there is no great literature without nationality', he took his themes largely from Irish history and legend, attempting to explore and express the inner spirit of Ireland. How far he discovered this spirit and how far he was inventing it himself is an open question. His book *The Secret Rose*, published in 1897, is a collection of stories and prose pieces set in periods ranging from mythical times to the 20th century and featuring characters such as Queen Dectira, Costello the Proud and Hanrahan the Red. 'So far as this book is visionary,' he wrote, 'it is Irish; for Ireland, which is still predominantly Celtic, has preserved with some less excellent things a gift of vision, which has died out among more hurried and more successful nations: no shining candelabra have prevented us from looking into the darkness, and when one looks into the darkness there is always something there.' The cover (opposite) was designed by Althea Gyles. Lovers kiss in the midst of the mystic rose which springs from death. (1)

THE SECRET ROSE

The search for a national identity found a voice in a weekly newspaper, the *Nation*, founded in 1842 and aimed at every social class. Above: *Reading 'The Nation'* by Henry MacManus. In an attempt to create a national art it advocated Irish subject matter, but no specifically Irish style emerged. Works like Frederick Burton's *The Aran Fisherman's Drowned Child* (above right), reflect serious research into local conditions, and Daniel Maclise's *Marriage of Strongbow and Eva* (detail below) dresses Irish history in the grand manner, with authentic touches of Celtic archaeology. Strongbow was Richard, Earl of Pembroke, who conquered Waterford and married the daughter of the King of Leinster in 1170. (2–4)

Ireland's past became an object of passionate study by those who were seeking to re-create an Irish culture. Many painters were also antiquarians. These three works combine scholarly accuracy with a romantic vision of legendary greatness. Above left: the West Cross of Monasterboice, from Henry O'Neill's *Sculptured Crosses of Ancient Ireland*, 1857 (see p. 55, pl. 18). Above right:

The Blind Girl at the Holy Well by Frederick Burton, prints of which were distributed to members of the Irish Art Union in 1839–40. Below: *Pilgrims at Clonmacnoise* by George Petrie, which brings together architectural detail and primitive peasant life. A kindred interest in these years was the collection of folk music, and Petrie was one of those who did valuable work in this field. (5–7)

A true Celtic Revival, as distinct from the mere choice of Celtic subjects, came only later in the century and found its greatest fruition in ecclesiastical art. The best work of this school is highly original yet remains uniquely Irish. The early 20th century tabernacle door of St Michael's church, Ballinasloe (left), is by Mia Cranwill; using various metals and coloured enamels, it is a vivid evocation, but not in the least a copy, of the great age of Celtic art. (8)

Stained glass saw further adaptations of traditional forms to new techniques. The windows made by Harry Clarke for the Honan Chapel in University College, Cork (opposite), begun in 1915, are among the finest. Small in scale but monumental in conception, they have a strength of design and a jewel-like brilliance of colour that is both totally Celtic and totally modern. (10)

For the cathedral at Loughrea, Co. Galway, built between 1897 and 1903, almost all the most talented artists of the Revival contributed work – Stations of the Cross by Ethel Rhind, sculpture by Michael Shortall, stained glass by A. E. Childe, Michael Healy, Sarah Purser and Evie Hone, and banners by Jack B. Yeats. The vestments (detail right) were designed by Evelyn Gleeson and made in her workshop at Dun Emer. Side patterns in the Celtic tradition are combined with more naturalistic ears of rye in the central circles. (9)

204

Architecture never freed itself from dependence upon historical models. The façade of the Honan Chapel is almost a straight copy of St Cronan's Church, Roscrea, Co. Tipperary. At Jordanstown, Co. Antrim, the church

of St Patrick, of the late 1860s, was an earnest attempt to 'revive the ancient architecture of Ireland'. The round tower, and the way it relates to the church, is based on Clonmacnoise. (11,12)

Hiberno-Romanesque remained a popular style for churches from the 1860s onwards. James Franklin Fuller's St Michael and All Angels, Clane, Co. Kildare, is scholarly in its sculptural motifs, but also relies heavily on decorative enrichment drawn from non-architectural sources. (13)

Glasnevin cemetery, Dublin, contains a monument to O'Connell in the form of a round tower, a mortuary chapel in the 'Irish-Romanesque' style and this tomb of Archbishop McCabe by G. C. Ashlin, built in 1887. The carved interlace comes from high crosses and manuscripts, and inside is a mosaic floor. (14)

The romantic skyline of Dromore Castle, Co. Limerick, by the English architect E. W. Godwin, incorporates a round tower growing incongruously from the middle of a 17th-century stronghold. The result is reminiscent of the Rock of Cashel. It was built between 1867 and 1869. (15)

Sculptors did not follow the historicist path with the same assurance as the architects, but they were concerned to evoke the past by other means. Below left: J. V. Hogan's monument, erected in 1874, to the bard Carolan, who had died over a century earlier. Below right: a capital from the nave of Loughrea Cathedral by Michael Shortall and an owl from the quadrangle of Deane and Woodward's University College, Cork. (16–18)

ERECTED
BY THE DESIRE OF SYDNEY LADY MORGAN
TO THE MEMORY OF
CAROLAN
THE LAST OF THE IRISH BARDS

OBIIT
A·D·MDCCXXXVIII · AETATIS · SVAE · AN·LXVIII

Present and past are equally alive in the best of Celtic Revival art. The forms may be those of 8th-century manuscripts but the feeling is often that of contemporary Symbolism or *art nouveau*. Left and right: two heroes of the early Irish Church, St Brendan and St Patrick. The first, who certainly founded the abbey of Clonfert, Co. Galway, in the 6th century, and is reputed to have crossed the Atlantic with a company of monks, appears in a stained-glass window by Sarah Purser at Loughrea. The second, portrayed in the act of banishing poisonous snakes from Ireland, is on one of the banners by Jack Yeats in the same cathedral. (19,20)

A radiant sun forms the central motif of the mosaic floor of the Honan Chapel, Cork (left). It is encircled by a Latin inscription in old Irish lettering, and this in turn is surrounded by the signs of the zodiac separated by Celtic interlace ending in animals' heads. (21)

The writing lines of Celtic illumination fill every surface inch of the Dominican chapel at Dun Laoghaire, Co. Dublin (far right). It was painted by Sister Concepta Lynch, and draws heavily on ancient manuscripts – the figure to the right of the window, for instance, is an enlarged detail from the *Book of Kells*. It is typical of the popular adaptation of Celtic ornament which flourished as late as the 1950s, though nowhere else is so overpowering an effect achieved. (24)

Angelic messengers on the tapestries of the Honan Chapel (right) are medieval in inspiration but not so uncompromisingly Celtic. (22)

Boldness of colour had been the hallmark of An Túr Gloine – the Tower of Glass – the workshop set up by Sarah Purser at the beginning of this century. And it persisted to the end. The cock by Evie Hone (below), one of its last recruits, was made as late as 1948. (23)

Literature succeeded in doing what the visual arts in the last analysis failed to do – create an Irish culture that was unquestionably international in stature. The early years of the Revival, under the influence of Young Ireland and the *Nation*, were marked more by patriotic feeling than literary excellence. But by the turn of the century, a whole galaxy of talent had arisen. John Synge (upper left, by John Butler Yeats) took his themes from Irish folk life but raised them to a universal level. The fact that he chose the drama as his medium was due to Lady Gregory (above), who helped found the Abbey Theatre, and made a heterogeneous group of writers into a unified movement. (25,26)

'Homage to Sir Hugh Lane' by Sean Keating. This group could be said to represent the artistic renewal for which Young Ireland had hoped. Lane (in the portrait at the back) had gathered together a notable collection of modern art and left it to the nation. Yeats is seated on the left. The others, from left to right, are Dermod O'Brien, Thomas Bodkin, George Russell ('AE'), W. Hutchinson-Poe, Thomas Kelly and R. Caulfield-Orpen. (27)

210

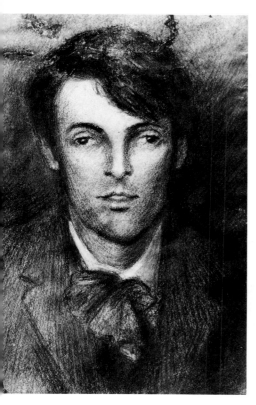

KATHLEEN-NI-HOULIHAN.

BRIDGET GILLANE,
MISS MARIE O'NEILL.

PETER GILLANE,
MR FRANK J. FAY.

KATHLEEN-NI-HOULIHAN,
MISS SARA ALLGOOD.

MICHAEL GILLANE,
MR J. M. KERRIGAN

William Butler Yeats was by nature introspective and drawn to mysticism, but he threw himself passionately into the practical task of creating a living Irish literature. The theatre was a means of reaching a great potential audience which would not read serious books. 'We believe', he wrote, 'that our desire to bring upon the stage the deeper thoughts and emotions of Ireland will insure for us a tolerant welcome.' *Cathleen ni Houlihan* was produced in Dublin in 1902; this illustration (above right) shows the Abbey Theatre production of two years later. Cathleen, the symbol of Ireland, seduces Michael Gillane away from his bride. The portrait of Yeats is by George Russell, known as 'AE', primarily a writer and, like Yeats, a mystic. (28,29)

Abbey Theatre

Lessees   THE NATIONAL THEATRE SOCIETY, Ltd.

Programme
Abbey Theatre Co.
Abbey Theatre

The Abbey Theatre opened in December 1904, and continued until it was burnt down in 1951, when it moved to other premises. Right: a scene from Synge's *Riders to the Sea*, 1906, with Brigit O'Dempsey, Sara Allgood and Maire O'Neill. (30,31)

211

James Joyce's Dublin is the aspect of Ireland which has probably lodged itself most securely in the world's imagination. Like so many Irish literary figures, Joyce's attitude to his native land was deeply ambivalent. He could neither live in Ireland nor forget it. And his greatest work, *Ulysses*, can be seen as a fittingly paradoxical end to the whole Celtic Revival. For the Ireland that it celebrates is not heroic but mundane, not idealistic but cynical, not simple and rural but sophisticated and urban. Below: Grafton Street, on a day that cannot be far from 'Bloomsday', 16 June 1904, when Leopold Bloom walked down it: 'Grafton Street gay with housed awnings lured his senses. Muslin prints silk, dames and dowagers, jingle of harnesses, hoofthuds lowringing in the baking causeway:' The tram, bound for Dalkey, is the one Stephen Dedalus would have caught to go to Sandycove, where he shared the Martello tower with 'stately, plump, Buck Mulligan'. Left: four generations of Joyces; the portrait is of Joyce's father and on the other side of the desk are his son Giorgio and grandson Stephen. (32, 33)

Chapter 7

THE CELTIC REVIVAL

Harp and shamrock – emblems from the title page of an anthology from the Nation called 'The Spirit of the Nation', published in 1843. Its patriotism and directness gave it popular appeal, but a man like AE felt 'in a frenzy' when he saw it referred to as literature. (1)

THE PROTESTANT ASCENDANCY had been a fertile period for the arts in Ireland, but they had not in any real sense been indigenous. The Celtic Revival marks a new departure. It depended for its existence upon the growth during the 1800s of an awareness of nationhood, encouraging the creation of a 'national' literature and a 'national' art.

Such aspirations Ireland shared with many other European countries seeking to reassert their historic identity. But Ireland faced peculiar difficulties. The number of native Irish speakers was steadily and rapidly declining in most of the country and the new literature would have to be in English. The movement looked back to and derived part of its inspiration and imaginative energy from the Celtic golden age; but in speaking of a 'Revival' we risk obscuring the crucial fact that the bulk of the modern literature was written in a different language, often by men and women whose ancestors had not even come to Ireland until long after the end of that remarkable medieval era.

In the visual arts, the situation was closely parallel. During most of the 19th century Irish artists were forced to make their careers abroad, usually in England. The bulk of the work they produced had nothing to distinguish its nationality.

Any that did manifested it in the choice of subject-matter, or in the revival of ancient Celtic art, rather than in any distinctly Irish style. The question is complicated by the fact that it is difficult to distinguish between those artists whose choice of Irish subjects, contemporary or ancient, was prompted by a search for the romantic or the picturesque, and those who were looking for a national identity.

The story of the Celtic Revival in literature is essentially the story of how these drawbacks were surmounted, and a vigorous and wholly authentic national culture brought into being. In the visual arts the final verdict must be one of qualified success only. But it is an exciting story, featuring strong, colourful personalities, memorable events, a closer involvement of art in the public world of politics than we can easily imagine today and of course a substantial number of literary and artistic master-pieces.

Literature and the Theatre
PHILLIP L. MARCUS

Poems written in English by Irishmen had begun to appear by the 14th century, but so long as Irish remained the primary language of most of the country no appreciable body of such literature could be expected. By the 1700s there were large numbers of 'new' settlers who considered themselves Irish but whose native language was English; and, while many authors of that era looked to England for their

subjects, form and style, others did take an interest in the indigenous culture. From the 1790s on, political ballads in English enjoyed wide circulation. The immensely popular *Irish Melodies* of Thomas Moore (1779–1852), which began appearing in 1808, gave a rather facile lyric expression to national themes, with a prevailing note of post-Union melancholy. It was only with the Young Ireland movement of the 1840s, however, that we find an organized, self-conscious effort to develop a literature that would be primarily English in language but distinctively national, 'racy of the soil', in character.

Nationality as the Young Irelanders defined it embraced all creeds and races and classes in the country. They wanted to bring together Irish-speaking Gaels, direct heirs of the pre-Norman people whose traditions the Penal Laws had driven into refuge in the impoverished world of the cabins and the turf fires; and men who were English in ancestry and language but identified themselves nevertheless with Irish political, economic and cultural interests. Literature was to be an important binding force. The leaders of the movement, the most famous of whom were Charles Gavan Duffy (1816–1903) and the revered Thomas Davis (1814–45), founded the weekly paper the *Nation* in 1842 to serve as a focal point for the encouragement of national literary effort and dissemination of the fruits of that effort. Because the leaders were strongly nationalistic in their politics, the most characteristic literature of the *Nation* and the 'Library of Ireland' (a series of inexpensive books for popular consumption) was often little more than anti-Unionist propaganda:

> *How thrive we by the Union?*
> *Look round our native land;*
> *In ruined trade and wealth decayed*
> *See slavery's surest brand;*
> *Our glory as a nation gone,*
> *Our substance drained away;*
> *A wretched province trampled on,*
> *Is all we've left today.*
> *Then curse with me the Union,*
> *That juggle foul and base –*
> *The baneful root that bore such fruit*
> *Of ruin and disgrace.*

Intended to be immediately intelligible to great masses of ill-educated readers, it was superficial and sometimes distorted in content, conventional and mechanical in style. Only a poet of real talent such as James Clarence Mangan (1803–49), author of 'Dark Rosaleen' and 'O'Hussey's Ode to the Maguire', was able to transcend the pressures of expediency. Thus, while the Young Ireland movement certainly did contribute greatly to the strengthening of national sentiment in Ireland, it could not by itself constitute the nucleus of a revival.

Realism and legend

At the same time, however, complementary forces were at work. One of these was a vein of acute realistic social observation in novels of Irish life, a vein which perhaps originated in 1800 with Maria Edgeworth's *Castle Rackrent*. The tradition was extended by such writers as Gerald Griffin, John Banim and William Carleton (best known for his *Traits and Stories of the Irish Peasantry*, 1830–33). Like Mangan, Carleton was for a time associated with the *Nation*, but never fully identified himself with its aspirations. *Knocknagow* (1879), probably the most popular Irish novel of the period, was contributed by the Fenian patriot Charles Kickham; it chronicled lovingly the life of a Tipperary village. The work of these novelists was sometimes low in quality or marred by class or religious bias, but it did significantly expand the range of appropriate subject-matter for national literature. The youthful W. B. Yeats would praise Banim and Carleton as writers who 'saw the whole of everything they looked at ... the brutal with the tender, the coarse with the refined ... [and] tried to make one see life plainly but all written down in a kind of fiery shorthand that it might never be forgotten'. While James Joyce would have had nothing but scorn for these native predecessors, his own fiction continues the tradition they helped begin and embodies the receptivity to a wide spectrum of experience for which Yeats had praised them.

Between them and Joyce the most powerful representative of that tradition was George Moore (1852–1933), who carried it on under the stimulus of Zola and French naturalism in his fine novel *A Drama in Muslin* (1886). It provides a panoramic view of contemporary Irish life and a merciless indictment of the entire country, urban and rural, Ascendancy and peasantry. His view of Dublin clearly prefigures Joyce's:

> The weary, the woebegone, the threadbare streets – yes, threadbare conveys the moral idea of Dublin in 1882. ... The Dublin streets stare the vacant and helpless stare of a beggar selling matches on a doorstep, and the feeble cries for amusement are like those of the child beneath the ragged shawl for the red gleam of a passing soldier's coat. On either side of you, there is a bawling ignorance or plaintive decay. Look at the houses! Like crones in borrowed bonnets some are fashionable with flowers in the rotting window frames – others languish in silly cheerfulness like women living on the proceeds of the pawnshop; others – those with brass plates on the doors – are evil smelling as the prescriptions of the threadbare doctor, bald as the bill of costs of the servile attorney. And the souls of the Dubliners blend and harmonize with their connatural surroundings.

This was the tract of Irish life that Joyce was to develop and make his own; and the virtual interpenetration of setting and character which Moore re-creates through metaphor was to receive its ultimate expression in the phantasmagoria of *Finnegans Wake*, the central character of which is both man and city.

A second major force which complemented Young Ireland efforts to create a national literature was a growing scholarly and imaginative interest in the Irish past, especially in the old Gaelic literature and legends. The Young Irelanders themselves encouraged this pursuit; but it had originated long before and many of its greatest enthusiasts were men who could not accept the nationalistic (as opposed to the merely national) elements in the Young Ireland political programme.

English-language accounts of Irish legends and bardic literature began appearing in the 16th and 17th centuries. Scholarly and literary attention increased rapidly during the later part of the next century, receiving a stimulus from the controversy over James Macpherson's alleged Ossianic 'translations'. (There was a corresponding concern with Irish traditional music, manifested in Edward Bunting's *General Collection of Ancient Irish Music* – a book which in turn influenced Moore's *Melodies*.) The Union caused only a temporary check; in the 19th century, massive contributions were made by the two great Gaelic scholars John O'Donovan (1809–61) and Eugene O'Curry (1796–1862), while the publication in 1825 of Thomas Crofton Croker's *Fairy Legends and Traditions of the South of Ireland* opened the rich related vein of Irish folklore. Meanwhile, the famine and its aftermath led to a drastic decline in the use of Irish, which had been under increasing pressure since the 1700s. By 1891, over 80 per cent of the population would speak no Irish at all.

Once these traditional stories were readily available in translation, their suitability as the basis for a new literature in English seemed obvious. They were fresh; had not been mined again and again like the Classical materials; and appeared virtually inexhaustible – 'the most plentiful treasure of legends in Europe', Yeats was to assert. Their distinctively Irish features offered Irish authors a way of breaking with the custom of merely echoing at a distance their counterparts in England. On the other hand, they represented a subject that, while intensely national, was uncoloured by modern politics and sectarian religious controversy and thus might appeal to a wider, more heterogeneous audience. Mangan, who contributed to the *Nation*, had worked as a copyist for O'Donovan and O'Curry and derived from them the strong interest in the Irish past which informs some of his best poetry. Aubrey de Vere (1814–1902), in contrast, refused to countenance agitation for independence and was very critical of what he termed Irish

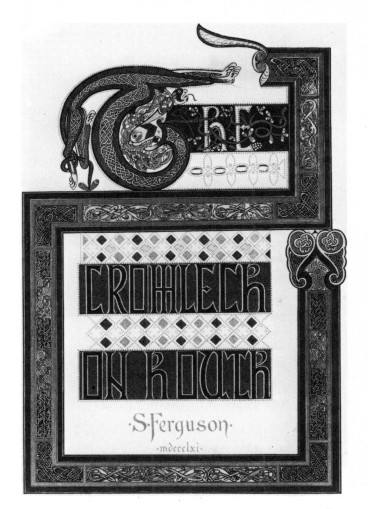

Sir Samuel Ferguson was among the first to make a serious effort to revive real Celtic forms. The title page of his 'Cromlech on Howth' of 1861, designed by Margaret Stokes, shows considerable appreciation of ancient manuscripts. (2)

'jacobinism'; but he produced a number of poetic adaptations of the early Gaelic tales. And the two most important predecessors of the Revival, Sir Samuel Ferguson and Standish James O'Grady, were both supporters of the Union.

Forerunners of the Revival

Ferguson (1810–86) briefly sympathized with some of the less extreme Young Ireland views, but before and after that era identified himself with the forces of the Unionist Ascendancy. He by no means considered himself a 'West Briton', however, and both as antiquarian and as poet he was deeply absorbed in the early literature and culture of the country. Clearly the motives underlying his interest in this material were different from Davis's; but he was a man of real, if limited, poetic ability, and thus was able to reveal as no one before him the potential of such material as a foundation stone for a national literature. His epic poem *Congal* (1872) had many flaws; but it, along with a number of poems based on legendary and folk subjects in *Lays of the Western Gael* (1865) and *Poems* (1880), constituted the most substantial body then available of work in which the fresh national subject-matter was combined with a high level of technical proficiency. It was primarily for this reason that Yeats was moved to praise him so extravagantly in 1886:

> The author of these poems is the greatest poet Ireland has produced, because the most central and most Celtic. Whatever the future may bring forth in the way of a truly great and national literature – and now that the race is so large, so widely spread, and so conscious of its unity, the years are ripe – will find its morning in these three volumes of one who was made by the purifying flame of National sentiment the one man of his time who wrote heroic poetry – one who, among the somewhat sybaritic singers of his day, was like some aged sea-king sitting among the inland wheat and poppies – the savour of the sea about him, and its strength.

The praise itself was certainly excessive, but Yeats was right in giving Ferguson so high a rank among his contemporaries; and the prediction that a new literary movement was at hand of course proved prophetic.

Yeats made even greater claims for Ferguson's friend O'Grady (1846–1928), asserting that his *History of Ireland* 'started us all'. His enthusiasm was matched by others, including T. W. Rolleston, who called the *History* 'the first book I ever read which convinced me that there was such a thing as a spiritual Ireland'; and George Russell, who declared that 'whatever is Irish in me he kindled to life'. What was the cause of this remarkable impact? It lay precisely in the vision of early Irish tradition embodied in O'Grady's famous work.

O'Grady's background, like Ferguson's, allied him with the Ascendancy; and only by chance did he discover that his country had a noble and inspiring past. Once he had made this discovery, however, he rapidly gave it memorable expression in his *History of Ireland* (1878–80). This was a strange book, partly prose epic and partly scholarly study, devoted to the deeds of the most famous of all Irish legendary heroes, Cú Chulainn. Some writers had already begun using the new source of subject-matter for less than elevated purposes: the Gaelic scholar P. W. Joyce, writing in 1879, spoke of stories which had been 'presented in a very unfavourable and unjust light – distorted to make them look *funny*, and their characters debased to the mere modern conventional stage Irishman'. In contrast, O'Grady regarded 'this age and the great personages moving therein as incomparably higher in intrinsic worth than the corresponding ages of Greece. In Homer, Hesiod, and the Attic poets, there is a polish and artistic form, absent in the existing monuments of Irish heroic thought, but the gold, the ore itself, is here massier and more pure, the sentiment deeper

and more tender, the audacity and freedom more exhilarating, the reach of imagination more sublime, the depth and power of the human soul more fully exhibit themselves.' For him Cú Chulainn's combat with his blood-brother Ferdiad was 'the most profoundly tragic scene in all literature', and Cú himself, 'the noblest character'.

This vision, too, involved distortion: in the Gaelic originals, the heroic and noble are mixed inextricably with the comic, the fantastic, the coarse. In his desire to give them the acclaim they deserve O'Grady did them the disservice of presenting only a partial – and thus a false – image. But appearing as it did during a period of burgeoning national consciousness, that was precisely the image which could most powerfully affect the minds of those who were to determine the course of subsequent Irish literature and history. For O'Grady, as for so many other Irishmen, the present moment was haunted by awareness of the past. In his own case the result was an obsession with the painful contrast between the modern landlord class, with whom he continued to sympathize, and what he imagined to be their enlightened and exemplary counterparts in the heroic period. For several other writers there would be material and inspiration for a new literary movement. And for Patrick Pearse, who was to declare that 'what Ireland wants beyond all other modern countries, is a new birth of the heroic spirit' and that 'we must re-create and perpetuate in Ireland the knightly tradition of Cuchulain', O'Grady's image combined with the words of Theobald Wolfe Tone, Robert Emmet, who led a brief rising in 1803, and Thomas Davis and John Mitchel to help form the consciousness behind the Easter Rising.

William Butler Yeats

The Irish critic Ernest Boyd hailed O'Grady as 'the father of the Literary Revival in Ireland'; and, as we have seen, Ferguson, Davis, and several other 19th-century authors could also take a share of the credit. But there is no doubt that the greatest contribution was made by William Butler Yeats (1865–1939). The poetry he wrote as a youth had imitated English models. In 1885 he met the old Fenian exile John O'Leary, and, under the influence of O'Leary's maxim that 'there is no great literature without nationality, no great nationality without literature', decided to become an *Irish* writer. Almost at once he transformed himself into the guiding force in contemporary Irish writing, giving cohesiveness and direction to the vague impulses that were in the air.

His first task was to define precisely what the distinguishing characteristics of a genuinely national literature might be. As he surveyed the efforts of his predecessors he found much to ponder. The most *popular* literature had come from the patriotic tradition inaugurated by the Young Irelanders, with whose radical political aims he was sympathetic; but he was offended by the weaknesses of that work and preferred on literary grounds the work of men like Ferguson and William Allingham, which lay outside the tradition epitomized by *The Spirit of the Nation* and was consequently little read yet seemed to him distinctively Irish. Resisting the pressures towards immediate political usefulness, he called for writing that would be Irish in subject and spirit and style but not necessarily politically nationalistic. Against the Young Ireland view that 'Patriotism . . . can *make* poetry' he argued that the writer must always put the demands of his art before those of politics. To counter the urge towards provincialism he asserted that 'a writer is not less national because he shows the influence of other countries and of the great writers of the world'. Foreign influences could be particularly valuable in the area of artistic craftsmanship, where so much of the 19th-century literature had been woefully deficient. As particularly important indigenous subject-matter he stressed legend, folklore and 'the spiritual life' – the last a manifestation of his own passionate life-long concern with the occult but which he nevertheless sought to establish as primally and essentially Celtic. And he expressed confidence that his country could 'build up a national tradition, a national literature, which shall be none the less Irish in spirit for being English in language'.

Yeats strove diligently to spread these ideals to others. In a steady stream of articles and reviews he propagandized for them and for writers whose work gave them substance. He defended the nascent movement against such critics as Gavan Duffy, who, returning to Ireland at the end of his life, wanted only patriotic writing in the old Young Ireland mode; and the famous Irish Shakespearean scholar and Trinity don Edward Dowden (a close family friend), who preferred the literature of England and the Continent to anything his own country might produce. As editor of a variety of anthologies, Yeats featured the work of the new authors and of those earlier writers who had prepared the way for them. He was also instrumental in founding Irish literary societies in Dublin and London, organizations which performed the important function of giving a sense of *group* effort, of a real *movement* in progress. Most dramatically of all, he provided a concrete illustration of his literary programme in his own increasingly prominent creative work.

His principal volumes before the turn of the century were *The Wanderings of Oisin and Other Poems* (1889), *The Countess Cathleen and Various Legends and Lyrics* (1892), *Poems* (1895), *The Secret Rose* (1897) and *The Wind Among the Reeds* (1899): narrative and

The *1881* issue of *Young Ireland* collects together all the familiar symbols and clichés: St Patrick, Ireland playing the harp, the wolfhound and the shamrock, held aloft by the eager young men in the foreground. (3)

lyric poems, stories, dramas – an impressive body of evidence that there was indeed something to his claims concerning the possibility of a great national literature. 'The Valley of the Black Pig', short enough to be given in its entirety, will serve to epitomize these early efforts:

The dews drop slowly and dreams gather: unknown spears
Suddenly hurtle before my dream-awakened eyes,
And then the clash of fallen horsemen and the cries
Of unknown perishing armies beat about my ears.
We who still labour by the cromlec on the shore,
The grey cairn on the hill, when day sinks drowned in dew,
Being weary of the world's empires, bow down to you
Master of the still stars and of the flaming door.

Here Yeats has subjected Young Ireland poetry to a kind of 'spiritual' sublimation process. The militancy of the earlier school is there, and many of the country people from whom Yeats had heard the legend upon which the poem is based saw in the battle a coming struggle between Ireland and England. But he himself makes the political subsidiary to the occult, identifying the poem in its original title as part of a group 'concerning Peasant

Visionaries' and (as his notes make clear) associating the legend with other mythological battles about which he knew from books of comparative anthropology such as Rhys's *Celtic Heathendom* and Frazer's *Golden Bough*. The resultant vision of apocalypse also draws upon the poet's Blakean and hermetic studies, and the poem is intensely national (even tied to the Sligo of Yeats's own youth) but not at all parochial. In technique, too, it shows a modification of the *Nation* tradition in the light of Yeats's contact with the literature of other countries. The subject of the poem (first published in the English *avant-garde* magazine *The Savoy*) demanded not the conventional energetic but mechanical ballad rhythms of Davis and his followers but rather 'wavering, meditative, organic rhythms' that would liberate the reader's mind from 'the pressure of the will' and make him receptive to communication by symbol and archetype. The sound patterns, the repetitions, the high percentage of monosyllabic words are designed to push audiences not to the barricades but rather to the quiet, awesome shores of trance.

Ireland in the 'nineties
The disillusionment with practical politics following Parnell's death in 1891 caused many sensitive minds to seek other outlets for their national impulses, and this obviously aided Yeats's efforts. Ireland in the 'nineties was becoming a lively place culturally. Most of the early stars in the literary firmament seem to us today to be distinctly minor talents: John Todhunter, Katharine Tynan, Nora Hopper, Lionel Johnson. But the mere fact of their involvement generated further interest and thus prepared for the advent of greater figures who might otherwise have written differently or not at all; and these years did see the emergence of one Irish writer of considerable ability and significance, George Russell (1867–1935), popularly known as 'AE'.

AE was in fact among the most remarkable and engaging personalities in the history of modern Ireland. He was an unlikely blend of mystic, artist and practical man, equally familiar with newspaper editing, the economics of co-operative farming, the Sacred Books of the East and the composition of poetry. He shared many of Yeats's occult interests and came to share his national ones, though he felt a tension between nationalism and 'the politics of eternity'. In 1898 Yeats observed that 'Dublin is waking up in a number of ways and about a number of things. Russell is doing a good part in the awakening.'

His poetry is generally inferior in quality to Yeats's work, perhaps because the fullness of his commitment to a transcendent reality made him less inclined to consider craftsmanship as an ideal. The folk subject (a fairy luring a mortal out of life), the apocalyptic note and the very language and verbal effects of the following stanza from his 'The Gates of Dreamland' remind us of the Yeats of 'The Valley of the Black Pig':

'Come away,' the red lips whisper, 'all the earth is weary now ;
'Tis the twilight of the ages and it's time to quit the plough.
Oh, the very sunlight's weary ere it lightens up the dew,
And its gold is changed and faded ere its falling down to you.'

Not surprisingly, Yeats praised such work as 'more Irish than any of those books of stories or of verses which reflect so many obviously Irish characteristics that every newspaper calls them, in the trying phrase of 1845, "racy of the soil"'. AE himself wrote 'I feel in a frenzy when I see the "Spirit of the Nation" referred to as literature' and praised Yeats in turn for providing an alternative. AE was also a great discoverer and encourager of young writers, including Joyce, Sean O'Faolain and Austin Clarke. Not all his 'finds' were so fortunate as these, and Yeats came to feel that his friend had also nurtured too many mediocre talents with whose contributions the movement could afford to dispense. Nevertheless, AE certainly played a key role in turning Irish literature away from the Davis tradition and keeping the new movement alive.

It seems appropriate at this point to emphasize that there were a number of writers of this era who did not follow the programme Yeats and his associates were championing. Oscar Wilde (1854–1900), for example, had by birth impeccable credentials for becoming involved with the Irish literary scene: his father Sir William Wilde was a noted Irish antiquarian and his mother, known as 'Speranza', had actually contributed verse to the *Nation*. But Wilde himself preferred a larger, cosmopolitan literary world. Similarly George Bernard Shaw (1856–1950), though he wrote frequently about social and political questions involving his homeland, made Ireland the subject of only one of his major plays. It would be possible to argue that his work and Wilde's reveal an 'Irish sensibility'; but clearly neither man wrote out of a conscious desire to contribute to the development of a national literature or identified himself integrally with the Revival. Considering their great creative abilities, the loss to that movement was a considerable one. Edward Plunkett, Lord Dunsany (1878–1957), provides another example. Although he sometimes came into contact with the Revival and was encouraged by Yeats to involve himself more closely, he was basically a 'West Briton' and thus out of sympathy with its aims.

Unlike these men, the fox-hunting cousins Edith Œnone Somerville (1858–1949) and Violet Martin (1862–1915), who as 'Somerville and Ross' collaborated on a number of novels, did make Ireland the primary concern of their work. Nevertheless, their relation to the movement was a tenuous and uneasy one. In 1894 they had published *The Real Charlotte*, which has been called the best Irish novel of the century, and it looked as if they might fit into Yeats's plans. But when their tremendously successful collection of stories *Some Experiences of an Irish R.M.* appeared in 1899 its comic treatment of Irish life reminded many readers of the 'stage-Irish' tradition and the patronizing works of the popular novelists Charles Lever (1806–72) and Samuel Lover (1797–1868). Somerville and Ross were in fact class-conscious members of the Ascendancy, though also shrewd observers of the social scene and often brilliant writers. Thus it was difficult for Yeats and his closest associates to claim them for the national effort, and they themselves were careful to remain detached. Yet their work, in contrast to that of the cosmopolitan writers, can indeed be studied profitably in the context of Irish literature.

At the opposite extreme from authors who did not share the intense national impulses of Yeats were others who felt that the movement he was fostering was not Irish *enough*. The key figure here was undoubtedly Douglas Hyde (1860–1949). As a child he had become fascinated with peasant life and with the Irish language. His collections of folklore soon brought him to Yeats's attention, and the bilingual *Love Songs of Connacht* which he published in 1893 seemed to Yeats a major step towards the development of a distinctively Irish form of English prose to replace the comic brogue that had been the staple of the novelists. But Yeats was mistaken in thinking that Hyde had any serious interest in creating a national literature in English. Hyde felt that the only way the modern nation could preserve its ancient Celtic heritage was through the Irish language, and it was towards saving and reviving the dying tongue that he devoted the greatest share of his energies. In November 1892 he gave these ideas memorable expression in his influential lecture on 'The Necessity for De-Anglicising Ireland', and when the Gaelic League was founded the following year he became its first president. Soon he was at the centre of a growing cultural movement of his own, and one that, at least implicitly, questioned the right of Yeats, AE and the others to call themselves *Irish* writers. Hyde himself, though he confessed in 1900 that he would rather have written one good poem in Irish than an entire volume of English verses, was indulgent towards their efforts, which he looked upon as a halfway house; but some of his followers, including the fiery journalist D. P. Moran, were not.

The stories of Somerville and Ross brought rural Ireland to life for a large circle of readers, but their approach was too patronizing to be acceptable to Irish nationalists. Edith Œnone Somerville's own illustrations successfully catch their spirit. (4)

Their 'Irish Ireland' programme asserted that the national literature *must* be in the native language. This position led to some vigorous clashes with Yeats and those identified with his ideals; it also contributed substantially to the militant nationalism which erupted in 1916.

An Irish theatre

The single most significant and well-known of Yeats's efforts to stimulate the development of a national literature was the Irish dramatic movement now universally associated with the Abbey Theatre, its home since 1904. Yeats had been drawn to the drama since the beginning of his literary career, and during the 1890s he became increasingly conscious of the suitability of the stage as a means of reaching the large potential audience who could not be interested in *reading* serious literature. A preliminary manifesto shows the way in which the theatre movement was conceived as a medium for the propagation of Yeats's literary ideals:

> We propose to have performed in Dublin in the spring of every year certain Celtic and Irish plays, which whatever be their degree of excellence will be written with a high ambition, and so to build up a Celtic and Irish school of dramatic literature. We hope to find in Ireland an uncorrupted and imaginative audience trained to listen by its passion for oratory, and believe that our desire to bring upon the stage the deeper thoughts and emotions of Ireland will insure for us a tolerant welcome, and that freedom to experiment which is not found in theatres in England, and without which no new movement in art or literature can succeed. We will show that Ireland is not the home of buffoonery and of easy sentiment, as it has been represented, but the home of an ancient idealism. We are confident of the support of all Irish people, who are weary of misrepresentation, in carrying out a work that is outside all the political questions that divide us.

At the time this manifesto was written there was, in addition to the old opposition of nationalist and Unionist, the new bitterness left by the split in the nationalist ranks following the fall of Parnell. Consequently the position that political relevance was not an essential requirement for national literature was particularly useful in providing a sufficiently broad basis of appeal for what was intended to be a national theatre. The claims of art were to come before all others; 'freedom to experiment' was to be essential. But the dramatic movement *would* be intensely national, drawing its strength from the heroic past and giving particular attention to mythological and early historical subjects. The playwrights, Yeats suggested in a contemporary essay, would be primarily authors 'who have never doubted that all things are shadows of spiritual things'.

Yeats himself energetically set about the task of realizing this programme. He plunged into the practical aspects of 'theatre business, management of men', and also wrote a number of plays, including *The King's Threshold*, *On Baile's Strand* and *Deirdre*, that showed growing mastery of theatrical techniques. Almost from the start, however, he encountered problems and disappointments. A controversy concerning the theology of his own *Countess Cathleen* (part of the programme in 1899, his Theatre's first year) was the first of many clashes with audiences that proved far less tolerant than the manifesto had predicted. There were also internal conflicts among the dramatists and the actors. Most seriously of all, the traditional romantic and heroic subjects that Yeats favoured as matter for the new drama failed to take hold. Among his associates in the early years of the movement, both Edward Martyn and George Moore preferred modern work in the vein of Ibsen. 'Peasant' plays became increasingly popular, and a strain of harsh realism emerged and began to dominate the stage.

The peasant material was primarily the province of two of the Theatre's greatest figures, Lady (Augusta) Gregory and John M. Synge. Lady Gregory (1852–1932), a woman of the 'Big House' and the Protestant Ascendancy, had immersed herself in the life and literature of her native land and became one of Yeats's closest friends and literary allies. Her Galway estate, Coole Park, served as a focal point and matrix for much of the new literary activity. The rich heritage of the house and the great natural beauty of the surrounding area impressed themselves deeply upon the imagination of Yeats and many others: their visits were memorialized by initials carved in the trunk of a great beech tree in the garden. Lady Gregory was attracted by Hyde's work, learned Irish, and in the cabins surrounding Coole she and Yeats sought to make contact with the living folk-mind. In her *Cuchulain of Muirthemne* (1902) and *Gods and Fighting Men* (1904) she synthesized the great cycles of early Irish legend and retold them in 'Kiltartan', an English prose coloured by Irish idiom and constructions:

> Then Cuchulain stood up and faced all the men of Ulster. 'There is trouble on Cuchulain,' said Conchubar; 'he is after killing his own son, and if I and all my men were to go against him, by the end of the day he would destroy every man of us. Go now,' he said to Cathbad, the Druid, 'and bind him to go down to Baile's Strand, and to give three days fighting against the waves of the sea, rather than to kill us all.'

This prose, though disparaged by some as artificial, was in Yeats's eyes the perfect medium for making the old stories part of the modern Irish consciousness.

Lady Gregory played from the first a major role in planning the theatre movement; she collaborated with Yeats on several plays, and, when it became apparent that appropriate works were in short supply, set about providing them herself. Her speciality was comedy, but she also wrote tragic-comedies, tragedies and 'wonder plays'. An element of fancy generally tinges the world of the country people depicted in her work. These plays appealed to a wide audience and thus helped keep the Theatre going in difficult times. Nevertheless, she shared Yeats's high standards and supported them vigorously: as she put it in *Our Irish Theatre*, her chronicle of the movement, 'we went on giving what we thought good until it became popular'.

John Synge (1871–1909) was yet another writer from an Ascendancy background who developed a deep commitment to Irish folk life; and the quality of the work he produced after foregoing a cosmopolitan career in Paris to write about the culture he had observed on the Aran Islands and elsewhere in his own country gave weight to Yeats's assertions that nationality was an essential element in great literature. But Synge was tenaciously sincere in his vision of that life ('what I write of Irish country life I know to be true and I most emphatically will not change a syllable of it because A. B. or C. may think they know better than I do'), and thus the plays in which he embodied it provoked tempestuous controversy. As a dramatist he believed that 'on the stage one must have reality, and one must have joy ...'. In most modern literature these qualities had bifurcated into the naturalistic and symbolist schools; but in countries such as Ireland, 'where the imagination of the people, and the language they use, is rich and living, it is possible for a writer to be rich and copious in his words, and at the same time to give the reality which is the root of all poetry, in a comprehensive and natural form'. This theory justified Synge's dramatic prose, which has general characteristics similar to Hyde's and Lady Gregory's but is even more vibrant and poetic:

Where now will you meet the like of Daneen Sullivan knocked the eye from a peeler, or Marcus Quin, God rest him, got six months for maiming ewes, and he a great warrant to tell stories of holy Ireland till he'd have the old women shedding down tears about their feet. Where will you find the like of them, I'm saying?

The reality underlying this passage from *The Playboy of the Western World* involved elements of violence, social decline and sexual frustration: the 'real men' are all gone and blooming girls have to make do with the runts who remain. Synge, preoccupied by death and actually destined to die in the fullness of his powers, was attracted by all manifestations of life lived to the utmost and did not feel compelled either to obscure or to condemn elements embarrassing to public morality or national self-images: 'the wildness and, if you will, vices of the Irish peasantry are due, like their extraordinary good points of all kinds, to the *richness* of their nature – a thing that is priceless beyond words'.

Many of the extreme nationalists could not admit that Synge's picture of Irish life had any truth in it. Their minds, conditioned by Young Ireland stereotypes, needed to see the English-Irish conflict in simple black-and-white terms; any admission that the Irish character had flaws would weaken the development of patriotic feeling and strengthen the oppressors' hand. So Synge, although his own national feeling probably ran deeper than that of most of his antagonists, became the target of virulent attacks. The powerful tragedy *Riders to the Sea* gave relatively little offence, but *The Shadow of the Glen* was considered 'a libel on Irish womanhood' and sparked a controversy in the newspapers. Another play, *The Tinker's Wedding*, was too strong even to be performed in Ireland; and there were riots in the theatre over *The Playboy* in 1907. (Hostile elements in the audience even sang Young Ireland ballads such as Davis's 'A Nation Once Again'.)

Yeats, who had been fighting the super-patriots since the 'nineties, took advantage of the *Playboy* controversy to reassert the supreme claims of art; but such quarrels made it harder and harder for him to believe in the possibility of a *popular* literary movement and helped produce his own gradual alignment with a very different strand of Irish tradition. Synge and Lady Gregory were themselves both strong-minded individuals who did not always agree with Yeats (or with each other), but the poetic retrospect of 'The Municipal Gallery Revisited' –

John Synge, I and Augusta Gregory, thought
All that we did, all that we said or sang
Must come from contact with the soil, from that
Contact everything Antaeus-like grew strong.
We three alone in modern times had brought
Everything down to that sole test again,
Dream of the noble and the beggar-man.

– shows that to Yeats their differences seemed insignificant in the face of their common enemy.

There were in fact other talented dramatists connected with the theatre movement, but the work of many of them portrayed with grim faithfulness areas of modern Irish life in which little or no joy could be discerned; and although Yeats recognized this work as satisfying his own requisites for national literature he could not fully sympathize with its vision. A strong element of that dark realism appeared in the plays of Padraic Colum (1881–1972), especially *The Land* and *Thomas Muskerry*. Lennox Robinson (1886–1958), often linked with T. C. Murray and R. J. Ray as 'Cork realists', explained this new mood as a direct reaction against their more romantic predecessors:

We young men, a generation later than Yeats . . . didn't see [Ireland] as a queen, didn't see her all fair in purple and gold, we loved her as truly as Yeats . . . and the rest – maybe we loved her more deeply, but just because we loved her so deeply her faults were clear to us. Perhaps we realists saw her faults too clearly, perhaps we saw her too often as a grasping, middle-aged hag. She was avaricious, she was mean, for family pride she would force a son into the Church against his will, she would commit arson, she would lie, she would cheat, she would murder and yet we would write all our terrible words about her out of our love.

To such observers as AE and Ernest Boyd the prominence of the realists was a sign that the theatre movement had entered a period of decadence; contemporary sensibilities conditioned by Joyce are less likely to be disturbed by the plays in this vein and can see that their vision of Irish life, although admittedly narrow, was a powerful and genuine one that needed dramatization.

Yeats's own discouragement with the theatre movement requires qualification. That the Abbey Theatre did not take the course he sought for it is undeniable, but it certainly catalysed concern with the development of a national literature. The activity it generated was abundant. Besides Yeats's own circle at the Abbey there were splinter groups, an Ulster dramatic movement, and plays in Irish. In addition to names already mentioned, Alice Milligan, AE, Hyde, Joyce, the Reverend Patrick S. Dinneen, James Cousins, William Boyle, George Fitzmaurice,

Drawing by Sir William Orpen showing Sir Hugh Lane and the three Directors of the Irish National Theatre, John Synge, W. B. Yeats and Lady Gregory, in 1907, soon after they had launched the Abbey Theatre. The aim was to present 'Celtic and Irish plays . . . and so to build up a Celtic and Irish school of dramatic literature.' (5)

Conal O'Riordan, W. F. Casey, Seumas O'Kelly, St John Ervine, Rutherford Mayne, Joseph Campbell, Thomas MacDonagh and Patrick Pearse were among those who tried their hand at writing plays. Prominent actors and actresses included Frank and W. G. Fay, Máire Ní Shiubhlaigh, Sara Allgood, Maire O'Neill, Arthur Sinclair, J. M. Kerrigan and Fred O'Donovan. Whatever the merits of individual plays and performances, their cumulative effect contributed substantially to increasing cultural (and political) awareness.

And it is a misconception to think that Yeats turned away from the Abbey. A study of the Theatre records and of his own correspondence reveals that he never surrendered active involvement in either the artistic or the business ends of play production. However, he was impressed by the failure of his own early plays to find a popular audience, and this led him to search for a dramatic form oriented towards performance but not tied to the public stage. By 1914 he had found what he sought in the aristocratic Noh theatre of Japan, brought to his attention by Ezra Pound. This mode seemed to him ideal for plays concerned with the supernatural, with legend and myth, and expressing their vision by means of symbol and esoteric allusion. It would

also free him from popular taste: he boasted that he had 'invented a form of drama, distinguished, indirect and symbolic, and having no need of mob or press to pay its way – an aristocratic form'. A minimum of props and scenery meant that the new plays were performable in a drawing room before a select, highly educated audience. (The appeal of private performance was enhanced when a 1914 crisis in Abbey finances made expensive experimental productions of Yeats's earlier plays temporarily impossible.) And certainly the plays he wrote under this influence, beginning with *At the Hawk's Well*, were too esoteric ever to become crowd-pleasers. Yet even as he turned in this new direction he felt he was 'working for my own country. Perhaps some day a play in the form I am adapting for European purposes shall awake once more, whether in Gaelic or English, under the slope of Slieve-na-mon or Croagh Patrick ancient memories. . . .' In 1916 he admitted to having the dream that such plays, perhaps translated into Irish, might be taken into the country districts. And plays of his, including some of the most esoteric ones, appeared on the Abbey stage right up to the time of his death.

'To create forms . . .'

When we move from the theatre to examine other aspects of Irish literature from the turn of the century to about 1920, we do so only to meet Yeats once more. Despite the fact that he devoted so much attention during these years to drama, he remained the central figure in Irish poetry. The new century brought a new emphasis to his vision, and thus to his work. He described the change in Nietzschean terms:

> I have always felt that the soul has two movements primarily: one to transcend forms, and the other to create forms. Nietzsche . . . calls these the Dionysiac and the Apollonic, respectively. I think I have to some extent got weary of that wild God Dionysus, and I am hoping that the Far-Darter will come in his place.

This statement was by no means a *renunciation* of the 'spiritual': the soul is still supreme. But whereas his poetry in the 'nineties had increasingly concerned itself with the soul's transcendence of the phenomenal world, now he would give more attention to its incarnation in that world. Writing for the theatre, which demanded language that men could *speak*, reinforced this shift in emphasis: it led him to seek for 'a more manful energy . . . and for clean outline, instead of those outlines of lyric poetry that are blurred with desire and vague regret'.

During this same period, Yeats was defending the primacy of art in controversies with the extremists among his nationalist political allies over such issues as *The Playboy* and the proposed gallery for the great collection of paintings which Lady Gregory's nephew Hugh Lane wished to give Dublin, and trying to keep the literary standards of the writers themselves as high as possible. The bitterness which so often resulted and his own increasing unpopularity brought him to see the value of his more 'masculine' style for *satiric* poetry and helped provoke him to a redefinition of his own national tradition. More and more he turned from the 19th-century nationalism with which he had originally identified back to the heyday of the Ascendancy in the decades preceding the Union. Grattan, Burke, Berkeley and Swift took on a new value in his eyes, became sources of political and philosophic and literary wisdom; and he saw himself and such congenial contemporaries as Synge, Lane and Lady Gregory as their heirs.

Both the satiric note and the sense of alienation from the nationalists are already discernible in poems like 'To a Wealthy Man . . .'

> *You gave, but will not give again*
> *Until enough of Paudeen's pence*
> *By Biddy's halfpennies have lain*
> *To be 'some sort of evidence',*
> *Before you'll put your guineas down,*
> *That things it were a pride to give*
> *Are what the blind and ignorant town*
> *Imagines best to make it thrive.*

His assertion in 'September 1913' that the revolutionary movement itself had lost its strength was disproved dramatically by the Easter Rising three years later. He recognized his misjudgment, and made brilliant art of the recognition in 'Easter 1916'; but he continued to pursue his new direction. It was a direction that he considered no less Irish, no less patriotic, than that chosen by the rebels; and it led him towards Thoor Ballylee, the Norman tower near Coole which he bought in 1917 and which became a dominant symbol in the great poetry of his mature years.

One of the disadvantages of a literary movement is that its most original authors almost invariably call forth imitators. By the first decade of the new century, a great many of the young poets were beginning to explore the early manner which Yeats had already moved beyond – an effect Joyce was to characterize in *Finnegans Wake* as the 'cultic twalette'. AE also had his disciples, and the new work often seemed to have drawn inspiration from both sources. Colum, 'Seumas O'Sullivan' (James Starkey), Ella Young and Susan Mitchell – who proved to be an excellent poetic satirist – were among the young writers emerging at this time. Ulster, of course, had its poets, including Alice Milligan and Joseph Campbell.

James Stephens (1880–1950), whose first volume of verse appeared in 1909, eventually developed into a poet of considerable stature; but after *The Crock of Gold* (1912) he was best known as a writer of prose romances. Oliver St John Gogarty (1878–1957), model for the notorious 'Buck' Mulligan of *Ulysses*, was actually a talented poet and another remarkable all-round man, involved in virtually every aspect of contemporary Irish life. He supported the Sinn Fein movement and later served with Yeats in the Senate of the newly established Free State. Much of his poetry, written out of a deep love of Classical literature and culture, seems by Yeatsian standards cosmopolitan; but he also produced witty satires on local themes.

Patrick Pearse, Thomas MacDonagh and Joseph Plunkett, three other poets whose work was becoming known during this era, were to achieve their greatest fame outside the sphere of literature. For them, their country literally meant more than life, but they too had been affected by the climate Yeats had created and did not repeat the Young Irelanders' mistake of confusing patriotism and poetry. Pearse, although like Hyde he really desired a national literature in Irish, praised Yeats as a 'great artist' and 'the poet who has most finely voiced Irish nationalism in our time'. Pearse did not feel that a writer who chose to advance a cause was automatically weakening his work, but neither did he believe that by doing so he would be strengthening it. In his study of Irish literature the scholarly MacDonagh observed that 'propaganda has rarely produced a great poem'. Each of these poets was a conscious craftsman and rigorously pruned his *oeuvre* with posterity in mind.

Nineteen-sixteen took all three men from the scene; in the following year Austin Clarke published his first volume, *The Vengeance of Fionn*. Clarke was to become arguably the best Irish poet after Yeats, but it was not until many years after this era that he developed the distinctive style found in his finest work. In retrospect the poetry of the 1900–20 period seems transitional: more sophisticated and self-conscious, attaining a generally higher level of artistry than the work of the formative years of the Revival; but providing nothing to equal the fullest flowering of the movement in Yeats's major lyrical volumes of the 'twenties and 'thirties.

The revival of prose: Moore and Joyce

To Ernest Boyd, writing in 1916, fiction seemed 'the weak point of the Revival'. However, he was among those who did not take Somerville and Ross seriously; he had only recently discovered Joyce; and Seumas O'Kelly had not yet published his great novella *The Weaver's Grave*. When one adds the contributions of these writers to the work of

Stephens, Moore and the Ulster novelist Shan F. Bullock, it becomes obvious that the prose of the first two decades of the 20th century is one of the strongest areas in modern Irish literature.

The fiction writers of this era struck every tonal note, from whimsical fantasy to brutal realism; lyricism, comedy and satire flourished; and there were major experiments in form and style. Somerville and Ross, O'Kelly, and Stephens all deserve more attention than they have received. For the purposes of this survey, however, Moore and Joyce must be given the fullest consideration – because their work, in addition to its excellence, embodies an appraisal of the Revival itself. Each of them produced a volume of stories chronicling the deadness of much of modern Irish life as they saw it (Moore focusing upon the countryside, Joyce upon the metropolis) and a novel that dramatized in detail a sensitive mind's efforts to escape this constricting environment; and each followed these works with a *magnum opus*, a Sacred Book, in which the entire Irish literary movement was subjected to a highly personal and generally negative scrutiny.

After writing *A Drama in Muslin* and *Parnell and his Island* in the 1880s, Moore had absented himself from his homeland until the turn of the century when the nascent theatre project aroused his national enthusiasm. In addition to his brief involvement with that project (which included collaboration with Yeats on the play *Diarmuid and Grania*) he took an interest in the language movement; the stories in *The Untilled Field* (1903) appeared also in Gaelic to serve as models for potential writers of fiction in Irish. It was almost certain, however, that the picture of Irish life presented in them would not be well received among the priests and Irish Irelanders who comprised the backbone of the Gaelic League. Moore depicts the country as debilitated by poverty and emigration, with its aristocracy in decay, the Church in control of people's lives, and no room for love, beauty or art. While some of the priests in the stories are treated sympathetically, the volume as a whole puts Catholicism in a very bad light.

Not surprisingly Moore's novel *The Lake* (1905), originally conceived as a story for *The Untilled Field*, charted the course of a priest's abandonment of his religion in order to seek 'life'. The book made an innovative contribution to the development of the psychological and symbolic novel. Father Gogarty's metamorphosis is effected by his plunging into a lake and swimming to freedom; the connection between the external and internal worlds is made explicit in his final reflection that 'There is a lake in every man's heart. ... And every man must ungird his loins for the crossing.'

Moore had come to feel that no artistic and cultural awakening was possible in Ireland so long as the country remained primarily Catholic. In addition to rather ostentatiously renouncing the faith himself, he made this perception the shaping principle in his fictional-autobiographical trilogy *Hail and Farewell* (1911–14). All his literary associates appeared under their real names, with no major figure spared from some degree of satire.

Moore's description of Yeats giving a speech about the Lane gallery provides a delightful counterpoint to Yeats's own poem on the subject:

> We . . . could hardly believe our ears when, instead of talking to us as he used to do about the old stories come down from generation to generation, he began to thunder like Ben Tillett himself against the middle classes ... and all because the middle classes did not dip their hands into their pockets and give Lane the money he wanted for his exhibition. . . . And we asked ourselves why Willie Yeats should feel himself called upon to denounce the class to which he himself belonged essentially: on one side excellent mercantile millers and shipowners, and on the other a portrait painter of rare talent. With so admirable a parentage it did not seem to us necessary that a man should look back for an ancestry, and we had laughed at the story . . . that on one occasion when Yeats was crooning over AE's fire he had said that if he had his rights he would be Duke of Ormonde, and that AE had answered, 'In any case, Willie, you are overlooking your father' – a detestable remark to make to a poet in search of an ancestry. . . . AE . . . should have guessed that Yeats's belief in his lineal descent from the great Duke of Ormonde was part of his poetic equipment. ... AE knew that there were spoons in the Yeats family bearing the Butler crest, . . . and he should have remembered that certain passages in 'The Countess Cathleen' are clearly derivative from the spoons.

There was genuine insight here about the importance of tradition for a writer like Yeats, but Moore scarcely did justice to Yeats's complex motives for attempting to realign himself and failed to see the extent of his achievement in stimulating a genuine Revival. Moore emerges as his own hero, the messianic artist who tried unsuccessfully to bring light to the Gentiles. The book was witty and beautifully written, but left much unhappiness among those who felt that the vision it presented was inaccurate and unfair. With the appearance of the first volume Moore emulated the protagonist of *The Lake*, leaving his house in Ely Place after a decade of residence and crossing the sea to London once again.

This pattern of voluntary 'exile' was echoed by James Joyce (1882–1941) in both his life and his work. When Joyce decided in 1902 to make himself known in Dublin literary circles, Yeats and AE thought that a highly promising young recruit had been found. Though they recognized his ability they did not know their man. Joyce admitted Yeats's greatness as a writer, but he could not accept what he saw as a catering to the 'rabblement' in the theatre movement. Already *au courant* with the latest Continental literary trends, he was suspicious of 'the folk' and feared that the Irish movement was essentially parochial. Thus he resisted the kindnesses and encouragement the older figures offered and in 1904 left the country to write abroad.

In the same year he had already begun the stories eventually collected as *Dubliners*. In them he left no doubt about his attitude towards the country he was fleeing: 'my intention was to write a chapter of the moral history of my country and I chose Dublin for the scene because that city seemed to me the centre of paralysis'. The volume begins with the death of a priest and each succeeding story adds images of sterility and corruption. The great final story, 'The Dead', does contain a positive picture of Irish hospitality and possibly some suggestions (more typical of Yeats than Joyce) of a greater vitality in the primitive west; but it too ends with death. The new movement is reduced to a handful of ludicrous images: a would-be poet who desires to be recognized as 'one of the Celtic school by reason of the melancholy tone of his poems'; a politician's bad patriotic verses about the death of Parnell; and a disastrous concert offered as emblematic of the contemporary musical scene. (The grasping Mrs Kearney of 'A Mother', the story in which the concert occurs, may be an ironic counterpart of Yeats's Cathleen ni Houlihan, who in his famous play has given up everything for Ireland.) Also in 1904 Joyce read *The Untilled Field*; although he called it a 'silly, wretched book', he must surely have recognized in it a response to Irish life very similar to his own, and he may well have absorbed from it certain images and situations.

Joyce was equally derogatory in his comments about *The Lake*, but a reading of his own *A Portrait of the Artist as a Young Man* reveals resonances everywhere with Moore's novel. Stephen Dedalus, the largely autobiographical hero of *A Portrait*, rejects a potential career in the priesthood in order to become an artist, a 'priest of eternal imagination'. Such values make him an outsider, virtually alone in a hostile milieu – a uniqueness Joyce dramatizes in part by showing Stephen's fellow college-students participating in the demonstrations against *The Countess Cathleen*. Stephen does care about Ireland, and desires to forge 'the uncreated conscience' of his race; but before he can do so he must leave, must escape the 'nets' of nationality, language and

'*Mr W. B. Yeats presenting Mr George Moore to the Queen of the Fairies.' Max Beerbohm had small sympathy with Yeats's mysticism, and was amused by his attempts to draw George Moore into the magic circle. Moore had escaped early from his Irish background and made his reputation with a series of realistic novels in the French tradition. (6)*

religion which threaten to hold back his soul from its full development. Thus the book ends with his preparations to depart for Paris.

But Stephen was to find (as had some of Moore's characters) that 'escape' is not so simple. In his next novel, *Ulysses*, Joyce brought him back to Dublin, sadder and possibly wiser but with little creative work to show for his efforts. The central question of whether his contact with Leopold Bloom, citizen of the city he had fled, will make him into the great artist who will go forth to write the novel in which he appears is beyond the scope of this essay. We may notice, however, that at last Joyce has deigned to acknowledge the Revival in progress in the Dublin of 1904 – Joyce's own *annus mirabilis* – to which Stephen returns. In doing so, however, Joyce's purpose was certainly not primarily historical verisimilitude. His deeper motives are suggested by a passage in which, during an interlude in Stephen's exposition of his theory about Shakespeare, the other characters discuss the literary movement: 'Our national epic has yet to be written, Dr Sigerson says. Moore is the man for it.'

At one level *Ulysses* can be read as Joyce's evidence that *he*, not Moore, was the man who would write 'the Irish epic'. Joyce suggested this not only by re-creating Homer's *Odyssey* in modern Dublin but also by embedding in his novel a sort of literary history of Ireland. Working primarily through parody, he destroyed all his chief competitors, leaving the field to himself. There are marvellous burlesques of Hyde, O'Grady, AE and Synge; an obscene parody of one of Yeats's most romantic poems; and satiric hits at Gogarty, at Moore himself and at lesser figures. In addition, medieval Irish literature, the folk tradition, the patriotic strain and the language movement are all found wanting. As Joyce had so ostentatiously dissociated himself from the Revival, the implication was that the efforts of Yeats and the others had been misguided, while the lonelier course elected by Joyce was the true course.

Yet half a century later we can see that in the end Yeats, too, was right. Joyce had left his country, but he never stopped writing about it; and perhaps no one ever gave it fuller expression in literature. Joyce's work was national if not nationalistic, and he avoided parochialism through his increasingly complex practice of telescoping the particular and the mythic or archetypal. Furthermore, he brought to the task of creating a national literature an incredible artistic sophistication which he developed, as Yeats had predicted would be necessary, by putting himself to school to the great European masters. Joyce, in so many ways Yeats's opposite, demonstrated that extremes often meet; and Yeats's tower in Galway and the Martello tower that dominates the opening chapter of *Ulysses* stand as twin symbols of the triumph of the modern Irish literary movement.

The Visual Arts

JEANNE SHEEHY

Since the late 18th century Irish connoisseurs had been paying increasing attention to the past. The taste for accurate archaeological investigation – the collection of manuscripts and *objets d'art*, the measuring and recording of ancient buildings – was important in Ireland, since it drew attention to a body of native art of very high quality which became the source of national pride. From about 1840 onwards it was the most powerful influence on the national aspect of Irish art.

There were attempts, from time to time, to create an Irish School. Thomas Davis, the leader of the Young Ireland movement, was interested in art, and tried to find a common cultural ground on which different classes and creeds could meet. The *Nation* published articles on art, reviews of exhibitions, and the antiquarian studies of such men as John O'Donovan, Eugene O'Curry and George Petrie. When the members of the Young Ireland group became involved in Daniel O'Connell's Repeal Association, they made their enthusiasm for art, on various levels, felt there as well. The membership cards of the Association, which had been 'as bare of sentiment as the price list of a commercial traveller' were embellished with national emblems – harps, shamrocks, portraits of historic figures such as Owen Roe O'Neill or Brian Boroimhe, the Old Parliament House in Dublin. The Repeal Wardens, who were in charge of the affairs of the Association in various parts of the country, were urged to watch over the historic ruins in their areas. The Association offered prizes for pictures and sculptures of

Irish historical subjects, and, later, for suitable designs for Catholic, Protestant and Presbyterian churches, and for public buildings. There was even a mild attempt at reform in dress – a hat of national character to replace the imported articles in general use. This was the inspiration of Charles Gavan Duffy, who obtained the help of the artist Henry MacManus to design 'an authentic cap of Irish origin' shaped like the old Milesian Crown. So that his example might give it currency it was presented to Daniel O'Connell, at his monster meeting at Mullaghmast in 1843, by a deputation led by the sculptor John Hogan and MacManus. Made of green velvet, and embroidered with artistic ornaments, it had 'a certain antique dignity' when placed on the commanding forehead of O'Connell. Unfortunately, in the fabric employed for common use – 'a sort of grey shoddy, relieved by a feeble wreath of green shamrocks' – it bore 'an awkward and fatal resemblance to a night cap' and did not achieve popularity.

Davis was particularly keen on the development of 'high art' which would contribute to the creation of a national spirit, and 'instruct and ennoble men'.

We entreat our artists as they love their country, as they owe it a service, as they pity its woes and errors, as they are wroth at its sufferings, and as they hope to share and aid its advance, to use this opportunity of raising the taste and cultivating the nationality of Ireland,

he wrote in the *Nation*, where he also published a list

of possible national subjects for painters, which he said, had been jotted down by a friend. These included *St Patrick brought before the Druids at Tara, Nial and his Nine Hostages, Shane O'Neill at Elizabeth's Court* and the rather inflammatory *Lifting of the Irish Flags of a National Fleet and Army*. His ideas seem to have gained a certain amount of currency, but, to judge by the annual exhibitions of the Royal Hibernian Academy, his hints for Irish historical paintings were not often taken up by artists. A rare example is Joseph Patrick Haverty's *Advocates in a Good Cause*, exhibited at the RHA in 1846, which shows Father Mathew administering the pledge (not to consume alcohol). Daniel Maclise's *The Earls of Desmond and Ormonde*, was another subject from the list.

Towards a national art

Davis consulted his friend Frederick Burton, the painter, on the possibilities of national art, and was not encouraged. Free, spiritual, high-aiming art, said Burton, could not be forced. Ireland should be given a decided national school of poetry, and other phases would follow. Burton was at one time the hope of the Young Irelanders. As a talented artist, with a keen interest in Irish life and antiquities, he was ideally placed to be the leading painter of the new Ireland. He was a friend of George Petrie, with whom he had many common interests, and of other antiquarians such as Lord Dunraven and Sir Samuel Ferguson. He was also involved in the foundation of the Archaeological Society of Ireland in 1841. Though he did not share the political opinions of Young Ireland, he did design (anonymously) the frontispiece for *The Spirit of the Nation*, with historic figures, national emblems and a Hiberno-Romanesque doorway decorated with chevron mouldings. There is quite a lot of Irish subject-matter among his early works. Around 1840 he painted a watercolour portrait (he is never known to have worked in oils) of Paddy Coneely, the blind Galway piper from whom Petrie collected traditional Irish airs. Engravings after his picture *The Blind Girl at the Holy Well* were distributed to members of the Royal Irish Art Union in 1839–40:

> the scene is laid amid the Romantic wilds of the Western Highlands. Before a time honoured well, overgrown with lichen and moss, surmounted by an ancient sculptured cross, kneel two female forms, clad in the rough but highly picturesque and characteristic garb of the peasantry of that district . . . the whole of the composition is elevated, without being so over refined as to destroy the reality of the scene. . . .

His *Aran Fisherman's Drowned Child*, the Art Union engraving for 1844, is full of highly Victorian

drama, but it is notable for the carefully observed details of interior and costume. We find Thomas Davis rejoicing that Irish subjects by an Irish artist should be so widely distributed in this way; but, as we have seen, Burton did not share his ideas about national art. It seems likely that Burton's choice of subject was prompted on the one hand by a scientific interest in folk customs, and on the other by the fashion for picturesque and unusual scenes, and not by any patriotic spirit. He left the country in 1851, working first in Germany, and then in England where he eventually became Director of the National Gallery and gave up painting.

Two other Irishmen became distinguished painters in England. Of these, William Mulready (1786–1863) can scarcely be considered in a national context – he left the country when he was six, and the nearest he ever comes to Irish subject-matter is *Choosing the Wedding Gown*, a scene from Goldsmith's *Vicar of Wakefield*. Daniel Maclise, however, did keep up his Irish connection – the circle of contributors to *Fraser's Magazine*, in which he moved, included several Irishmen, and in the 1840s, along with John Doyle, the cartoonist, and Patrick MacDowell (1799–1870), the sculptor, he was a member of the Irish Society in London, an extension of the Young Ireland effort. Like Burton, he probably chose some of his Irish subjects because they accorded with the medievalizing or picturesque fashions of his time, but he does show more evidence of national awareness. The largest and most ambitious of his Irish paintings, *The Marriage of Strongbow and Eva*, was a subject set by the Fine Arts Commissioners in charge of the decoration of the Houses of Parliament at Westminster, but there is a certain patriotic drama in the way he chose to treat it: Strongbow's victorious foot resting on a fallen cross ornamented with Celtic interlace; the sacrificial posture of his bride; and especially the most conspicuous figures in the picture, a writhing mass of fallen warriors, whose garments show evidence of Maclise's researches into Celtic art. A carved slab in the central foreground bears the inscription *oroit do Mac* (pray for Mac . . .) often found on ancient crosses and memorials.

Maclise's last oil, *The Earls of Desmond and Ormonde*, treated one of the subjects suggested almost thirty years earlier by Thomas Davis: *Kildare 'On the Necks of the Butlers'*, which tells the story of the Earl of Desmond, carried off the battlefield by his victorious enemies, taunted by them about his position, and replying that he was where Desmond ought to be, 'on the necks of the Butlers'. Maclise also drew on another popular source of patriotic sentiment, the *Melodies* of Thomas Moore, and illustrated the Longman edition in 1845.

Of the artists who stayed in Dublin, we find one

The harp that once through Tara's halls
   The soul of music shed,
Now hangs as mute on Tara's walls,
   As if that soul were fled.—
So sleeps the pride of former days,
   So glory's thrill is o'er,
And hearts, that once beat high for praise,
   Now feel that pulse no more.

Thomas Moore's purpose in 'Irish Melodies', 1808, was 'to interpret the voice that spoke in my country's music'. But Daniel Maclise's illustrations to the edition of 1846 show clearly that for him the Celtic Revival was still purely literary; there is as yet no awareness of real Celtic art. (7)

or two with patriotic leanings. As already mentioned Haverty's painting of Father Mathew administering the pledge depicts a subject suggested by Thomas Davis. His interpretation is rather a sentimental one, whereas Davis had probably envisaged a more heroic crowd scene. He painted a *Limerick Piper* in several versions, and a large number of portraits of Daniel O'Connell. Henry MacManus had closer national links. He was from Monaghan, and an Orangeman, but friendship with Charles Gavan Duffy, who was a fellow townsman, and association with Young Ireland won him to national opinions. He illustrated a pictorial history of Ireland, which was written by John Cornelius O'Callaghan, part of Young Ireland's drive to educate the Irish people. He painted quite a large number of Irish subjects, both historical and contemporary. His *St Patrick Expounding the Trinity at Tara* received favourable notice at the Dublin Exhibition of 1853. Among his contemporary subjects is *Reading 'The Nation'*, in the National Gallery, Dublin.

There were a number of artists who were also antiquarians – most prominent among them George

Petrie (1790–1866) and Henry O'Neill (1798–1880), who exhibited regularly at the RHA. Both were chiefly topographical artists, who brought their archaeological skills to bear in their views of Irish ruins. Petrie's *Pilgrims at Clonmacnoise* combines a picturesque rendering of peasant costume and ruins against the sunset with an accurate delineation of architectural and sculptural detail. Henry O'Neill was a member of the Repeal Association, and did portraits of O'Connell, and of the Young Irelanders. In 1857 he published *Illustrations of the Most interesting of the Sculptured Crosses of Ancient Ireland*. Like Petrie's work, the plates combine antiquarian accuracy with romantic settings. The book was an important source for the Celtic crosses which became increasingly popular as monuments and gravestones.

The antiquarian Margaret Stokes illustrated a luxurious edition of *The Cromlech on Howth*, by Samuel Ferguson, published in 1861. It is lavishly decorated with borders and capitals in scarlet, gold, green and purple, taken from the *Book of Kells* and *Book of Durrow*. It is interesting to find Celtic interlace, used decoratively in such profusion, at so early a date.

Sculptors and architects

Among the sculptors who made reputations abroad, there is little evidence of interest in things Irish. John Henry Foley, it is true, designed monuments to Henry Grattan, and to Daniel O'Connell – but the making of monuments was his chief occupation, and these cannot be taken as any more evidence of national feeling than the bronze of Manochjee Nesserwanjee which he executed for Bombay. Patrick MacDowell left Ireland when he was twelve, and like that of William Mulready, his work is not particularly Irish. Only John Hogan (1800–58) shows Irish interests in his work. He spent part of his working life in Rome, but visited Ireland, and returned to live there in 1848. He executed a number of monuments to national figures though not as many as his talents deserved – the commission for the Thomas Moore statue in College Green, Dublin, went to Christopher Moore, with unhappy results. Hogan had connections with O'Connell and Young Ireland – he was one of the artists who presented the green velvet cap to O'Connell at Mullaghmast. One of his most interesting works is the monument to James Doyle, Bishop of Kildare and Leighlin (known as JKL), in Carlow Cathedral. It was described in the following terms by Petrie in the *Irish Penny Journal*, December 1840:

The subject is the last appeal of a Christian prelate to heaven for the regeneration of his country. Erin is represented resting on one knee, her body bent and humbled, yet in her majestic form retaining a fulness of beauty, and dignity of character; her turret-crowned head resting on one arm, while the other, with an expression of melancholy abandonment, reclines on and strums her ancient harp. In the male figure which stands beside her in an attitude of the most unaffected grace and dignity we see a personification of the sublime in the episcopal character.

The situation in architecture was, on the whole, similar to the other arts – changes in style generally followed developments in England. Some architects, however, did study the remains of medieval buildings, stimulated by an interest which was a fundamental part of the Gothic Revival. A large number of ancient churches were restored in the 19th century, and this, too, led to a study of ancient architecture. One of Ireland's most talented architects, Benjamin Woodward, made studies of Holy Cross Abbey, Co. Tipperary, early in his career; perhaps some reference to this is to be found in the little owl forming the label-stop on one of the quadrangle windows at University College, Cork, which echoes a very similar owl at Holy Cross. A. W. N. Pugin, who did quite a lot of work in Ireland in the 1840s, studied the ruins of Dunbrody Abbey, Co. Wexford, and had decided views about the qualities proper to Irish churches.

It was the round towers which early attracted attention as a peculiar feature of Irish architecture. Interest in them was stimulated by the controversy – were they belfries, baptistries, or merely phallic symbols? – which raged for the second half of the century. The monument to Daniel O'Connell, which was begun in Glasnevin Cemetery, Dublin, shortly after the Liberator's death in 1847, is a round tower. The original project, suggested by George Petrie, consisted of a group of buildings – the tower, a chapel in the earliest style of Christian architecture in Ireland and a stone cross – but the tower was so colossal that there was no money left for anything else, and even if there had been the scale would have been impossible. There is a round tower, not very archaeological in character, which was added, in 1848, to the Church of Ireland chapel at Old Court, Co. Down. When E. W. Godwin built a castle for the Earl of Limerick, at Dromore, in the 1860s, he incorporated a round tower on the skyline, giving the composition a silhouette like that of the Rock of Cashel.

James Joseph McCarthy was an architect who had close links with the Young Ireland movement. He was a friend of Charles Gavan Duffy, and probably belonged to the Repeal Association. Gavan Duffy said of him that he had 'built more Celtic churches than any man of Irish birth since the *Gobán Saor* taught our ancestors to construct the round towers', and that he had caught the first

impulse to revive Irish Gothic in ecclesiastical architecture from his reading of the *Nation*. The reference to Gothic is significant – it was not, in general, until later in the century that Hiberno-Romanesque became the specific Revival style. In the 'forties and 'fifties architects were content to borrow from other periods – indeed there is some indication that the Gothic Revival as a whole was, for the Roman Catholic population, a return to a Celtic past of saints and scholars. As the *Catholic Directory* expressed it, in 1845,

> We hope yet to see the day when the zealous piety of the people, guided by educated taste, will once more cover the face of the 'Island of Saints' with structures that shall emulate the sacred splendour of the august fanes which were the boast of 'Cashel of the Kings' or of Holy Mellifont, and whose ruins remain to attest the ruthless atrocity of our Saxon invaders.

McCarthy quite frequently used elements borrowed from medieval buildings. At Ardfert, Co. Kerry, begun in 1853, he based all of his window heads on a trefoil example in the transept of the nearby cathedral. At Kilmallock, Co. Limerick, the entire east end of the church he designed is based on the neighbouring Dominican priory, including a line for line copy of the reticulated tracery in one of the priory windows.

We occasionally find McCarthy using round towers, though the effect is never particularly Irish: at Thomastown, Co. Kilkenny, the round staircase turrets, set into the transepts, look Germanic, and at Lixnaw, Co. Kerry, the bell turret on the west front is reminiscent of a round tower, but in a position never found in an ancient church.

One remarkably early instance of Hiberno-Romanesque revival is to be found at Glenstal Castle, Co. Limerick – a copy of the highly ornate doorway at Killaloe Cathedral, executed in 1841, perhaps under the influence of the antiquarian Lord Dunraven. The first attempt to revive the style for an entire building seems to have been W. H. Lynn's, at St Patrick's Church, Jordanstown, near Belfast. Erected in the late 1860s, it was described as 'the first attempt in modern times to revive the ancient architecture of Ireland'. The architect gave a great deal of attention to archaeological accuracy, especially the placing of the round tower.

> To Mr Lynn is due this adaptation of a most characteristic feature of the ancient architecture of Ireland to the purposes of modern building, and its entire suitability suggests that of the many theories advanced as to the original intention of the round towers not the least reasonable is that they were used as in the present instance, as bell

One of the signs of a growing awareness of the national heritage was the appearance of reproduction Celtic brooches and Ardagh Chalices, illustrated here from a periodical of 1896. The Chalice is transmogrified into a sugar bowl and provided with tongs to match. (8)

towers. The idea of reproducing a building of this kind was suggested by a study of the ruins at Clonmacnoise, where in the remains of the church called *Teampull Finghin* a round tower is found in somewhat similar connexion with the ancient chancel.

An interesting feature of Jordanstown is the stained glass. It was made by Clayton and Bell of London, and a good deal of trouble was taken 'to endeavour to represent our Irish saints as an artist of their own time would have delineated them'. Careful searches were made among monuments and illuminations for examples of costume and treatment – St Patrick's crozier was copied from an ancient Irish crozier in the British Museum, and the borders round the windows were designed after the ornamentation of the *Book of Durrow* and other ancient examples.

The Revival and popular taste

In the applied arts growing national sentiment manifested itself strongly. Beleek porcelain, with its decoration of harps and shamrocks, still a familiar sight in the Dublin souvenir shops, was already being produced in the 1860s. Bohemian engravers, working in Dublin in the second half of the century, ornamented the glass on which they worked with wreaths of shamrocks. The production of copies of ancient Irish jewellery and other objects was stimulated by the discovery of the Tara Brooch in 1850, and of the Ardagh Chalice in 1868. The manufacture of souvenirs in bog wood (usually oak) reached enormous proportions.

The history of bog oak ornaments is an interesting one. It seems that when George IV visited Ireland in 1821, a person of the name of M'Gurk presented him with an elaborately carved walking stick of bog oak, the work of his own hands. The object was much admired, and M'Gurk obtained many orders. Some time later a man called Connell began to do a more regular business, carving the bog wood which was to be found plentifully near Killarney, where he lived, and selling it as souvenirs to tourists, and the craft was soon taken up by other carvers. The Queen, the Prince Consort and other members of the Royal Family bought some of the finest specimens, and the carving of bog oak attained the position of a native art. By the mid-'sixties Johnson, a leading Dublin jeweller, was selling between £4,000- and £5,000-worth of bog oak ornaments a year and he was only one of many producers – it was so popular that an imitation, in deal, stained and stamped, was produced in England, and sold as Irish bog oak. Exhibits of bogwood carving figure largely in the industrial exhibitions which took place in Ireland from 1852 onwards. They mostly consisted of copies of Celtic crosses in high relief, round towers, abbeys, copies of antique ornaments – brooches and fibulae, harps, shamrocks and other national emblems. Articles of a rather more dubious 'Irish' nature were also popular – pieces illustrative of *Donnybrook Fair*, or *Paddy and his Pig* 'in which the pig, proverbial for going the contrary way to that which it is wanted to go, is deceived, with a knowing leer, by Paddy, who pretends that he is going the wrong way, and thereby induces the pig to go right'.

Copies or interpretations of antique ornaments were also very much in evidence at the exhibitions. This revival seems to go back to 1842, when Waterhouse and Company, by the addition of a pin, converted antique Irish fibulae into brooches. Some time later the Royal Irish Academy gave Dublin jewellers access to their collections, and drawings and models were made. When the Tara Brooch was discovered, it became extremely popular, and a Tara

Bracelet was designed as a companion piece. The Catalogue to the Dublin International Exhibition of 1865 claimed that 'Ireland can now boast of the continued use of peculiarly national ornaments worn by her princes and nobles in ages long since past.'

Furniture, too, took a Celtic turn, though generally of a popular kind, at the exhibitions. At the Irish Industrial Exhibition of 1853 we find Mr Clarke, of St Stephen's Green, exhibiting 'a Davenport, on richly carved consoles with guard on top representing the round towers of Ireland . . .', and Mr Jones an 'omnium of three plateaus with statuette of Brian Borimhe'. The Exhibition of the Fine Arts and Ornamental Art by the Royal Dublin Society in 1861 included a 'Cabinet of Irish oak, richly carved, to represent the Temple of Music; the figure on the summit is Ollamh Folla, the Irish lawgiver; one panel represents the triennial convention of the Irish Chiefs in the great hall of Tara; in the other the harpers performing before the king and court in Tara's Hall.'

In all of this production both in the fine and in the applied arts, two kinds of motif are discernible, though sometimes they are combined. On the one hand there is the revival of ancient Celtic art, evident in the use of interlace designs, and the revival of jewellery and architecture. On the other are the national emblems: shamrock, harp, wolfhound, Hibernia, some of which date from the late 18th century. The round tower is common to both categories. In the course of the century antiquarian motifs became increasingly popular, so that eventually Celtic interlace, high crosses and the Tara Brooch joined the harp and shamrock as patriotic devices. There are some splendid examples of popular national imagery in the latter part of the century. Pat McAuliffe (1846–1921) was a builder and plasterer who embellished a great number of houses in Listowel, Co. Kerry, with polychrome tableaux which make use of Hibernias, wolfhounds, harps and so on. In Dublin one of the most interesting examples of the same genre was O'Meara's The Irish House, a pub on Wood Quay now, alas, demolished. It was decorated in stucco and Portland cement by Burnet and Comerford, and had a skyline composed of six round towers. Its walls were ornamented with reliefs of Irish scenes: Grattan's last address to the Irish Parliament; Erin weeping over her harp; Daniel O'Connell; each scene separated by niches with wolfhounds and methers (ancient Irish drinking cups) of colossal size. The skyline ironwork said 'Céad Míle Fáilte, Erin go Bragh', and the date 1870.

A later, and, as befits its location, more restrained example crowns the top of the erstwhile National Bank in College Green – Eire, with her wolfhound

'This casket,' says the description in the Art Journal of 1853, 'is especially an Irish work, and is made entirely of native materials. The wood is the black bog oak, and is enriched with silver-gilt mountings and national emblems, the jewels being Irish diamonds and amethysts, which have a peculiarly brilliant effect when mounted on the dark bog wood.' (9)

and crowned harp, on a pedestal decorated with crowns and shamrocks, and inscribed 'Eire go Bragh'. This was carved in 1889 by the firm of Pearse and Sharp. The Pearse in question was the stone-carver father of Patrick and William Pearse.

Into the 20th century

Though the plastic arts in Ireland by no means kept pace with the cultural, political and literary revival which got going towards the end of the 19th century and came to fruition in the 20th, they did absorb a certain amount of vitality from it. In so small a community, people involved in literature, the theatre, the Gaelic League, even politics, inevitably had some contact with art and artists, and the applied arts pervaded the lives of most people. Hugh Lane, who founded the Municipal Gallery of Modern Art, was the nephew of Lady Gregory. Lane was more interested in bringing European art to Ireland than in the creation of a national school, but he did encourage a number of Irish painters, including John Butler Yeats (1839–1922). He organized an exhibition of Irish painting at the Guildhall, London, in 1904, and was so anxious to widen its scope that any painter who admitted to the most remote Irish connections was included. Lily and Elizabeth Yeats, sisters of the poet, were at the centre of the Arts and Crafts movement, one as an embroidress, the other producing superbly printed books. The poet AE was also a painter, and was involved in the movement to foster home industries, which included lace-making and weaving.

Interest in the arts of pagan and early Christian Ireland, which had been growing steadily since the 'forties, received new impetus, and Celtic interlace ornament appeared everywhere – on the covers of books, in the productions of the Arts and Crafts Society, and in the Gaelic costume which was affected by literary and patriotic figures. The men – among them were Willie and Patrick Pearse, and William Gibson, who, as Lord Ashbourne, insisted on addressing the House of Lords in Irish – wore green or saffron kilts, and each had a *brath* (a large square of fabric) pinned to the shoulder of his jacket with a silver or copper brooch of the Tara pattern. The female costume is vividly described by Mary Colum in her memoirs:

A girl poet, friend of mine . . . never wore any other garb. She would appear in the Abbey in gorgeous purple and gold, a torc on her forehead, a Tara brooch fastening her brath, and various other accouterments of the ancient Irish, including the inevitable amber. . . . For dressy wear I had a white garment with blue and green embroidery, a blue brath, copper brooches and other archaeological adornments. For more ordinary wear I had the Irish costume in blue green, a brath of the same colour, with embroideries out of the Book of Kells.

The more conventional contented themselves with wearing Irish materials. Lady Fingal helped at an Irish Exhibition in London around 1903 – she sold a cigar of Irish manufacture to Edward VII – dressed in a coat and skirt of bright emerald green Irish tweed.

Just as the interest in things ancient and Celtic had been stimulated earlier in the century by a romantic interest in the past that was common to the whole of Europe, so the craze for Celtic interlace at the beginning of this century was not unaffected by the fact that it coincided with the *art nouveau* style, which indulged in similar sinuosities. The mystical movements in vogue in England and France were also manifested in Ireland, in the form of the Irish Theosophical Society, where they mingled with the Celtic twilight, to the confusion of some sections of the public: 'let our young men and maidens compose mystic verses, savouring of Bhudism, and converse in what we have no manner of doubt is execrably bad Irish', and Ireland would be regenerated, according to an editorial in the *Irish Builder* in 1901, which attacked the unworldliness of the Revival. What Ireland really needed was the inculcation of sound commercial principles.

Artists and architects

Among the leading painters active in the last quarter of the century there was, once again, not much that was markedly Irish. Nathaniel Hone (1831–1917) was a painter whose style derived from the Barbizon landscapists, among whom he had worked. His landscapes evoke an aspect of the Irish countryside –

lush pastureland with cattle – which is no less typical than bog and mountain with donkeys, but it might just as well be in England or France. His preoccupations are painterly rather than patriotic. The same is true of Walter Osborne (1859–1903). He associated with people like Yeats, Maud Gonne and Douglas Hyde, and his family were Home Rulers. He painted scenes in Co. Galway – *The Horse Fair*, *The Fish Market* – showing girls in red petticoats and old women in shawls; but his choice of these subjects was probably dictated by the same spirit which sent him and his contemporaries to Pont Aven in Brittany, and Newlyn in Cornwall – the search for picturesque subjects far from the cities.

John B. Yeats painted a great many of the leading figures of the day – his sons William and Jack, Lady Gregory, George Moore, Douglas Hyde, AE, Synge – a catalogue of his portraits reads like a literary history of the period. John Lavery and William Orpen, younger men, both made successful careers as portrait painters in England. Neither is particularly Irish in his early work, which shows a strong French Impressionist influence, but both were affected by the political atmosphere of the second decade of the century. Lavery (1856–1941) painted the portraits of leading political figures – Redmond, Carson, Collins, de Valera – and made his studio 'neutral ground where both sides might meet' during the Treaty negotiations. He found Michael Collins a patient sitter, but noticed that he liked to sit facing the door. For William Orpen (1878–1931) interest in the national heritage took a satirical turn, in the three extraordinary allegorical pictures which he painted between 1913 and 1916. One of these, *Nude Pattern – Holy Well, Ireland*, in which some of the figures are nude, and others are clothed in the traditional costume of the inhabitants of the west, is a rather savage jibe at the religious customs of the country people.

Jack Yeats, on his own account, and through his family, was very much involved in Irish cultural activity. His early paintings, and the prints he made for his sister Elizabeth's Cuala Press, contain many references to life in Co. Sligo – fairs, races, country scenes – where he spent much of his childhood. Later, some of his work has distinct political references: *Bachelor's Walk, In Memory* (1915) shows the location of an encounter, on 20 July 1914, between a group of Volunteers and the King's Own Scottish Borderers. *Communicating with the Prisoners* (1924), which shows women outside Kilmainham jail shouting to prisoners inside, is a memory of the War of Independence.

It was a pupil of Orpen's, Sean Keating (*b.* 1889), who drew most on the struggles of 1916–22. His *Men of the West*, exhibited at the RHA in 1917, is a highly romanticized view of rebels of the period, in

'Anna Liffey', the personification of Dublin's river, a woodcut printed in 1907 by Elizabeth Yeats's Cuala Press to illustrate a poem by E. R. McClintock-Dix. (10).

picturesque western costume, with guns, a tricolour and lean, intent, bearded faces. Paul Henry (1876–1958) translated the western landscape, with its thatched cottages, bogs, blue mountains and brown turf stacks, into a flat, decorative pattern which was very effective. Unfortunately it was taken up by less talented artists, and survives to this day as a hackneyed formula.

Sculpture early in this century was distinguished by the number of national monuments erected, even before independence. Some of the most vigorous were designed by Oliver Sheppard (1864–1941). One of his finest works is *Cuchulainn* in the General Post Office, Dublin, which serves as a memorial of 1916, but was executed several years earlier. Sheppard also designed the fine 1798 memorial in Wexford.

In architecture, by far the most vigorous of the arts in Ireland, interest in the Hiberno-Romanesque style grew steadily. J. J. McCarthy designed a mortuary chapel, using Romanesque 'of that character which is peculiarly Irish', erected at Glasnevin in 1878. He made liberal use of 'chevron and billet mouldings modelled on Irish Romanesque examples'. The style was chosen to harmonize with the round tower of the O'Connell monument. Nearby is the memorial to Cardinal McCabe, designed by G. C. Ashlin, and erected in 1887. This is elaborately treated in Irish Romanesque, with carved interlace

designs, and a floor of ceramic mosaic showing emblems of the four Evangelists. Ashlin had been a pupil and partner of Edward Welby Pugin, and usually built in early French Gothic. Late in the century he became interested in Irish Romanesque, and when he was elected President of the Royal Institute of the Architects of Ireland in 1902, his inaugural address was on *The Possibility of the Revival of the Ancient Arts of Ireland, and their Adaptation to our Modern Circumstances.*

For the Church of Ireland, James Franklin Fuller designed several buildings in the style: St Michael and All Angels, Clane, for example, opened in 1883. The antiquarian Miss Stokes was consulted about the building 'and brought her profound knowledge to bear in many useful suggestions'.

During the first thirty years of this century, Hiberno-Romanesque was very popular indeed, partly because of the interest in Ireland's past, but also because its sturdiness, and the simplicity of its structural forms, were a welcome contrast to the thinness and fussy detail of late Gothic Revival. It had a number of exponents, but the architect who took it up with most effect was W. A. Scott. His church at Spiddal, Co. Galway, dedicated in 1907, uses the round openings and simple shapes of Romanesque but avoids the pitfall of too much carved decoration.

An interesting clue to changes in architectural taste is to be found in the buildings put up for industrial exhibitions, at home and abroad. At first, like their prototype, the Crystal Palace, they were of iron and glass. Later, however, attempts were made to give them a more specifically national character. The Irish Industries section of the World's Columbian Exposition, Chicago, in 1893 was housed in an Irish village. The entrance was a reproduction of the north doorway of Cormac's Chapel, Cashel, through which one debouched into a copy of the cloisters of Muckross Abbey, Co. Kerry. There was a reproduction of Blarney Castle, and of several thatched cottages. The Irish Pavilion at the Glasgow Exhibition of 1901 was a thatched house, designed by Sir Thomas Deane. The most grandiose display of all was at the Louisiana Purchase Exposition, St Louis, in 1904. It included St Lawrence's Gate, Drogheda; a reduced facsimile of the Old House of Parliament (Bank of Ireland), Dublin; a facsimile, exterior and interior, of Cormac's Chapel; the Cross of Muiredach, Monasterboice; the Round Tower of Clonmacnoise; and the cottage of President McKinley's ancestors, Dervock, Co. Antrim – all constructed in expanded metal and plaster.

The applied arts

The most valuable and permanent way in which

the artistic revival manifested itself at the beginning of the 20th century was in the applied arts, particularly in church decoration. The Arts and Crafts Society of Ireland held its first exhibition in 1895. It was largely amateur, and uneven in quality, but included furniture from small workshops in places like Killarney and Abbeyleix; and lace, the manufacture of which was also being fostered. There were several exhibits of reproductions of Celtic jewellery, the great stand-by of exhibitions from 1852 onwards. Edmond Johnson showed copies of the Tara Brooch, the Cavan Torc, the Shrine of St Molaise – and a sugar bowl copied from the Ardagh Chalice, with sugar tongs to match. Another exhibitor showed two silver muffineers, adapted from the Charter Horn of the Kavanaghs.

By the third exhibition, in 1903, the quality had improved enormously, and the exhibitions were enriched with work from Elizabeth Yeats's Dun Emer Bindery, carpets with Celtic designs from the workshop at Dun Emer run by Miss Gleeson and stained glass from Miss Purser. Exhibitions from then on contained work by many of the artists who were contributing at the same time to an exceedingly rich development of church decoration. This revival was largely due to the energy and organization of Edward Martyn, George Moore's friend, who was also interested in the reform of church music. He was instrumental in having classes in stained-glass-making set up in the Metropolitan School of Art, Dublin, and he persuaded Sarah Purser to set up a workshop, called An Túr Gloine, or the Tower of Glass, where former members of this class, and their master, A. E. Childe, might practise their craft. Most important of all, he persuaded successive bishops of Clonfert to allow the artists to work on the cathedral at Loughrea – with the result that it is a monument to the Revival. It has glass by members of An Túr Gloine, ranging from Miss Purser herself to Evie Hone (1894–1955), a late recruit to the studio. The metalwork was designed by W. A. Scott; the carving was done by Michael Shortall; and the banners where designed by Jack Yeats and embroidered by his sister and her assistants. There are also magnificent vestments at Loughrea, and at Ballinasloe, in the same diocese, made under the direction of Miss Gleeson at Dun Emer. At Ballinasloe too, there is a tabernacle door in enamel and metalwork, designed like a medieval book-cover, by Mia Cranwill, and stained glass by Harry Clarke (1889–1931), an outstandingly talented artist – though not a member of An Túr Gloine. The Honan Chapel, in University College, Cork, is another repository of rich decoration from the same sources.

There are quite strong native elements in most of this ecclesiastical art: Scott's metalwork uses Celtic

The Celtic Revival retained its vigour well into the 20th century. This 'Éire Page' by Art O'Murnaghan was designed in 1922 as part of a never-realized project for an illuminated book that was to be an Irish Republican Memorial. The text comes from the Vision of St Brigid, the 6th-century abbess of Kildare. The words in large lettering are various names for Ireland. The decorative patterns are almost an anthology of Early Christian ornament. (11).

motifs, and so do the Dun Emer vestments and embroideries. The stained glass often shows Irish saints, and uses images and symbols from early accounts of them. Mia Cranwill's enamel has interlace and spiral patterns. The decorative sense, with flat patterns and strong simple shapes, which the work displays, was, however, common to the rest of Europe at the period, and was a reaction against the extreme detail and realism of Victorian art.

Art did not stop with the securing of national independence, and painting, sculpture and architecture have by now firmly adopted the international style. There are still, however, powerful reminders of the Celtic Revival. Until quite recently school books, Christmas cards and illuminated texts were decorated with ornaments and initials from ancient manuscripts – and Irish coinage, postage stamps and telephone directories still are. Irish costume, as concocted in the 19th century (a dress with Celtic designs embroidered on it, or a kilt, and a *brath* secured at the shoulder with a 'Tara' brooch), is still worn. It is still possible to buy imitations of the Tara Brooch, and of ancient crosses – though bog oak has been replaced, as a common material for the manufacture of souvenirs, by Connemara marble – and harps and shamrocks are still as popular expressions of national sentiment as they were throughout the 19th century.

8

THE IRISH IN AMERICA

Starvation, struggle and success

WILLIAM V. SHANNON

So adieu, my dear father, adieu, my dear mother,

Farewell to my sister, farewell to my brother;

I am bound for America, my fortune to try,

When I think on Bunclody, I'm ready to die.

From *The Streams of Bunclody*. Anonymous ballad

The Irish who landed in America in the 1850s and 60s were almost entirely country people used to a rural life. In America they went not to the country but to the towns. The peasant became a labourer, a factory worker, a businessman. A new type of Irishman, unknown at home, emerged: aggressive, competitive and tough.

In New York immigrants disembarked at Castle Garden, on Manhattan (Ellis Island did not become an immigrant station until 1892). This painting by Samuel Waugh makes us rather patronizingly aware of the ship's place of departure by the inscription on the trunk on the right: 'Pat Murfy for Ameriky'. From here they went to the overcrowded poor quarters of the big cities, provoking resentment and hostility from those already established. The Irish formed a well-defined group who were not allowed, and did not desire, to forget their identity. They were also Catholic (until then sparsely represented in the States) and very poor, since they were fleeing to avoid starvation. Later in the 19th century this same pattern was to be repeated with other ethnic groups from Europe, but by that time the Irish had moved up in the social scale and acquired a measure of power. (1)

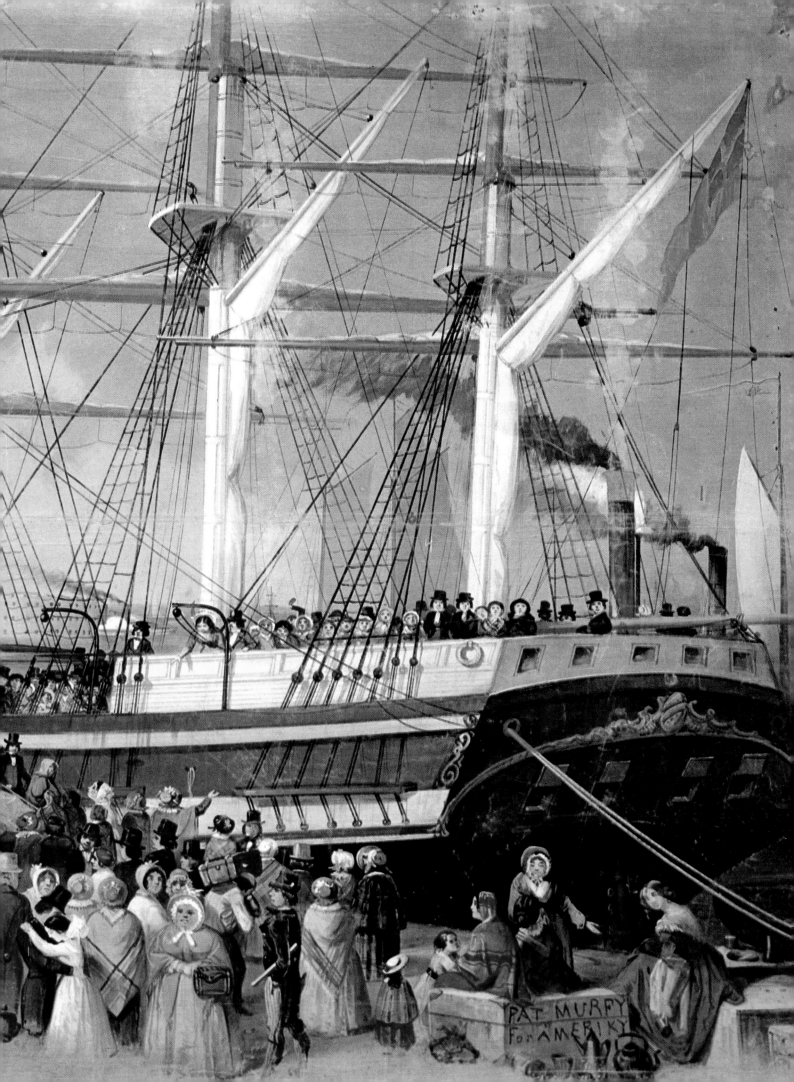

PAT MURFY
For AMERIKY

Nine men of Irish ancestry signed the Declaration of Independence. The grandfather of Charles Carroll (below) had emigrated in 1688 in quest of religious freedom. The family prospered, and Carroll signed on behalf of Maryland. (2)

It was Irish labour which built many of the greatest engineering works of the 19th century in America. Huge projects like the Brooklyn Bridge (right) depended upon them, and 'Irish power' was counted alongside water power and steam power. (3)

Two phases in the rise of Irishmen to positions of power (right). Andrew Jackson was the son of Protestant ('Scots–Irish') immigrants from Carrickfergus. His election to the presidency in 1828 marked a new era in American politics, the end of the gentleman-president and the beginning of populist rule. The accusation of 'kingship' levelled against him became a cliché. Later in the century the powers behind the 'throne' of New York were represented as the Tammany politicians Tweed and Sweeny. 'Tammany' was a political machine which could protect Irish–Americans at the price of some corruption and some manipulation of the law. (4,5)

238

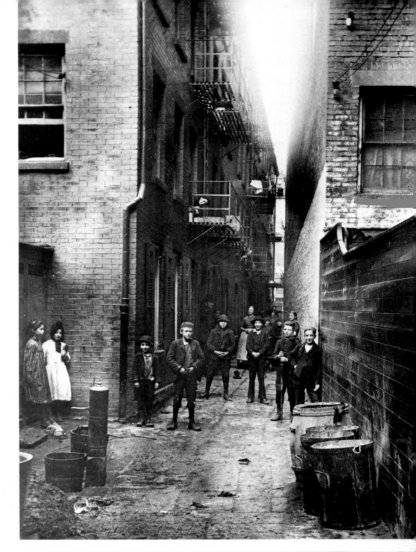

The Catholic Church held the Irish community together, giving it a focus of loyalty and a means of improving its status. By sacrifice and hard work, hospitals and schools were founded, churches built and a numerous priesthood maintained. Perhaps the grandest affirmation of Catholic prestige was St Patrick's Cathedral, New York (above). Designed by James Renwick in 1859 it stands in Fifth Avenue, and is still one of the major works of the Gothic Revival in America. (6)

New York, Boston and Philadelphia were the three East Coast cities which received the largest influx of Irish immigrants after the famine. In New York they crowded into the slums of Manhattan and Brooklyn, unable to escape the stereotype of ignorance and squalor imposed on them by the middle classes. These boys (above right) are in Mullen's Alley, 1888. (7)

Philadelphia, like most big American cities, was built with Irish muscle and skill. These steelworkers, 'flirting with death' (in the words of the photographer) are on the Lincoln Liberty Building, thirty-seven stories high. (8)

Arrival. PADDY O'ROURKE.

2d Year. PAT O'ROURKE.

5th Year. OFFICER O'ROURKE.

240

St Patrick's Day parades reinforced an Irish sense of unity and nationality. This one (left) is at New York in 1874. Harper, maidens and warriors in traditional costumes conduct a bust of O'Connell through the streets. Note too the float belonging to the St Patrick's Benevolent Society. (9)

The rise to power of Irishmen inevitably provoked unfriendly comment. Below: ten years' progress, from penniless immigrant to prosperous businessman. (10–13)

Irish causes were of intense concern to the Irish in America. In 1880, at the height of the Home Rule agitation, Parnell visited America and attempted to rally support. The magazine *Puck* (right) saw this as an unjustified disruption of American public life. A bedraggled eagle looks down sourly from its perch marked 'Monroe Doctrine'. (14)

More Irish than Ireland. Sir John Lavery, born in Belfast in 1856, painted his Irish–American wife as the national heroine Kathleen ni Houlihan (below right)—epitome of both the Ireland of legend and of the new race of Irishmen across the Atlantic. (15)

'Lace curtain Irish' became a new target for satire at the end of the century. Not poverty but social pretensions were now held up to ridicule. Among a series of 'New York Salons' featured in *Life* in 1892 was 'At Mrs Assistant Dock Commissioner O'Hara's'. It was at this period, too, that the Protestant Scots–Irish began consciously to distinguish themselves from the Catholic Irish who were lower on the social scale. (16)

At a national level Irish influence grew steadily. The first Catholic to be nominated for the presidency by a major party was Alfred E. Smith, who had risen through the Tammany system from working-class beginnings to be Governor of New York. Honest, energetic and popular, he was adopted as the Democratic candidate in 1928 (left). His contest with the Republican Herbert Hoover provoked the last major manifestation of anti-Irish and anti-Catholic bigotry. (17)

A future Pope—Cardinal Pacelli—visited New York in 1936. Kissing his ring is the redoubtable Mrs Nicholas Brady, Irish, rich, pious and powerful. (18)

Having made a fortune in Wall Street, Joseph P. Kennedy entered government service in 1934 and was made ambassador to London (below) in 1938. (20)

Irish America found its voice in such men as Eugene O'Neill and George M. Cohan, seen here in a montage photograph evoking O'Neill's *Ah Wilderness*. (19)

Grace Kelly, the film star, arrives for her wedding to Prince Rainier of Monaco on the arm of her father, who began life as a construction worker. (21)

'A Time for Greatness', Norman Rockwell's specially commissioned cover-painting for *Look*, July 1964, sums up the surge of optimism that greeted the election of John F. Kennedy, Joseph Kennedy's son. For the Catholic Irish, it marked their final acceptance by America. Kennedy, the grandson of an immigrant, was the first Catholic to hold supreme office, and his political style was recognizably both Catholic and Irish. (22)

Chapter 8

Starvation, struggle and success

WILLIAM V. SHANNON

'*Welcome to all!' In Joseph Keppler's lithograph from Puck, 1880, the oppressed nations of Europe mount the gangplank to Uncle Sam's Ark, the Irish in the lead. (1)*

AS THE IRISH IMMIGRANTS OF THE 1840S SAILED into New York harbour, they first caught sight of the meadows and forests of Staten Island, a rural vista not so different from the green-clad hills of home. But if Staten Island was and for a long time remained a sylvan retreat, the America in which the Irish soon found themselves was decidedly urban. Penniless or nearly so, the immigrants were in need of jobs, and these could most readily be found in the rapidly growing cities of the Atlantic seaboard – New York, Boston, Philadelphia and Baltimore. A predominantly rural people in the old country, the Irish were to become an urban people in the new.

The Irish entered a society that was undergoing fantastic growth. A people of barely 5 million persons in 1800, America would number approximately 76 million by the end of the 19th century, a fifteen-fold increase unprecedented in human history. The recurrent potato famines of the 1830s and 1840s in Ireland coincided with a particularly remarkable commercial and industrial expansion in the United States. In the twenty years between 1840 and 1860, as population leaped upward from 17 million to 31 million, the miles of railroad built grew from 2,800 to 30,000 and production of iron and other metals soared.

Not at first, but gradually over the generations, this transplantation from a stagnant, overcrowded rural society to a wide open, rapidly changing urban and industrial society transformed the Irish character. What Americans, whether of Irish or non-Irish ancestry, usually find startling when they first visit Ireland is the soft speech, the gentle courtesy and the leisurely style of life. These qualities seem startling because they are not the characteristics associated with Irish-Americans. In the United States, the Irish are usually thought of as aggressive, competitive and swaggering, sentimental but tough. There is nothing shy or feckless in the Irish-American image,

no hint of the leprechaun's drollery or the countryman's slow rhythm of life. It is as if the shift from a static and deeply religious society to a thriving and largely secular society liberated hidden energies and turned the Irish mind from the metaphysical to the real. The aggression that had occasionally burst forth in sporadic acts of vengeance and terrorism against hated landlords could now find a legitimate and rewarding channel.

The struggle to survive

The hundreds of thousands of Irish who crowded into the eastern cities in the post-famine years did not, of course, undergo this transformation all at once. At first, they were the bewildered denizens of the slums, struggling desperately to find their footing on alien territory. Like the Greeks, Turks and other Mediterranean people who have migrated to Western Europe in the post-World-War-II boom, those early Irish filled the interstices of the industrial and commercial system. They were the casual labourers who did the hardest and most menial tasks; they were the last hired and the first fired. When at work, they were poorly paid and often exposed to danger. Health conditions in the Irish neighbourhoods were appalling, with tuberculosis and infant mortality rates particularly high. A modern historian has calculated that the average age at death in Boston in 1850 was twenty-two.

The American cities to which the Irish came were straggling, overgrown colonial towns ill prepared

245

During the 1840s and 50s the Irish were mainly employed as labourers. It was a stereotype that took a generation to live down: this cartoon is of 1882. (2)

to cope with the social and physical effects of an industrial revolution and a population explosion. Irish labour contributed importantly to building the streets, sewers and water conduits, the bridges and reservoirs, and later the gas and electric systems that made these big towns into modern cities. Many of them contributed not only their sweat but their lives. Several of the landmark public works projects in the United States – the Erie Canal linking New York City with the inland Great Lakes, the Croton Dam and Reservoir providing New York City with its first dependable water supply, the Brooklyn Bridge tying Manhattan with Long Island, and the first transcontinental railroad – were paid for not only in money but in Irish lives lost in accidents and hazardous tasks. 'There are several sorts of power working at the fabric of this Republic,' a newspaper commented in 1847, 'waterpower, steampower, horsepower, and Irish power.'

This Irish involvement in public works had two lasting effects that persist into the present. Every city that was a terminus or major transfer point of a railroad or canal became a centre of Irish settlement – Buffalo, Cleveland, Chicago, St Paul, Omaha and San Francisco. The other result was that the Irish

came to dominate the building trades. Many Irish-American fortunes, some of them quite sizable, were made in the construction industry, while the labour unions of bricklayers, carpenters, plumbers and labourers are usually Irish-led. In recent decades, the Irish have had to share their hegemony in this field of labour with Italian immigrants, but George Meany, who heads the federation of American labour unions, started life as a plumber and many of his senior colleagues in the labour movement are Irish-Americans.

More important than their enormous contribution to the physical construction of the growing cities, however, was the Irish social contribution. The social institutions evolved by the Irish determined the human quality of life in the cities; they transformed urban and industrial wastelands into genuine human communities. First, the Irish built their churches. The mere erection of a simple brick edifice and the coming among them of a priest, usually imported from Ireland, changed a few grey city blocks into that warmer, friendlier place called a parish. To build these churches and maintain them, the early Irish immigrants had to scrimp and sacrifice, contributing their pennies each week. Since the state-supported schools in those days often observed certain Protestant customs such as the use of the King James rather than the Douay version of the Bible, battles erupted between the Catholic clergy and city officials. As a result, Catholic communities in the eastern cities gradually began the gigantic additional task of constructing their own network of Catholic schools, without public funds to assist them. From the nucleus of the church and the school, there proliferated other institutions such as orphanages, hospitals, and homes for the aged. So intense has been the identification between Irish Catholics and their Church that in big cities down to the present, they often identify themselves as coming not from a particular neighbourhood but from a particular parish.

To cope with the common hardships, the immigrants formed benevolent societies that sold sickness insurance and funeral benefits. These societies incorporated or overlapped with purely social marching-and-chowder groups that existed to hold picnics and excursions in the summer and dances in the winter.

What marked off the Irish most notably from native Americans in the 19th century was their differing attitudes towards beer and alcohol. There had always been public houses in America where liquor was sold and consumed, but in the 1830s and 1840s, when the Irish began arriving in ever greater numbers, a strong temperance movement was sweeping through the nation. The Irish saloons were obvious targets. This temperance movement

'The Greek Slave' as seen by the generally anti-Irish and anti-Catholic Thomas Nast. Having been induced to emigrate, the Irishman is kept chained to Tammany, the Democratic Party, the ballot box and drink. (3)

As the Irish rose in the social scale they attracted just as much hostility, but for different reasons. Here, in 1884, an imperious Irish cook, entertaining her policeman (also Irish), turns the mistress of the house out of her own kitchen. (4)

surged again early in the 20th century and crested in 1919 when a constitutional amendment was adopted which for fifteen years until its repeal made the manufacture, sale and consumption of liquor illegal. Although there have always been Irish teetotallers, the great majority of Irish saw nothing wrong in taking 'a drop o' the creature' and have been in the forefront of opposition to restrictive legislation.

Links with home

To outsiders, the Irish were one indistinguishable mass. But within the Irish community, the immigrants thought of themselves not as 'Irishmen' but as men from Clare or Kerry or Cork or Wicklow. Nationalism was still a novel idea in Europe in the first half of the 19th century, particularly among immigrants from isolated, rural areas. It was the reaction of native Americans to them that made the immigrants conscious of their Irishness. Realizing that they were strangers in their new country and that older Americans often regarded them with hostility or suspicion, the immigrants had to ask themselves the perennial American questions – Who am I? If I am different, in what ways am I different?

In the effort to answer these questions, the immigrants evolved numerous fraternal, patriotic and social organizations, the best-known being the Ancient Order of Hibernians. Other Americans then and for many decades afterwards saw these

organizations as expressions of 'divided loyalties' on the part of 'hyphenated Americans'. But the Irish were not 'birds of passage' planning to earn enough money to retire to the old country and live well. On the contrary, their commitment to America was intense and their patriotism of an aggressive, flag-waving, jingoistic kind. They gave America the highest letters of recommendation when, despite the hardships and frequent loneliness, they wrote to their relatives and friends urging them to emigrate to this new country.

But in learning about their new country and experiencing it, they inevitably tried to translate what they learned and felt back into the older European setting. They wanted Ireland to have its own republic and its own George Washington; they wanted Ireland to be united as the United States is around the ideals of Thomas Jefferson and Andrew Jackson. Thus, the Irish in America have always been a major source of money for nationalist independence movements in Ireland. The 'Forty-Eighters' such as Thomas D'Arcy McGee and Thomas Francis Meagher were acclaimed as heroes in New York when they arrived after the collapse of the revolution they had tried to make. In 1867, the Fenians tried to liberate Ireland by launching an armed invasion of Canada. In later periods, Charles Stewart Parnell and Eamon de Valera raised large sums among Irish-Americans for their political

'The Knave and the Fool': a cartoon of 1868, when Fenian activity was at its height. The Knave (note horns and tail) is the American Irishman tempting his simple brother back home to violence, promising the cap of liberty but delivering a noose. (5)

Whole regiments of the American army were made up of Irishmen. This recruiting poster, complete with harp and shamrock, is of 1851. During the Civil War thirty-eight Union regiments had the word 'Irish' in their names. (6)

crusades. This money-raising, gun-running tradition lingers today, although support for the IRA's activities in Northern Ireland comes from a tiny minority of post-World-War-II emigrants, mostly from the North. Ninety-nine per cent of Irish-Americans give no financial and relatively little political support to the IRA's campaign to unite Ireland by force.

In addition to their churches, schools, mutual aid societies and nationalist organizations, the Irish also organized their own volunteer fire companies and armed militia. These were important institutions in 19th-century America, which had no professional fire-fighting forces and only a very small peacetime army. Since the established volunteer fire companies and militia companies made the Irish feel unwelcome, the immigrants formed their own. There were Emmet Guards, Irish Rifles, Irish-American Guards, Hibernia Guards and many others. These militia units marched on the Fourth of July in splendid uniforms and also celebrated St Patrick's Day with far more pomp and flamboyance than it had ever been observed in Ireland. In peacetime,

these units were as much social as military. But when the American Civil War broke out in 1861, they joined the Union Army and fought with conspicuous gallantry. When President John F. Kennedy addressed the Irish Dail in June 1963, he presented the battle flag of one of these units to the Irish nation. Again, in the Spanish-American War of 1898 and World War I, these regiments and brigades enhanced the legend of 'the fighting Irish'.

Fire-fighting in those days was also as much a social event as a grim necessity. The volunteer fire companies competed to see who could get to the scene of a fire first. Since the water was then pumped by hand, they also competed to see who could get their stream of water highest – occasionally rupturing the hose in the process. Whiskey and beer were freely served to renew the energies of exhausted firemen during a major fire. Firehouses were neighbourhood gathering places where men of varying ages met to trade stories and gossip. Fire companies also marched in municipal parades, and they liked to attend popular theatres in a body to cheer their favourite actors and singers.

Tammany: the politics of self-preservation

From these distinctive immigrant neighbourhoods with their churches, schools, mutual aid societies, nationalist organizations, volunteer fire companies, militia units and saloons, there emerged a new style of politics in America, founded upon ethnic and neighbourhood loyalty. Although the Germans had also emigrated to the United States contemporaneously with the Irish and there were German politicians active in evolving this political style and 'the German vote' was a considerable factor in some cities, the Irish generally proved to be more enterprising and more adept at urban politics. In Boston, New York, Philadelphia, Baltimore, Chicago, St Louis and San Francisco, the Irish took effective political control of all or significant parts of the city.

This was issueless politics. It had little to do with national problems or party platforms, although a substantial majority of Irish-Americans were enrolled in the Democratic party. It had everything to do with gaining local power which translated into jobs and contracts for an ill-educated, impoverished but ambitious and numerous group. In almost every other way, their numbers were a curse; there were always too many mouths to feed, too many applicants for the job, too many families in the overcrowded tenement houses. But, politically, their swarming numbers were a blessing. Every man could vote, and votes meant political power.

This kind of politics was based on personal acquaintance, on family friendships, on voting for someone who was from the same village in the old country. Political sentiment was formed in conversations in firehouses, militia meetings and saloons. In New York City, this style of politics achieved its most highly organized form in Tammany Hall. The Irish took over this long-existing political organization, named for an Indian chief, in the 1840s and for the next ninety years used it as their political vehicle. Much later, the Chicago Irish developed a similar machine which continues to control the nation's second largest city down to the present.

Tammany and similar political organizations had a strict hierarchical structure. Every city block had one or more active political workers, known as 'wardheelers', who kept in touch with local sentiment. A group of blocks formed a precinct headed by a captain, and a group of precincts formed a district headed by a district leader. The district leaders elected an executive committee whose chairman was the party leader or 'boss'.

These political machines formed, in effect, a shadow government paralleling the legal, official regime. Government then had no social service agencies and no pensions or other financial aid to dispense to the unemployed and the unlucky. The labourer looking for a job, the family facing eviction by the landlord, the widow unexpectedly deprived of her husband's wages, the truant boy in trouble with the police, the worker crippled on the job, the illiterate trying to compose a letter – these and others were in need of help that was direct, immediate and compassionate. The political machine operating through its wardheelers in every block and its party clubhouses in every district provided that kind of help. It was inefficient, inadequate and haphazard but it was the only system available, and it was one the Irish immigrants worked out themselves.

The machine depended for much of its strength on its control of jobs on public works projects – streets, sewers, water lines, bridges, tunnels and public buildings – and with private utilities such as gas, electric and transit companies dependent on government franchises. The machine collected its 'taxes' through various forms of corruption. There were bribes paid in exchange for franchises, kickbacks on construction contracts, and insurance and bonding arranged through politically connected firms. Machine insiders knew where public improvements were to be made and profited by buying the land in advance, or they owned sand-and-gravel companies and were employed as sub-contractors.

The machine also depended for power on its control of police and thereby its ability to influence the enforcement of laws against gambling and prostitution and those requiring the closing of saloons at midnight and on Sunday. Insofar as the machine controlled the lesser criminal courts, it could 'fix' cases and arrange reduced and suspended sentences.

Despite recurring scandals and intermittent re-

More anti-Irish ridicule. Here 'Mr John Kelly' has joined the fire-service 'where his strength and natural influence over men give him a prominent position.' (7)

To celebrate the Centennial of 1876 the 'Irish World' published these portraits of Irish signers of the Declaration of Independence. Only one, Charles Carroll, was a Catholic. The rest were Scots-Irish from Ulster. (8)

form administrations, the machines that began to appear before the Civil War survived and flourished for many decades. To the non-Irish, these political machines were noisome, offensive, even sinister institutions, and the political bosses – James Michael Curley of Boston, Richard Croker and Charles Murphy of Tammany Hall, Frank 'I am the law' Hague of Jersey City, Tom Pendergast of Kansas City and Richard Daley of Chicago – have seemed exotic figures. But seen in terms of the community life that bred them, they were wholly natural. The people who provided the votes were satisfied with what they received in jobs, in help in time of need, in picnics and Sunday excursions, in access to those in power at City Hall and in a sense of belonging.

The old machines began to disappear in the 1930s, but not because of their inner weaknesses or the assaults of reformers; those had always existed. The development of a welfare state directed and financed from Washington met many of the human problems that the local political machines had once coped with. At the same time, the Irish and other European immigrants had become increasingly middle class in education, economic status and political outlook. As they did so and moved out of the inner cities to the suburbs, Tammany and its many counterparts began to wither and die. Politically aspiring Irish-Americans detached themselves from the old organizations and renounced the old style in favour of the new. Politics passed from the age of the bosses to the age of Kennedy.

The national scene

The Irish had been present on the American scene from almost the earliest colonial times. Although the majority of them were Calvinist Protestants from Ulster, little distinction was then made between Protestant and Catholic Irish. Nine of the fifty-seven signers of the Declaration of Independence were of Irish birth or ancestry, as were several generals in Washington's army. The only Catholic signer was Charles Carroll of Carrollton, Maryland, who was also the wealthiest and proved to be the longest-lived. One of his cousins was a delegate to the Constitutional Convention of 1787 and another was the first Catholic bishop in the United States.

Individual Irish Catholics attained eminence in the years before 1830. Matthew Carey became the country's most important publisher. Edward Kavanagh served as Governor of Maine and represented that state in Congress. Dominick Lynch, a wealthy wine merchant and music patron, was regarded as the leader of New York society. Two exiles from the rising of 1798 – Dr James McNeven, a Catholic, and Thomas Addis Emmet, an attorney and a Protestant – achieved professional success in New York.

But the Irish as a group were not significant in those early years. The first census, in 1790, listed only 44,000 persons of Irish birth; in addition, there were perhaps another 150,000 of Irish ancestry out of a total population of 3 million. In that same year, the first Catholic bishop estimated that there were only 35,000 Catholics in the country. There was almost no emigration during the Napoleonic wars. But in the rural distress of the 1830s, about 650,000 left Ireland for Canada and the United States, and that number rose sharply in the years of 'the great hunger' and after.

It was during these middle decades of the 19th century that the predominantly Catholic Irish made their profound impact on the growing cities of America and began to shape them in their own image. Professor Thomas N. Brown of the University of Massachusetts has well described how, while this process was under way, the larger American society regarded these newcomers:

A new Irish stereotype arose. Accepting the image of the good-natured, whisky-loving, thriftless paddy from the novels of Lever and the pages of *Punch*, Americans satisfied themselves that the Irish, however incapable of serious responsibilities, were honest and loyal in discharging menial ones. By 1870 the Wild Irishman had become the Comic Irishman. In the two following decades the Comic Irishman was enormously popular in the American theater, where he was laughed at by native and immigrant alike. And magazines like *Harper's*, although unfriendly to more pretentious Irishmen, celebrated the ignorant good humor of Irish servants and the sentimental valor of Irish soldiers.

In 1890, Edward Harrigan, writer, producer and actor, presented his last great success in this vein of popular theatre. It was *Reilly and the Four Hundred*. This show about a newly rich, social-climbing Irish family had a hit song, 'Maggie Murphy's Home':

*There's an organ in the parlor, to give the house a tone
And you're welcome every evening at Maggie Murphy's
home.*

As well as any date, this marks the rapid decline of the Comic Irishman, wearing rags, keeping a pig in the parlour and speaking with a pronounced brogue, and the emergence of the increasingly numerous and newly prosperous middle class, the 'lace curtain Irish'. These were merchants, lawyers, doctors, school teachers and higher-ranking civil servants. Paradoxically, it was also at this time that the distinction between Protestant and Catholic Irish became well defined. Because of the influx of what was then called the 'new immigration' from Italy, Eastern Europe and Russia, the older Anglo-Saxon Protestant elements in America retreated into a veritable orgy of ancestor worship. Organizations such as Sons of the American Revolution, Daughters of the American Revolution, the Order of the Cincinnati, and the Colonial Dames were either freshly organized or gained greatly in significance. As part of this drawing apart, the Protestant Irish began to characterize themselves as Scots-Irish in order to distinguish themselves from the masses of famine-stricken Catholic Irish who had emigrated later. This distinction has generated much confusion in historical discourse with regard to the meaning of the term 'Irish', but it has nevertheless hardened and become first usage. Several American Presidents, including Andrew Jackson, James Knox Polk and Woodrow Wilson, were Scots-Irish. Normally in the United States today, the only people who identify themselves as 'Irish' are Catholic Irish and, in this sense, the first Irish, as well as the first Catholic, President was John F. Kennedy.

The Irish began to make their presence in American life notably felt in many fields of activity in the 1890s and even more so in the first decade of the 20th century. In the world of sport, 'the Great John L.' Sullivan won the heavyweight championship and established boxing as a respectable and highly popular sport. In 1896, when the Olympic Games were revived, the first American gold medal was won by Irish-born James Connolly. In subsequent Olympics, Irish-Americans were to win many times, particularly in track events. The Irish were outstanding in baseball in these decades when that sport was becoming established as the national game. Michael Kelly's base-running feats were immortalized in the song, 'Slide, Kelly, Slide'. John Joseph 'The Little Napoleon' McGraw managed

the New York Giants for thirty years and led them to ten championships. Charles A. Comiskey, the son of an Irish immigrant, was a long-time player, helped organize the American League and owned the Chicago White Sox.

In business, Michael Cudahy developed one of the nation's major meat-packing firms and shared in the evolution of refrigeration, long-distance transportation and other methods that revolutionized American eating habits. In finance, Thomas Fortune Ryan and Nicholas Brady amassed immense fortunes. James Brady, a notably successful steel salesman, bedecked himself with diamond studs and diamond cufflinks, thus entering popular folklore as 'Diamond Jim' Brady.

Irish-Americans were dominant in the nascent American labour movement. Peter J. McGuire, long-time secretary-treasurer of the Brotherhood of Carpenters, was successful in persuading Congress to establish the first Monday in September as Labor Day.

In the arts in the 1890s, two great figures emerged, both Dublin-born: the composer Victor Herbert and the sculptor Augustus Saint-Gaudens. Herbert, like the singer John McCormack, bridged the worlds of serious and popular culture. He was strongly conscious of his Irish heritage, composing pieces such as 'Irish Rhapsody' and serving as president of various organizations including the Friends of Irish Freedom and the Friendly Sons of St Patrick.

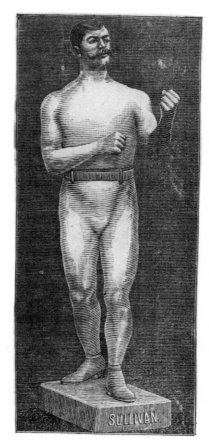

John L. Sullivan became world heavyweight boxing champion in 1883. These statuettes, 25 inches high, were offered at 5 dollars each. Sullivan was only one of many Irishmen to make their mark in the world of American sport. (9)

The Irish in America 251

As the Irish came into prominence in many different fields and exercised an ever larger measure of political power in the major cities, it became impossible any longer to patronize them as wild or comic or feckless. They were becoming too powerful for that. Because many of them entered journalism, the Irish were able, subtly but importantly, to alter their own image in the national mind. One of them was Mark Sullivan, a famous 'muckraking' investigative reporter in the early 1900s, later the author of the six-volume popular history of the United States from 1900 to 1925, *Our Times*, and still later the dean of American political commentators.

Another great journalist was Finley Peter Dunne who as a young Chicago newspaperman introduced his comic alter ego, 'Mr Dooley', in a sketch in 1893 and, with interruptions, kept him alive for more than twenty years. Martin Dooley, described as 'a bachelor, a saloon-keeper, and a Roscommon Irishman', became a famous national character; and President Theodore Roosevelt and many other leaders of the period became devoted readers. The Dooley sketches featured a lengthy monologue usually set off and sometimes interrupted by comments or questions from a slow-witted customer, Hennessy.

Mr Dooley skilfully satirized figures in the Irish community such as the corrupt alderman or the windy nationalist orator. Referring to the many parties and picnics held to raise money for the cause of Irish freedom, he observed: 'Be hivins, if Ireland could be freed be a picnic, it'd not only be free today, but an impire, begorra.'

He was equally adept at penetrating national hypocrisy and self-delusion, such as the wave of imperialist sentiment that swept the country in 1898 and led to the annexation of the Philippine Islands. He gibed at the imperialist slogan, re-stating it as: 'Hands acrost th' sea an' into somewan's pocket.' America's message to the Filipinos, he said, was: 'We can't give ye anny votes because we haven't more thin enough to go around now, but we'll treat ye th' way a father shud treat his childher if we have to break ivry bone in ye'er bodies. So come to our arms.'

Mr Dooley's popularity symbolized the sunny relationship that prevailed between the Irish community and the rest of the American nation in those years from 1890 to 1914. Except for a severe economic depression from 1893 to 1896, the United States was enjoying a sharply rising curve of prosperity. Despite strikes, lockouts and sweatshops, the real income of workers was rising, and the general public mood was one of optimism and confidence. Americans of every background sang and whistled the tunes of the great Irish-American song-writer and actor, George M. Cohan, who wrote, 'Mary', 'It's A Grand Old Flag', 'Give My Regards to Broadway', 'I'm a Yankee Doodle-Dandy' and many others.

World War I and after

The prolonged struggle that preceded America's entry into World War I in 1917 opened a slight rift in this solidarity. The Irish were unenthusiastic about entering the war on the side of the British, their hereditary enemy. Once the decision was made, however, the Irish volunteered for military service in large numbers. Although the modern army no longer permitted men to join up in ethnic units, some regiments nevertheless were preponderantly Irish. Joseph Clarke's poem about the martial qualities of the Irish, 'The Fighting Race', was once again popular. Unlike the German-Americans, who had also opposed the decision to enter the war, the Irish were not fighting against their original homeland. Cohan wrote 'Over There', the war's most popular song, and the Irish rallied along with other Americans 'to make the world safe for democracy'.

With the war's end came disillusionment. Ireland's bid for independence in the winter of 1918–19 turned into two years of warfare with the British. It soon became clear to the American-Irish that Ireland was not one of the small nations that was going to benefit from democracy's triumph on the battlefield. President Wilson was notably unsympathetic to the cause of Irish independence and refused to meet with de Valera and the other leaders of Ireland or to make even small gestures to conciliate Irish-American opinion. As a result, Irish opinion turned vehemently hostile to the Versailles Peace Treaty and became a significant element in the coalition that defeated America's proposed entry into the League of Nations.

A deeper disillusionment was to follow. In the early 1920s, the Ku Klux Klan was revived in the South. Originally established after the Civil War to intimidate the newly freed Negroes, this organization consisted of roving bands of men who wore white hooded costumes, burned fiery crosses and terrorized those who disagreed with their doctrine of white supremacy. For decades, it had been semidefunct, but when new leadership revitalized it, the KKK began to spread to the North and to preach an anti-Catholic as well as an anti-Negro message.

Meanwhile, Irish political hopes had come to focus upon Alfred E. Smith, the Governor of New York. A poorly educated youth from a working-class family, Smith had entered politics for the same reason as many other poor boys; it was a career that promised a future. After performing routine errands as a wardheeler and holding minor office, Smith was elected to the State Assembly in Albany by the Tammany machine. But after a few terms, he showed that he was considerably more than the usual Tammany stalwart. By reading every proposed bill and diligently attending committee sessions, he educated himself on the intricacies of state government and on many complex social problems. Since he was scrupulously honest, his integrity as well as his native intelligence commended him to many liberals and reformers who were not usually enamoured of Tammany politicians. He became a leader in the legislature, was elected Governor in 1918, was narrowly defeated in the Republican landslide of 1920, but triumphantly returned to office in 1922.

In 1924, the Democrats held their national convention in Madison Square Garden in New York. Smith was a candidate for the presidential nomination. His chief opponent was William Gibbs McAdoo, who had been Secretary of the Treasury in the Wilson administration. The principal issue before the convention was whether the party would condemn the Ku Klux Klan for its incitement of violence and bigotry. Since McAdoo had some KKK support, he was in favour of evading the issue, while the Catholic and liberal forces backing Smith strongly supported the condemnatory resolution. After a bitter debate, the resolution failed by a few votes. The convention then settled into an embittered, two-week stalemate with neither Smith nor McAdoo able to muster the two-thirds majority that was then required for nomination and with neither willing to yield to the other. Ultimately, John W. Davis, a former ambassador to Great Britain but little known to the public, received the nomination on the hundred-and-third ballot and suffered a severe defeat in the general election.

Smith, however, was re-elected Governor that fall and again two years later. By 1928, a consensus had developed that he was the party's ablest leader and that he should receive the nomination, which he did on the first ballot. But with the country prosperous and at peace, Smith had no issue with a cutting edge. Herbert Hoover, the Republican candidate, was famous as the man who had fed the starving Belgians during World War I and who as Secretary of Commerce for the previous eight years had helped engender the nation's economic boom. He was a formidable opponent.

Unfortunately, the Smith–Hoover contest became an occasion for a dismal display of resurgent bigotry. Smith was the first Catholic to be nominated for national office by either of the two major parties. The vicious fears and fantasies that had envenomed the Ku Klux Klan debate of 1924 once again crackled to the surface. Hoary anti-Catholic propaganda themes dating back to the Reformation once more entered general circulation. Some Pro-

testant ministers solemnly warned that if Smith were elected, the Pope would come to the White House and rule America.

Smith made a respectable showing at the polls, but he and many of his fellow Irish Catholics experienced his electoral rejection as a personal and cultural repudiation of themselves. An Irish Catholic, they felt, was somehow 'not good enough' to be President of the United States. In placing Smith's name in nomination, Franklin D. Roosevelt had dubbed him 'the Happy Warrior', but Smith's career ended in a most unhappy anti-climax and the consequent bitterness and resentment lingered for many years in the Irish community.

The road to the presidency
The Irish might be said, however, to have been fortunate in Smith's defeat, for within six months of Hoover's taking the oath of office, the stock market crashed and the Great Depression of the 1930s began. If Smith had been in office, Catholicism might have been made the scapegoat for this débâcle. As it was, the Irish and other Catholics bore no blame for the breakdown of the old order in business and politics, an order largely led and controlled by Protestant Anglo-Saxon elements, for whom the unfortunate Hoover became the symbol. When the opposition Democrats swept the election of 1932 under Franklin Roosevelt's leadership and began what proved to be a twenty-year reign, the Irish were part of the winning coalition and for the first time were able to move up from the municipal to the national level of political power. Individual Irishmen in the past had held high office – such as Joseph McKenna, who was President McKinley's Attorney-General, and Joseph Tumulty, who was President Wilson's executive secretary – but these had been isolated exceptions. In the twenty years of the Roosevelt and Truman administrations, the Irish attained positions in the cabinet, on the Supreme Court and in major embassies abroad. Politically, they had arrived.

James A. Farley, a big, genial, professional politician from New York, was Roosevelt's national party chairman and became Postmaster-General. Thomas G. Corcoran, a brilliant half-Irish, half-Yankee lawyer from Rhode Island, became the star of Roosevelt's entourage of intellectuals, known as 'the brains trust'. Frank Murphy of Michigan served as Governor-General of the Philippines and as Attorney-General; in 1939 he was named to the Supreme Court. James V. Forrestal, a Wall Street banker who was Roosevelt's last Secretary of the Navy, became first head of the unified Defense Department in the Truman administration and was a major policy-maker in the early years of the Cold War.

In the Congress, meanwhile, from the 1930s onward Irish figures also played major roles. Senator David I. Walsh of Massachusetts became chairman of the Senate Naval Affairs Committee and was instrumental in building up the nation's naval strength prior to World War II. Representative John W. McCormack of Massachusetts was the long-time majority floor leader and later Speaker of the House of Representatives. Subsequently, Representative Thomas P. O'Neill of Massachusetts was elected to these same offices, while Senator Mike Mansfield of Montana was Senate Majority Leader from 1961 to 1977. Senator Brien McMahon of Connecticut, his career tragically cut short by death in 1952, wrote the basic law establishing civilian control of nuclear energy.

One of the most spectacular careers of the Roosevelt era was that of Joseph P. Kennedy. The son-in-law of John F. 'Honey Fitz' Fitzgerald, an early Irish Catholic mayor of Boston, Kennedy left New England to become a notably successful Wall Street speculator. Entering government in 1934, he served as the first chairman of the Securities and Exchange Commission, a regulatory body set up to purge the financial community of various iniquitous practices, some of which he himself had used to grow rich. He next headed the Maritime Commission, which oversaw the nation's chronically sick merchant marine and then was rewarded with the ambassadorship to the Court of St James. He was the first Irish Catholic to hold this office. His diplomatic career ended on a sour note, in 1940, since he resigned during the London Blitz, making no secret of his belief that the British, notwithstanding their gallantry, were doomed to defeat unless the Americans rescued them, a course of action he did not favour. Policy disputes aside, however, the symbolism of Kennedy's appointment made him a figure of lasting significance to the American-Irish, a people sensitive to their status in British eyes.

It was historically fitting, therefore, that Ambassador Kennedy's son should be the man to break the barrier against a Catholic serving in the White House. Unlike Alfred E. Smith, who wore a brown derby, smoked big cigars, talked in a marked East Side of New York accent and belonged to the nation's most notorious political machine, John F. Kennedy entered the national political scene trailing no cultural clichés and bearing no stigmata from the Irish community's painful past. Slim, handsome, wealthy, a war hero, he had no discernible idiosyncrasy except his Harvard-and-Boston accent. He was an extraordinarily adept political performer, having inherited an instinct for the jugular from his tough, competitive forbears and having acquired a canny insight into the uses of television and the national press – a most important attribute in a period when the mass media have become a powerful political influence.

Kennedy defeated Richard Nixon for the presidency in 1960 by less than two-tenths of one per cent of the popular vote. The narrowness of his plurality reinforced Kennedy's tendency to be cautious and to husband his popularity as if it were a wasting asset. But gradually he grew in confidence and in his hold on the public imagination. The showdown with the Soviet Union over the emplacement of Soviet missiles in Cuba in October 1962 consolidated his reputation as a cool and skilful practitioner of high-stakes diplomacy. It also impelled him to move away from the Cold War posture of his earlier years towards more energetic peacemaking efforts with the Russians. In 1963 he negotiated a limited nuclear test-ban treaty and the first major sale of grain to the Soviet Union. On the domestic front, the civil rights movement reached a crisis in June 1963. Kennedy responded by proposing a far-reaching civil rights bill which was moving towards enactment into law at the time of his death.

Kennedy's assassination in Dallas on 22 November 1963 was a traumatic event not only for the American-Irish but for the whole American national community. It had a brief and equally tragic sequel. Robert F. Kennedy resigned the Attorney-Generalship, took up his older brother's fallen standard, was elected to the US Senate in 1964 and four years later sought the presidency. He, too, was cut down by an assassin's bullets, in June 1968. A third brother, Edward, is also a member of the US Senate – the Kennedys are the only family in American history to have three brothers serve in the Senate – but whether he will ever lead a Kennedy restoration in the White House is problematical.

The memory of John Kennedy, of his wit, his physical beauty, his taste in brilliant companions in public service, his soaring rhetoric and his valour in war lingers in the American imagination. The first Irishman to reach the apex of American and world power, he too soon was hurried into the pantheon of fallen heroes. He became a legend before he could completely fulfil his promise as a man. Ireland's history is so much a tale of sorrows and of young leaders foredoomed to defeat and death. It is perhaps inescapably Irish that even in America, this confident and thrusting society where Irish immigrants and their descendants have enjoyed so much material success and warming recognition, here, too, their history strikes a tragic note. To the goodly company of Sarsfield, Emmet, Parnell, Pearse, Barry and Collins, there are added the names of John and Robert Kennedy and the accomplishments of reality are again misted over by the romance of what might have been.

9

MODERN IRELAND

The birth and growth of the new state

KEVIN B. NOWLAN

'Religion's never mentioned here', of course.
'You know them by their eyes' and hold your tongue.
'One side's as bad as the other', never worse.
Christ, it's near time that some small leak was sprung
in the great dykes that always barricade
the dutchmen from the jacobites among us.

. . .

Yet I live here, I live here too, I sing,
expertly civil-tongued with civil neighbours
on the high wires of first wireless reports,
sucking the fake taste, the stony flavours
of those sanctioned, old, elaborate retorts:
'Oh it's disgraceful, surely, I agree.'
'Where's it going to end?' 'It's getting worse'.
'They're murderers', 'Internment, understandably . . .'
The 'voice of sanity' is getting hoarse.

From *Whatever You Say, Say Nothing* by Seamus Heaney

A free Ireland – dreamed of for centuries, almost achieved by Parnell, rashly proclaimed at the Easter Rising – became a reality in January 1922. The Irish Free State, as it was called, came into being as a dominion of the British Commonwealth. Although this meant that it was virtually self-governing there were two features that made it unacceptable to the republican wing of Sinn Fein – an oath of allegiance was required to the Crown, and Northern Ireland was given the right to secede from the rest of the country (which it immediately did). The first led to a bitter civil war which lasted until 1923, when the republican leader de Valera agreed to a cease fire. The second – the continued separation of Ulster – was not so easily solved, and is today by far the most serious problem facing Ireland.

This photograph was taken not in 1916 but at a subsequent commemoration of the Easter Rising. Beside the symbolic figure of Hibernia with her traditional harp, the republican flag flies proudly over the rebuilt Post Office. (1)

Three years of war preceded the treaty of 1922. The election of November 1918 (above) returned a majority of Sinn Feiners who refused to sit at Westminster and constituted themselves a republican government, promptly suppressed by Britain. The result was a struggle between the IRA and the British Army – the hated 'Auxilaries', seen (below) searching a postman and escorting the coffin of Terence MacSweeney, the republican Mayor of Cork who had died on hunger-strike. (2–4)

The North, which was strongly Protestant and had no republican ambitions, viewed the prospect of domination by the South with alarm and fear. From the very moment when Home Rule had become a possibility Northern opposition had not wavered. Partition, whatever its drawbacks, seemed therefore the only way out. In June 1921, the Northern Ireland Parliament was inaugurated by George V (above: painting by William Conor). But the six counties contained a substantial Catholic and nationalist minority who never accepted partition as permanent. Secretarian violence flared up immediately, an intimation of troubles to come. Below: York Street, Belfast; Catholic workers attacked by Protestant. (5,6)

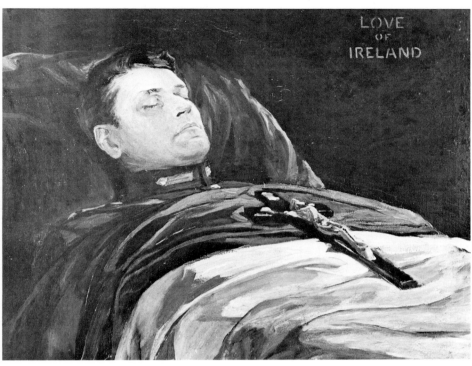

Michael Collins had played a leading role in the war against the British, but became convinced that the settlement offering dominion status should be accepted. He accompanied Arthur Griffith to London to negotiate with Lloyd George. After the ratification of the treaty in 1922 he was elected Chairman of the Provisional Government and Commander of the Army. Six months later he was killed in an ambush by republicans. Brave, dashing and attractive, he was perhaps the best loved of the Irish patriots. The portrait is by Sir John Lavery. (7)

Eamon de Valera repudiated the treaty, and Sinn Fein split into two. In the elections of 1922 (below left) he argued fervently for a full republic but failed to convince more than a minority of his countrymen. After the civil war, however, he retreated from his extreme position, re-entered the Dail with a new party, Fianna Fail, and in 1932 became prime minister, holding that office, with breaks, until 1959. In 1933 he abolished the oath of allegiance; in 1937 replaced the Irish Free State with the 'independent sovereign state' of Eire; and in 1949 formally declared it a republic. Below right: de Valera with Douglas Hyde, the first President of Eire, in 1938. It was de Valera who guided his country through the difficult times of World War II, keeping to a policy of strict neutrality. In 1959 he succeeded to the presidency himself and died, aged 92, in 1975. (8,9)

259

Irish art of the period just after independence was still closely involved with history. Sean Keating belongs to the world of Synge and O'Casey, portraying Irishmen, especially from the more remote areas, as heroic and romantic patriots. Above: *Men of the South*, guerilla fighters of 1916–20. A new generation, however, is freeing itself from such preoccupations and giving Ireland a place in the mainstream of Western culture. But as in the 19th century, literature has succeeded in doing this more confidently than painting or sculpture. (10)

Lady Longford, Hilton Edwards and Micheál Mac Liammóir inherited the mantle of Lady Gregory and Yeats, and at the Gate Theatre generated something of the excitement of the old Abbey. The painting is by Muriel Brandt. (11)

Seamus Heaney (right), born in 1939, is among the most stimulating of the younger poets and literary critics. Portrait by Edward McGuire. (12)

260

Sculpture and architecture show an awareness of trends all over the world. Below: untitled sculpture in steel by Brian King at Goff's, near Dublin. Right: St. Aengus Church, at Burt, Co. Donegal, designed in 1967 by Liam McCormick and Partners. The stone wall alludes to the past, the bold upward thrusting roof to the future. (13,14)

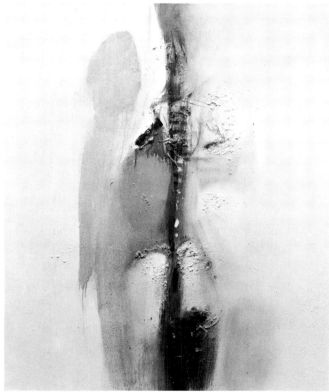

Woman, by Louis le Brocquy. Painted in 1959, it takes representational art to the verge of, but not quite into, abstraction. (15)

Behan and Beckett both, in contrasting ways, continue the Irish tradition of laughter at the wake – tragedy inextricably mixed with comedy. Behan was photographed during the American run of *The Hostage*. Right: Beckett's *Endgame* – mankind consigned to the dustbin, still swapping memories and funny stories. (16,17)

Today's Ireland is still in many ways bound to its past, perhaps because progress has so often been seen in terms of a return, not an outward voyage. Quick solutions and clean breaks are distrusted, but this very slowness to change brings its own advantages. Ireland has held on to the human scale and to the links between men and the land in a way that other nations are beginning to envy. In a town like Killorglin, Co. Kerry (above left), the old pattern of life persists, and Puck Fair (see p. 178) can still be celebrated there without a sense of self-conscious revivalism. Modern housing (above: 'Sylvan Homes', Kilkenny) supplements and sometimes replaces the crumbling Georgian terraces (right). Above all, the Catholic Church has not only retained an unusual degree of influence but has used it with unusual conservatism. A shop-window at Roscommon (left) and a pilgrim at the summit of Croagh Patrick, Co. Mayo (below), may perhaps stand for religion at its most mundane and its most spiritual. (18–22)

Turf still burns in Ireland, either in the traditional way (above, in rural Galway) or by more modern methods in one of eleven new power-stations. This one (below) is at Rhode, Co. Offaly. By 1973 a quarter of Ireland's electricity was being supplied by these stations. The turf is excavated mechanically on a large scale and processed in drying plants. It is highly inflammable, some varieties firing at a temperature of 200°C, but is much bulkier than coal and contains more non-combustible matter that is deposited as ash. (23,24)

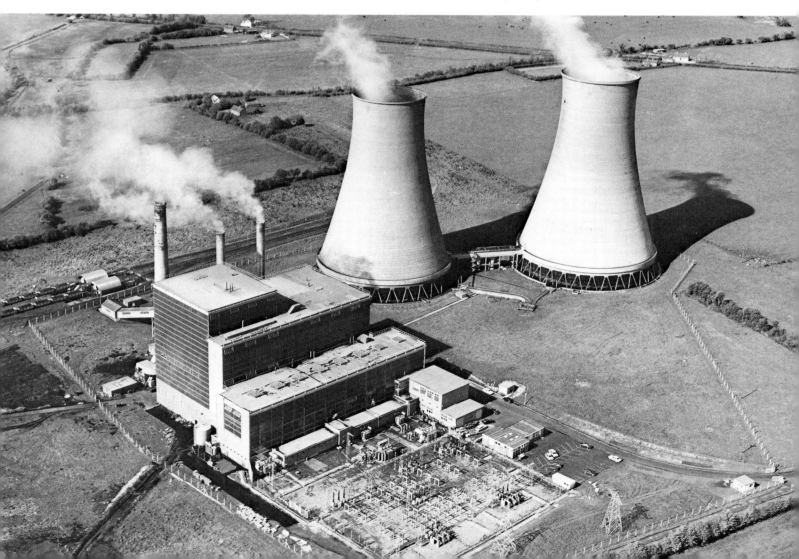

The tragedy of Ulster began with demands by Catholics for equal treatment in areas such as housing and employment. (25)

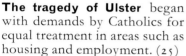

The Unionists include two militant extremes – patriotism, like the lady covered in Union Jacks, and Protestantism, represented by the Rev. Ian Paisley. (26,27)
The Republicans: Their involvement in physical force has freed them from moral scruples. Far left: IRA men at the funeral of a hunger-striker in London, 1974. The predictable reaction has been an equally fanatical Protestant force, the Ulster Volunteers. Here hooded leaders talk to the press, 1975. (28,29)
The majority of the inhabitants of Northern Ireland belong to neither extreme, deplore the killings and long for peace. The latest initiative has come from women. Below: Peace March in the Shankill area of Belfast, and the two leaders, Betty Williams and Mairead Corrigan, August 1976.(30,31)

Chapter 9

The birth and growth of the new state

KEVIN B. NOWLAN

The new Ireland, trampling on the British flag against a background of the Dublin Post Office in flames: an image of the IRA which was an inspiration in the 20s, a cliché in the 30s (when this poster was printed) and an increasingly hollow gesture thereafter. (1)

THE YEAR 1917, IN IRELAND, was marked by a swing in popular sympathy towards the radicals. Sinn Fein candidates, pledged to abstain from attending Parliament at Westminster, defeated the moderate Redmondites in the parliamentary by-elections. In particular, the return of Eamon de Valera for the constituency of East Clare was an indication of the change taking place in Ireland. Born in 1882 in New York, of a Spanish-Cuban father and an Irish mother, de Valera was brought up in Ireland and became closely associated with the Gaelic cultural movement and with the Irish Volunteers. He narrowly escaped execution in 1916 for his part in the Rising. His American birth and the fear of the adverse effect of his execution on a still neutral United States may have induced the British to spare his life. Released from prison in June 1917, he quickly became the leading figure in the republican ranks, especially in terms of political policy and tactics. His election as president of the Sinn Fein movement and also of the Irish Volunteers not only strengthened his personal position but helped to bring closer together the civil and military wings of the advanced nationalist movement. Sinn Fein and the Volunteers, however, remained separate bodies. There was room for misunderstandings between Sinn Fein, the Volunteers and the Irish Republican Brotherhood, especially as some Volunteer officers questioned the value of the IRB and saw it as a secret and divisive factor. Though the internal differences did not reach very serious proportions, they were not resolved before the Anglo-Irish settlement of 1921–22 and they may well have contributed to the personal tensions within the nationalist movement during the long-drawn-out controversy about that settlement.

The reorganization of Sinn Fein and the Volunteers came at an opportune time. For reasons of obvious political prudence, the British government had not extended compulsory military service to Ireland. Faced, however, with the pressing demand for reinforcements to meet the new German offensive in March 1918 and sensitive to criticism in Britain, the government decided in April to seek powers from Parliament to conscript young Irishmen. This decision provoked an immediate outcry throughout nationalist Ireland. The conscription threat was denounced in very strong terms by the Catholic hierarchy and in protest against such a move the members of the Irish Parliamentary party withdrew from Parliament and returned to Dublin to make common cause with Sinn Fein in the anti-conscription campaign. This situation and the arrest of many prominent republicans, who were alleged to be engaged in a 'German Plot' (May 1918), kept Ireland in a state of political tension. The gainers, in political terms, were the leaders of Sinn Fein, and not the Irish Parliamentary party, which had virtually to admit the defeat of its methods by having to withdraw from Parliament. The Armistice of November 1918 brought the conscription crisis to an end, but the general election of that year was a measure of the changes which had taken place in Ireland since 1916. The once great Irish Parliamentary party was reduced to a mere six seats, while Sinn Fein candidates won seventy-three seats. It was, however, a clear reminder of the unbroken strength of the Unionist party that it was able to consolidate its position in north-east Ulster by winning twenty-six seats. Though a substantial number of voters (nearly one-third of the electoral roll) did not vote and though some voters may have hesitated to vote against Sinn Fein, the scale and significance of the republican victory can hardly be exaggerated.

Ireland's Solemn League and Covenant. A National Pledge

Denying the right of the British Government to enforce compulsory service in this country, we pledge ourselves solemnly to one another to resist Conscription by the most effective means at our disposal.

The above was signed by me at _Kilthnagh Co. Mayo_ on the day of _April 21st_ 1918. Name _____ Address _____

MAYNOOTH COLLEGE. CO. KILDARE
Where the Prelates of Ireland received the Deputation from the Mansion House

HIS EMINENCE CARDINAL LOGUE Archbishop of Armagh and Primate of all Ireland

HIS GRACE THE MOST REV^d J. WALSH^{DD} Archbishop of Dublin and Primate of Ireland

EAMON DE VALERA M.P. representing SINN FEIN

JOHN DILLON, M.P. representing Irish Parliamentary Party

ARTHUR GRIFFITH representing SINN FEIN

JOSEPH DEVLIN, M.P. representing Irish Parliamentary Party

WILLIAM O'BRIEN (Dublin) President Irish Trade Union Congress

WILLIAM O'BRIEN M.P. representing 'All for Ireland League'

M. EGAN, J.P.T.C Cork

THE RIGHT HON LAURENCE O'NEILL THE LORD MAYOR who presided at the Mansion House Conference Ireland's Envoy to Washington

MANSION HOUSE. DUBLIN Where the Conference assembled.

also present T. JOHNSON. BELFAST.

T.M. HEALY M.P representing 'All for Ireland League'

The years after 1916 saw a steady hardening of public opinion against British rule. Revulsion against the executions after the Easter Rising marked one stage. De Valera's election as president of Sinn Fein in 1917 was another. The attempt to impose conscription on Ireland in March 1918 provoked a third. Leaders of almost every party and of the Catholic Church united to oppose it. This proclamation is of interest not only for what it says but also for its way of saying it, with Old Irish lettering and Celtic ornament. (2)

Dominion or Republic?

The way was now open for bringing the Sinn Fein programme a stage further. All the members elected for Irish constituencies were summoned to meet in Dublin, on 21 January 1919, to constitute the Dail or national assembly of the Irish Republic. Those Sinn Fein members who were not imprisoned attended. The Unionists ignored the new assembly, which had no standing in British law and was soon to be proscribed as illegal. Republican resistance had now secured at least the semblance of constitutional forms of government. Significantly, Irish republicans, as much as the more moderate nationalists, were influenced by the customs and traditions of the British constitution, as British law and administrative practice had become a part of the Irish political inheritance. The republicans, however, were no more successful than the old parliamentarians in devising a formula which would reconcile their claims to independence for the whole

island with the aspirations of the Ulster Unionists to remain firmly within the structure of the United Kingdom. The republican concept of a united and possibly Gaelic Ireland was not in accord with the political realities and, to a surprising degree, republicans discounted the seriousness and strength of the Ulster Protestant position.

The Dail was primarily an instrument of republican defiance since it lacked, initially, the normal machinery of administration. It sought, without success, to secure a hearing for the Irish case at the Paris Peace Conference, but it did make some progress in other ways. 'Republican Courts' were set up to replace the official ones and when de Valera escaped from prison (3 February 1919), he was elected President of the Dail government and set out on a very successful fund-raising mission in the United States. From 1920 onwards, the Dail government was able to control local administration through the newly elected councils.

Clashes between units of the Irish Volunteers and the British forces, especially the armed Royal Irish Constabulary, became sharper and more frequent in 1920. It was during this period that the influence of Michael Collins was consolidated within the revolutionary movement. A young man of charm and determination, he became Dail Minister for Finance, a key figure in the Volunteers and subsequently President of the Supreme Council of the IRB. The assassination, in the course of 1920, of the republican Lord Mayor of Cork, the death on hunger strike of his successor, Terence MacSweeney, and the recruitment by the British of the ill-disciplined 'Black and Tans' were further stages in the deterioration of Anglo-Irish relations. The response to the new measures of the British was an intensification of guerrilla fighting and reprisals by the Volunteers, who were now being described increasingly as the Irish Republican Army (IRA).

It is difficult to assess the attitude of the local populations to the prolonged and destructive hostilities, but sustained guerrilla activities could hardly have been possible without a fair measure of popular sympathy or at least a muted goodwill. The lack of discipline among the 'Black and Tans', the shootings and house burnings and raids by Crown forces, all helped to alienate many in the traditionally nationalist parts of the island from the British authorities. The 'Man on the Run', the republican 'flying columns', the successful ambushes, captured the popular imagination. The incidents were to be remembered in ballads and in literary form, too, in the writings of a Frank O'Connor or the memoirs of an Ernie O'Malley. The Volunteer in trench coat and leggings was to become part of the symbolism of a militant Irish nationalism.

By the summer of 1920, the Royal Irish Constabulary had to abandon many of the smaller outposts and the British hold on local administration was clearly weakening. At the same time, however, the Irish Republican Army had its problems. Its resources were limited and the active service force was hardly more than three thousand men. Funds, too, were in short supply and the Irish population was growing weary of a conflict which could result in no clear-cut victory over the British. For his part, Lloyd George, as Prime Minister, had to take into account the sharp criticisms of British policy which were being voiced in both Britain and America. More drastic measures to bring the Irish troubles to a speedy end would only have provoked still greater criticism in liberal circles at home and abroad. By the summer of 1921 a settlement seemed opportune to realists on both sides, and there were such. But on what terms could a settlement be reached?

In yet another attempt to meet the Irish problem, Lloyd George's ministry put the Government of Ireland Bill through Parliament in 1920. This measure made provision for the creation of two Irish parliaments, one for Northern and one for Southern Ireland. It was intended that each would enjoy a limited measure of legislative autonomy while remaining an integral part of the United Kingdom. Provision was also made for a Council of Ireland in the fond hope that it would be a prelude to a single Irish parliament. The 1920 Act, the last of the 'Home Rule' measures, was also the first to give effective form to the partition of Ireland. The territorial division made in Ireland by the 1920 legislation was not to be altered by any of the subsequent developments. But at the time, this apparently timid attempt to resolve the political difficulties of Ireland was ignored by the republicans and reluctantly accepted by the Ulster Unionists who, however, came to recognize that, within the six counties which comprised Northern Ireland, they would be able to exercise an effective political control, despite the presence within the territory of a substantial nationalist and Catholic minority. Already, in 1920–21, sectarian and political violence of a particularly bitter kind, in Northern Ireland, was a grim intimation of the troubles which were to beset the region.

In the South, the republicans' demands continued to be presented in terms of independence for all Ireland and when elections were held, in May 1921, under the provisions of the Government of Ireland Act, they were simply treated by Sinn Fein as new elections for Dail Eireann, the assembly which, of course, they claimed was entitled to speak for the whole country. In Northern Ireland, the local 'Home Rule' parliament was duly elected, with the Unionists gaining forty out of the fifty-two seats in the Lower House. Sinn Fein controlled the Dail, the Unionists were now established in the North. The lines of division in Ireland were being more sharply drawn than ever before.

While the Government of Ireland Act provided no solution, the negotiations between the British government and the representatives of the Dail, which finally began in the summer of 1921, seemed to offer some hope of a settlement. An important preliminary to the discussions was the truce of 11 July 1921, which officially brought the fighting to a halt.

The protracted negotiations extended over the closing months of that year. The essential issues at stake were the nature of Ireland's future relations with the United Kingdom and the place of the new Northern Ireland in any settlement. The astute British Prime Minister, Lloyd George, argued in favour of dominion status, with due recognition of

Speech bubble: YOU HAVE GOT TO SWALLOW THIS — OR ELSE!

Labels: THE TREATY / IRISH CITIZEN / MILITARISM

The Anglo-Irish treaty of 1922 set up the Irish Free State as a Dominion, but still within the Empire and owing allegiance to the British crown. Moderate opinion, led by Michael Collins, saw it as a 'stepping stone' to the Republic, but others, including de Valera, believed it to be forced on Ireland by English military strength. (3)

the right of Northern Ireland to remain within the United Kingdom if it so wished. Such a proposition fell far short of Irish republican aspirations, but de Valera and his colleagues began to formulate the proposition that an independent Ireland could be associated with the British Empire, through a 'treaty of free association', as de Valera put it. There was present, therefore, an important willingness to modify the absolute claims to a republic. The difficulty was to find a formula which would satisfy both the British and the Irish.

On 11 October 1921, the republican government was invited to send yet another mission to London to determine how 'the association of Ireland with the community of nations known as the British Empire may be reconciled with Irish national aspirations'. This carefully worded invitation was accepted, but this time de Valera did not lead the mission, a decision which was later to give rise to much political controversy. In place of de Valera, it was led by the moderate, Arthur Griffith; and Michael Collins, the most influential figure in the armed resistance, was also a member of the five-man delegation.

Though Lloyd George and the British negotiators were prepared to make concessions on minor points, they held to the position they had already established. Griffith and Collins believed that a compromise could still be found, but they returned to London with apparently no clear mandate to accept a settlement which would involve

allegiance to the British sovereign as King of Ireland – particularly objectionable to republican feeling – or full incorporation in the Empire. Their instructions, however, were not well defined. Faced, on the one hand, with renewed assurance from the British negotiators that great pressure would be exerted on Northern Ireland to come into a new Irish state, and the offer of greater financial independence for Ireland and, on the other hand, with a threat of a renewal of war, the Irish delegates, without consulting Dublin, decided to accept an agreement with Great Britain. In the early hours of 6 December 1921 the 'Articles of Agreement for a treaty between Great Britain and Ireland' were signed.

The Irish signatories argued that it was the best settlement that could be obtained and that economic pressure and a border revision would soon bring Northern Ireland into a united Ireland. For the pragmatic Collins, the Agreement brought full independence a stage nearer. To the advanced republicans, however, the Agreement was unacceptable, especially the provision of an Oath of Allegiance to the British Crown. De Valera's position was more flexible: external association with the Empire was acceptable, full membership was not. His rejection of the December settlement tended, in practice, to bring him closer to the advanced republicans in 1922 and 1923; but his willingness to seek a solution other than total separation from the Commonwealth was to influence his approach to Anglo-Irish relations on later occasions, especially in the 1930s.

Allegiance to the Crown and the abandonment of the external signs of republicanism, rather than the Ulster problem as such, provided the material for the bitter debates in the Dail on the Anglo-Irish Agreement, which ended on 7 January 1922 with a narrow vote in favour of the treaty: sixty-four votes to fifty-seven. De Valera, once defeated, resigned and was succeeded by Arthur Griffith. The treaty found widespread support. The Catholic bishops, the principal newspapers and moderates generally showed their approval. The bulk of the IRB supported their leader, Collins, in regarding the treaty as opening the way to greater independence at a later date: a 'stepping stone' to the Republic.

The establishment, with British approval, of a Provisional government of Ireland allowed the United Kingdom government to transfer authority to a regime which enjoyed a legitimate status in British law. The membership of the Provisional government overlapped with that of the Dail ministry, and Collins was chairman. But the peace in Ireland was fragile. The tensions between the pro- and anti-treaty military elements grew. Hasty attempts were made, in May, to bring the rival sections of Sinn Fein into an election pact. The arrangements collapsed and it became increasingly clear that no constitution for an Irish state could be drafted which would be acceptable to the British and the republicans. The election in June showed clearly the strength of the pro-treaty elements. Out of 128 seats in the Dail, pro-treaty Sinn Fein and other groups willing to accept the treaty won 93 seats. The anti-treaty Sinn Fein share was only 35 seats. Thereafter the drift into open conflict was rapid. British pressure on the pro-treaty administration and an increasingly defiant stand by the anti-treaty IRA led to the outbreak of fighting on a serious scale from the end of June onwards. The shelling of the Four Courts, Dublin, where the republicans had established themselves in defiance of the Provisional government, raised the curtain on a civil war. More than the precious archives of hundreds of years of Irish history were destroyed in the siege of the Four Courts.

The Civil War was bitterly fought and it was seriously divisive in its long-term effects. Collins, as commander-in-chief of the pro-treaty forces, was killed in an ambush in August 1922, and in the same month an ailing Griffith died. Reprisals and executions marked the ten-month war, but with the defeat of the main republican forces in the south of the island, they were ordered to cease fire by de Valera, as head of the republican administration, on 24 May 1923. The Civil War was over, but it left a sad legacy of bitterness. By December 1922, however, the new Saorstat Eireann (the Irish Free State) had come into existence. The Free State was a full member of the British Commonwealth and the British were guaranteed naval and other military facilities in Ireland in times of peace and war. The republicans did not recognize the Free State or its parliament and the cease-fire of 1923 made no difference on this point. It was, therefore, against a background of civil strife and disunity that the Free State government, with William T. Cosgrave as President of the Executive Council (Prime Minister), began the task of national reconstruction.

The new Irish state

Cosgrave was helped considerably in the task of reconstruction by the fact that the Irish government was able to take over from the departing British a reasonably intact administrative structure, and many Irishmen in the British public service opted to serve the new state and were very welcome. The organization of the Cumann na nGaedheal party, in 1923, gave W. T. Cosgrave, a man of considerable political judgment, a firm basis on which to build up a political structure. With a civil police force successfully organized, and parliament functioning, the Free State administration had reasonable

grounds for a cautious optimism. There were, however, the signs of danger. The anti-treaty IRA and Sinn Fein were unreconciled and there was still some sporadic violence. When elections were held, in August 1923, the republicans won forty-four seats compared with Cosgrave's sixty-three. As before, the republicans refused to enter the Dail, and it was left to the small Labour party to serve in the role of a parliamentary opposition. Again, March 1924 saw symptoms of serious unrest in the Free State army. Demobilization, at a time when civilian jobs were scarce, and a belief that Collins's basic republicanism was being abandoned by the Cosgrave ministry led to a near mutiny. The danger was quickly averted; but the incident was an indication both of a latent republicanism among a section of the army and of a growing conservatism in government circles. The government came to accept dominion status as a satisfactory end in itself and it also worked to win the loyalty of such minority groups as the Anglo-Irish landed gentry and the Protestant middle class, who had traditionally supported the British connection. The revolutionary past was being quietly put to one side by the new rulers of the Irish Free State.

For the Anglo-Irish gentry and, to a lesser extent, the professional classes, however, the process of accepting the new order was not always easy. Despite the increasingly conservative face of government in the Free State, the age of the Viceregal Lodge had obviously passed. The new civil service, the emphasis on things Gaelic, the land legislation, the burning of some 'Big Houses' during the Civil War by the 'Insurgents', all added to the sense of unease about the future. But though some of the 'Garrison', as they were often described in nationalist circles, quitted the country for ever, in time the Protestant minority, in town and country, came to terms with the Free State. Protestants continued to hold a position of influence out of proportion to their numbers in banking, insurance, shipping and the professions generally. And though the recent Land Acts marked the end of landlordism in Ireland, the Anglo-Irish continued and, indeed, still continue, to play an important role in the valuable livestock industry. The Irish revolution may have changed some social patterns. The surprising thing about it was how few those changes were in practice. There is still a Royal Dublin Society and a Royal Hibernian Academy.

Another critical test for the new Cosgrave administration was the Boundary Commission which had been set up under the terms of the Anglo-Irish Agreement. The Irish negotiators in 1921 had believed that boundary revisions would make almost impossible the economic and political survival of Northern Ireland. When, however, the

'Dividing up the Estate, or the Land Commission goes crazy': a cartoon from 'Dublin Opinion' highlights the changes that marked the break-up of the old estates and the end of landlordism. (4)

Commission finally met, in 1924–25, the outcome was unsatisfactory in terms of the aspirations of the Free State but suited well the interests of the Northern Ireland administration. The South African chairman (Feetham) ruled that only minor frontier revisions could be made. In determining any such limited exchanges it was proposed that the Commission would work on the assumption that Catholics were nationalists and Protestants were Unionists. Rather than accept so controversial a settlement, the Free State government hastily made an agreement with Great Britain, on 3 December 1925, which preserved the status quo on the border, released the Free State from certain financial obligations to Great Britain and made some vague provisions, which were never implemented, for consultations on common interests between the Free State and Northern Ireland. This setback on the border issue provoked sharp criticism of the Irish government in republican circles, though the critics provided no practical suggestions as to how Catholic and Protestant, nationalist and Unionist interests in the North could be effectively reconciled in the context of a united Ireland.

De Valera, as head of the republican Sinn Fein movement, came to the conclusion, in 1926, that Sinn Fein should leave the political wilderness and contest the next Dail elections and that the republican candidates should announce their in-

tention to take their seats in the House, if elected, but to refuse the hated Oath to the Crown. The Dail, de Valera argued, was not the legitimate parliament of the Republic, but it could be used to achieve full independence. Unable to secure a clear mandate for his new policy from Sinn Fein, de Valera and his supporters left it and established Fianna Fail (the 'Soldiers of Destiny'). Only a small group remained loyal to the uncompromising republicanism of Sinn Fein. The Oath of Allegiance continued to be a problem even after the June elections of 1927, when Fianna Fail won forty-four seats; but, in the end, by treating the Oath as an 'empty formality', de Valera and his supporters took their seats in the Dail on 11 August 1927. This decision to go into parliament was to be of the highest importance in the history of the survival and development of parliamentary democracy in Ireland and it altered drastically the power structure in the House. Cosgrave's administration could no longer command a clear majority. Further elections in the autumn of 1927 saw Cosgrave's Cumann na nGaedheal win sixty-two seats and Fianna Fail fifty-seven. The gap was narrowing rapidly, but Cosgrave, supported by the additional votes of two small parties and some independents, was able to survive in office until 1932.

Throughout the period 1923 to 1930, Cumann na nGaedheal pursued a rather conservative course in the fields of economic policy and social legislation. The Cosgrave ministry tended to support Free Trade rather than protection and economic self-sufficiency, though a certain move towards industrial protection became evident during the world crisis from 1929 onwards. It is true that far-seeing measures were taken to develop hydro-electric power and land legislation to speed up the transfer of land from the estate owners to the farmers was sponsored by the government. It is well to remember, however, that the Free State did not inaugurate the programme of land reform. The Land Acts of the 1880s and 90s, put through Westminster by Liberal and Conservative governments, had opened the way for the changes in land ownership in Ireland. But legislation, from 1924 onwards, had speeded up the process of compulsory acquisition of land for redistribution. The Land Commission's policy had, in the long term, the effect of creating a class of working farmers who owned their lands subject to the repayment, in the form of an annuity, of the purchase price. All this legislation helped to strengthen the conservative quality of life in rural Ireland, and it may have imposed too rigid a structure of land-holding, making it too unresponsive to modern market and technical demands. The debate still goes on.

Emigration, especially to North America, had

long been seen as a dire proof of British misgovernment in Ireland. Alone among Western nations, it seemed, the Irish were declining in numbers in their own country from the 1840s onwards into the new century. Sinn Fein had asserted that political and economic freedom would change this situation for the better. The establishment of the Free State, however, brought with it no significant changes in the pattern of emigration. Interrupted by World War I, emigration overseas resumed again in the 1920s, and to the numbers who left the country for social reasons were added those republicans who were unwilling to accept the Free State. Emigration then remained rather high throughout the 1920s and 30s, running at an average rate of 5·6 per 1,000 inhabitants. In 1926, the census year, the total population of the Free State was 2,971,992.

The survival of traditional Ireland

On a cultural level, measures were taken by the Cosgrave ministry to encourage the more widespread use of the Irish language. It was given constitutional status as the national language; the teaching of Irish was made compulsory in the schools; and a knowledge of the language was required for admission to the public services. This language policy was continued by subsequent administrations, but the results were to be of only a very limited kind in terms of making Irish the normal medium of communication outside the small traditionally Irish-speaking districts. Yet there was a positive side to the Gaelic Revival policy. The establishment of the Irish Folklore Commission helped to save a great fund of rural tradition which was, in many ways, unique in Western Europe. Within another generation and with the breakdown of rural isolation, this corpus of folklore might have been lost for ever. The popular interest in Irish traditional music and dance was to grow; and it has become a remarkable feature of Irish life in the years since World War II. Again, though the reading public for literature in the Irish language was a limited one, prose and poetry of much strength and beauty continues to be written in Irish down to the present time. Mairtín Ó Cadhain's prose and the poetry of Seán O Riordáin, Micheál MacLiammóir and Máire Mhac an tSaoi are reminders of the quality of the Gaelic literary tradition. There is, today, no rigid dividing-line between writers in English and in Irish. Gaelic creative writers have produced accomplished works in English, and Thomas Kinsella's fine translation into English of the Gaelic epic, the *Táin Bó Cuailnge*, was an important contribution to Irish literature in the English language.

The 1920s saw the first tentative efforts to set up a national broadcasting service. It was not until 1926

Electricity comes to the cabins of Ireland. In many ways Ireland remained a mixture of modernity and tradition. 'This improvin' of rural life is wonderful', says the farmer. 'Now, the children'll be able to study till all hours of the night for the Civil Service.' (5)

that a national service was finally put on the air. In determining broadcasting policy, the British pattern, in general terms, was adopted. Broadcasting was to be a public utility, not a commercial enterprise. It was, however, characteristic of the new state and its cautious approach to innovation that Irish radio was given no liberal charter like that won by the British Broadcasting Corporation. The Ministry of Posts and Telegraphs kept a firm control over radio policies and funds. It was only slowly that Irish radio, and, in the post-war period, Irish television, began to escape from the close embrace of the Post Office. The continuing controversies about the effective independence of the broadcasting service suggest that the story may not yet be ended.

In its basic educational policies, in relation to the prohibition of divorce, the control of indecent publications, the banning of the sale of contraceptives and of the distribution of publications advocating birth control, the Cosgrave ministry was responsive to the considerable, if usually indirect, influence of the Catholic Church. As a recent writer, J. H. Whyte, put it: 'From its early days, the government proved willing to use the power of the state to protect Catholic moral values.' The influence of the Church was part of the daily life of the community. The death of a bishop merited headlines in the secular newspapers. Religious festivals and pilgrimages were important public occasions. The ecclesiastical seminaries and the convents had no shortage of novices and the contribution made by Irish clerics to the spread of Catholicism in Africa and the Far East in the 1920s and 30s and, indeed, even later, was remarkable. With the Second Vatican Council and the more critical spirit generally in the Catholic Church in the 1960s and 70s, the atmosphere in Ireland changed to some extent. Vocations for the religious life became fewer, and bishops are now more frequently contradicted in public; but the churches still attract large congregations and the statements of the Catholic hierarchy continue to command much attention in the press. The voice of dissent has grown on such issues as divorce and birth control, but an essentially conservative Church has retained much of the popular status it enjoyed in those years of faith in the 1920s and 30s. Only the more rash among politicians tangle with the Church in modern Ireland; but it may be argued that the number of the more rash is growing slowly. At the same time, since its establishment, the Irish state has shown a wide measure of respect for religious and political minorities. Despite the strong clerical influences present in Ireland, the separation between Church and state has remained a basic factor in Irish constitutional practice. The form of the state remained secular, and clerical influence was kept within fairly well-defined limits under Cosgrave and, perhaps, even more so under his successor, de Valera.

The new imagination

Though the high literary achievements of the opening years of the century were hardly equalled, in general terms, in the 1920s and '30s, new writers were making very important contributions to literature in English, especially in the form of the short story. Frank O'Connor brought realism and humour to his stories of the Civil War and after. As one critic put it: 'Ideals, political, cultural and religious, are never in O'Connor's world quite secure from booby-traps and apple-pie beds, are seldom for a moment immune from the poke in the ribs that preludes laughter.' Another Corkman, Sean O'Faolain, could write with intricate clarity and precision of an Ireland full of contradictions. But O'Faolain is more than a novelist of great power. His masterly studies of Hugh O'Neill, the

great Earl of Tyrone, in the 16th century, and of Daniel O'Connell, the Liberator, are reminders of his wide grasp of the factors which helped to make modern Ireland. The period produced other works of brilliance and often of conflict: an inner conflict between the writer and a new Ireland more cautious and flat than the dream. Liam O'Flaherty's *The Informer*, *Famine* and other works, the strange world of Patrick MacGill, the strength and beauty of Kate O'Brien's stories, were all capable of throwing light on the complexities of Irish life. There were others who came from that Anglo-Irish world which had contributed much to the literary revival: Elizabeth Bowen, and Lord Dunsany, novelist, poet and patron of the talents of others. James Joyce's great, difficult and obscure *Finnegans Wake* was to appear in 1939, and Samuel Beckett was showing his insight into the absurdity of the human condition in works like *Murphy*. The tradition of the novel and short-story-telling was carried on into the 1940s and the post-war years by writers such as Mary Lavin, Francis MacManus, Francis Stuart, Benedict Kiely and Flan O'Brien, with his echoes of Joyce.

By the 1920s, the Dublin theatre tradition had been well established; indeed, some might say that it had become too established and lacked the spark and originality of earlier years. There were, however, forces which challenged the creation of a rigid canon of Irish drama. Sean O'Casey's bold and vigorous portraits of Dublin life, Denis Johnston's vision and the dramatic and poetic works of Austin Clarke were signs of life and character among Irish playwrights. The Gate Theatre, under the imaginative guidance of Hilton Edwards, Micheál MacLiammóir and Lord Longford, and the Lyric Theatre and other groups, in the 1930s and later, helped to make some amends for a certain staleness in what the Abbey Theatre had to offer.

W. B. Yeats died in 1939; but a new generation of poets had emerged. Padrac Colum, Austin Clarke, F. R. Higgins, Robert Farren and Patrick Kavanagh helped to give a critical, often astringent quality to Irish poetry. They were to be followed by others, often seeking a new definition of an Irish vision in a rapidly changing society: Valentin Iremonger, John Montague, Thomas Kinsella, Denis Devlin and Roy McFadden. Journals such as the *Bell* and, later, *Envoy* and *Irish Writing* served well the needs of creative writing in Ireland. Difficulties did, however, confront the Irish writer in the years before and for some time after World War II. The censorship of publications, with its heavy hand, disturbed many creative writers. Again, the Irish market was small and the readers generally conservative in their views. Not a few of the younger writers were to follow James Joyce's example and live and write about Ireland abroad.

If, despite difficulties and frustrations, Irish letters had an international reputation as a self-reliant and independent element in the English-speaking world, the visual arts tended to have a more provincial character. Indeed, the clear primacy of letters remained a constant factor throughout the whole modern period. The artists of the Celtic Revival have already been described in a previous chapter, but there were other artists of originality and quality who began to attract attention: Patrick Tuohy, whose haunting portraits were his great strength, Norah McGuinness and, in a more established mode, Maurice MacGonigal. They were to be followed by a group of accomplished painters whose work, though very individual and informed by Ireland, reflected the current trends in the British and Continental schools: Patrick Hennessy, Louis le Brocquy and Gerard Dillon, to name a few.

Sculptors, perhaps because they lacked patrons in a new and rather poor state, did not really flourish. But artists such as Seamus Murphy, Albert Power and Jerome Connor had talent and high craftsmanship. Later sculptors like Oisin Kelly and Hilary Heron have shown an originality which seems to have given a new impetus to sculpture in Ireland.

In architecture, there is little to remember from the pre-World-War-II period except the commendable restoration of the great public buildings in Dublin which had been severely damaged during the years of conflict. The 1930s did see, however, a great deal of house-building in the new suburbs around Dublin. In design, these houses were essentially copies of contemporary British types, and town planning, in the Ireland of the 1930s, was a little-known art. Dublin grew out of its earlier order and elegance into ribbon building and scattered developments. The full implications of an absence of serious thinking about architecture and planning only became really evident in the boom years of the 1960s, once the post-war recession had passed.

The politics of division

It was in the field of external affairs, and especially in relation to the strengthening of the constitutional status of the Dominions within the Commonwealth, that the new Irish state had some of its most significant successes. The Free State became a member of the League of Nations; it opened diplomatic missions abroad; and, along with Canada and South Africa in particular, pressed hard to put the Dominions on a basis of equality with Great Britain. At the Imperial Conference of 1926 and in the negotiations leading up to the Statute of Westminster (1931), the Irish did much to win legal recognition of the fact that the British Commonwealth had become an association of virtually independent states. This diplomacy made possible the more radical changes of a constitutional kind which de Valera was able to make once he came to power in 1932.

The world economic crisis and a sharp revival of revolutionary republicanism in the period 1929–31 added to the difficulties facing a conservative government. Fianna Fail, with its policies of agricultural and industrial self-sufficiency, its promise of progressive social legislation and of a steady move, by constitutional means, to the republic, seemed to offer an exciting and acceptable alternative to a government which had been in office since 1922. Fianna Fail, too, with its republican objectives, seemed more likely to hold in check the radicals of the IRA and of a newly established socialist republican group, Saor Eire ('Free Ireland'). The elections of February 1932 returned Fianna Fail with seventy-one seats as the largest party in the new Dail, though without an absolute majority. In an age of growing threats to parliamentary democracy elsewhere in Europe, it was a measure of the strength of the Irish parliamentary system that, within a decade of the Civil War, Cosgrave made way for the man who had opposed the treaty, Eamon de Valera, the leader of Fianna Fail.

The Northern parliament had been inaugurated by King George V, in Belfast, in June 1921. The predominant position of the Ulster Unionists was evident from the beginning; out of the fifty-two seats in the Lower House (the House of Commons), forty were held by Unionists under the determined leadership of Sir James Craig (created Lord Craigavon, 1927), who was to remain Prime Minister of Northern Ireland until his death in 1940. The Unionists also dominated the Upper House (the Senate). It was a measure of the monolithic character of the Northern Ireland political system that the share of seats held by the Unionists in the House of Commons seldom varied from election to election.

Though the Unionist party was to control Northern Ireland until the political crisis of the late 1960s created a new situation, the opening years of Northern Ireland's existence as a political entity were troubled ones. Serious sectarian riots and reprisals (some two hundred killed and nearly a thousand wounded in 1922) and clashes with the IRA on the border with the Free State dominated the political scene in 1921 and 1922. Special armed paramilitary units were recruited from among the Protestant population and the sense of uncertainty in the North was heightened by the fact that the boundaries of the territory were not immediately settled. The authority of the local parliament was limited to the internal affairs of Northern Ireland. The financial controls exercised by London were considerable and, in theory, the Westminster

Parliament could override the subordinate legislature in Belfast. In practice, Westminster proved reluctant to discuss the affairs of Northern Ireland or to interfere with the decisions of the Northern administration. With excessive optimism, as we now know, it was hoped in British political circles that the settlement of 1921–22 would put an end to the Irish question. Though pushed all too readily into the background, Northern Ireland continued to be represented in the Parliament of the United Kingdom by twelve members in the Commons, of whom ten were usually members of the Unionist party and worked in close alliance with the British Conservatives.

The Catholic and generally nationalist element in the Northern population regarded the partition of Ireland with dismay and, to begin with, even the moderate nationalists were hesitant about participating in the new system of government. From 1925 onwards, following the controversial Anglo-Irish boundary agreement, which appeared to give a measure of permanency to the frontiers of Northern Ireland, nationalists began to take their places in the Northern parliament, where their share was usually about ten seats. Committed republicans, however, refused to sit in the parliament, which they regarded as having no legal validity.

From the beginning, the pattern of development in Northern Ireland differed in certain ways from that of a normal parliamentary democracy. The Catholic or nationalist minority, which constituted some 30 per cent of a population of 1,256,561 in 1926, regarded Northern Ireland as being essentially Protestant in character. They argued that the Northern administration only existed to maintain the social and political ascendancy of the Unionist party and of the powerful Orange Order. There seemed to the minority little hope that this situation would be altered as long as Northern Ireland retained a separate identity. The nationalist aspiration remained, therefore, the achievement of Irish unity, though it was easier to express such a wish than to indicate how unity could possibly be brought about. The Ulster Unionists, for their part, argued that, were the Catholic minority to accept partition loyally and demonstrate their allegiance to the United Kingdom, they could participate fully in the life of the province. It was a case which failed to acknowledge economic and social realities in Northern Ireland and the force of history and tradition in the life of a community. The suspicions between Catholic and Protestant in Northern Ireland were old, involving cultural factors, too, and memories of defeat and conquest. The divisions crossed the lines of class distinction to a considerable extent. It is significant that, during the economically depressed years of the 1930s, when the rate of unemployment in Northern Ireland was over 20 per cent of the insured population, popular unrest was expressed not in terms of class war but of sectarian riots in industrial Belfast.

There were intransigent elements in both the nationalist and Orange camps; the IRA and Sinn Fein continued to demand an all-Ireland republic. The new Fianna Fail party, too, was committed to the ideal of the republic, and when it came to power in the South in 1932, the Northern Unionists quickly saw a threat to their entrenched position. In 1933, the Special Powers Act, a temporary measure which had given extensive powers of search and arrest to the police, was made a permanent part of the law of Northern Ireland. The 1930s, characterized by an unwillingness to make concessions on both sides, saw a strengthening rather than a weakening of divisions within Northern Ireland and between the North and the South.

With the support of the Labour party's vote, Fianna Fail took office, after the elections of January 1932, and quickly introduced a measure to end the controversial Oath of Allegiance to the British Crown. This was, in effect, the first attack on the structure of the Anglo-Irish Agreement of 1921 which de Valera had regarded as an unacceptable limitation on Irish independence. The office of Governor-General, the representative of the Crown in the Free State, was stripped of all formal status and the right of appeal from the Irish courts to the Privy Council in London was abolished. Another long-standing grievance, in republican circles, had been the annual payments made to the United Kingdom exchequer to recoup the British government for the substantial advances made to landlords whose estates had been purchased by the tenant-farmers under the land legislation of the pre-1922 period. Republicans argued that Ireland had been over-taxed in the past and that it was only just that the 'land annuities', as they were called, should be withheld. The new Irish government refused to pay the annuities when the negotiations with London broke down. The British retaliated by imposing a heavy tariff on Irish agricultural imports and countermeasures were then taken by the Irish government. These tariffs on imports from Britain helped, in practice, to strengthen a basic objective in the Fianna Fail programme: to encourage the industrial development of what had been essentially an agricultural economy. Starting from a virtually Free Trade situation, Ireland became in the course of a few months 'one of the most heavily tariffed countries that could be found'.

Despite the hardships of the 'economic war' with Great Britain which bore particularly heavily on the agricultural community, de Valera was able to consolidate his position politically. In the Dail elections of January 1933, his party won seventy-seven seats. This gave him, for the first time, a small overall majority. In contrast, Cosgrave's party only won forty-eight seats, the remainder of the seats going to a number of smaller parties. The 'economic war' had brought with it a measure of tension and unrest in some rural areas, especially among the opponents of the new government, and a further complicating factor was a resurgence of violence on the part of the IRA before and during the 1933 elections. To protect, it was claimed, public order, and to defend Cumann na nGaedheal (Cosgravite) meetings from attack, a corps of former members of the Free State army was organized. Known initially as the Army Comrades Association (ACA), its members wore a 'Blueshirt' uniform, and under the leadership of General Eoin O'Duffy, who had been dismissed from his post as Commissioner of Police by de Valera, the ACA became the 'National Guard'. For a brief period, O'Duffy enjoyed a measure of power. He became the head of the new Fine Gael party, which represented a union of the old Cumann na nGaedheal party with some lesser groups. His opponents accused him of fascist leanings, and the National Guard certainly adopted some of the external trappings of fascism. It would be wrong, however, to conclude that the Fine Gael party was committed to totalitarian aims. Fine Gael, in practice, remained essentially a conservative parliamentary party. Fascism and Marxism made only a marginal impact on the Ireland of the 1930s. Specifically Irish issues such as the Civil War and partition continued to dominate Irish political considerations. By 1935, Fine Gael, now under Cosgrave's prudent leadership, was moving back into the pattern of political practice which had been established by its predecessor, Cumann na nGaedheal.

De Valera's government took firm and effective action to curb the activities of O'Duffy's National Guard. Equally firm action was taken against the IRA, which, though divided now into left- and right-wing factions, was becoming more aggressive and dissatisfied with the government. De Valera was determined to show that there could be no doubt where authority lay. In 1936, the IRA was banned as an illegal organization. A further indication of the determination of the Fianna Fail government to assert its leadership of nationalist Ireland was the new constitution of 1937, which became law following a referendum. The constitution claimed all Ireland as the national territory, contained no reference to the British Crown and made provision for a popularly elected President of Ireland. The name Irish Free State was dropped in favour of Ireland or, in the Irish language, Eire, again emphasizing the claim to jurisdiction over the whole

De Valera's Fianna Fail party won a small majority in the Dail election of January 1933. Opposition came from the right wing Cumann na nGaedheal party led by William T. Cosgrave, who tried to represent de Valera as an ineffectual latter-day emperor. (6)

island. The British government was quick to stress that the new constitution had no effect on the status of Northern Ireland as a part of the United Kingdom or on the validity of the Anglo-Irish Agreement of 1921. The British reservations made little impact on the situation: de Valera had made a further move towards the realization of his concept of 'external association' with the Commonwealth.

Measures to encourage tillage and some modest social legislation were other aspects of the Fianna Fail programme. Pension schemes for widows and orphans were introduced, the scope of unemployment assistance was widened and considerable advances were made in providing housing for the lower-income groups. But neither in the field of social reform nor in that of banking and monetary policy did the Fianna Fail government engage in any radical adventures. De Valera remained a reformer rather than a revolutionary. The negotiated settlement, if the terms were right, pleased him. This was well illustrated by the course of the negotiations between the British and Irish governments in 1938, as a result of which the British gave up all their military and harbour rights in Ireland (other than in Northern Ireland), a concession which was to be of major significance for Ireland during World War II. The financial disputes between the two countries were resolved, and the resulting Anglo-Irish Trade Agreement opened the British market to Irish exporters with few restrictions. It also allowed the British gradually to build up their industrial exports to Ireland. The liberalization of trade between the two countries, in the post-World-War-II period, should be seen as a consequence and a development of the 1938 Trade Agreement. The era of prohibitive tariffs in Ireland proved a short one.

Ireland and World War II

When World War II began, de Valera made it quite clear that Ireland would not permit her ports to be used as a base for an attack on Great Britain; but he made it equally plain that Ireland would not willingly abandon neutrality as long as British forces occupied Northern Ireland. Some doubts were expressed in the Dail about the practical possibilities of remaining neutral, although the Fine Gael party, the one most committed in the past to the Commonwealth connection, quickly accepted neutrality as both feasible and desirable. In this they were in agreement with Fianna Fail and the Labour members.

In the first nine months of war, Ireland, as a neutral, had no serious problems in her relations with the belligerents. The fall of France, however, brought about a new situation. Some, such as Winston Churchill, argued that Britain should demand back the port and military facilities which they had given up under the 1938 agreements. The limited capacity of Ireland, in military terms, and the hostile attitude of the IRA, were causes of concern in London. Though the risk of a German invasion of Ireland declined from the summer of 1941 onwards, such considerations as the submarine war and the suspicion that pro-Axis elements were engaged in espionage in Ireland all worked to maintain British pressure on the Irish government. The entry of the United States into the war, in December 1941, created new complications for Ireland. The American authorities proved both persistent and unsuccessful in their efforts to secure facilities for their forces, and de Valera responded to the presence of American troops in Northern Ireland with a sharp protest. American and British pressure for the expulsion of the Axis diplomatic missions from Ireland reached quite serious proportions in February 1944, and there was some fear in Ireland of military intervention by the Allies. The

crisis passed, and, with the changing character of the war, the need for access to the Irish ports diminished rapidly.

Neutrality made heavy demands on the Irish economy. The British imposed a limited range of economic sanctions against Ireland and the shipping resources of the country were small. Lack of industrial raw materials led to an increase in unemployment and to higher prices. Though wartime needs saw an intensification of agricultural activity, Ireland emerged from the war beset by the problems of shortages, a weakened economy and high prices. In political terms, neutrality left Ireland a rather isolated state outside the Allied camp and helped to still further separate her from the other member states of the Commonwealth.

The effect of World War II on Northern Ireland was to strengthen its ties with Great Britain and to help consolidate the power of the ruling Unionist party. Northern Ireland provided an important staging area for American and British troops, and though Belfast suffered severely in air raids in 1941, the Northern economy benefited from the wartime demands on agriculture and industry, especially shipbuilding. Employment in the Belfast shipyards rose from about 7,000 workers in 1938 to 20,600 in 1945. The close links between the economy of Northern Ireland and that of Great Britain were further emphasized by the acceptance of the principle that social services in the North should be of the same standard as in Great Britain. This, in practice, was to involve substantial subsidies from the British exchequer, and it achieved more impressive results than were possible in the South, with its limited resources.

Problems of the new Republic

Fianna Fail emerged from the war years still in command of an overall majority in the Dail. A number of factors, however, worked to undermine its strong position. The economy made, at best, only a halting recovery and emigration remained a serious and unresolved problem. In the circumstances, the foundation, in July 1946, of a new political party, Clann na Poblachta, seemed to offer to moderate republicans an attractive alternative to Fianna Fail. The leader of the new party, Sean MacBride, had been a chief of staff in the IRA and his father had been one of the 1916 men, but now MacBride turned to parliamentary methods as a more acceptable way than arms to win national unity. Uneasy at the danger presented by the Clann, de Valera called a general election in February 1948. The Clann did not succeed as well as some observers had expected, but the ten seats it won helped to deprive Fianna Fail of its majority in the Dail. Surprisingly, the disparate opposition parties came together in a coalition government which broke Fianna Fail's long political ascendancy. The new Taoiseach (Prime Minister) was John A. Costello of Fine Gael. MacBride became Minister for External Affairs.

The coalition government showed some enterprise in the economic and constitutional fields. A new Anglo-Irish Trade Agreement, in 1948, strengthened the economic links between the two countries and special agencies were set up to encourage industrial investment in Ireland. The Irish state began to emerge from its wartime isolation and became a participant in the Marshall Aid Programme and a founder member of the Council of Europe. But it was characteristic of the now established neutralist attitude that Ireland did not subscribe to the Treaty of Brussels or join NATO. The British presence in Northern Ireland was still an inhibiting factor.

Possibly the most dramatic step taken by the first coalition government was the decision finally to end all constitutional ties between the Irish state and the Commonwealth. The influence of Clann na Poblachta can be seen in this decision, but it also reflected Costello's hope, as Prime Minister, that a clear republican status would 'take the gun out of Irish politics'. Though Fianna Fail expressed the fear that a formal withdrawal might make the unification of Ireland more difficult, the party gave its support to the Republic of Ireland Act, which became law on Easter Sunday 1949. Great Britain readily accepted the Irish decision, but the Labour government put through the Westminster Parliament the Ireland Act, 1949, which, while providing for the recognition of the Republic, assured Northern Ireland that 'in no event will Northern Ireland or any part thereof' cease to be British territory without the express consent of the parliament of Northern Ireland. For the Ulster Unionists it seemed that partition was being given a more enduring foundation than ever before. The decision to leave the Commonwealth did not, in fact, 'take the gun out of Irish politics', but it put on a more logical basis the international position of the Irish state and it gave recognition to the fact that Commonwealth membership had little emotional value in Irish nationalist terms.

The first coalition, an unsteady combination of five parties, broke up in 1951. A variety of factors contributed to its fall, not least the still depressed condition of the Irish economy. The most controversial issue, however, was a conflict about the provision of certain health and maternity services under the Health Act of 1947. The Catholic hierarchy questioned the regulations as encroaching on the rights of the family and the individual, and they argued that the terms of this free-for-all scheme

'Begob, Eamon', says Queen Victoria, about to be removed from her pedestal, 'there's great changes around here.' Ireland formally withdrew from the British Commonwealth in April 1949. (7)

would, in practice, limit the patient's choice of doctor. They were particularly alarmed by the provision for the biological education of children and the instruction of mothers, as such education and instruction could involve such issues as birth control, on which the Church had well-defined teachings. The Minister for Health in the coalition, Dr Noel Browne, in reply contended that the scheme would be a voluntary one. His assurances did not satisfy the Church leaders and his whole project also encountered the bitter opposition of the medical profession and of many members of the coalition parties. Browne belonged to Clann na Poblachta and internal tensions and leadership rivalries within the Clann further undermined his position. In the end, the government rejected Dr Browne's scheme and the Dail was assured by the Prime Minister that future health measures would be in conformity with Catholic social teaching. Under strong pressure from MacBride, as leader of the Clann, Browne resigned from the Costello ministry.

The political crisis centering on the Mother and Child scheme underlined yet again the powerful influence of a conservative Church, watchful of any suggestion of state encroachments in the moral sphere. There was a great deal of public controversy and debate in the press on the merits and demerits of Dr Browne's case and on the role of the Church national affairs, but there was little doubt where immediate victory lay. For Clann na Poblachta, the recriminations and internal disputes led to the rapid decline and the ultimate extinction of the party.

Following the break-up of the coalition government, and new elections, Fianna Fail, under de Valera, returned to office from 1951 to 1954. Though Fianna Fail succeeded in putting through a modified health scheme, they were just as unsuccessful as their predecessors in resolving the chronic economic problems or in stemming the tide of emigration.

The general election of 1954 gave the Republic its second coalition government, with Costello again as Prime Minister; but, as on the previous occasion, economic problems, especially inflation, undermined the new coalition's position. Its tasks were made more difficult by a sudden upsurge of IRA and radical republican activity in 1956. The IRA was very much a minority group, but its campaign may have reflected a measure of discontent in republican circles following the collapse of Clann na Poblachta. It was also a reminder of the tenacity of the belief that Irish unity could be achieved by force regardless of the political realities in Northern Ireland. The IRA offensive took the form of attacks across the border on military and police barracks in Northern Ireland. In the Republic, IRA activities were effectively brought under control from 1957–58 onwards and by 1962 the IRA campaign had petered out. The militancy of the republicans was, however, a warning of the constant danger of a radicalization of the Ulster question.

The collapse of the second coalition made the way free for a remarkable resurgence of Fianna Fail, which provided the government of the Republic from 1957 to March 1973. The second period of Fianna Fail predominance was marked by a number of significant developments not least in the economic sphere, where there had been so little improvement since the end of World War II. The First and Second Programmes for Economic Expansion opened the way for a more flexible approach to state investment in industry with particular emphasis on the expansion of exports. Tax concessions to manufacturers, a greater involvement of the Irish banks in financing new enterprises and attempts to stimulate agricultural production were aspects of these coordinated schemes for economic expansion. The 1960s were marked by a decided upswing in the Irish economy, and a flow of foreign capital, too, was attracted into the country. It was an indication of a changing pattern in Irish life that emigration dropped substantially in the 1960s and though the opening years of the 1970s have seen in Ireland, as elsewhere, a falling off in the rate of economic growth, emigration has been replaced by a modest net inflow

of people into Ireland. The 1966 census made the interesting point that the Irish population was increasingly a young population and the evidence suggests that its marriage trends are moving more into line with patterns elsewhere in Western Europe. A sustained increase in the population, it is feared, may bring with it problems unless the range of employment opportunities is widened. With about a third of the Republic's population crowding into the Dublin region, the assumption that Ireland is a predominantly rural country began to lose much of its meaning in the 1960s.

In social terms, the 'sixties and early 'seventies have been characterized by a greater openness in Irish society, and by a greater willingness to debate social and moral issues such as family planning and the constitutional ban on divorce. These particular issues have tended to take the place in public controversy that was occupied in the 1950s by the Mother and Child scheme. The voice of dissent is louder, but, at the same time, traditionalist influences remain strong and parliament has been unwilling to alter existing prohibitions. Irish society has, however, become more sensitive on the subject of social welfare and the need for improvements; rural isolation has been lessened by the advent of television, and the Gaelic Revival movement has encountered a persistent apathy in, as some would argue, an increasingly materialistic environment.

The years from the mid-1960s onwards have been characterized by a significant movement of funds, local and foreign, into speculative office-development, especially in the Dublin region. This has brought with it much undistinguished building which largely seems to reflect British provincial standards. Good new buildings are sadly few, and the old and beautiful inner areas of Dublin, the Georgian streets and squares, have been brought under serious pressure. It remains to be seen how much of this architectural heritage from the 18th and early 19th centuries will survive. The conservation groups are active, but town planning in Ireland has long been timid and limited in its achievements in the field of conservation.

In the arts, the 1960s and early 1970s were marked by a measure of renewal. Artists such as Louis le Brocquy, Colin Middleton, Brian Henderson and Cecil King have given substance to the Irish presence in modern painting, while Brian King and Deborah Brown have progressed far in experimental sculpture. Occasions such as the imaginative *Rosc* exhibitions of contemporary art help to put the Irish achievement in a wider international context. Possibly the most exciting developments, in cultural terms, have been in poetry. The new generation of Irish poets have a great deal to say and some say it well. Out of the pain and tension of Ulster new voices have come. Seamus Heaney is probably the most significant of the younger poets and he often turns to his Ulster experiences. Michael Longley, another Ulster poet, brings a clarity and deep compassion to his writings. Again, the Ulster presence in poetry is much strengthened by the work of Seamus Deane, John Montague and Derek Mahon. Among the Southern poets, Thomas Kinsella ranks high in scholarship and poetic insight, while Brendan Kennelly's strong, intense lines and Eavan Boland's explorations add something new to the Irish poetic tradition. The novel and the short story are still strongly represented. Established writers such as Mary Lavin, Edna O'Brien, Benedict Kiely and James Plunkett continue to produce good work and there are new names such as Aidan Higgins, Jennifer Johnston, John McGahern, Thomas Kilroy – a playwright as well – and John Banville, with his sophisticated experimental fictions.

The 1960s saw important changes in political leadership. Eamon de Valera, old and virtually blind, retired from active politics, and was elected to the largely titular office of President in June 1959. He was replaced as Prime Minister by the pragmatic and energetic Sean Lemass, who had been for long de Valera's Minister for Industry and Commerce. Lemass's interest was essentially in the economy and it was under him that the programmes for economic expansion took practical shape. The era dominated by de Valera had come to an end and though voices were still to be heard critical of his stand at the time of the Civil War, his skill and diplomatic patience during the years of World War II were generally recognized. Devoted to the Gaelic ideal, which he never saw realized, de Valera had helped to shape a rather conservative Irish state committed not to revolution but, at most, to cautious social and political change.

In foreign policy, Ireland's admission to the United Nations, in 1955, opened the way for the Republic to pursue a moderately independent line. Ireland was acceptable to many of the 'emergent nations' because of her history and Irish troops saw service with the UN in such areas as the Middle East, the Congo and Cyprus; but there was no fundamental change in the Irish unwillingness to join military alliances. In the immediate European context, of even greater importance was the admission of Ireland to the Common Market at the beginning of January 1973. This decision to enter the European Community was backed by massive popular approval in a national referendum. Supported by the two main parties, Fianna Fail and Fine Gael, entry into the EEC could be seen as another and, perhaps, the decisive step away from the old Sinn Fein dream of economic as well as political independence. The opponents of membership, drawn mainly from Labour and republican circles, failed to convince the electorate that there was any viable alternative.

The tragedy of Ulster

A welcome development within the country was an apparent improvement in the poor level of communication between the Northern and Southern governments. This change was marked by the friendly meetings, in 1965, between the two Irish heads of government. They were the first exchanges of their kind between Dublin and Belfast.

The Northern Premier, Terence O'Neill, a member of an old Ulster landowning family, and a man of moderate views, had succeeded Brookborough as leader of the Unionist party and Premier of Northern Ireland in 1963, at a time when British-style welfare legislation and substantial British financial aid were achieving more impressive results than were currently possible in the Republic, with its limited resources. In Northern Ireland, however, the control of public affairs remained firmly in Unionist and Protestant hands and the Catholics, in general, remained in varying degrees alienated from Northern Ireland as a political entity. They had specific grievances about discrimination in employment, educational facilities, housing and the control of local councils. O'Neill hoped to lessen sectarian differences and improve North-South relations while retaining the existing constitutional and financial links with Great Britain. The rate of liberalization remained too slow to satisfy Catholic aspirations, while among right-wing Unionists, the members of the Orange Order and militant Protestants such as the Reverend Ian Paisley, any change was seen as a threat to Protestant interests and to the constitutional position of Northern Ireland within the United Kingdom.

The closing years of the 1960s were marked by a high measure of political stability in the Republic of Ireland; but there was in 1968 a rapid deterioration in the situation in Northern Ireland. There, the increasing assertiveness of the ultra-Unionists was matched by a growing defiance in Catholic and nationalist circles. The Northern Ireland Civil Rights Association (February 1967) was essentially moderate and middle class in its origins, but it attracted to its ranks small but very vocal radical elements, socialists as well as members of the IRA. The IRA, soon to be split again into left-wing ('Official') and right-wing ('Provisional') factions, saw in its involvement in the protest movement a means of recovering the influence it had lost as a result of the futile campaign against military and police posts in the late 1950s. The Civil Rights movement was largely concerned with

UNITED ULSTER UNIONIST COUNCIL

You Can't Have It Both Ways

COUNCIL OF IRELAND

BRITISH HERITAGE

Northern Ireland at the crossroads. For the Unionists there can be no compromise between the British and Irish choices. The middle way, if it exists, has yet to be found. (8)

reform within the Northern Ireland context, but it came increasingly to have political and nationalist implications. These trends became more obvious following serious clashes involving the police and civil rights marchers in Londonderry, in October and November 1968. It remained, however, possible to distinguish between the supporters of moderate change and the sustained and violent efforts of the IRA, though small in numbers, to transform the troubles in Northern Ireland into a revolutionary confrontation with British military power. The failure of O'Neill to secure a clear support for his policies in the Unionist party; his consequent resignation in 1969; and the serious rioting in Londonderry and Belfast in August 1969, opened the way for a tragic increase in political crime in Northern Ireland and a deepening of the divisions between the communities there.

The year 1970 was characterized by still greater violence, especially in Belfast, where relations between the British army and sections of the Catholic population in the working-class areas took on a hostile aspect. The Northern Ireland administration showed an increasing instability, with the Unionist party breaking down into moderate and extreme factions. Bombing campaigns launched by the Provisional IRA brought a new dimension of tragedy into Northern life and there followed equally destructive counter-attacks by the Protestant paramilitary groups. The introduction of internment for political suspects, in August 1971, only added new tensions and helped to alienate the nationalist population still further from the Northern Ireland administration. The confrontation

between the warring factions and the British army took on a more controversial form following the grim events of 'Bloody Sunday' in Londonderry on 30 January 1972, when thirteen people were shot dead in an encounter with paratroopers. The political crisis and the obvious inadequacy of the party in power, led the British Prime Minister, Edward Heath, to announce, in March 1972, the effective end of a Northern Ireland parliament and the imposition of direct rule from Westminster. It was the end of that ascendancy of Unionist power which had dominated the political and social life of Northern Ireland since its creation. But neither direct rule nor the subsequent disappointing attempts to give Northern Ireland a new and more equitable constitution provided the people of the North with the peace and order they had been denied for almost a decade. Though voices of moderation and reconciliation have been raised by Catholic and Protestant churchmen, the positive reactions to their appeals has been minimal among the militant factions. The Women's Peace Movement, which in 1976 had crossed sectarian boundaries, still offers some hope that reason rather than the assassin's gun will ultimately prevail.

In the Republic, the tragic and brutal events in Northern Ireland have had their repercussions, though, on the whole, the impact has been more muted than might have been expected, with relatively little popular involvement except when emotions ran high following 'Bloody Sunday'. There have been bombing incidents involving the loss of life in Dublin and a few border towns, and emergency measures have had to be taken by the government to curb the activities of the illegal IRA. Though all the major political parties have stressed that only a peaceful settlement in the North can ensure justice, the events in the North have had political consequences in the Republic. They led directly to a crisis within the Fianna Fail party in 1970, which resulted in the resignation or dismissal of ministers from the government against the background of a rather dramatic arms trial and allegations that people in high places were assisting the IRA militants in the North. The recriminations that followed and the echoes of a power struggle within the party contributed to the fall of Fianna Fail from office in March 1973. Jack Lynch, a Cork lawyer, who had succeeded Lemass on his retirement as Prime Minister, had to give way to Ireland's third coalition government. This time it was a combination of Fine Gael and the small Labour party with Liam Cosgrave, the leader of Fine Gael and the son of a founder of the old Irish Free State, as Taoiseach. Continuity still counted for much in Ireland even in disturbing, perhaps revolutionary times.

SELECT BIBLIOGRAPHY

1 Prehistoric Ireland

CASE, HUMPHREY 'Settlement-patterns in the North Irish Neolithic' in *Ulster Journal of Archaeology* 32 (1969), pp. 3–27

DE VALERA, R., and S. Ó NUALLÁIN *Survey of the megalithic tombs of Ireland*, Vols. 1–3 (Dublin, 1960, 1964, 1971)

DILLON, M., ed. *Early Irish Society* (Dublin, 1954)

EOGAN, G. 'Excavations at Knowth, Co. Meath' in *Proceedings of the Royal Irish Academy* 66c (1968), pp. 299–400; 74c (1974), pp. 11–112

EVANS, E. E. *Prehistoric and Early Christian Ireland* (London and New York, 1966)

—— *The Personality of Ireland* (London, 1973)

HARBISON, E. *The Archaeology of Ireland* (London and New York, 1976)

HERITY, M. *Irish Passage Graves* (Dublin and New York, 1974)

JACKSON, K. *The Oldest Irish Tradition: A Window on the Iron Age* (London and New York, 1964)

NEVILL, W. E. *Geology and Ireland* (Dublin, 1963)

NORMAN, E. R., and J. K. ST JOSEPH *The Early Development of Irish Society* (London, 1969)

O'KELLY, C. *Illustrated Guide to New Grange* (Wexford, 1967)

O'RIORDAIN, S. P. *Tara: The Monuments on the Hill* (Dundalk, 1954)

—— and G. DANIEL *New Grange and the Bend of the Boyne* (London and New York, 1964)

ORME, A. *Ireland* ('The World's Landscapes' 4) (London and Chicago, 1970)

PIGGOTT, S. *The Druids* (London and New York, 1975)

RAFTERY, J., ed. *The Celts* (Dublin, 1964)

2 The Early Irish Church

BYRNE, F. J. *Irish Kings and High-Kings* (London and New York, 1973)

HENRY, FRANÇOISE *Irish Art in the Early Christian Period to AD 800*

—— *Irish Art during the Viking Invasions, 800–1020 AD*

—— *Irish Art in the Romanesque Period, 1020–1170 AD* (London and New York, 1965–70)

HUGHES, KATHLEEN *The Church in Early Irish Society* (London, 1966, and New York, 1967)

—— *Early Christian Ireland: Introduction to the Sources* (London and New York, 1972)

—— and ANN HAMLIN *The Modern Traveller to the Early Irish Church* (London, 1976): aims to give an introduction to non-specialists who want to look intelligently at the sites

KENNEY, J. F. *The Sources for the Early History of Ireland: Ecclesiastical* (New York, 1929,

reprinted with addenda 1968): a fully annotated bibliography with substantial introductions to each section; still indispensable

Ó CORRÁIN, DONNCHA *Ireland before the Normans* (Dublin and London, 1972)

Translations of Irish poetry

CARNEY, J. *Medieval Irish Lyrics* (Dublin and Los Angeles, 1967)

GREENE, D., and F. O'CONNOR *A Golden Treasury of Irish Poetry, AD 600–1200* (London, 1967)

JACKSON, KENNETH *A Celtic Miscellany* (revised ed. Harmondsworth, 1971)

MEYER, KUNO *Ancient Irish Poetry* (London and New York, 1911)

MURPHY, GERARD *Early Irish Lyrics* (Oxford, 1957)

3 The Long Middle Ages

CHAMPNEYS, A. C. *Irish Ecclesiastical Architecture* (Dublin, 1910; reprinted Shannon and New York, 1970)

CONWAY, C. *The Story of Mellifont* (Dublin, 1958)

CURTIS, E. *A History of Medieval Ireland* (London, 1938)

GWYNN, A., and N. HADCOCK, *Medieval Religious Houses: Ireland* (London, 1970)

HENRY, F. *Irish Art in the Romanesque Period, 1020–1170 AD* (London and New York, 1970)

HUNT, J. *Irish Medieval Figure Sculpture, 1200–1600* (Dublin and London, 1974)

LEASK, H. G. *Irish Churches and Monastic Buildings*, 3 vols. (Dundalk, 1955–60)

—— *Irish Castles and Castellated Houses* (2nd ed. Dundalk, 1944)

LYDON, J. F. *The Lordship of Ireland in the Middle Ages* (Dublin, 1972)

—— *Ireland in the Later Middle Ages* (Dublin, 1973)

NICHOLLS, K. *Gaelic and Gaelicised Ireland in the Middle Ages* (Dublin, 1972)

OTWAY-RUTHVEN, A. J. *A History of Medieval Ireland* (London and New York, 1968)

STALLEY, R. A. *Architecture and Sculpture in Ireland, 1150–1350* (Dublin, 1971)

WATT, J. A. *The Church and the Two Nations in Medieval Ireland* (London, 1970)

—— *The Church in Medieval Ireland* (Dublin and London, 1972)

4 The End of the Old Order

BAGWELL, R. *Ireland under the Tudors*, 3 vols. (London, 1885–90; reprinted 1963)

BURKE, WILLIAM P. *The Irish Priests in the Penal Times* (Waterford, 1914; reprinted Shannon, 1968)

DE BREFFNY, B., and R. FFOLLIOTT, *The Houses of Ireland* (London and New York, 1975)

—— and G. MOTT *The Churches and Abbeys of Ireland* (London and New York, 1976)

DOWLING, P. J. *A History of Irish Education* (Cork, 1971)

EDWARDS, R. DUDLEY *Church and State in Tudor Ireland* (Dublin and New York, 1935)

FALLS, C. *Elizabeth's Irish Wars* (London, 1958)

FITZGERALD, B. *The Geraldines, an Experiment in Irish Government, 1169–1601* (London, 1951)

HILL, GEORGE *An Historical Account of the Plantation of Ulster at the Commencement of the Seventeenth Century, 1608–20* (Belfast, 1877)

MacCURTAIN, MARGARET *Tudor and Stuart Ireland* (Dublin and London, 1972)

MacLYSAGHT, EDWARD *Irish Life in the Seventeenth Century* (Cork, 1939; 3rd ed. Shannon, 1969)

MALINS, E. and THE KNIGHT OF GLIN *Lost Demesnes: Irish Landscape Gardening, 1660–1845* (London, 1976)

MAXWELL, CONSTANTIA *Irish History from Contemporary Sources, 1509–1610* (London, 1923)

MOODY, T. W. *The Londonderry Plantation, 1609–41* (Belfast, 1939)

MORTON, GRENFELL *Elizabethan Ireland* (London, 1971)

MURRAY, R. H. *Revolutionary Ireland and its Settlement* (London and New York, 1911)

PRENDERGAST, J. P. *Ireland from the Restoration to the Revolution, 1660–1690* (London, 1887)

QUINN, D. B. *The Elizabethans and the Irish* (New York, 1966)

RONAN, M. V. *The Reformation in Ireland under Elizabeth, 1558–80* (London and New York, 1930)

SILKE, J. J. *Ireland and Europe, 1559–1607* (Dundalk, 1966)

SIMMS, J. G. *The Williamite Confiscation in Ireland, 1690–1703* (London, 1956)

—— *Jacobite Ireland* (London, 1969)

5 The New Culture

ARNOLD, B. *Concise History of Irish Art* (London, 1969; reprinted 1977)

BENNETT, DOUGLAS *Irish Georgian Silver* (London, 1972)

BODKIN, THOMAS *Four Irish Landscape Painters* (Dublin and London, 1920)

CLARK, W. S. *The Irish Stage in the County Towns, 1720–1800* (Oxford and New York, 1965)

CRAIG, MAURICE *Dublin, 1660–1860* (London, Dublin and New York, 1952)

—— and THE KNIGHT OF GLIN *Ireland Observed* (Cork, 1970)

CROOKSHANK, ANNE, and THE KNIGHT OF GLIN *Irish Portraits, 1660–1860* (Paul Mellon Foundation for British Art, 1969)
—— *The Painters of Ireland, c. 1660–1920* (in the press)
CURRAN, C. P. *Dublin Decorative Plasterwork of the Seventeenth and Eighteenth Centuries* (London and New York, 1967)
DE BREFFNY, B., and R. FFOLLIOTT *The Houses of Ireland* (London and New York, 1975)
DIXON, HUGH *An Introduction to Ulster Architecture* (Belfast, 1975)
GUINNESS, DESMOND *Portrait of Dublin* (London and New York, 1967)
—— and W. RYAN *Irish Houses and Castles* (London, 1971)
JONES, BARBARA *Follies and Grottoes* (London, 1974)
PHELPS, WARREN *Irish Glass* (London, 1970)
STRICKLAND, W. G. *A Dictionary of Irish Artists*, 2 vols. (Dublin, 1913)
TASQUIN, ANTHONY (i.e. John Williams) *Memoirs of the Royal Academicians and an Authentic History of the Artists of Ireland* (first published 1796; reprinted with introduction by R. W. Lightbown, London, 1970)
TICHER, KURT *Irish Silver in the Rococo Period* (Shannon, 1972)
WALSH, T. J. *Opera in Dublin, 1705–1797: the Social Scene* (Dublin, 1973)

Specialist Articles
Apollo, October 1966: special issue on 'The Arts in Ireland'
BOYDELL, MARY 'Made for Convivial Clinking: 19th-century Anglo-Irish Glass' in *Country Life*, 26 September 1974
COLERIDGE, ANTHONY and DESMOND FITZGERALD 'Eighteenth-century Irish Furniture' in *Apollo*, October 1966
CONNER, née LONGFIELD, ELIZABETH 'Visits to Longueville, c. 1805–15' in *Irish Georgian Bulletin*, July-August-September 1960
CRAIG, MAURICE 'Irish Bookbinding' in *Apollo*, October 1966
FFOLLIOTT, ROSEMARY 'Household Stuff' in *The Irish Ancestor*, 1971
GLIN, THE KNIGHT OF 'A Family of Looking-Glass Merchants' in *Country Life*, 28 January 1971
GOODBODY, OLIVE C. 'Quaker Inventories' in *The Irish Ancestor*, 1971
GUINNESS, MRS DESMOND 'The Deliberate Follies of Ireland' in *Ireland of the Welcomes*, January-February 1972
LONGFIELD, ADA K. 'Early Irish Printed Fabrics' in *Country Life*, 7 December 1972
—— 'Irish Delft' in *Irish Georgian Bulletin*, July-December 1971
—— 'Samuel Dixon's Embossed Pictures of Flowers and Birds' in *Irish Georgian Bulletin*, October-December 1975
McPARLAND, EDWARD 'The Wide Streets Commissioners: their importance for Dublin architecture in the late 18th-early 19th century' in *Irish Georgian Bulletin*, January-March 1972
MORTIMER, MARTIN 'The Irish Mirror Chandelier' in *Country Life*, 16 December 1971
RUCH, JOHN 'Coade Stone in Ireland' in *Irish Georgian Bulletin*, October-December 1970
SEABY, WILFRED A. 'Finest Irish Williamite Glass' in *Country Life*, 9 December 1965
TOWNSHEND, FRANCIS 'Silver for Wine in Ireland' in *Country Life*, 29 June 1967

6 The Distressed Society
CONNELL, K. H. *Irish Peasant Society* (London, 1968, and New York, 1969)
CULLEN, L. M. *Life in Ireland* (London and New York, 1968)
—— *An Economic History of Ireland since 1660* (London and New York, 1972)
DE BREFFNY, B., and R. FFOLLIOTT, *The Houses of Ireland* (London and New York, 1975)
DONNELLY, JAMES S., JR *The Land and People of Cork in the Nineteenth Century* (London, 1975)
LEE, JOSEPH *The modernisation of Irish society, 1848–1918* (Dublin and London, 1973)
LYONS, F. S. L. *Ireland since the Famine* (London and New York, 1971)
MARTIN, F. X. (ed.) *Leaders and Men of the 1916 Rising* (London and New York, 1967)
MOODY, T. W. *The Ulster Question, 1603–1973* (1974)
—— and J. C. BECKETT (eds.) *Ulster since 1800* (second series, London, 1957)
NOWLAN, K. B. (ed.) *Travel and Transport in Ireland* (Dublin and New York, 1973)
O'BRIEN, C. C. (ed.) *The Shaping of Modern Ireland* (London, 1960)
Ó TUAMA, SEÁN (ed.) *The Gaelic League Idea* (1972)
Ó TUATHAIGH, GEARÓID *Ireland before the Famine, 1798–1848* (Dublin, 1972)
ZIMMERMANN, G. D. *Songs of Irish rebellion: political street ballads and rebel songs, 1780–1900* (Dublin, 1967)

7 The Celtic Revival
Literature
BOYD, ERNEST *Ireland's Literary Renaissance* (Dublin, London and New York, 1916)
BROWN, MALCOLM *The Politics of Irish Literature* (London and Seattle, 1972)
BUCKNELL UNIVERSITY PRESS (Lewisburg, Pa.) 'Irish Writers' series (in progress, 1970–)
ELLIS-FERMOR, UNA *The Irish Dramatic Movement* (London, 1954)
ELLMANN, RICHARD *James Joyce* (London and New York, 1959)
—— *Yeats: the Man and the Masks* (New York, 1948 and London, 1949)
FLANAGAN, THOMAS *The Irish Novelists, 1800–1850* (New York, 1959, and London, 1960)
GREGORY, LADY (AUGUSTA) *Our Irish Theatre* (London and New York, 1914)
HOGAN, ROBERT, and JAMES KILROY *The Irish Literary Theatre, 1899–1901* (Dublin, 1975)
HOWARTH, HERBERT *The Irish Writers* (London and New York, 1958)
KAVANAGH, PETER *The Story of the Abbey Theatre* (New York, 1950)
LOFTUS, RICHARD J. *Nationalism in Modern Anglo-Irish Poetry* (Madison, Wis., 1964)
MALONE, ANDREW E. *The Irish Drama* (London and New York, 1929)
MARCUS, PHILLIP L. *Yeats and the Beginning of the Irish Renaissance* (London and New York, 1970)
O'DRISCOLL, ROBERT, ed. *Theatre and nationalism in twentieth-century Ireland* (London, 1971)
ROBINSON, LENNOX *Ireland's Abbey Theatre* (London, 1951, and New York, 1952)
SKELTON, ROBIN, and ANN SADDLEMYER, eds. *The World of W. B. Yeats* (Seattle, 1967)
YEATS, W. B. *Autobiographies* (new ed. London, 1955)
—— *Explorations* (London, 1962, and New York, 1963)

The Visual Arts
BARRETT, CYRIL 'Irish Nationalism and Art' in *Studies* LXIV (Winter 1975), p. 256
BELL; BLETT; MATTHEW *Survey of Portaferry and Strangford* (Ulster Architectural Heritage Society, Belfast, 1969)
CURRAN, C. P. *Dublin Decorative Plasterwork of the Seventeenth and Eighteenth Centuries* (London and New York, 1967)
DAVIS, THOMAS *Literary and Historical Essays* (Dublin, 1846)
DUFFY, CHARLES GAVAN *Young Ireland* (London, 1869)
GAUGHAN, J. ANTHONY *Listowel and its Vicinity* (Naas, 1973)
A Guide through Glasnevin Cemetery (Dublin, 1879)
GWYNN, DENIS *Edward Martyn and the Irish Revival* (London, 1930)
KILLANIN, LORD, and MICHAEL V. DUIGNAN *The Shell Guide to Ireland* (London, 1967)
A Notice of St Patrick's Church, Jordanstown (privately published, 1868)
POTTERTON, HOMAN *Irish Church Monuments* (Belfast, 1975)
ROYAL IRISH ART UNION (Dublin), *Report, 1839–40*
RYNNE, ETIENNE 'The Revival of Irish Art in the Late Nineteenth and Early Twentieth Century' in *Topic* 24 (Washington and Jefferson College, Washington, Pa., Fall 1972)
STANTON, PHOEBE *Pugin* (London and New York, 1971)
STRICKLAND, W. G. *A Dictionary of Irish Artists* (reprinted Dublin, 1969)
TIERNEY, MARK, and JOHN CORNFORTH 'Glenstal Castle, Co. Limerick' in *Country Life* (3 October 1974)
WHITE, JAMES, and MICHAEL WYNNE *Irish Stained Glass* (Dublin, 1963)

Exhibition catalogues
Irish Industrial Exhibition, Leinster Lawn, Dublin, 1853 (building demolished)
Dublin International Exhibition, Leinster Lawn, Dublin, 1866
Irish Art in the Nineteenth Century, Rosc., 1971; Crawford Municipal School of Art, Cork, 31 October–29 December 1971
Irish Art 1900–1950, Rosc., 1975; Crawford Municipal School of Art, Cork, 1 December 1975–1 January 1976
Jack B. Yeats: A Centenary Exhibition, National Gallery of Ireland, Dublin, September–December 1971
Daniel Maclise, National Portrait Gallery, London, 3 March–6 April 1972; National Gallery of Ireland, Dublin, 5 May–18 June 1972

8 The Irish in America
ADAMS, W. F. *Ireland and Irish Emigration to the New World from 1815 to the Famine* (New York and London, 1932)
BOWEN, CROSWELL, and SHANE O'NEILL *The Curse of the Misbegotten: A Tale of the House of O'Neill* (New York, 1959, and London, 1960)
CLARK, WILLIAM BELL *Gallant John Barry* (New York, 1938)
DIBBLE, ROY F. *John L. Sullivan: An Intimate Narrative* (Boston, Mass., 1925)
ELLIS, ELMER *Mr Dooley's America* (New York, 1941)
ELLIS, MONSIGNOR JOHN TRACY *The Life of James Cardinal Gibbons*, 2 vols. (Milwaukee, 1952)
GIBSON, FLORENCE E. *The Attitudes of the New York Irish Toward State and National Affairs, 1848–1892* (New York, 1951)
KAHN, E. J. *The Merry Partners: The Age and Stage of Harrigan and Hart* (New York, 1955)
ROVERE, RICHARD *Senator Joe McCarthy* (New York, 1959, and London, 1960)
SCHLESINGER, ARTHUR *A Thousand Days* (Boston, Mass., and London, 1965)
SMITH, ALFRED E. *Up To Now – An Autobiography* (Garden City, New York, 1929)
TURNBULL, ANDREW *Scott Fitzgerald* (New York and London, 1962)

Select Bibliography 283

WERNER, M. R. *Tammany Hall* (New York, 1928)

WHALEN, RICHARD *The Founding Father: The Story of Joseph P. Kennedy* (New York, 1964, and London, 1965)

9 Modern Ireland

General surveys

LYONS, F. S. L. *Ireland since the Famine* (London and New York, 1971)

MURPHY, JOHN A. *Ireland in the Twentieth Century* (London, 1975)

Special studies

BARRITT, D. P., and C. F. CARTER *The Northern Ireland Problem* (London and New York, 1962)

BELL, J. BOWYER *The Secret Army: History of the IRA, 1916–1970* (London, 1970)

CARROLL, JOSEPH T. *Ireland in the War Years, 1939–1945* (New York and Newton Abbot, 1975)

CHUBB, BASIL *The Government and Politics of Ireland* (Stanford, 1970)

DE PAOR, LIAM *Divided Ulster* (Harmondsworth, 1970)

HARKNESS, D. W. *The Restless Dominion* (London and New York, 1969)

LONGFORD, EARL OF, and THOMAS P. O'NEILL *Eamon de Valera* (London, 1970, and New York, 1971)

MacMANUS, FRANCIS, ed., *The Years of the Great Test, 1926–39* (Cork, 1967)

MANNING, MAURICE *Irish Political Parties* (Dublin and London, 1972)

—— *The Blueshirts* (Dublin, 1970)

MEENAN, JAMES *The Irish Economy since 1922* (Liverpool, 1970)

MOODY, T. W., and J. C. BECKETT, eds. *Ulster since 1800* (first and second series, London, 1955 and 1957)

NOWLAN, KEVIN B., and T. DESMOND WILLIAMS, eds. *Ireland in the War Years and After, 1939–51* (Dublin, 1969, and Notre Dame, Indiana, 1970)

RIDDELL, PATRICK *Fire over Ulster* (London, 1970)

WHYTE, J. H. *Church and State in Modern Ireland, 1923–1970* (Dublin and New York, 1971)

SOURCES OF ILLUSTRATIONS

The page on which an illustration appears is shown by the first set of numerals in bold type, its plate or figure number by the second. Sources of photographs are given in italics. The following abbreviations have been used: BL, British Library, London; BM, British Museum, London; CPWI, Commissioners of Public Works in Ireland; GM, George Mott; ITB, Irish Tourist Board; NGI, National Gallery of Ireland, Dublin; NLI, National Library of Ireland, Dublin; NMI, National Museum of Ireland, Dublin; NPG, National Portrait Gallery, London; PB, drawn by Peter Bridgewater; V & A, Victoria and Albert Museum, London.

Frontispiece. Hibernia; engraving by W. Hollar from *De Hibernia et Antiquitatibus eius* by Sir James Ware, 2nd edition, 1658.

Introduction
9 1. Cliffs at Horn Head, Co. Donegal. *J. Allan Cash*
10 2. Bantry Bay, Co. Cork. *Edwin Smith*
3. Bog by the Military Road, near Sally Gap, Co. Wicklow. *Edwin Smith*
11 4. Luggala, Co. Wicklow. *ITB*
12 5. Ben Bulben from West Glencow, Co. Sligo. *Edwin Smith*
6. Upper Lake, Killarney, Co. Kerry. *ITB*

1 Prehistoric Ireland
21 1. Portal-dolmen, Proleek, Co. Louth; c.2000 BC. *CPWI*
22 2. Oval court of court-grave, Malinmore, Co. Donegal. *R. J. Welch, Ulster Museum, Belfast*
3. Saddle-quern, from New Grange, Co. Meath; c.2500 BC. *NMI*
4. Passage-grave interior, Fourknocks, Co. Meath; c.1800 BC. *CPWI*
23 5. Corbelled roof of main chamber, New Grange, Co. Meath; c.2500 BC. *ITB*
6. Entrance stone to passage-grave, New Grange, Co. Meath; c.2500 BC. *CPWI*
7. Main chamber of passage-grave, New Grange, Co. Meath; c.2500 BC. *CPWI*
24 8. Gold collar or gorget, from Gleninsheen, Co. Clare; c.700 BC. *NMI*
9. Gold lunula, from Mangerton, Co. Kerry; 1800–1500 BC. *BM*
25 10. Gold boat, from Broighter, Co. Londonderry; probably 1st century AD. *NMI*
11. Gold torque, from Inishowen, Co. Donegal; c.1200–900 BC. *BM*
12. Decorated hollow gold collar, from Broighter, Co. Londonderry. *NMI*
26 13. Decorated stone, Knowth, Co. Meath; c.2500–2000 BC. *CPWI*
14. Detail of ornament on gold dress-fastener, from Clones, Co. Monaghan. *NMI*
15. Decorated stone, Knowth, Co. Meath; c.2500–2000 BC. *CPWI*
16. Decorated stone, Knowth, Co. Meath; c.2500–2000 BC. *CPWI*
17. Decorated stone, Knowth, Co. Meath; c.2500–2000 BC. *CPWI*
18. Decorated stone basin, Knowth, Co. Meath; c.2500–2000 BC. *CPWI*
27 19. Cairn cemetery looking west, Carnbane West, Lough Crew, Co. Meath; c.3000 BC to 1st century AD. *Director in Aerial Photography, University of Cambridge*
20. Hill of Tara, Co. Meath. *Director in Aerial Photography, University of Cambridge*
21. Cultivation ridges in the townland of Carrownaglogh, Co. Mayo; probably Bronze Age. *Robin Glasscock*
28 22. Staigue Fort, Co. Kerry; probably Early Iron Age. *ITB*

29 23. Carved stone figure with two faces, Boa Island, Lough Erne, Co. Fermanagh. *Robin Glasscock*
24. Hill-fort Grianan of Ailech, Co. Donegal, probably first centuries AD. *Supplied by E. Estyn Evans*
30 25. Standing stones, Waterville, Co. Kerry; probably Bronze Age. *J. Allan Cash*
26. Cairn, Ballymacgibbon, Co. Mayo; Stone Age. *Edwin Smith*
27. The Long Stone, Punchestown, Co. Kildare. *CPWI*
28. Ogham stone, Kilcoolaght East, Co. Kerry; after 300 BC. *CPWI*
31 29. Stone Circle, Drombeg, Co. Cork; 1st century BC–1st century AD. *CPWI*
30. Navan Fort (called Emain Macha in Irish), Co. Armagh; built probably c.300 BC. *Director in Aerial Photography, University of Cambridge*
32 31. Dun Aengus, Aran Island, Co. Galway. *Director in Aerial Photography, University of Cambridge*
32. Three-faced stone head, from Corleck, Co. Cavan; Early Iron Age. *NMI*
33. Decorated stone, Turoe, Co. Galway; probably 3rd–2nd century BC. *CPWI*
33 1. Detail of spiral pattern on entrance stone, New Grange, Co. Meath; c.2500 BC. PB
35 2. Plans of four types of court-graves. PB
36 3. Plans of three passage-graves. PB
38 4. Plan and sketch of typical wedge-grave, with remains of cairn. Drawn by E. Estyn Evans
39 5. Diagram of Ogham alphabet. PB
44 6. Plan and section of a souterrain, Donaghmore, Co. Louth. PB

2 The Early Irish Church
49 1. The Arrest of Christ; miniature from Book of Kells, second half of 8th or early 9th century, f. 114r. Trinity College Library, Dublin. *Green Studio*
50 2. Initial from the *Cathach* of Saint Columba; early 7th century. *Royal Irish Academy, Dublin*
3. Tinned bronze ringbrooch and pin; 500–600 AD. *NMI*
4. Detail of Ardagh Chalice; silver and millefiore glass, early 8th century. *NMI*
5. The Crucifixion; cast bronze plaque, probably a book cover, 8th century. *NMI*
6. Detail of belt-shrine from Moylough, Co. Sligo, showing the buckle counter-plate; 8th century. *NMI*
51 7. Strainer from Moylarg, Co. Antrim; bronze, c.500–600 AD. *NMI*
8. North cross, Ahenny, Co. Tipperary; 8th century. *ITB*
52 9. Page from Book of Durrow, 7th century, f. 3v. Trinity College Library, Dublin. *Green Studio*
53 10. St John; miniature from

MacDurnan Gospels, which belonged to MacTornain, abbot of Armagh, at end of 9th century, f. 170v. *Lambeth Palace Library, London*
11. David and Goliath; miniature from Southampton Psalter, 10th century. *Courtesy of Master and Fellows of St John's College, Cambridge*
12. Detail of Tara Brooch; decorated gilt bronze, early 8th century. *NMI*
54 13. Gallarus Oratory, Dingle peninsula, Co. Kerry. *Edwin Smith*
14. Male figures; detail of book shrine *Breac Maodhóg*, 11th or 12th century. *NMI*
15. Female figures; detail of book shrine *Breac Maodhóg*, 11th or 12th century. *NMI*
16. Monastic site of Kiltiernan, Co. Galway. *Director in Aerial Photography, University of Cambridge*
55 17. Relief showing Adam and Eve, and murder of Abel; detail from cross of Abbot Muiredach (died 922), Monasterboice, Co. Louth. *Edwin Smith*
18. Cross of Abbot Muiredach (died 922), Monasterboice, Co. Louth. *CPWI*
19. Detail of crozier of abbots of Clonmacnoise; early 12th century. NMI. *ITB*
56 20. Temple Benen, Inishmore, Aran Islands, Co. Galway. *GM*
21. Monastery on Skellig Michael looking towards Little Skellig, Co. Kerry. *ITB*
57 1. Gravestone from Clonmacnoise, Co. Offaly, with inscription *Orait do Dainéil*, 'A Prayer for Daniel'. PB
60 2. Interlaced animal motif from Book of Durrow, mid-7th century, f. 192v. Trinity College Library, Dublin. PB
61 3. Initial from Book of Durrow, St Mark's Gospel, mid-7th century. *Trinity College Library, Dublin*
62 4. Animal relief from Ardross, 8th century. Inverness Museum. PB
5. Animal; detail from Book of Kells, late 8th or early 9th century. Trinity College Library, Dublin. PB
65 6. The four symbols of the Evangelists; page from Book of Armagh, early 9th century, f. 32v. *Trinity College Library, Dublin*
69 7. Reconstruction of a 12th-century monastery; after a painting by Brian O'Halloran. PB

3 The Long Middle Ages
73 1. View through arch of fountain house, c.1200, to cloister, Mellifont, Co. Louth. *Tony Stone Associates – Photo Noel Habgood*
74 2. Detail of door, c.1167, Nun's Church, Clonmacnoise, Co. Offaly. *Belzeaux*
3. Round tower at Timahoe, Co. Laois; 12th century. *ITB*
4. East face of high cross with figure of bishop, Dysert O'Dea, Co. Clare; 12th century. *CPWI*
5. Detail of shrine of St Patrick's Bell; between 1094 and 1105. *NMI*

285

75 6. Detail of chancel arch, late 12th century, Tuam Cathedral, Co. Galway. *Belzeaux*

7. Gable above west door, late 12th century, Clonfert Cathedral, Co. Galway. *Belzeaux*

8. Interior of Cormac's Chapel, Rock of Cashel, Co. Tipperary; 1127–34. *Belzeaux*

9. St Molaise; oak statue from Inishmurray, Co. Sligo, c.1250–1300. *NMI*

76 10. Trim Castle, Co. Meath; c.1220. *Tony Stone Associates – Photo Noel Habgood*

11. Richard II sailing for England; miniature from Jean Creton's chronicle, French, c.1405. MS. Harley 1319 f. 18. *BL*

77 12. Detail of Cross of Cong, from Co. Mayo; made for Turlough O'Connor, High King of Erin, c.1122–36. *NMI*

13. Irish king and subjects eating mare's flesh; miniature from *Topographia Hiberniae* by Giraldus Cambrensis, English, 13th century. MS. Laud. Misc. 720 f. 226r. *Bodleian Library, Oxford*

14. Irishman decapitates mare; miniature from *Topographia Hiberniae* by Giraldus Cambrensis, English, 13th century. MS. Laud. Misc. 720 f. 225v. *Bodleian Library, Oxford*

78 15. Nave, early 13th century, Christ Church Cathedral, Dublin. *GM*

16. Vaulted ceiling of the Shrine of the True Cross, mid-15th century, Holy Cross Abbey, Co. Tipperary. *GM*

17. Tomb niche, 15th century, Kilconnell Friary, Co. Galway. *Roger Stalley*

79 18. Ross Erilly Friary, Co. Galway; begun c.1498. *GM*

19. Donor kneeling before archbishop and saints Peter and Paul; 15th-century tomb sculpture, Strade, Co. Mayo. *CPWI*

20. 8th Earl of Ormonde and Countess; tomb effigy, St Canice's Cathedral, Kilkenny. *ITB*

21. St James the Less; tomb panel, Jerpoint, Co. Kilkenny, from workshop of Rory O'Tunney. *J. Fiennes*

80 22. Detail of crozier of Conor O'Dea, Bishop of Limerick; probably by Thomas O'Carryd, 1418. Bishop of Limerick. *Goldsmiths Company, London*

23. Initial; from the Psalter of Stephen de Derby, between 1349 and 1382. MS. Rawl. G. 185 f. 81v. *Bodleian Library, Oxford*

81 1. City of Cork; illustration from *Pacata Hibernia* by Stafford, 1633. PB

82 2. Plan of Cistercian abbey of Mellifont, Co. Louth. PB

86 3. Irish foot-soldier of the reign of Edward I (1272–1307). Chapter House Liber/A. *Public Record Office, London*

88 4. Athenry Castle, Co. Galway; illustration from *Antiquities of Ireland* by Grose, vol. I, 1791.

93 5. The meeting of Thomas, Earl of Gloucester and Art MacMurrough; miniature by French painter, c.1401–5, to Jean Creton's chronicle. MS. Harley 1319 f. 9. *BL*

94 6. Tower houses at Carrickfergus, Co. Antrim; detail of drawing by John Dunstall, 1612. MS. Cotton Augustus I ii f. 41. *BL*

95 7. Castle of Glin; detail of drawing, early 17th century. MS. Carew 635, f. 141a. *Lambeth Palace Library, London*

97 8. Initial; from Book of Ballymote, made for MacDonogh, Lord of Coran, c.1390, f. 22 *Royal Irish Academy, Dublin*

4 The End of the Old Order

101 1. Walter Devereux, 1st Earl of Essex (1541?–76); English School, 1572. Montacute House, Yeovil. *NPG*

102 2. Obverse of the Great Seal of Ireland,

c.1585; drawing by Nicholas Hilliard (c.1547–1619). *BM*

3. Charles Blount, Lord Mountjoy, Lord Lieutenant of Ireland (1563–1606); engraving, c.1603, by T. Cockson. *BM*

4. View of Carrickfergus; drawing, late 16th century. *BL*

103 5. A group of Irish; watercolour by Lucas de Heere, c.1575. *University Library, Ghent*

6. Soldier, from the Charter of Queen Elizabeth I to the City of Dublin, 1582–3, illustrated in Gilbert's Facsimiles, 1874–84

7. Irish kerns, c.1540–50; woodcut, 16th century. Douce Collection, *Ashmolean Museum, Oxford*

104 8. Fort and castle of Charlemont, built 1624 by Sir Toby, later Lord, Caulfield; watercolour. MS. Add. 24200 f. 39. *BM*

9. The fort of Culmore. MS. Carew 634 f. 11v, 1624. *Lambeth Palace Library, London*

10. The siege of Enniskillen, 1594; contemporary watercolour. MS. Cotton Augustus I ii f. 39. *BL*

105 11. Sir Thomas Lee (d.1601), Captain General of Kern of Ireland, dressed in Irish garb; painting by Marcus Gheeraerts, 1594. Collection Captain Loel Guinness, on loan to Tate Gallery, London. *E. Tweedy*

106 12. Oliver Plunkett, Catholic Archbishop of Armagh (1629–81); painting attributed to Garrett Morphey (fl.1680–1716). *NGI*

13. James Butler, 1st Duke of Ormonde (1610–88); detail of painting after Lely, c.1665. *NPG*

14. James II landing at Kinsale, 1689; contemporary Dutch engraving. *BM*

107 15. The Battle of the Boyne, 1690; painting by Jan Wyck (c.1640–1702). *NGI*

16. Louis XIV welcoming James II and his entourage to St Germain-en-Laye, 1690; etching by Romeyn de Hooghe (1645–1708). *BM*

108 17. The Loftus Cup; silver, made 1593 from Great Seal of Ireland, commissioned by Adam Loftus, Lord Chancellor of Ireland and Archbishop of Armagh (1553?–1605). *Ulster Museum, Belfast*

18. Adam Loftus, Lord Chancellor of Ireland, 1st Viscount Loftus (1568?–1643); anonymous English painting, 1619. *NGI*

19. Richard Boyle, first Earl of Cork (1566–1643); miniature by Isaac Oliver (c.1568–1617). *NPG*

109 1. The Seal of the Catholic Confederacy, 1642

110 2. Irish feasting in the open air; illustration from *Image of Irelande* by John Derrick, 1581

111 3. Three armed Irishmen; detail of drawing by Albrecht Dürer, 1521. *Bildarchiv Preussischer Kulturbesitz*

112 4. Irish friar blessing Irish thief; detail of illustration from *Image of Irelande* by John Derrick, 1581

5. Profile of Irish solidier; illustration from *De Hibernia et Antiquitatibus eius* by Sir James Ware, 2nd edition 1658

114 6. Initial with portrait of Queen Mary Tudor, from patent bestowing Earldom of Kildare on Gerald FitzGerald, 1554, illustrated in Gilbert's Facsimiles 1874–84

115 7. Catechism in Irish, published in Louvain, 1645. *NLI*

117 8. Page from Council Book of town of Galway, 1632, illustrated in Gilbert's Facsimiles, 1874–84

118 9. Hugh O'Neill, Earl of Tyrone; illustration from *La Spada d'Orione Stellata nel Cielo di Marte* by Primo Damaschino, 1680

120 10. Plan of the London Vintners' Company township of Bellaghy, Ulster, 1622. MS. Carew 634 f. 74 (detail). *Lambeth Palace Library, London*

121 11. View of Trinity College, founded 1592. MS. Dinely 392. *Trinity College Library, Dublin*

122 12. 'Irelandes Lamentation'; broadsheet published London, 1647, 669 f. 11/4. *BL*

123 13. Attack on Drogheda, 1649; contemporary print. *BM*

124 14. Tyrconnell arming Papists; satirical playing card, c.1689. Willshire cat E 191. *BM*

5 The New Culture

129 1. Speaker Foster with his family outside Oriel Temple, Drogheda, 1786; watercolour by J. J. Barralet (c.1747–1815). Collection Viscount Massareene and Ferrard, *NPG*

130 2. View of Waterford; painting by William van der Hagen (fl.1715–45). Collection Waterford Corporation. *Ulster Museum, Belfast*

3. View of Stradbally, Co. Leix: detail of anonymous painting, c.1740. Collection Major E. A. S. Cosby. *Harsch*

131 4. Leinster House, Dublin; engraving by James Malton (c.1766–1803) from his *Picturesque and Descriptive View of the City of Dublin*, 1794. V & A

5. Interior of Trinity College Library, 1793; engraving by James Malton (c.1766–1803) from his *Picturesque and Descriptive View of the City of Dublin*, 1794. V & A

6. View of Carton, Co. Kildare; painting by William van der Hagen (fl.1715–45). Collection Nall-Cain. *Harsch*

132 7. View of Powerscourt, Co. Wicklow; painting by George Barret (1728–84). Collection Mr and Mrs P. Mellon, *Yale Center for British Art*

8. Mount Ievers Court, Co. Clare; designed by John Rothery, built 1731–7. *William Ryan*

133 9. Castletown, Co. Kildare; designed by Alessandro Galilei and Edward Pearce, built 1719–32. *Brian Lynch, ITB*

134 10. Group with Tom Conolly and his friends hunting, 1768; black and white chalk on paper by Robert Healy (c.1743–71). Collection Hon. Desmond Guinness

11. The family of Thomas Bateson, 1762; painting by Philip Hussey (1713–83). *Ulster Museum, Belfast*

12. Sheet of water at Carton, Co. Kildare, with 2nd Duke of Leinster and his Duchess about to board a boat; painting by Thomas Roberts (1749–78). Collection Hon. Desmond Guinness. *Harsch*

135 13. Windham Quin (1717–89) with his dog; painting by Stephen Slaughter (1697–1765). Collection the Dunraven Limerick Estates Co. *NPG*

14. Two ladies at a harpsichord, c.1740; painting by James Latham (1696–1747). Collection John Leslie. *NPG*

15. Lord Granard having his wig powdered; painting by Herbert Pugh (fl.1758–88). Collection Earl of Granard

136 16. North Gate, Cork, with Lord Barrymore's carriage and pair; painting by Nathaniel Grogan (c.1740–1807). Collection Alan White. *Harsch*

17. State Ball at Dublin Castle in the 1730s; anonymous painting. Collection Colonel N. G. Stopford-Sackville. *Eileen Tweedy*

137 18. Miss Sarah Cosby, c.1740; painting by James Latham (1696–1747). Collection Major E. A. S. Cosby

19. Charles Coote, Earl of Bellamont

(1738–1800) in robes of the Order of the Bath; painting by Joshua Reynolds, 1773. *NGI*

138 20. Plaster decoration by Robert West, *c*.1755, 20 Lower Dominick St, Dublin. *GM*

21. Figure of Faith; plaster statue by Bartholomew Cramillion, 1755, Rotunda Hospital Chapel. *ITB*

22. Detail of quilt embroidered and signed by Martha Lennox, 1712. *Ulster Museum, Belfast*

23. Silver coffee pot; Dublin, *c*.1765. Private collection

24. Archbishop Cobbe's mammoth glass goblet, with figure of William III; *c*.1745. *Ulster Museum, Belfast*

25. Wood carving on organ balcony; attributed to John Houghton, *c*.1725. St Michan's Church, Dublin

139 26. Dining room, Bantry House, Co. Cork. *Edwin Smith*

140 27. Capel Street, Dublin, 1800; detail of watercolour by James Malton (*c*.1766–1803). V & A

141 28. 2nd Lord Aldborough, on his horse Pomposo, reviewing the Volunteers in Belan Park; detail of painting, 1780–81, by Francis Wheatley (1747–1801). National Trust, Waddesdon Manor. *Eileen Tweedy*

142 29. The Custom House built by James Gandon, 1781–91; detail of watercolour by James Malton (*c*.1766–1803). *NGI*

30. The Casino, Marino, Clontarf, built by William Chambers for Lord Charlemont, *c*.1760; engraving after F. Wheatley, 1783, from T. Milton's *Views from seats in Ireland*, 1783–93

31. James Gandon; portrait by William Cuming (1769–1852) and Tilly Kettle (1735–86). *NGI*

143 32. The River Bann; one of fourteen colossal heads, *c*.1802, by Edward Smyth (1749–1812), on the Custom House, Dublin. *CPWI*

33. Rutland Square with Charlemont House, 1793; engraving by James Malton (*c*.1766–1803) from his *Picturesque and Descriptive View of the City of Dublin*, 1794. V & A

144 34. Self-portrait of the artist and his wife, *c*.1800–3; painting by Robert Fagan (1767–1816). Collection Mrs John Hunt. *Harsch*

35. *Battle of Ballinahinch*, 1798; painting by Thomas Robinson (d.1810), signed and dated 1798. *NGI*

145 36. Self-portrait (head *c*.1780, the remainder 1804); painting by James Barry (1741–1806). *NGI*

37. An old gentleman; miniature on ivory signed and dated 1805 by John Comerford (*c*.1770–1832). V & A

146 38. The 4th Earl of Bristol, Bishop of Derry (1730–1803) on the Janiculum Hill, Rome; pastel by Hugh Douglas Hamilton (*c*.1739–1808). Collection the Marquess of Bristol. *NPG*

39. The Earl of Charleville; detail of monumental tomb by John Van Nost the Younger (d.1787), Tullamore, Co. Offaly. *Courtauld Institute of Art, London*

40. Christopher Hewetson (*c*.1739–98) with the bust of Gavin Hamilton; painting by Anton Raphael Mengs (1728–79). Wallraf-Richartz Museum, Cologne. *Rheinisches Bildarchiv*

147 41. Canova in his studio with the painter H. Tresham, R. A., *c*.1790; pastel on paper by Hugh Douglas Hamilton (*c*.1739–1808). Collection H. Farmar. *NPG*

42. Pope Clement XIV, 1773; detail of marble bust by Christopher Hewetson (*c*.1739–98). V & A

43. Jonathan Swift (1667–1745); marble bust by John Van Nost the Younger (d.1787). *NGI*

148 44. Cover of *The Gentleman and Citizens Almanack*, Dublin, 1779. V & A

45. Detail of pulpit; designed by Francis Johnston, carved by Richard Stewart, St Werburgh's Church of Ireland, Dublin. *GM*

46. Irish mirror chandelier, 1785–90. Courtesy Delomosne and Son, London

47. Goblin mask; carved detail on table, *c*.1740. NMI. *GM*

48. China bowl with open basket-work sides, decorated in blue; by Peter Shee, Dublin, 1752–7. *BM*

49. Mask; carved on table, *c*.1750. *GM*

50. Decanter with inscription *Ireland for Ever*; Irish glass, *c*.1800. *Courtesy Delomosne and Son, London*

51. Silver dish ring; by David Peter, Dublin, 1763. *Private collection*

52. Silver tea caddy with hinged lid surmounted by ivory finial; by Matthew West, Dublin, 1773. *Private collection*

149 1. Design for a country house from *Useful and Ornamental Designs* by Richard Morrison, 1793. *NLI*

152 2. The Conolly Folly, designed 1740, probably by Richard Castle; engraving from Noble and Keenan's map of Co. Kildare, 1752

155 3. Colganstown, Co. Dublin (detail). *Drawn by Maurice Craig and Derry O'Connell*

157 4. 'Taste à la Mode'; illustration from *Hibernian Magazine*, Dublin, 1790. *BL*

160 5. Three-decker pulpit similar to one in Kilbixy Church, Co. Westmeath; drawing by Francis Johnston. *NLI*

163 6. Review of Volunteers in Phoenix Park, 1781; detail of linen furniture fabric, Leixlip factory, 1782. *NMI*

6 The Distressed Society

173 1. *The Emigrant*; painting, 1871, by Erskine Nicol (1825–1904). *National Gallery of Scotland, Edinburgh*

174 2. Machinery for flax bleaching; print by W. Hincks, 1791. V & A

3. *The Blind Piper*; painting by J. P. Haverty (1794–1864). *NGI*

4. *The Festival of the Seven Churches, Glendalough*; painting, *c*.1813, by Joseph Peacock (1783–1837). *Ulster Museum, Belfast*

175 5. Kitchen Interior; painting by J. G. Mulvany (*c*.1766–1838). *NGI*

6. Bianconi long car; print, 1856, after a drawing by M. A. Hayes. *NGI*

176 7–11. Five scenes of peasant life near Youghal, Co. Cork; drawings by Sampson Twogood Roch, 1831. Private collection

177 12. Evicted family. Lawrence Collection, *NLI*

13. Eviction scene. *NLI*

178 14. Cutting turf. *NLI*

15. Puck Fair, Killorglin, Co. Kerry. *NLI*

179 16. Fisherman with coracle, Co. Donegal. *NLI*

17. Spinning wool, Cliffony, Co. Sligo, *c*.1900. Stone Collection, *Birmingham Reference Library*

18. Irish harvester's dinner. *Ulster Folk and Transport Museum, Belfast*

19. Grinding corn in quern, Inishmurry, Co. Sligo, *c*.1900. Stone Collection, *Birmingham Reference Library*

180 20. O'Connell Street, Dublin, after 1916 Easter Rising. *NLI*

21. Anti-Home-Rule big gun brigade of Portadown, Co. Armagh, September 1912. *Radio Times Hulton Picture Library, London*

181 1. 'The Triple Alliance – Famine,

Eviction, Coercion'; Cartoon from *Weekly Freeman*, 1885–6. *BM*

182 2. Portrait of an Irish chief; cartoon by James Gillray, published 10 July 1798. *BM*

183 3. Pattern for handwoven damask cloth; *c*.1790–1820, for Coulson of Lisburn. *Public Record Office of Northern Ireland*

184 4. Irish cabin, from *Agriculture Ancient and Modern* by S. Copland, London, 1866

188 5. Daniel O'Connell as Hercules; cartoon from *Fireside Journal*, London, 12 August 1843. *BL*

190 6. Famine in Ireland – funeral at Skibbereen; engraving after a sketch by H. Smith, from *Illustrated London News*, 30 January 1847

191 7. 'A terrible record'; cartoon from *Weekly Freeman*, 2 July 1881

194 8. 'The genius of the bill'; cartoon from *Weekly Freeman*, 16 April 1881

195 9. 'An old story retold'; cartoon from *Weekly Freeman*, 10 January 1885

7 The Celtic Revival

201 1. Cover of *The Secret Rose* by W. B. Yeats, 1897; design by Althea Gyles

202 2. *Reading 'The Nation'*; painting by Henry McManus (*c*.1810–78). *NGI*

3. *The Aran Fisherman's Drowned Child*; painting, 1843, by Frederick Burton (1816–1900). *NGI*

4. *The Marriage of Strongbow and Eva*; painting, 1854, by Daniel Maclise (1806–70). *NGI*

203 5. The west side of the West Cross, Monasterboice, Co. Louth; illustration from *Sculptured Crosses of Ancient Ireland* by H. O'Neill, 1857

6. *The Blind Girl at the Holy Well*; engraved by H. T. Ryall from a watercolour of 1840 by Frederick Burton (1816–1900). *BM*

7. *Pilgrims at Clonmacnoise*; painting by G. Petrie (1790–1866). *NGI*

204 8. Tabernacle door at St Michael's Church, Ballinasloe; by Mia Cranwill, *c*.1900. *GM*

9. Detail of vestment from Loughrea Cathedral, Co. Galway; designed by Evelyn Gleeson and made in Dun Emer workshop *c*.1903–10. *GM*

205 10. Detail of stained glass window at Honan Chapel, University College, Cork; designed *c*.1915 by Harry Clarke (1889–1931). *GM*

206 11. West front of Honan Chapel, University College, Cork; by James F. McMullen, 1915. *GM*

12. St Patrick's, Jordanstown, Co. Antrim; 1866, by W. H. Lynn. *Historic Monuments Branch, Belfast*

13. Interior of St Michael and All Angels, Clane, Co. Kildare, 1833; by James Franklin Fuller. *GM*

14. Tomb of Archbishop McCabe, Glasnevin cemetery, Dublin; built by G. C. Ashlin, 1887. *GM*

207 15. Dromore Castle, Co. Limerick; built by E. W. Godwin, 1867–9. *GM*

16. Monument to Carolan (1670–1738), St Patrick's Cathedral, Dublin; relief by John Valentine Hogan, erected 1874 by Sydney, Lady Morgan. *Courtauld Institute of Art, London*

17. Capital, by Michael Shortall, *c*.1900, in nave of Loughrea Cathedral, built 1897–1903. *GM*

18. Stone owl in quadrangle, University College, Cork, by Benjamin Woodward. *GM*

208 19. St Brendan; stained glass window by Sarah Purser (1848–1943), Loughrea Cathedral, Co. Galway. *GM*

20. St Patrick; sodality banner designed 1903 by Jack Butler Yeats (1871–1957), Loughrea Cathedral, Co. Galway. *GM*
21. Mosaic floor; *c.*1915, Honan Chapel, University College, Cork. *GM*
209 22. Symbol of St Matthew, detail of dossal, *c.*1916, by Evelyn Gleeson and Dun Emer Guild. Honan Chapel, University College, Cork. *GM*
23. Cockerel; stained glass, 1948, by Evie Hone (1894–1955). *Municipal Gallery of Modern Art, Dublin*
24. Wall painting in Dominican chapel, Dun Laoghaire, Co. Dublin; by Sister Concepta Lynch, *c.*1920. *GM*
210 25. J. M. Synge, April 1905; print by E. Walker after drawing by John Butler Yeats (1839–1922), published by Cuala Press. Private collection
26. Lady Gregory, 1913; lithograph by Flora Lion (1852–1932). *NPG*
27. *Homage to Sir Hugh Lane* (W. B. Yeats, D. O'Brien, T. Bodkin, 'A.E.' (George Russell), W. Hutcheson-Poe, T. Kelly, R. Caulfield-Orpen); painting by J. Keating (b.1889). *Municipal Gallery of Modern Art, Dublin*
211 28. A scene from *Cathleen ni Houlihan*, by Yeats, Abbey Theatre, with Marie O'Neill as Bridget Gillane, Frank J. Fay as Peter Gillane, Sara Allgood as Cathleen ni Houlihan and J. M. Kerrigan as Michael Gillane; drawing by Ben Bay. *NGI*
29. W. B. Yeats, 1903; pastel by George Russell. *NGI*
30. Abbey Theatre programme
31. Scene from *Riders to the Sea* by J. M. Synge, Abbey Theatre, 1906, with Brigit O'Dempsey, Sara Allgood and Maire O'Neill
212 32. Grafton Street, Dublin, *c.*1900. Lawrence Collection. *NLI*
33. Four generations of Joyces, Paris, 1938: James Joyce with his son Giorgio and grandson Stephen under the portrait of his father John Stanislaus by Patrick Tuohy. *Gisèle Freund – John Hillelson*
213 1. Title page detail of *Spirit of the Nation*, 2nd edition, 1843
215 2. Title page, by Margaret Stokes, of *Cromlech on Howth* by Samuel Ferguson, 1861
217 3. Title page of *Young Ireland*, March 1881. *BL*
219 4. Illustration from *A Patrick's Day Hunt*, by Martin Ross and E. Oe. Somerville, published Archibald Constable and Co. Ltd, Westminster
222 5. Sir Hugh Lane, J. M. Synge, W. B. Yeats and Lady Gregory, 1907; cartoon by William Orpen (1878–1931). *NPG*
225 6. W. B. Yeats presenting G. Moore to the Queen of the Fairies; cartoon by Max Beerbohm, *c.*1900. *Municipal Gallery of Modern Art, Dublin*
228 7. Illustration by Daniel Maclise (1806–1870) to *Irish Melodies* by Thomas Moore, 1866 edition
230 8. Ardagh Chalice sugar bowl with matching tongs, by E. Johnson in *The Artist*, January 1896. *NLI*
231 9. Casket of bog-oak with silver-gilt mountings; from *Illustrated Catalogue to Exhibition of Art and Industry*, Dublin, 1853, reproduced *Art Journal*, 1853
233 10. Anna Liffey; illustration from *A New Song called Anna Liffey*, printed for E. R. McClintock Dix by Cuala Press, 1907
234 11. 'Éire Page' by Art O'Murnaghan, 1922. *NMI*

8 The Irish in America
237 1. Immigrants disembarking at the Battery, Castle Garden; detail of painting by

Samuel Waugh, *c.*1855. *Museum of the City of New York*
238 2. Charles Carroll of Carrollton (1737–1832); painting, *c.*1830, by William James Hubard (1807–62). *Metropolitan Museum of Art, Rogers Fund*
3. The building of Brooklyn Bridge; drawing by W. P. Snyder from *Harper's Weekly*, 24 November 1877
4. *King Andrew The First* (President Andrew Jackson); lithograph, 1832. *Library of Congress, Washington D.C.*
5. 'The Power Behind the Throne': John T. Hoffman seated with 'Boss' William Tweed to his right and Peter Sweeny to his left; cartoon by T. Nast from *Harper's Weekly*, 29 October 1870
239 6. St Patrick's Cathedral; photograph, 1894. *Museum of the City of New York*
7. Mullen's Alley; photograph by Jacob A. Riis, *c.*1888–9. *Museum of the City of New York*
8. Steelworkers erecting Lincoln Liberty Building, Broad and Chestnut Streets, Philadelphia, 1926. *O. E. Hoppé, Mansell Collection, London*
240 9. St Patrick's Day parade at Union Square, New York; lithograph, 1874. The J. Clarence Davies Collection, *Museum of the City of New York*
10–13. Paddy O'Rourke, Pat O'Rourke, Officer O'Rourke, Hon. Mr Rourke; cards, copyright 1882 by Geo. Topp. Collection J. J. Appel
241 14. Charles Stewart Parnell in the House of Representatives; cartoon by J. A. W. from *Puck*, 28 January 1880
15. Lady Lavery as Cathleen ni Houlihan; painting by Sir John Lavery (1856–1941), commissioned 1923 for use on Irish banknotes. Collection Central Bank of Ireland
242 16. 'The Salons of New York: At Mrs Assistant Dock Commissioner O'Hara's'; illustration from *Life*, December 1892
17. Alfred E. Smith (1873–1944), Governor of New York. *Radio Times Hulton Picture Library*
243 18. Mrs Nicholas Brady, Papal Duchess, kissing the ring of Cardinal Pacelli, the future Pope Pius XII, New York, October 1936. Mrs Brady, née Genevieve Garvan, received the title of Duchess from the Pope. *Associated Press*
19. Eugene O'Neill (1888–1953) with George M. Cohan (1878–1942) in 1933 when he acted in O'Neill's play *Ah Wilderness*; montage by Edward Steichen. Collection Joanna T. Steichen
20. Joseph P. Kennedy (1888–1969), United States Ambassador, accompanied by Sir Sydney Clive, on his way to present credentials to King George VI, March 1938. *Radio Times Hulton Picture Library, London*
21. Grace Kelly arriving with her father for her wedding to Prince Rainier III of Monaco, 4 April 1956. *Radio Times Hulton Picture Library, London*
244 22. 'A Time for Greatness'; lithograph by Norman Rockwell, cover for *Look* magazine, 14 July 1964
245 1. 'Welcome to all!'; detail of cartoon by Joseph Keppler from *Puck*, 28 April 1880
246 2. 'American gold'; detail of cartoon by F. Opper from *Puck*, 24 May 1882
247 3. 'The Greek Slave'; detail of cartoon from *Harper's Weekly*, 16 April 1870
4. 'The Irish maid in America'; detail of cartoon by F. Opper from *Puck*, 30 January 1884
248 5. 'The Knave and the Fool – Fenian Brothers'; cartoon from *The Razor*, 1 January 1868. *BL*

6. Recruitment poster of Corcoran Legion. *New York Historical Society*
249 7. John Kelly, member of the Volunteer Fire Department; detail of cartoon from *Puck*, 20 October 1880
250 8. Irish American signers of the Declaration of Independence; illustration from *Irish World*, centennial edition, New York, July 1876. *BL*
251 9. John L. Sullivan; advertisement for statuette by Wilson Macdonald from *New York Illustrated Times*, 28 July 1883. *BL*

9 Modern Ireland
257 1. Roof of Dublin Post Office during Easter parade commemorating 1916 Easter Rising. *V. Gorter – Camera Press*
258 2. Campaigning in Dublin for the General Election, November 1918. *Collection George Morrison*
3. A Black and Tan soldier searching a postman, 1920. *Collection George Morrison*
4. Auxiliaries surround coffin of Terence MacSweeney on its arrival at Cork, 1920. *Collection George Morrison*
259 5. The inauguration of the Northern Ireland Parliament by King George V in June 1921; painting by William Conor, Stormont. By courtesy of J. W. Vitty
6. Battle of York Street, Belfast: Catholic workers attacked. *Collection George Morrison*
7. *Love of Ireland* (Michael Collins, killed 1922); painting by Sir John Lavery (1856–1941). *Municipal Gallery of Modern Art, Dublin*
8. Eamon de Valera speaking on behalf of the Republican (Sinn Fein) party during the election campaign, June 1922. *Collection George Morrison*
9. Dr Douglas Hyde, first President of Eire, with de Valera, 5 May 1938. *Keystone Press*
260 10. Men of the South, guerrilla fighters of 1916–21 period; painting by Sean Keating (b.1889). *Crawford Municipal Art Gallery, Cork*
11. Lady Longford, Hilton Edwards and Micheál MacLiammóir; painting by Muriel Brandt. Gate Theatre, Dublin. Reproduced by permission of Hilton Edwards and Dr Micheál MacLiammóir. *Harsch*
12. Seamus Heaney; painting by Edward McGuire, 1974. *Ulster Museum, Belfast*
261 13. Untitled sculpture in steel by Brian King, at Goff's, near Dublin. *Harsch*
14. St Aengus Catholic church, Burt, Co. Donegal; built 1967 by Liam McCormick and Partners. *GM*
15. *Woman*; painting, 1959, by Louis le Brocquy (b.1916). *Tate Gallery, London*
16. Brendan Behan (1923–64) in New York during the American run of *The Hostage*. *Laon Maybanke – Camera Press*
17. Frances Cuka and Jack MacGowran in Beckett's *Endgame*, 1958. *Reg Wilson*
262 18. Street in Killorglin, Co. Kerry, *c.*1965. *Edwin Smith*
19. Modern housing, Sylvan Homes, Kilkenny. *Mark Fiennes*
20. Shop window in Roscommon, *c.*1965. *Edwin Smith*
21. Pilgrim on summit of Croagh Patrick, Co. Mayo. *Rod Tuach/Source*
263 22. Children in Dublin slum. *Tom Kennedy/Source*
23. Turf carrier near Gortmore, Co. Galway. *ITB*
24. Electricity generating station at Rhode, Co. Offaly, opened in 1960. *Tom O'Malley Pictures Ltd*
264 25. Catholic women protesting in Ulster. *Brian Aris – Camera Press*

26. Loyalist woman marcher, Ulster, 14 July 1976. *Irish Times*
27. The Reverend Ian Paisley, MP, outside his Belfast church, the Martyrs' Memorial Free Presbyterian Church. *Harsch*
28. IRA march with coffin of hunger-striker Michael Gaughan, 8 June 1974. *D. Newell-Smith – Camera Press*
29. Hooded leaders of Ulster Volunteer Force telling of killings, March 1975. *Press Association*
30. Women's Peace Movement march, Shankill area of Belfast. *Harsch*
31. Peace march with Mrs Betty Williams and Miss Mairead Corrigan, August 1976. *Topix*

265 1. IRA recruitment poster, 1933. *NLI*
266 2. Anti-conscription pledge, 1918. Among the signatories, pledged to oppose conscription, are the Catholic Primate, the Lord Mayor of Dublin, MPs and leaders of the Sinn Fein and Trade Unions. *NLI*
268 3. Cartoon attacking treaty of 1922. *NLI*
270 4. 'Dividing up the Estate'; cartoon from *Dublin Opinion*
271 5. Rural electricity; cartoon from *Dublin Opinion*
275 6. Anti-de Valera poster issued by Cumann na nGaedhael party, 1933
277 7. Removal of Queen Victoria's statue; cartoon from *Dublin Opinion*, 1948

280 8. Ulster Unionist poster, 1974. *NLI*

Acknowledgments
The publishers are grateful to the following for permission to include the quotations which precede each chapter: Cuala Press (pp. 20 and 48); Lady Longford (p. 72); Oxford University Press (p. 100); Faber and Faber Ltd, Richard Murphy and OUP, New York (pp. 128 and 256); and Faber and Faber Ltd (pp. 6 and 172).

INDEX

Page numbers in *italics* refer to illustrations